The North Sea World in the Middle Ages

The North Sea World in the Middle Ages

Studies in the Cultural History of North-Western Europe

*Thomas R. Liszka and
Lorna E.M. Walker*

EDITORS

FOUR COURTS PRESS

Set in 10.5 pt on 12.5 pt Ehrhardt by
Carrigboy Typesetting Services, for
FOUR COURTS PRESS LTD
Fumbally Lane, Dublin 8, Ireland
e-mail: info@four-courts-press.ie
http://www.four-courts-press.ie
and in North America for
FOUR COURTS PRESS
c/o ISBS, 5824 N.E. Hassalo Street, Portland, OR 97213.

© The various contributors and Four Courts Press 2001

A catalogue record for this title is available from the British Library.

ISBN 1-85182-561-4

All rights reserved. No part of this publication may be reproduced, stored in or introduced into a retrieval system, or transmitted, in any form or by any means (electronic, mechanical, photocopying, recording or otherwise), without the prior written permission of both the copyright owner and publisher of this book.

Printed in England
by MPG Books, Bodmin, Cornwall.

Contents

LIST OF CONTRIBUTORS	7
LIST OF ILLUSTRATIONS	9
INTRODUCTION	11

PART ONE: TEXTS AND IMAGES: HISTORICAL PERSPECTIVES

1. *Insigne Crucis:* A European Motif in a Nordic Setting — 15
   Haki Antonsson
2. Points of Law at the Point of a Sword: Tristan's Duel with Morolt in the North Sea World — 33
   Vickie Ziegler
3. Lydgate's *Troy Book* and the Confusion of Prudence — 52
   Robert R. Edwards
4. The Rider on the Sea-Monster: *Quid gloriaris in malitia …* — 70
   Rosemary Muir Wright

PART TWO: THIS WORLD: CULTURAL CONTACTS

5. North Sea Language Contacts in the Early Middle Ages: English and Norse — 88
   Paul Bibire
6. Hákon *Aðalsteins fóstri:* Aspects of Anglo-Saxon Kingship in Tenth-Century Norway — 108
   Gareth Williams
7. Culture and Contacts in the Scottish Romanesque — 127
   Lorna E.M. Walker
8. Seafaring and Trade in East Fife — 164
   Colin J.M. Martin

PART THREE: THE OTHER WORLD: HAGIOGRAPHICAL STUDIES

9. The Cult of St Fillan in Scotland — 175
   Simon Taylor
10. Brendan the Navigator: a Twelfth-Century View — 211
    Clive R. Sneddon

11	Shrine Rivalry in the North Sea World *Robert Worth Frank, Jr*	230
12	The *South English Legendaries* *Thomas R. Liszka*	243

ST JOHN'S HOUSE PAPERS 281

INDEX 283

Contributors

HAKI ANTONSSON, Lecturer in Mediaeval History, University of St Andrews

PAUL BIBIRE, Honorary Lecturer in the School of History, University of St Andrews

ROBERT R. EDWARDS, Distinguished Professor of English and Comparative Literature, Pennsylvania State University

ROBERT WORTH FRANK, JR, Professor Emeritus of English, Pennsylvania State University

THOMAS R. LISZKA, English Program Coordinator, Altoona College, Pennsylvania State University

COLIN J.M. MARTIN, Reader in Maritime Archaeology, University of St Andrews

ROSEMARY MUIR WRIGHT, Senior Lecturer in Art History, University of St Andrews

CLIVE R. SNEDDON, Lecturer in French, University of St Andrews

SIMON TAYLOR, Anderson Research Fellow in Early Mediaeval Scottish Sources, University of St Andrews

LORNA E.M. WALKER, Honorary Senior Lecturer in Mediaeval History, University of St Andrews

GARETH WILLIAMS, Curator of Early Medieval Coins, British Museum

VICKIE ZIEGLER, Director, Center for Medieval Studies, Pennsylvania State University

Illustrations

Except where otherwise indicated in the captions, the illustrations are museum or library photographs, reproduced with permission, here gratefully acknowledged.

CHAPTER 4: THE RIDER ON THE SEA-MONSTER

Figures

4.1	Initial 'Q' from the opening to Psalm 51. The Corbie Psalter: Amiens, Bibl. mun., MS 18 C, fol. 46	71
4.2	The opening to Psalm 51. Psalter: Troyes, Cathedral Treasury, MS 12, fol. 41v	73
4.3	Antichrist on Leviathan. *Liber Floridus*: Ghent, University Library, MS 92, fol. 62	75
4.4	Illuminated Initial. St Gregory, *Homilies on Ezekiel*: The Pierpont Morgan Library, New York, MS G. 6, fol. 39 (photo David Loggie)	79
4.5	Initial 'D'. St Augustine, *Commentary upon the Psalms*: Valenciennes, Bibl. mun., MS 39, fol. 8 (photo G.P. Simon)	83

CHAPTER 7: CULTURE AND CONTACTS IN THE SCOTTISH ROMANESQUE

Maps

7.1	The British Isles and Normandy	128
7.2	Selected sites in Scotland	129
7.3	Selected sites in the Cotentin	156

Figures

7.1	Abercorn Church: south doorway	131
7.2	Abercorn hogbacks and cross-shafts	132
7.3	Inchcolm hogback with traces of end-beasts	133
7.4	The St Andrews sarcophagus	135
7.5	St Rule's Church, St Andrews	136
7.6	St Rule's Church: chancel arch	138
7.7	Dunfermline Abbey: north nave arcade	144
7.8	Dunfermline Abbey: west doorway	146
7.9	Dalmeny Church: south doorway	149

7.10	Dalmeny Church: (a) apse; (b) corbels nos. 4 and 5 at the head of the apse; (c) no. 4 (left); (d) no. 5 (right); (e) no. 6 (apse, south)	150, 151
7.11	Church of St Étienne, Caen: corbels in the nave	154
7.12	Durham Cathedral: corbels in the nave	155
7.13	Tollevast Church: view from the south-east	157
7.14, 7.15	Tollevast Church: interior corbels	160
7.16	Pictish grave-marker: Meigle Museum, Perthshire, no. 26	161
7.17, 7.18	Carved animal-head posts from the Oseberg ship burial	162

CHAPTER 8: SEAFARING AND TRADE IN EAST FIFE

Figures

8.1	The modern town of Crail	167
8.2	Lighthouse on the Isle of May	168
8.3	Merchants' houses at Pittenweem	171
8.4	A Fife merchant ship from the tombstone of Robert Ford of Kilrenny	173

CHAPTER 9: THE CULT OF ST FILLAN IN SCOTLAND

Maps

| 9.1 | Scotland showing the distribution of Fillan place-names and dedications | 177 |
| 9.2 | The mediaeval parish of Killin, including Strath Fillan | 187 |

Figures

9.1	View across Strath Fillan	185
9.2	Helmet with the armorial bearing of the family of Bruces of Annandale	188
9.3	Carving which may have marked the grave of one of the dewars of St Fillan's arm-reliquary	189

The North Sea World in the Middle Ages: Studies in the Cultural History of North-Western Europe

INTRODUCTION

For many years we looked at large bodies of water on a map and saw boundaries: as, for example, those separating Europe from Africa, Mexico from the Caribbean, Great Britain from the Continent. But especially in recent years, encouraged by the recognition of such disciplines as 'Mediterranean studies', we have become more aware that seas are connecting bodies. They facilitate contact, friendly and hostile. Like superhighways, they can be fraught with danger. Merchants, pilgrims, visitors, and family can cross them. Languages, religions, literary and artistic motifs, and commodities can cross them. So can invaders. Pirates can inhabit them. Storms can wreak havoc on all.

In 1996, a Conference was held in St Andrews, Scotland, on the shores of the North Sea. It was organized jointly by the Center for Medieval Studies at Penn State University and the Department of Mediaeval History at St Andrews University. The purpose of the Conference was to explore the medieval 'world' centred upon the North Sea in particular, and the north-western European littoral in general. The Conference received some obvious inspiration from one held in Leiden a year earlier, focused on the North Sea and Culture in the early modern era.[1] However, the St Andrews conference gave greater emphasis to cultural and literary contacts than to those of the world of work. Several of the papers in this volume were among those presented at St Andrews. Subsequently, the collection has benefited from the processes of revision, selection, and addition of material.

Like the solar system, the world around the North Sea is a series of circles: some closer, some farther. Take one look, and you see a Scotland, an England, or a Norway in contradistinction to all around. Take another look, and you see these locales in natural association with each other, and as naturally with Ireland, Normandy, Germany, and beyond. Look again, and you see connections with both the classical past and the world of eternity. A world of contact cannot be captured in a single book, even in a much larger volume than this one. We present our studies in three parts: the first reflective of the past; the second focusing more sharply upon the

---

1 See *The North Sea and Culture (1550–1800): Proceedings of the International Conference held at Leiden 21–22 April 1995*, edited by Juliette Roding and Lex Heerma van Voss (Hilversum, 1996).

medieval present; and the third moving towards eternity. But such categorization is, of course, artificial. Discussions of kingship, travel and trade, literary and artistic symbol, cult and hagiography, Christian and classical association, law, and the subsequent study of scholars cut across the tri-partite division.

In Part One the emphasis is on historical perspective and the links between literature, history, and art. Haki Antonsson shows how the European motif of a cross appearing on the shoulder or between the shoulder blades is transformed for use in *Njáls saga*. In French crusader histories, the miraculous sign indicates that the bearer is now a saint. In English, French, German, Netherlandic, and Scandinavian settings, it can be a miraculous indication of royal status. Aware of these associations, King Eysteinn, facing death, asked for the sign to be hacked on himself as a heroic, but non-miraculous assertion of his royalty.

Vickie Ziegler explores the links between Germanic law, Germanic court procedure, and Christian doctrine relevant to unilateral and judicial ordeals, and sheds new light upon the interpretation of important Tristan literature along the north-western littoral. In Gottfried von Straßburg's Middle High German version, Tristan emerges as an adherent of right conduct. Brother Robert's Old Norse version of the story casts the issue in terms of tyranny versus the rights of free men. And Malory's Middle English text transforms French source material to present the ordeal as a chivalric test of Tristram's own skill in arms.

Robert Edwards looks to England's Henry V, who desperately desired reconciliation with his rivals, both across the channel in France and at home. With the commissioned poem *Troy Book*, Lydgate recommends prudence to Henry as a defining quality of a good king, one that led to a reconciliation of rivals in the old Troy. But the lesson has come a long way to the new Troy – from the pagan near east of Dares and Dictys, through the Christian Mediterranean of Lydgate's source, Guido delle Colonne's *Historia Destructionis Troiae*, to medieval England. In the journey, the meanings of 'prudence' became confused and somewhat contradictory. Nevertheless, Lydgate suggests that Henry, as a Christian prince, can transcend the limitations of his pagan predecessors to bring peace to his corner of the world.

Finally, Rosemary Muir Wright explains the presence of the image of a human riding backwards on a sea monster in the northern French Corbie psalter. The artist has used an image whose source is not Carolingian or classical. Instead, this depiction of the Antichrist enthroned upon Leviathan may be distinctly northern, linked both with the Vikings and with their fellow-sailors, the Irish missionary monks, who associated powers of darkness with the dangers of the untamed ocean.

Part Two focuses upon the cultural contacts to which seafaring, travel, conquest, and pilgrimage contributed so much. Paul Bibire discusses both the relationships among the Germanic languages and dialects of early England and Scandinavia, and their subsequent contacts during periods of English settlement, Viking invasion, and the Danelaw. He addresses the problem of bilingualism subsequent to Norse settlement in England and the question why Norse vocabulary enters English some three or four centuries after the Norse settlements.

Gareth Williams considers accounts of the rule of Hákon the Good of Norway given in Icelandic sagas and Latin histories of the late twelfth and thirteenth centuries. The later works emphasize Hákon's upbringing in England at the court of his 'foster father' Athelstan, and Williams argues that Hákon's subsequent actions as king were based on the English model of kingship to which he was exposed. In addition to exploring this medieval cross-sea connection, Williams offers scholars corrective advice upon the evaluation of sagas as historical evidence.

In a paper written initially to provide a context for a tour of selected sites in Fife and Lothian Lorna Walker looks at evidence and arguments which challenge the received derivation of Scottish architecture and sculpture. The significance of Abercorn with its hogback monuments and stone crosses is discussed, together with pre-Davidian accomplishment at St Andrews, and influences upon Dunfermline Abbey, not only from Durham but also from Dalmeny. Focusing upon the imagery of the animal head, she shows us a world of Pictish, Northumbrian, Scandinavian and Norman cultural contact. Colin Martin concludes the section by providing a glimpse of the long history of seafaring, prior to, through, and after the medieval period in East Fife. He introduces the people who made the voyages, the products they shipped, and the perils they faced.

In Part Three, devoted to hagiographical studies, we move from the medieval present to the future and to eternity. Simon Taylor examines the cult of the saint known as Fillan in Scots and English. A survey of the place names, church commemorations, and fair-days associated with Fillan shows that the cult extended to every area of Scotland except, notably, the north-east and the old province of Moray. The saint's origins may be traced to Ireland and to as many as eighteen separate saints named Fáelán whose histories and legends became inter-associated over time. The study of the Fillan's cult is like the study of many saints 'who have left us little more than their name'. Accretions to the finally recognized legend may derive from genuine tradition, from misinterpretation of the early liturgical sources, and from the political realities of the times. In these ways a circle which began life as focused around the Irish Sea moved eastwards to touch the North Sea World.

Clive Sneddon asks why Brendan, a sixth-century Irish saint, considered in the second rank of Irish saints, would be chosen as the subject of a twelfth-century poem 'written for a queen of the Anglo-Norman King of England Henry I'. As an Irish missionary to Scotland, Brendan is a participant in the interwoven histories of the nations of the British Isles, and as such may be seen as indicating that England emerged in an insular context, independently of the later claims of France and Scandinavia. If the *Navigatio Brendani* regards the saint as worthy of seeing Paradise in his life-time, the twelfth-century poet shows him to be acting on behalf of all mankind, thus enhancing his significance in the spiritual and secular worlds.

Robert Frank demonstrates how miracle records kept at Canterbury, Durham, Finchale, St Andrews, and shrines along the coast of Norway reflect competition for pilgrim visitation. They record a wealth of detail-names of minor characters, places, days of the week, the identity of objects, the number of times things happened, names of witnesses – in order to convince their audience of the validity of their saint's miracles. If a shrine's miracles were doubted, the shrine could suffer serious financial consequences. Such records give us close-ups of life at all levels, demonstrating a kind of reportage not readily available elsewhere in mediaeval sources.

Finally, Thomas Liszka presents a case study of a Middle English work. We know about earlier worlds, like that around the North Sea, largely from the documentary evidence left to us. And how that evidence has been preserved for us, or edited, influences our perceptions. The first editor of the *South English Legendary*, Carl Horstmann, defined an identity for the work which was useful, but hardly inevitable. And later *SEL* scholars built on the framework of his definition. However, a look at the surviving manuscript evidence shows us that the *SEL* was one of many medieval texts that were considered open, texts that not only could, but should be adapted, improved, and suited to local use. As a result, there were produced many *South English Legendaries* that deserve to be better known.

Even so, in the context of the cultural history of North-Western Europe in the Middle Ages, does the North Sea World deserve to be better known and understood, a world centred upon the North Sea, but washed also by the waters of the Baltic and the Irish Seas and the English Channel. At a time of greater European awareness and integration the focus of this volume of essays has relevance not only for specialist academics but for all who are interested in the common cultural inheritance of the western world. Wide-ranging in scope, the conference which gave birth to the collection brought together experts in several fields: history, language and literature, religion and hagiography, law and iconography. Such interdisciplinary enterprises do much to enrich the work of scholars and to make that work accessible to a wider audience.

The editors would like to take this opportunity of thanking all those who contributed to the organization of the Conference, and in particular Dr Barbara Crawford of St Andrews and Dr Vickie Ziegler of Penn State. Without their dedicated leadership and vision neither the Conference nor this publication would have come about. We express the gratitude of the conference organizers and all involved then or subsequently in this editorial undertaking for the substantive support of the Department of Mediaeval History and St John's House at the University of St Andrews, and of the College of the Liberal Arts, the Office of the Provost, the Department of English, the Institute for the Arts and Humanistic Studies, the Office of Interdisciplinary Research Programs, and the Office of International Cooperative Programs at Penn State University. And we are particularly grateful for the generous support of AT&T. Finally we give special thanks to those whose generous financial assistance has contributed to the publication of this volume, namely Penn State Altoona College, the Carnegie Trust for the Universities of Scotland, the Research Committee of the School of History at the University of St Andrews, and the Russell Trust.

Insigne Crucis: A European Motif in a Nordic Setting

HAKI ANTONSSON

'And if the brother dies doing his penance, he should be treated like any other brother, and the cross should be sewn on him as on any other brother.'

The Rule of the Templars[1]

'I am branded with this sign so that, conforming to the Crucified in His suffering, I may be found worthy to share in the glory of His resurrection.'

Peter Damian[2]

I

An episode from the most celebrated of the Icelandic Family sagas, *Njáls saga*, is my point of departure.[3] This epic of the late thirteenth century focuses on events that allegedly took place in the first half of the eleventh century or shortly after the conversion of Iceland to Christianity. The saga is constructed around two climactic death scenes: the slaying of the valiant Gunnar Hámundarson and the burning of his best friend, the wise and conciliatory Njáll Þorgeirsson. Outnumbered, Gunnar meets his fate in a heroic manner whereas, in contrast, Njáll faces his end in a passive frame of mind. As his farmstead is set ablaze he makes no effort to protect himself or seek clemency.

---

1 *The Rule of the Templars: The French Text of the Rule of the Order of the Knights Templar*, tr. and introduced by J.M. Upton-Ward, *Studies in the History of Medieval Religion*, IV (Woodbridge, 1992), p. 124.   2 'Ego hoc stigmate signatus inveniar, ut crucifixo configuratus in poena, consors fieri merear resurgentis in gloria', S. Petri Damiani, *Carmina sacra et preces*: Oratio 26, in *Opera Omnia*, II, *Patrologiae cursus completus*, series latina, CXLV (Paris, 1853), p. 927.   3 *Brennu-Njáls Saga*, ed. by Einar Ól. Sveinsson in *Íslenzk Fornrit*, 12 (Reykjavík, 1954), pp 342–44. The translation is from *The Complete Sagas of Icelanders. Including 49 tales*, ed. by Viðar Hreinsson, III (Reykjavík, 1997), pp 162–64. For a good introduction to the Icelandic Family sagas see Carol J. Clover, 'Icelandic Family Sagas', *Old Norse-Icelandic Literature. A Critical Guide*, ed. by Carol J. Clover and John Lindow, *Islandica*, 45 (Ithaca and London, 1985), pp 239–316.

Njáll's stoic attitude is memorably expressed in his famous utterance that 'God will not let us [referring to himself and his wife] burn both in this life and the next.' In a world consumed with misplaced pride and the often twisted logic of feuding, Njáll's resignation at a moment of dread demonstrates his moral superiority. Njáll's own conscience is clear; the burning of his farmstead is the culmination of a process initiated and escalated, not by him, but by his immediate relatives; his wife Bergþóra and his violent and enigmatic son, Skarphéðinn.

Following the burning, the earthly remains of Njáll's family and retinue are recovered from the rubble. A certain Hjalti, a well respected and pious man, is entrusted with this task. Beforehand he is told that 'everybody will believe what you say you have seen.' Hjalti assumes here a role familiar to readers of hagiography, the inspector of corporal relics. He and his men first discover the bodies of Njáll and Bergþóra, completely untouched by the fire, underneath an oxhide. Astounded by this sight, Hjalti asks those present what they make of it:

> þeir svǫruðu: 'þinna atkvœða vilju vér at bíða.' Hjalti mœlti: 'Ekki mun mér verða einarðarfátt um þetta. Líkami Bergþóru þykki mér at líkendum ok þó vel. En Njáls ásjána ok líkami synisk mér svá bjartr, at ek hefi engan dauðs manns líkama sét jafnbjartan.' Allir sǫgðu, at svá væri.

> They answered, 'We'll wait for what you have to say.' Hjalti said, 'I'll be frank about this. Bergthora's body is as I would have expected, though well preserved. Njal's countenance and body are radiant, and I've never seen such radiance in a dead man's body.' They all agreed that this was the case.

The attention of the group now turns to Skarphéðinn who is found standing upright by a wall with his legs burned up to his knees: 'He had bitten into his upper lip. His eyes were open and not swollen. He had driven his axe into the gable wall so hard that half the blade was buried and it had not lost its temper.' When Skarphéðinn has been stripped of his unburnt clothes the following is revealed:

> Hann hafði lagit hendr sínar í kross ok á ofan ina hœgri, en tvá díla fundu þeir á honum, annan meðal herðanna, en annan á brjóstinu, ok var hvárrtveggi brenndr í kross, ok œtluðu menn, at hann mundi sik sjálfr brennt hafa.

> He had folded his arms in a cross, with the right arm above, and they found two marks on him, one between his shoulders and the other on his chest, both burned in the shape of a cross, and people thought he had probably burned these marks himself.

At this point the attitude of those attending the grim spectacle is highlighted. Regarding the appearances of Njáll and Bergþóra it is Hjalti again who calls the tune. With a brief and somewhat understated speech he indicates that there is something extraordinary about Njáll's countenance. The reader is clearly meant to conclude that Njáll's soul is saved and that he now reaps his just reward in heaven. His serene appearance partly vindicates his last words that 'God will not make us burn in this life as well as in the next.' Only partly though, for he speaks in the plural and includes his wife in his optimistic utterance, but regarding the posthumous fate of Bergþóra, we are left in the dark. When the men first behold the well-preserved bodies they 'thought it a great miracle.' As we have seen, Hjalti qualifies this opinion for he sees nothing extraordinary about Bergþóra's body surviving the fire unscathed; its good preservation is simply due to chance or luck.

Matters are hardly less ambiguous in relation to Skarphéðinn. The contrast between his tortured appearance and Njáll's calm exterior is dramatic; it is as if Skarphéðinn, trapped between the collapsing walls and facing certain death, was forced to confront his uncertain fate in the afterlife. This impression is enhanced by the mysterious crosses found on his body, not least by the statement that Skarphéðinn himself made them: 'people thought he had probably burned these marks himself.'

Einar Ól. Sveinsson, arguably the most influential commentator on *Njáls saga*, interpreted Skarphéðinn's act as a christianized version of a ritual in which warriors branded themselves with the point of a spear as a dedication to the Germanic God of war, Óðinn/Wotan. Thus doing 'he expiates the heinous crime he committed against Höskuldur [that is, the single act which more than anything led to the burning] by burning it away. Now everything is complete.'[4] Margaret Cormack has also stressed the penitential side of Skarphéðinn's behaviour. Precisely because of his violent deeds in the past nothing less than a striking sign of his piety and penance was sufficient.[5] Indeed it is tempting to interpret the marks as representing an outward illustration of a profound shift in Skarphéðinn's spiritual outlook at his hour of death. It designates his belated baptism to Christianity and thus in a sense signifies his rebirth. It may be of some relevance that in the thirteenth-century Norwegian law-code of Frostaþing it is decreed that a women who delivers a child alone shall 'take spittle and make the sign of the cross with it on the breast and the shoulder'.[6] The parallel with the marks on Skarphéðinn is evident.

The interpretations of Einar Ól. Sveinsson and Margaret Cormack rest on the assumption that the common verdict – that Skarphéðinn burnt the two crosses on himself – is the only conceivable one. However the fact that the author does not explicitly claim that this was the case but rather steers us

---

[4] Einar Ól. Sveinsson, *Njáls Saga: A Literary Masterpiece*, ed. and trans. by Paul Schach, with an introduction by E.O.G. Turville-Petre (Lincoln, 1971), p. 155.
[5] Margaret J. Cormack, 'Saints and Sinners: Reflections on Death in some Icelandic Sagas', *Gripla*, 8 (1993), p. 190. [6] *The Earliest Norwegian Laws being the Gulathing Law and the Frostathing Law*, trans. by Laurence M. Larson (New York, 1935), pp 226–27.

towards this interpretation by referring to common opinion, suggests that an alternative interpretation is possible, namely that the crosses appeared on Skarphéðinn's body as a result of divine intervention.

Rory McTurk in his study of the supernatural in *Njáls saga* argues that the reference to the crosses should be classified with supernatural incidents that we are to believe to be genuine. In this category we find phenomena such as the appearances of Gunnar's ghost and the miraculous healing power of King Brian Boru's corpse following the battle of Clontarf. Moreover the fact that these incidents 'are narrated on the first level [that is, told by the narrator directly] *as well as* focalized in the first degree [that is, without references to witnesses] suggests that the author wishes them to be regarded as more unambiguously supernatural than any of the other incidents considered here.'[7] However, as already mentioned, matters are not so straightforward regarding the crosses on Skarphéðinn's corpse. Most notably Rory McTurk's interpretation must be modified in the light of the fact that the author chose specifically to underline the opinion of those attending. Although the narrator tells us directly that crosses were found on the corpse, we are subtly drawn to the interpretation that they were not of supernatural origin.

It has been observed that the author felt no need to dwell on the symbolic implications of Njáll's appearance. A medieval reader well versed in hagiography would certainly have associated it with the salvation of the soul. Indeed we need scarcely speculate on this matter for it has been noted that in a *Vita Eustaci*, translated into Old-Norse in the early twelfth century, the Roman martyr and his family are placed inside a brazen ox which is then set on fire. When the ox is opened the corpses are found perfectly preserved.[8] The similarities here with the scene in *Njáls saga* are clear. In other words, we are left in no doubt as to the posthumous fate of Njáll. Even in death he assumes the centre stage and no other member of his family is allowed to cast a shadow over this hero, or rather anti-hero, of the saga. This much is clear and needs no further comment.[9]

Still we have an unsolved problem on our hands. Namely, why did the author find it necessary to stress the apparently obvious point that Skarphéðinn branded himself with the crosses?

---

[7] Rory McTurk, 'The Supernatural in Njáls Saga: A Narratological Approach', *Saga-Book of the Viking Society*, 23 (1990), p. 43.   [8] Lars Lönnroth, 'Kroppen som själens spegel', *Lychnos* (1963–64), p. 32; *Heilagra manna søgur*, ed. by C.R. Unger, II (Christiania, 1877), p. 203.   [9] It is thus only Njáll's appearance which is presented as miraculous. This distinction has been overlooked by scholars: see, for instance, Richard F. Allen, *Fire and Iron. Critical Approaches to Njáls Saga* (Pittsburg, 1971), pp 156–57; Einar Ól. Sveinsson, *Njáls Saga*, p. 178.

II

On 5 April 1097, a fleet under the leadership of Count Stephen of Blois embarked from Sicily and headed for the Holy Land. The ships, all loaded with crusaders, had barely left the harbour when one 'suddenly cracked through the middle for no apparent reason' and 'four hundred of both sexes perished by drowning'. The same vessel was then washed ashore and

> Nam quum corpora jam mortua qui circumstabant pro posse collegissent, repertae sunt in carnibus quorumdam super spatulas scilicet cruces insignitae. Nam quod in pannis suis vivi gestaverant, competebat, Domino volente, in ipsis servitio suo sic praeoccupatis idem signum victoriosum sub pignore fidei permanare; simul etiam tali miraculo patefieri considerantibus merito dignum erat, ipsos defunctos sub misericordia Dei jam quietem vitae perennis adeptos fuisse.

> When those standing round about had collected as many bodies of the dead as possible, they found crosses actually imprinted in the flesh of some of them, between the shoulders. For it was fitting that this same symbol of victory, which they had worn on their clothes while living, should remain by the will of God as a token of faith upon those occupied in His service. At the same time it was also proper that such a miracle should show those who witnessed it that the dead had now attained by the mercy of God the peace of eternal life.

This account appears in the *Historia Hierosolymitana*, written around 1100 by a French participant in the First Crusade, Fulcher of Chartres.[10] In it Fulcher transforms the dismal failure of the crusaders in question into victory. Their death by drowning is presented in terms of martyrdom. From Fulcher's perspective, the appearance of the miraculous crosses between their shoulders is a divine revelation that the crusaders were saved, that they 'had now attained by the mercy of God the peace of eternal life.'

About a decade or so later Fulcher's compatriot, Guibert of Nogent, commented on both the symbolic significance of this particular incident, and,

---

10 Fulcher of Chartres, *Historia Hierosolymitana*, I, viii, in *Recueil des Historiens des Croisades: Historiens Occidentaux*, III (Paris 1865), p. 330. The translation is from *Fulcher de Chartres Historia Hierosolymitana. A History of the Expedition to Jerusalem 1095–1127*, trans. by Frances Rita Ryan and ed. with an introduction by Harold S. Fink (Knoxville, 1969), p. 65. On the significance of this description in the context of the development of stigmata in the Middle Ages see Giles Constable, *Three Studies in Medieval and Religious Thought. The Interpretation of Mary and Martha; The Ideal of the Imitation of Christ; The Orders of Society* (Cambridge 1995), p. 220. On martyrdom and the First Crusade see Jonathan Riley-Smith, 'Death on the First Crusade', in *The End of Strife*, ed. by D. Loades (Edinburgh, 1984), pp 14–31; Colin Morris, 'Martyrs on the Field of Battle before and during the First Crusade', *Martyrs and Martyrologies*, ed. by D. Wood, *Studies in Church History*, 30 (Oxford, 1993) pp 93–105; H.E.J. Cowdrey, 'Martyrdom and

interestingly, Fulcher's interpretation of it.[11] In his *Gesta Dei per Francos* Guibert found his version of this event both naive and lacking in critical acumen. Although Guibert conceded that if he had so wished God might well have imprinted the marks on the crusaders' bodies, he pointed out that in the early stages of the crusade 'men of the lowest social class, and even worthless women' claimed that such signs appeared on their bodies:

> Ille paulisper intextas ex suffusione sanguinis rigas, crucem astruens, ostentabat in oculo; iste pupillarem, qua faede caecutiebat, masculam, eundi sibi commonitorium perhibens, pro caelesti exhibebat oraculo. Alius, aut novorum pomorum succis, seu quolibet genere fuci, cuilibet particulae corporis moliebatur speciem crucis; ut sicut oculorum subsellia pingi solent stibio, ita divini in se spectaculi vel vireret vel ruberet, fraude facta et commentis, ostensio.[12]

> One man scratched his cheeks, drew a cross with the flowing blood, and showed it to everyone. Another showed the spot on his eye, by means of which he had been blinded, as a sign that a heavenly announcement had urged him to undertake the journey. Another, either by using the juices of fresh fruit, or some other kind of dye, painted on some little piece of his body the shape of a cross. As they used to paint the area below the eyes with antimony, and deceitful exhibition, they might claim that God had showed himself in them.[13]

In line with his generally cautious attitude towards matters supernatural,[14] Guibert thought it more prudent to conclude that the marks were made by those involved. Those familiar with Guibert's general frame of mind will probably suspect that the humble status of the crusaders in question was not an insignificant factor in shaping his opinion on this issue.

Thus in two quite different medieval settings and sources we find the sign of the cross appearing on the bodies, more specifically between the shoulder-

---

the First Crusade', *Crusade and Settlement*, ed. by P.W. Edbury (Cardiff, 1985), pp 45–65. 11 Guibert of Nogent, *Gesta Dei per Francos*, VII, xxxii, in *Recueil des Historiens des Croisades: Historiens Occidentaux*, IV (Paris, 1869), p. 251. 12 *Ibid.* p. 251. 13 *The Deeds of God through the Franks: Guibert de Nogent's 'Gesta Dei per Francos'*, trans. by Robert Levine (Woodbridge, 1997), pp 155–56. 14 His attitude is most clearly expressed in his treatise on relics in which he criticised the ease with which miracles were proclaimed and incipient cults emerged in this period: *De pignoribus sanctorum* in *Patrologiae cursus completus*, series latina, *CLVI* (Paris, 1844–46). See Benedicta Ward, *Miracles and the Medieval Mind. Theory, Record and Event 1000–1215* (Aldershot, 1982), pp 126–27. On the curious championing of Guibert as a rationalist by modern critics see John F. Benton, *Self and Society in Medieval France* (New York, 1970), p. 8; *A Monk's Confession. The Memoirs of Guibert of Nogent*, trans. with an introduction by Paul J. Archambault (Pennsylvania, 1996), p. xx.

blades, of people who came to a violent or an unexpected and tragic death, in a late thirteenth-century Icelandic saga telling of an event which took place in the first half of the eleventh century, and in a near contemporary account of an incident that occurred in the early stages of the First Crusade.

Indirectly, the French accounts may hold a key to the unanswered question of why the author of *Njáls saga* chose to emphasize the non-miraculous nature of Skarphéðinn's cross-marks. For without this reference to the communal voice the medieval reader could easily have interpreted the marks in a different fashion, namely that the two crosses were of miraculous origin and implied that Skarphéðinn's soul was saved. Moreover, in both the French and the Icelandic sources, one can detect a certain tension between the natural and the supernatural, explicit in the former but latent in the latter. The Icelandic author is aware that it is possible to explain the appearance of the crosses in terms of both the ordinary and the extraordinary.[15] But, as I emphasized earlier, he wants to present Njáll as the outstanding figure. Of Njáll alone can it be said with certainty that he reaped the fruits of his exemplary life. In order to bring out the difference between Skarphéðinn and Njáll in this respect, the author resorts to a simple but effective stylistic device that precludes the reader from interpreting the crosses as signs of divine grace.

III

In 1157 King Eysteinn Haraldsson of Norway was executed by a supporter of Ingi, his brother and co-regent. *Heimskringla*, a compilation of Kings' sagas composed by the Icelandic historian Snorri Sturluson in the fourth decade of the thirteenth century, describes the scene of his death in the following manner:

> Konungr bað, at hann skyldi hlyða messu áðr [en hann var tekinn af lífi], ok þat var. Síðan lagðisk hann niðr á grúfu ok breiddi hendr frá sér út ok bað sik hǫggva í kross á milli herðanna, kvað þá skyldu reyna, hvárt hann mundi þola járn eða eigi, sem þeir hǫfðu sagt lagsmenn Inga. Símun mælti við þann, er hǫggva skyldi, bað hann til ráða, kvað konung hǫlzti lengi hafa kropit þar um lyng. Hann var þá hǫggvin ok þótti verða við prúðliga. Lík

---

[15] On the ambiguous appearance of the supernatural in the Icelandic sagas (including the contemporary sagas) see J. Lindow, 'Þorsteins þáttr skelks and the verisimilitude of the Supernatural Experience in Saga Literature', *Structure and Meaning in Old Norse Literature: New Approaches to Textual Analysis and Literary Criticism*, ed. by John Lindow et al. (Odense, 1986), pp 264–80. Lindow's words that the 'individual and later the community will test the supranormality of the experience, and if interpreted generally as supernatural, the experience will reinforce the value of the broken norm' are particularly appropriate regarding the evaluation of Njáll's and Skarphéðinn's corpses, ibid. p. 270.

hans var flutt til Fors, en fyrir sunnan kirkju undir brekkunni var lík hans náttsœtt. Eysteinn konungr var jarðaðr at Forskirkju, ok er leg hans á miðju kirkjugólfi ok breiddr yfir kǫgurr, ok kalla menn hann helgan. Þar sem hann var hǫggvin ok blóð hans kom á jǫrð, spratt upp brunnr, en annarr þar undir brekkunni, sem lík hans var náttsœtt. Af hváru tveggja því vatni þykkjask margir menn bót hafa fengit. Þat er sǫgn Víkverja, at margar jarteinir yrði at leiði Eysteins konungs, áðr óvinir hans steypði á leiðit hundssoði.[16]

The king asked to hear mass [before being slain], and that was granted him. Then he laid himself with his face down, spreading out his arms, and asked them to slash him crosswise between his shoulders – then they would find out whether he could stand cold steel as King Ingi's followers said he could not. Símun spoke to the man who was to hew him, asking him to go to work, and saying that the king had crept all too long through the heather. Then he was beheaded and was considered to have behaved manfully. His body was brought to Fors and placed for the night under the hill south of the church. He was interred in Fors Church, with the resting place in the middle of the church floor, and a rug spread over it. Men called him holy. At the spot where he was beheaded and his blood touched the ground, a spring came up, and another one, under the hill where his body had been placed for the night. Many consider that they regained their health from the water of either spring. People from Vík have said that many miracles happened at the tomb of King Eystein before his enemies poured broth made from dog on it.[17]

For those acquainted with Old-Norse literature the tone of this scene is not an unfamiliar one. Confronted with imminent death, the main protagonist, in this case King Eysteinn of Norway, keeps his composure and, for good measure, taunts his executioner with a sharp remark. It hardly needs emphasising that the ability to leave this world manfully, preferably with a witty quip on the lips, was a particularly potent way of expressing manhood in medieval Norse society. In brief, King Eysteinn conducts himself in a manner befitting a hero and, at the same time, a martyr.

The martyr-like feature of the scene is underlined by the physical stance which Eysteinn assumes before Símun's retainer wields the axe: 'he laid himself

---

16 *Heimskringla*, III, ed. by Bjarni Aðalbjarnarson, *Íslensk Fornrit*, 28 (Reykjavík, 1951), p. 345. Snorri is here partly following *Fagrskinna*, an early thirteenth-century Norwegian Kings' saga compilation, which includes Eysteinn's wish to be hacked cross wise between the shoulders. However, *Fagrskinna* neither mentions his spreading out of the arms or his saintly reputation, *Ágrip af Noregskonunga Sögum. Fagrskinna – Noregskonunga tal.*, ed. by Bjarni Einarsson, *Íslensk Fornrit*, 21 (Reykjavík 1985), pp 294–95.   17 *Heimskringla: Sagas of the Norse Kings*, trans. by Samuel Laing; revised with introduction and notes by Peter Foote (Dent, 1961), p. 261.

with his face down, spreading out his arms ... ' Eysteinn thus confronts his executioner with his body shaped in the sign of the cross. The Norwegian king was not the first to have reportedly made this gesture of *imitatio Christi* for it has been associated with martyrs from the earliest centuries of Christianity. For instance the apologist Eusebius of Caesarea, writing around AD 308, tells in his *Ecclesiastical History* of a certain youth who was caught up in the persecution of Christians in Palestine in the second half of the third century:

> [He was] ... not twenty years of age, standing unbound and stretching his hands in the form of a Cross ... while bears and leopards almost touched his flesh. And yet their mouths were restrained, I know not how, by a divine and incomprehensible power.[18]

According to the so-called *Tabula Othiniensis*, an inscribed copper-plate made on the occasion of Knud II's (*d*.1086) *elevatio* in 1095, the martyred Danish king fell before the altar with his hands outstretched in the shape of a cross before he was killed.[19] As also, reportedly, did Earl Waltheof of Northumbria, executed at the orders of William the Conqueror in 1076 and subsequently venerated as a martyr. *Fagrskinna*, a Norwegian work of the early thirteenth century, tells how the earl gave his silver-tunic to the executioner and then spread himself on the ground in the shape of a cross. The saga states that the informant for this scene was the Icelander, Þorkell Þórðarson, a member of Waltheof's retinue.[20] Although Ordericus Vitalis's description of the same execution differs in many important details from the Icelandic account, it is noteworthy that the earl is said to have 'stretched out his arms' at the moment he faced the sword.[21] In light of these two independent accounts of Waltheof's behaviour at his hour of death it is difficult to avoid the conclusion that in reality he did strike this particular pose. Here it is worth noting the appearance of this hagiographic commonplace in the near-contemporary *Sturlunga saga* which states that three thirteenth-century Icelanders made an identical gesture before their execution.[22] It is tempting to conclude that we are here faced with life imitating art, or rather hagiography.

There is an obvious penitential side to this form of *imitatio Christi*. Note can be taken, for example, of the curious behaviour of Henry III of Germany at the

---

18 Eusebius, *The Ecclesiastical History*, VIII, 7, trans. by J.E.L. Oulton, II (Loeb Classics: Cambridge Mass./ London, 1932), p. 273. **19** 'ante aram manibus solo tenus expansis in modum crucis latere lancetus', *Vitae Sanctorum Danorum*, ed. by M. Cl. Gertz (København, 1908–12), p. 61. **20** *Íslenzk Fornrit*, 21, pp 294–95. **21** 'Illis autem permittentibus surrexit et flexis tantum genibus oculisque in caelum fixis et manibus tensis.' *The Ecclesiastical History of Ordericus Vitalis*, Book IV, ed. and trans. by Marjorie Chibnall, II (Oxford, 1969), p. 323. **22** *Sturlunga saga*, ed. by Guðbrandur Vigfússon (Oxford, 1878), I, pp 256, 265; II, pp 339–40. For these and other examples from Old-Norse literature see Johan Fritzner, *Ordbog over det gamle norske sprog*, II (Kristiania,

funeral of his mother in 1043 where the emperor, according to a letter written by Abbot Bern of Reichenau, threw off his purple and assumed the mourning habit of penitence. In the presence of all the people, Henry sank to the ground with his hands stretched out in the shape of a cross. On another occasion, before a battle against the Huns, the emperor set aside his mantle and regalia, dressed in penitential clothing, and prostrated himself, assuming a cross-like shape.[23] A ritualized display of humility of this sort must be placed within the context of the christological perception of the medieval ruler, most illuminatingly displayed in Ottonian iconography where attributes of the suffering Christ are often associated with the office of emperor.[24] A correspondence between a secular ruler and the *passio* of Christ is also manifest in an *Ordo* for the coronation of Roger II on Christmas Day 1130, where the prospective king of Sicily is required to cast himself before the altar in the shape of a cross: 'ibi humiliter totus in cruce prostratus iaceat.'[25]

If King Eysteinn's posture displays a form of penitence and an identification with the crucifixion of the Saviour, the same can hardly be said of his final request – that the executioner should hack the sign of the cross between the shoulder-blades. On the contrary, Eysteinn makes this curious request in order to display his courage and manliness at the hour of death, or as we are told, so that 'they would find out whether he could stand cold steel as King Ingi's followers said he could not.'

Eysteinn's strange request represents, I believe, a variation of the cross motif found in *Njáls saga*, and in Fulcher's account of the First Crusade. However, the context in which it appears in *Heimskringla* is quite different from those two cases. The penitential aspect is absent and so is the miraculous. To comprehend the latent meaning of King Eysteinn's request we need to place it within an altogether different framework.

The key to that undertaking is Eysteinn's royal status. Marc Bloch in his study *The Royal Touch* discusses the medieval belief that those rightly born to kingship had a mysterious birthmark upon their bodies as a proof of rightful pedigree.[26] The most common sign is the cross, usually found on the right shoulder of the person in question or, alternatively, between the shoulder-blades. According to

---

1886), pp 351–53. **23** For a discussion of these two scenes see Karl Schnith, 'Recht und Friede: Zum Königesdanken im Unkreis Heinrichs III', *Historisches Jahrbuch*, 81 (1962), pp 22–57. For ritualised humility of royal figures in general see Geoffrey Koziol, Begging *Pardon and Favour. Ritual and Political Order in Early Medieval France* (Ithaca & New York, 1992). **24** Robert Deshman, '*Christus rex et magi reges*: Kingship and Christology in Ottonian and Anglo-Saxon Art', *Frühmittelalterliche Studien*, 10 (1976), pp 367–406, esp. pp 381–90. **25** Reinhard Elze, 'The Ordo for the Coronation of King Roger II of Sicily: An Example of Dating from Internal Evidence', *Coronations: Medieval and Early Modern Monarchic Ritual*, ed. by János M. Bak (Berkeley/Los Angeles/Oxford, 1990), p. 171. **26** Marc Bloch, *The Royal Touch. Sacred Monarchy and Scrofula in England and France*, trans. by J.E. Anderson (London/Montreal, 1978;

one troubadour, Charles of Anjou is said to have born the cross on his body. Likewise, around the year 1260 a contemporary chronicler notes that people saw the cross between the shoulders of Frederick II's grandson and namesake. At the end of the fifteenth century the leading members of the Hapsburg family all allegedly had this mark on their backs. The sign is usually associated with reigning kings or pretenders to the throne who were cut off from their rightful inheritance at birth but were nevertheless destined to occupy it in the future. Although the earliest example Bloch could find was from the early thirteenth century, he assumed, quite correctly as we shall see, that the motif in its royal context originated in the twelfth century.

Seven years after *The Royal Touch* saw the light of day Arthur Dickson published his study of *Valentine and Orson*, a relatively obscure late medieval romance.[27] In this work, which has survived in both the English and a Swedish version, the royal pedigree of the two main protagonists of the story is revealed by a birthmark: a cross between the shoulder-blades. Dickson pointed out that this motif appears in numerous late medieval romances from England, France, Germany and the Netherlands. In an extended footnote he criticized Bloch for not having sufficiently emphasized its ubiquity in medieval literature and folklore. The criticism was not altogether a fair one, for in fact Bloch had drawn attention to the appearance of the motif in the *Lay of Havelock the Dane*, an English Romance from around the year 1300, where the royal status of the hero is confirmed by a blazing cross on his right shoulder, and in the German thirteenth century poem, *Kudrun* where Hagen the Irish bears a cross mark between his shoulder-blades. Thus the sign is attributed to both fictitious and historical figures; it crosses the boundaries between reality and art.

Marc Bloch suggested, almost as an afterthought it seems, that the origin of this belief was Isaiah 9:5, 'the government shall be upon his shoulders', which Christians have through the ages interpreted as a prophecy relating to the coming of Christ. Hence the positioning of the cross on the shoulder, the back or between the shoulder-blades in medieval tradition. This explanation leaves matters hanging in the air for it does not address the question why the motif cannot be found in the medieval sources before the turn of the twelfth century. A different approach is called for, one which takes into account the two-dimensional nature of the motif in question: its atemporal dimension and its historical one.

In the most diverse cultures we encounter a strong belief that a physical peculiarity of some sort designated from birth a person of inherent importance or quality. Particularly common is the belief that a child born with a caul around its neck will later in life possess powers out of the ordinary. For instance, in the Inquisitorial trials conducted in the last decades of the sixteenth century, over the so-called *benendanti* from the region of Friuli in Italy, the

originally published 1923), pp 142–46; see the references given there.   [27] Arthur Dickson, *Valentine and Orson. A Study in Late Medieval Romance* (New York, 1929), p. 49.

accused claimed that a child born with a caul around its neck was destined to become a witch (albeit a benign one).[28] In Greek mythology and legend lameness or malfunction of one foot is often associated with fated heroes who linked with the world of the dead.[29] Considering that the king was ultimate symbol of hereditary privilege, it is not surprising that there was a strong tendency to associate his inherent invisible qualities with corporal peculiarities of some nature. A browsing of Stith-Thompon's motif index for folklore bears this out clearly. In an Indian tale the golden hue of a certain boy's body denotes his royal status. In an African tale it is a red tooth that does the same job. In one Irish saga a luminous face is a sign of royal pedigree and in Old-Norse literature it is frequently the shining eyes or blond hair which mark the king, or the future king, from the rest. It is worth noting that in the case of royals the distinguishing mark is frequently shining, luminous or otherwise appropriate to their exalted status.[30] Whereas the peasants of Friuli were marked from birth by a somewhat earthly sign, that is, a caul around their neck, the heroes of the fifteenth-century English romance, *Cheuelere Assigne*, six princes and one princess, were born with silver necklaces around their neck.[31] Similarly in an Indian folk-tale, eight princesses and one prince were brought into the world with golden necklaces strung around their heads.[32]

There is nothing particularly Christian about these identifying peculiarities or even particularly pagan for that matter. We are here in the realm of folklore and folk-customs, where the person who is destined to fulfil a role beyond the ordinary carries a corporal sign of some nature.

This is the atemporal or ahistorical dimension relevant to the motif under discussion. Let us now turn to the temporal one. As mentioned above, Marc Bloch believed that the motif in its royal context originated in the twelfth century. This was the century in which the cross, not least as a result of Pope Urban II's exhortation, was adopted by the crusaders to the Holy Land as a visible demonstration of their undertaking.[33] Crusaders frequently had the sign imprinted on their garments and, according to contemporary or near-contemporary commentators some, in the wake of the religious enthusiasm which followed the first crusades, literally imprinted the crosses on their

---

28 Carlo Ginzburg, *The Night Battles: Witchcraft and Agrarian Cults in the Sixteenth and Seventeenth Centuries*, trans. by John and Anne Tedeschi (London, 1983), pp 9–10.
29 Carlo Ginzburg, *Ecstasies: Deciphering the Witches' Sabbath*, trans. by Raymond Rosenthal (London, 1992), pp 230–40.   30 *Motif-index of Folk-literature*, ed. by Stith Thompson, III (Copenhagen, 1956), pp 79–380; Riti Kroesen, 'Hvessir augu senn hildingar The Awe-Inspiring Eyes of the King', *Arkiv för nordisk filologi*, 100 (1985), pp 41–58.   31 *The Romance of the Cheuelere Assigne*, ed. by Henry H. Gibbs, Early English Text Society, extra series, VI (London, 1868), lines 42–44.   32 *The Oral Tales of India*, ed. by Stith Thompson and Jonas Balys, Indian University Publication: Folklore Series, no. 10 (Bloomington, 1958), p. 215.   33 See James A. Brundage, '"Cruce Signari": The Rite for Taking the Cross in England', *Traditio*, 22 (1966), pp 289–91.

bodies.[34] Thus, in his *Itinerarium Kambriae, The Journey through Wales*, Gerald of Wales tells how in 1188 Archbishop Baldwin of Canterbury exhorted people on Anglesey to take up the cross to free Jerusalem from Saladin. 'Many of the common people were persuaded' but a band of youths, whom the archbishop addressed personally, were unmoved and did not follow their example. Within three days the same young men were beaten, and some killed, by a band of robbers. Seeing this as a divine retribution for their indifference to the archbishop's exhortation, the cross 'which they had previously scorned they now of their own free will marked on their own bodies.'[35]

Gerald does not specify here where the Welshmen in question imprinted the crosses on their bodies. Here, however, we may recall Fulcher of Chartres's statement that the drowned crusaders carried the sign between the shoulder-blades. This particular positioning of the mark is naturally highly symbolic for it evokes the scene of Christ carrying the cross to Golgotha which in turn highlights the pilgrim status of the crusaders. One of the earliest surviving eye-witness accounts of the First Crusade, the *Gesta Francorum et aliorum Hierosolimitanorum*, describes how during Bohemond's siege of Amalfi in Southern Italy the Norman war-lord was informed that the crusaders were 'all well-armed, they wear a badge of Christ's cross on their right arm or between the shoulders.'[36] In Reginald of Durham's twelfth-century *Life and Miracles of St Godric* we read that a certain pilgrim carried the sign of the cross between his shoulder-blades.[37]

The hypothesis can be put forward that the enhanced status of the cross as an outward symbol of *individual* piety in the twelfth century had a part to play in the simultaneous emergence of our motif as a sign of royal legitimacy. In this respect it can be placed within the general shift towards a more physical, humanising, expression of Christian spirituality in the course of the twelfth and thirteenth century; here we can see a certain correspondence with the development of *stigmata* in the same era.[38] As to the placement of the cross between the shoulders, it is worth noting that this part of the body had a strong association with royal succession. In an *Ordo* for the Roman emperor dating

---

34 See Jonathan Riley-Smith, *The First Crusade and the Idea of Crusading* (London, 1986), pp 34, 81–2, 114. See also the references to such acts during the First Crusade, ibid. p. 187. 35 *Gerald of Wales, The Journey through Wales and The Description of Wales*, Bk. II, *c*.7, trans. by Lewis Thorpe (London, 1978), pp 185–86; 'crucem quam antea spreverant in carne sibi invicem jam ultronei affixerunt.' Giraldi Cambrensis, *Itinerarium Kambriae et Descripto Kambriae*, II, 7, ed. by James F. Dimoch (RS. 1868), p. 126.   36 'Deferunt arma ad bellum congrua, in dextra uel inter utrasque scapulas crucem Christi baiulant', *Gesta Francorum et aliorum Hierosolimitanorum*, ed. by Rosalind Hill (Edinburgh/Oxford), p. 7. On the role of the cross sign in the *Gesta* see Colin Morris, 'The *Gesta Francorum* as Narrative History', *Reading Medieval Studies*, 19 (Reading, 1993), pp 64–65.   37 'et scapulis signum peregrinantium bajulavit', *Libellus de Vita et Miraculis S. Godrici, heremitae de Finchale*, auctore Reginaldo Monacho Dunselmensi, ed. by J. Stevenson (SS, 20; London, 1848), p. 166. 38 Constable, *Three Studies*, pp 213–16.

from the tenth or eleventh century, the ruler is anointed with the oil of catechumens on the right arm and between the shoulders.[39] According to the coronation rite by which Frederick Barbarossa was crowned in 1155, the prospective emperor first lay prostrate before the altar of St Peter before being anointed on the right arm and between the shoulder-blades.[40] Similarly, in a tenth-century French *Ordo*, the Capetian king is anointed both on the shoulders and between the shoulder-blades.[41]

It is possible to detect three stages of increasing symbolic intensity in the cases examined so far: the cross worn on the clothes, the cross branded on the body by human hands and, finally, the cross appearing as a sign of divine grace. In the royal context, however, the mark is there from birth as a tangible expression of an invisible quality: the sanctity of royal blood. In view of the apparently well known belief in the cross on the back or between the shoulder blades as denoting royalty, Eysteinn's last words acquire a highly sarcastic tinge. By requesting this potent symbol of kingship to be hacked on his shoulder at the time of his death the request becomes a defiant statement of his royal status.

Could I be reading too much into Eysteinn's final words by placing them within the context I have expounded above? Although Marc Bloch assumed that the cross motif had emerged in the twelfth century, the oldest example he could find is from the early thirteenth century. Moreover he did not list a single example from the nordic sphere.

IV

The political situation in Norway in the three decades following the killing of King Eysteinn was highly volatile. The royal line of Eysteinn exhausted itself in internal strife and in 1179 an outsider by the name of Sverrir Sigurðarson appeared on the scene and, after a long and fierce campaign, usurped the throne.

His reign was marked by sporadic opposition to his rule as one pretender after another stepped forward. One of the less distinguished figures of this sort, Þorleifr *breiðskeggr*, a former monk, is mentioned in the near-contemporary *Sverris saga*. The short chapter telling of Þorleifr begins thus:

> Þat sama sumar er iarll hafði andaz var floccr a Marcum austr. En firir þesom flocki var sa maðr er callaðr var Þorleifr breiðscegr oc væri son Eysteins konungs Haralds-sonar oc þat til iartegna at a meðal herða honom var eyr groit i cros.[42]

---

39 Melchior Hittorp, *De divinis Catholicae Ecclesiae officiis* (Paris, 1610), pp 153–54.
40 E. Martène, *De antiquis ecclesiae ritibus* (Antwerp, 1763), p. 212.   41 Ibid. p. 630.
42 *Sverris saga etter Cod. AM 327 4o*, ed. by Gustav Indrebø (Kristiania, 1920), p. 121.

> The same summer that the earl [Eiríkr *skakki*] had died a band appeared east in the Marker region. The leader of this band was a man named Þorleifr *breiðskeggr*; he was said to be a son of King Eysteinn Haraldsson, and as a sign of that he bore between his shoulders the scar of a wound healed in the shape of a cross.[43]

Þorleifr attracted a substantial following not least, we are told, because of his alleged wisdom and scrupulous morals: 'his life resembled a monk's life, subject to the rules of his order, rather than a layman's. Þorleifr's appearance on the Norwegian political stage was a brief one as he and most of his followers were killed in a surprise attack by king Sverrir's forces. However, following his death, a rumour was spread abroad that he was a saint', a notion that the author of *Sverris saga* dismisses outright.

The interesting feature here is Þorleifr's claim that a cross-shaped scar between the shoulder blades can prove that he is the son of King Eysteinn. It is noteworthy that the author of *Sverris saga* felt no need to explain why this peculiarity was able to prove anything of the sort. As we have seen, a cross-mark between the shoulder-blades was associated with royal status in medieval Europe. If this tradition was known in Norway as early as the late twelfth century – as I think one must assume – Þorleifr's reference to the cross on his body becomes more comprehensible. Moreover, it is the echo between his own claim – substantiated by a scar that had healed in the shape of a cross – and the tradition of his father's execution that particularly captures the attention. It is as if the wound hacked between the shoulder-blades of his father was, by miraculous intervention, stamped on his own body. Here the mark not only proves royal descent but also kinship with another person of royal pedigree associated with a similar mark.

In the late medieval romance of *Valentin und Namenlos* the sign is used for similar purposes.[44] Phila, the sister of the king of France, and newly married to the king of Hungary, gives birth to twin sons. At their birth, however, they are exposed by a wicked bishop and the king's mother who, spurred on by the prediction of an astronomer, both fear that the twins will be a threat when they come of age. The infants survive and one, Valentin, is found in a box floating on the river and rescued by Clarina, Phila's sister, who instantly recognizes that the child is of noble descent by the cross between its shoulders.[45] Some years later Valentin meets his twin brother Namenlos and observes that both have identical marks on their body.[46] This discovery convinces them that they are closely related, and together they set out to find their royal parents which, of course, they eventually do after various colourful adventures.

---

[43] My own translation. [44] *Namnlös och Valentin, en Medeltidsroman.* (*Namenlos und Valentin*). *Efter gamla handskrifter*, ed. by G.E. Klemming, *Svenska Fornskrift-Sällskapet*, Samlingar, Del III, Häft 1 (Stockholm, 1846). [45] Ibid. ll. 261–64. [46] Ibid. ll. 1208–10.

Thus Valentin and Namenlos finally came into possession of their rightful inheritance. The fairy-tale ending of their story is in stark contrast with the fate of the historical figure of Þorleifr *breiðskeggr*. Nevertheless, in both narratives, the motif of the cross between the shoulder-blades fulfils a similar double role: as a proof of royal pedigree and a sign of kinship between two members of a kingly dynasty.

The notion that an acquired corporal mark could be handed down from father to son was not unknown in the Middle Ages. Gerald of Wales in his *Itinerarium Kambriae* tells the following story:

> Militem quoque in Anglia vidimus, ex Devoniae finibus oriundum, cui nomen Erchembaldus: de quo contigit, ut dum matris in alvo gestaretur patre partum penitus abnegante, et matrem zelotypiae causa ex sola suspicione fortiter accusante, puero in lucem prodeunte, sola litem per se natura diremit. Fissuram namque, quam ictu lanceae militari exercitio per medium sub nare superius labrum genitor olim susceperat, laudabili naturae miraculo eodem in loco genitura praetendit. Erchembaldi quoque filium vidimus, cui nomen Stephanus, eodem indicio patrissantem ; casuali laesione tanquam in naturam jam conversa.[47]

> In England I once saw a knight called Erchembald, who came from Devonshire. While he was still in his mother's womb, his father refused to recognize him as his son. For reasons of jealousy, he accused his wife of adultery because he was suspicious of her. At the boy's birth nature settled the argument. As the result of a blow from a lance which he had received in battle, the father had a scar just below his nose in the middle of his upper lip. By some miracle of nature, when the child was born, he, too, had a scar in the same place. I myself saw Erchembald's son, whose name was Stephen, and there is no doubt that he had the same mark.[48]

Here we encounter clearly a similar phenomenon to the one found in *Sverris saga*: in both cases an acquired physical peculiarity is transmitted to the next generation and in turn functions as proof of particular ancestry. However, the case of the Norwegian pretender carries a much clearer supernatural connotation. The mark on Eysteinn's body is imprinted (if it ever was) *after* he (allegedly) conceived Þorleifr and thus can only be explained within a miraculous context. The incident recorded by Gerald of Wales, however, is a clear case of a marvel, that is, a remarkable occurrence or a strange phenomenon which was nevertheless a work of nature[49] rather than an example of divine intervention. A comparable

---

[47] Giraldi Cambrensis, *Itinerarium Kambriae*, pp 131–32. [48] Gerald of Wales, *The Journey through Wales*, Bk. II, *c*.7, pp 190–91. [49] 'The crucial distinction in Gerald's mind between a marvel and a miracle was that the miracle was produced by divine

Insigne Crucis: *A European Motif in a Nordic Setting*

attitude towards a similar phenomenon can be found in Pliny the Elder's *Historia Naturalis* where we are told that 'a thought suddenly flitting across the mind of either parent is supposed to produce likeness or to cause combination of features' in the offspring.[50] It appears more than possible that Gerald of Wales was influenced by Pliny in his discussion of hereditary peculiarities in *Itinerarium Kambriae*.[51]

The curious echo between the Eysteinn's death scene in *Heimskringla* and the reference to Þorleifr *breiðskeggr* in *Sverris saga* strongly indicates that the motif of the cross between the shoulder-blades as a sign of royal pedigree was known in Norway around the turn of the twelfth century. It is important to emphasize that the motif does not appear in the two Icelandic Kings' sagas as a literary embellishment or stylistic device. Rather it seems to serve a very real political purpose in a society where succession to the throne was disputed and there was a clear need for outward symbols to legitimize royal authority. Indeed King Sverrir Sigurðarson himself justifies his claim to kingship by telling about a dream in which St Ólafr Haraldsson, *rex perpetuus Norvegiae*, appears to him and promises to aid him in his struggle against the then reigning king, Magnús Erlingsson.[52] It is this peculiar situation in Norway which may explain the surprisingly early appearance of the cross-motif in the Kings' sagas.

Moreover we are dealing here with an oral tradition associated with two leaders who were venerated as martyrs following their death; it is not difficult to envisage how their cults could function as rallying points for their supporters. Indeed the veneration of Eysteinn and Þorleifr appears to have taken deeper roots than the cursory references to their veneration in the Old-Norse sources may lead us to believe. Thus it is known that in the sixteenth century '*Hellig Thorlofs Capel*' (St Þorleifr's Chapel) was located at Elverums in the Marker region.[53] No other saint is known by that name, and considering that that chapel was located in the region where Þorleifr *breiðskeggr* was active, it is safe to assume that it was dedicated to him. Similarly, in a nineteenth-century source, 'St Østeins kilde' (St Eysteinn's spring), is recorded to have been situated near the place where the king was executed,[54] information which squares with the reference in *Heimskringla* to the healing spring which emerged following Eysteinn's execution. Thus through the manifestation of the cross-

---

power, usually, though not exclusively, working through a saintly man or woman, while the marvel, however remarkable it might be, was a work of nature.' R. Bartlett, *Gerald of Wales 1146–1223* (Oxford, 1982), p. 106.   50 'cogitatio etiam utriuslibet animum subito transvolans effingere similitudinem aut miscere existimatur.' Pliny, Natural History, Bk. VII, *c*.12, trans. by H. Rackham, II (*Loeb Classics*: Cambridge Mass., 1962), pp 540–41. 51 'It is possible that physical peculiarities of this sort my be produced in a child because the mother remembers something which she has seen, concentrating on it and thinking of nothing else.' Gerald of Wales, *The Journey Through Wales*, p. 191.   52 *Sverris Saga*, pp 4–5.   53 L. Daae, *Norges helgener* (Christiania, 1879), p. 129.   54 Ibid. p. 192.

motif in relation to King Eysteinn Haraldsson and his alleged son, Þorleifr *breiðskeggr*, we get a decidedly rare glimpse of a sort of 'oral hagiography' which could sustain and enhance the saintly reputation of martyred secular leaders in the absence of official promotion of their cults.

In the medieval period the enigmatic Skarphéðinn of *Njáls Saga*, the crusaders drowned on their way to the Holy Land, the defiant king Eysteinn, Þorleifr the failed pretender to the Norwegian crown, and many other figures, imaginary or real, were associated with a special sign: a cross on the shoulder or between the shoulder-blades. It is the manner in which this mysterious sign appears in different contexts that makes it a motif of interest. In the historical works of two Frenchmen, Guibert of Nogent and Fulcher of Chartres, writing at the turn of the twelfth century, the origin and nature of the sign reveals their different attitude towards the miraculous. In *Njáls saga* the sign illuminates an unexpected side of the violent Skarphéðinn: the seemingly unflappable hero etches it on his body as he faces his ultimate judgement. In *Heimskringla* the mark – appearing in a novel form – neither carries with it notions of penance nor of salvation but rather those of royalty and heroism at the hour of death. Ironically, of the three Scandinavian examples, it is only in the case of Þorleifr, the obscure and somewhat pathetic pretender, that the sign appears in its most common form: as an indication of royal status. In his case and that of his alleged father, King Eysteinn Haraldsson, the motif shows how the boundaries between political propaganda, literary motifs and folkloric beliefs could overlap – even in the far North.

Points of Law at the Point of a Sword: Tristan's Duel with Morolt in the North Sea World

VICKIE ZIEGLER

Of all the aspects of medieval life that have been held up to ridicule by the cultural Darwinists, the concept of the ordeal has been among the most disparaged. These critics, however, fail to understand the position that the ordeal occupied in the range of legal proofs available. It was considered a last resort, an appeal to God in a final attempt to establish justice when all other avenues were exhausted. In the Middle Ages, people were well aware that this last resort sometimes failed to achieve real justice – just as we too could point to modern notorious miscarriages of justice despite our supposedly more enlightened proceedings. Indeed, they recognized that the ordeal was susceptible to human manipulation. For that reason, the condemnation by the Fourth Lateran Council for all intents and purposes stopped the use of such unilateral ordeals as trial by fire and trial by water, which had come to be seen as attempts to manipulate God.[1] Nevertheless, trial by battle, a bilateral ordeal, persisted as a valid judicial proceeding for a much longer time. It is perhaps easier for us to understand why it survived so long if we look at the belief at the core of both sorts of judicial ordeal – a belief shared among the three monotheistic religions: that God supports the side that is in the right, or at least, more in the right. The latter type of ordeal persisted because medieval society drew an important theological distinction between asking for God's support in a situation in life, whether in court or on the battlefield, and asking God to render an independent and verifiable verdict on demand through the natural order.

While both sorts of ordeal are evident in the various surviving versions of the Tristan and Isolde stories, scholars have invariably paid more attention to Isolde's unilateral ordeal. This study, however, will examine the trial by battle or judicial duel, the bilateral ordeal, that figured in the Tristan material as it appeared in several locales about the North Sea during the high and late Middle

---

[1] Robert Bartlett, *Trial by Fire and Water: The Medieval Judicial Ordeal* (Oxford, 1986), pp 116–22. See also Gerhard Buchda, 'Der Beweis im mittelalterlichen sächsichen Recht', in *La Preuve*, Recueils de la Société Jean Bodin (Bruxelles, 1964), pp 531–32. Hermann Nottarp, *Gottesurteile* (Munich, 1956), p. 265, notes that, in the case of a duel, the secular judge, not a priest, decides on guilt or innocence.

Ages – in works in Middle High German by Gottfried von Straßburg, in Old Norse by Brother Robert, and in Middle English by Sir Thomas Malory. The works are different in significant ways. Gottfried's work, the oldest chronologically, seems here to reflect elements of the MHG Charlemagne/Roland tradition and contains a significant use of allegory, in contrast to both Brother Robert's and Malory's works. Brother Robert's Old Norse translation of Thomas' version of the Tristan material, on which Gottfried also based his adaptation, contrasts with Malory's account, which was based on the very different Old French prose *Tristan*. And Malory's version, coming as it does at the end of the Middle Ages, discards the religious and ethical elements so prominent in Gottfried's version in favor of a late medieval English portrayal of an ideal knight. Nevertheless, a comparative analysis of the handling of this judicial duel will provide some interpretative clues to larger literary issues in the Tristan material and shed some light on the larger legal context.

Drawn both by the heat of the iron and Isolde's passion in *Tristan*, scarcely any scholar dealing with the judicial ordeal in the Middle Ages avoids mentioning Gottfried von Straßburg's version of Isolde's ordeal. Forced to carry the hot iron to defend herself against an accusation of adultery, Isolde's careful formulation of her oath results in an acquittal. Yet the other ordeal in the work, the judicial duel between Tristan and Morolt, languishes in relative critical obscurity. Even the leading German legal dictionary does not cite it as a source, though the legal learning that Gottfried demonstrated in his portrayal of the ordeal by fire is no less in evidence in the judicial duel between Tristan and Morolt.[2] This neglect is even more surprising, since Gottfried's approach to each ordeal could not be more different. Missing are sardonically ironic commentaries, missing are attempts to pervert the process of justice through oaths that are literally true but at the heart false. Instead the language of legend and the chanson de geste as well as allegorical elements, which Gottfried uses at significant and serious parts of the work, such as Tristan's knighting and the love grotto, clothe the judicial duel with narrative approbation. Not only the type of ordeal and the presentation differ, but also the legal matters in question contrast sharply. The judicial issue in the Morolt narrative concerns the terms of a political and financial contract. While the first ordeal centers on interpretation of the facts, the point of emphasis in the second is on true or false oaths in a case of adultery. As such, the theological questions that hang in the charged air around Isolde during her ordeal are not at issue here.

A particular interpretative point at issue is the character of Tristan and its relation to Gottfried's opinion of chivalry. Certain critics, such as Jackson, Green, Stein etc., belong to what might be called the 'Tristan the Trickster' school; in their view, his perceived manipulative and deceptive behavior constitutes

[2] Ruth Schmidt-Wiegand, *Handwörterbuch zur deutschen Rechtsgeschichte*, 34. Lieferung (Berlin, 1992), cols 364–70. (Hereafter referred to as *HWBDR*.)

an attack on chivalry; they believe there is support for their interpretation in the judicial duel with Morolt. Their indifference to legal history makes this exercise easier than it might be. They conflate unilateral and bilateral ordeals and are not familiar with medieval legal realities or courtroom procedure.[3] This lack of knowledge leads both to mis- and overinterpretation, as we shall see in the course of this paper.

A vital link in the chain of events that bring Tristan to Ireland, the judicial duel with Morolt is the only judicial duel in the work that actually comes about. Tristan dispatches Morgan in a fight, while the proposed duels in the Truchseß and Gandin episodes never actually happen. The legal issue provoking this battle involved the tribute that Cornwall had to pay Gurmun of Ireland. This tribute, described as 'zins' in the original text (ll. 5930, 5942), was a result of Cornwall's subjection by Gurmun of Ireland. The word *zins*, Lat. census, was a well-established legal term in the Middle Ages, used in commercial as well as in governmental affairs.[4]

The payment of the tribute had been established in a treaty. Tristan and Morolt use four words with legal meanings to describe the guarantees and terms of this relationship: *sicherheit*, *eit*, *gelübede*, and *triuwe*. All four can mean a promise or an agreement, yet there are different shades of meaning.[5] *Sicherheit* could mean the treaty itself, while the *eit* (oath), in addition to denoting a promise, was also the means through which an agreement received legal standing. The oath owed its force and standing to its function as a kind of self-curse, which called down penalties on violators. The Christianization of the oath only increased its gravity for the individual.[6] The oath in question here is not a purgative oath, such as Kunegunde swore, but a promissory one. These types of oaths, common in the Middle Ages, came in a variety of forms, some

---

3 W.T.H. Jackson, *The Anatomy of Love: The Tristan of Gottfried von Straßburg* (New York, 1971), pp 148–50. Dennis Green, *Irony in the Medieval Romance* (Cambridge, 1979), pp 60–61, 88–89. Peter K. Stein, 'Tristans Schwertleite: Zur Einschätzung ritterlich-höfischen Dichtung durch Gottfried von Straßburg', *Deutsche Vierteljahrsschrift für Literaturgeschichte und Geistesgeschichte*, 51 (1977), pp 340–43. Walther Haug, 'Âventiure in Gottfried von Straßburgs Tristan', in *Festschrift für Hans Eggers zum 65. Geburtstag*, ed. by Hubert Backes (Tübingen, 1972), pp 109–11. 4 *Deutsches Wörterbuch*, ed. by Jacob and Wilhelm Grimm (Leipzig, 1956), XV, cols 1476–78, col. 1477: 'als zeichen politischer abhängigkeit und botmäszigkeit, vom oberherrn unterworfenen Völkern auferlegt [. . .] diese bedeutung überwiegt in der ahd. und mhd. literatur'. Grimm cites line 5979 of Gottfried's *Tristan*, from the Morolt episode, as an example of this meaning, col. 1478. 5 Matthias Lexer, *Mittelhochdeutsches Handwörterbuch*, I (Leipzig, 1872) *eit*, col. 534; *gelübede*, col. 828; II (1876), *sicherheit*, cols 902–03; *triuwe*, col. 1520. 6 Hans Hattenhauer, 'Der gefälschte Eid', in *Fälschungen im Mittelalter: Internationaler Kongreß der Monumenta Germaniae Historica, Teil II: Gefälschte Rechtstexte: der bestrafte Fälscher* (Hannover, 1988), pp 659–89. Ruth Schmidt-Wiegand, 'Eid und Gelöbnis, Formel und Formular im mittelalterlichen Recht', in *Recht und Schrift im mittelalterlichen Recht*, ed. by Peter Classen, Vorträge und Forschungen, XXIII (Sigmaringen, 1977), pp 55–56.

of them, such as the subject's oath, probably modeled on Roman law. Many came from conquered regions, such as the one we have here.[7]

From the thirteenth century on, *Gelübede* is well documented as a legal term for obligation; renunciation incurred the loss of reputation as well as legal rights and was equated with perjury. Morolt's line of defense is therefore a potent one: choosing those parts of the agreement that corroborate his legal position, he accuses Tristan and thereby the rest of the nobles of oath-breaking, which was a kind of perjury, as well as of breaking their *triuwe* (fidelity) and *sicherheit*. In the Middle Ages, the breach of any kind of formalized promise was considered a breach of fidelity.[8] These charges were laden with most serious legal implications, which is why Tristan immediately goes on the counter-attack.

Tristan immediately punctures Morolt's legal strategy, which, like most legal strategies, is long in the tooth: you don't have a case. The hope is always that an uninformed or dull-witted opponent will accept the other's statement at face value and give up. Tristan, however, knows the terms of the treaty and in a cogent and precise response, seizes the legal initiative from Morolt. Refusal to pay tribute does not break *triuwe unde eit*: Tristan points out that the terms of the agreement provided for either the tribute or a duel between champions or a battle between two armies as fulfillment of Cornwall's legal obligations (6359–76). Not only does Tristan have the specific treaty on his side, but he also could have called on tradition: the right to dissolve an oath to an unjust lord had existed since Germanic times.[9]

Faced with the facts, Morolt still tries to place his opponent at a moral disadvantage. The choice of a battle or duel is no choice, since he came alone, expecting no hostility. He intended to leave Cornwall as he had always done, with 'rehte und ouch mit minnen' (6404), legal obligations fulfilled in a peaceful atmosphere. This phrase, a legal term whose first appearance in a German dialect was in the *Sachsenspiegel*, reveals that for Morolt, *reht*, or law, still means the tribute with no other options.[10]

In this case, Morolt's interpretation of the treaty differs irreconcilably from that of Tristan and the nobles; the fact that a duel takes place at all indicates

---

7 Gerhard Dilcher, 'Eid', *HWBDR*, I (Berlin, 1971), cols 866–70. 8 Ekkehard Kaufmann, 'Treue', *HWBDR*, 34. Lieferung (Berlin, 1992), col. 328. Gerhard Buchda, 'Gelöbnis', *HWBDR*, col. 1493. Heinz Holzhauer, 'Meineid', *HWBDR*, III (Berlin, 1984), col. 452. 9 Julius Planck, *Das deutsche gerichtsverfahren im mittelalter* (Braunschweig, 1879), II, p. 147. See Dilcher, 'Eid', *HWBRG*, I, col. 869. 10 Hermann Krause, 'Minne und Recht', *HWBDR*, III (Berlin, 1984), cols 582–88, esp. cols 584–85, where he cites the passage from *Tristan*, noting that *minne* here has a legal sense. See also Hermann Krause, '*Consilio et iudicio*: Bedeutungsbreite und Sinngehalt einer mittelalterlichen Formel', in *Speculum Historiale: Geschichte im Spiegel von Geschichtsschreibung und Geschichtsdeutung*, ed. by Clemens Bauer, Laetitia Boehm, and Max Mueller (Freiburg/Munich, 1965), p. 436. Further evidence that Morolt holds fast to the position that Cornwall is obliged to pay the tribute comes in his reply to Tristan (6443–49).

that Morolt's position rests on interpretation and not incontrovertible fact. Like the ordeals of fire and water, the judicial ordeal was used in cases where the truth could not be established in other ways. Since there can be no compromise between the two positions on the legality of the tribute, the issue must be settled through a judicial duel.[11] This fact of medieval legal life has been overlooked by those scholars critical of Tristan, who see the judicial duel as a tactical ploy that Tristan originates, evidence of his lack of principle.[12] In actual fact, there were definite procedural rules about sufficient reasons for judicial duels; moreover, as the only serious analysis of law in *Tristan* points out, the fact that something needs to be proved places the duel in the category of a *judicium Dei*.[13] It would seem dangerous to base an interpretation of this event on a lack of basic knowledge of legal procedure, particularly when Gottfried incorporates so much of it here and elsewhere.

This form of the ordeal, trial by battle, was part of the warp and woof of the judicial fabric of the Middle Ages.[14] This legal procedure had its roots in Germanic times, when a fight was the remedy of choice for dispute settlement, though it did not establish truth in the way that the *judicium Dei* was intended to do. In pre-Christian times, divine intervention was thought to occur on the side of the protagonist with the best magic and not on that of the party who was in the right from an abstract point of view.[15] The fight does not establish this fact, but reveals it, since God intervenes on behalf of the right.[16] God's

---

11 Planck, *Gerichtsverfahren*, II, p. 147.   12 See, for example, Haug, 'Gottfried', p. 111: 'wenn er von daher die Auseinandersetzung zum gerichtlichen Zweikampf stilisiert, so ist das Taktik'. Green, *Irony*, p. 88, citing Haug, says: 'Tristan converts a single combat into one concerned with the justice of the case for his own shrewdly calculated purposes'.   13 See Planck, *Gerichtsverfahren*, II, p. 147. Rosemary Norah Combridge, *Das Recht im 'Tristan' Gottfrieds von Strassburg* (Berlin, 1964), p. 52. Jean–Marie Carbasse, 'Le Duel judicaire dans les coutumes méridionales', *Annales du Midi*, 87 (1975), p. 388.   14 Discussion of the question of the relation of the ordeal by battle to the other ordeals appears in Bartlett, *Trial*, pp 106–26, and in Heinz Holzhauer, 'Der gerichtliche Zweikampf', in *Sprache und Recht: Beiträge zur Kulturgeschichte des Mittelalters: Festschrift für Ruth Schmidt-Wiegand zum 60. Geburtstag* (Berlin, 1986), pp 270–01.   15 Henry Charles Lea, *The Duel and the Oath*, ed. by Edward Peters (1866; Philadelphia, 1974), pp 112–32. Kurt Georg Cram, *Iudicium Belli: Zum Rechtscharakter des Krieges im deutschen Mittelalter* (Münster/Cologne, 1955), pp 8–9. Holzhauer, 'Zweikampf', discusses the origins of the judicial duel, which seems to have been found in other cultures as well (pp 265–74). See also G. Baist, 'Der gerichtliche Zweikampf, nach seinem Ursprung und im Rolandslied', *Romanische Forschungen V* (*Festschrift Konrad Hoffmann zum 70. Geburtstag*), 92 (1980), pp 437–38. Since this analysis concerns itself primarily with the legal function of the trial by battle in its Western European context, particularly in the German lands, questions of origins and parallels in other societies lie outside its scope. The issue has been hotly debated; for a useful summary of nineteenth-century legal scholars' opinions on the original nature of the duel, see Alexander Gal, 'Der Zweikampf im fränkischen Prozeß', *ZRG GA*, 28 (1907), pp 238–41.   16 Cram, *Iudicium*, p. 11, distinguishes between a duel as *Entscheidungsmittel* and as

active involvement appears from the beginning of Tristan's conversations with the nobles (6085–133, 6138–92). He expressly states that if the battle turns out in his favor, it will be because God wills it so (6171–72). These passages deserve some close attention, because in them Tristan lays out the issues involved and the outlines of the personification that Gottfried later expands prior to the battle. When Tristan returns to Mark's court, full of cringing barons preparing to sell their children into slavery to save their own lives, he bases his amazement on religious grounds, saying that it was completely against God's commandments to behave this way (6105–10). Only one man plus a duel are needed to change this situation; that man is assured of divine rewards immediately if he loses and later if he wins. God's commandments and their own reputations should impel them to find a champion who will put his fate in God's hands and not fear Morolt's strength too much. Tristan's references to divine intervention become much more frequent as it becomes apparent that he is the only noble ready to take on this task. If they leave matters to God and himself, he entreats God to let matters fall out well and restores them to their rights. If the battle has a positive outcome, then that is due to the power of God, who alone deserves thanks if Tristan succeeds. He mentions God, justice, and his own strength of feeling as his three helpers who go with him into battle and who compensate for his lack of experience (6138–92). This reference sets the stage for the personification that Gottfried introduces during the battle.

The role of God as the guarantor of justice (6170–72) and Tristan's protector (6155, 6158, 6184) appears frequently in Tristan's speeches throughout the Morolt section. Similar statements figure prominently in the speeches of saintly characters about to undergo ordeals; Kunegunde and Richardis come to mind.[17] In this regard, Tristan's statements, reminiscent as they are of legend material, serve several functions. Like the courageous and holy figures of legend, Tristan stands unequivocally in the right. In other ordeal material in literature, only the figures who are right in a religious sense and who will emerge victorious speak so calmly about losing. Similar speeches are missing from the section involving Isolde's trial by fire. The absence of such speeches during Isolde's trial is not the only difference between Gottfried's treatment of the two ordeals. Throughout the quarrel with Morolt, God's role in the rule of law appears in a much different light than in the later court scene. Tristan describes God here as the supreme arbiter who ensures that right triumphs. The contrast could not be more marked with the famous commentary of Gottfried's on the pliant Christ.

One of the major functions of the ordeal by battle was to combat perjury, which is why we find it often in cases connected to oaths or treaties, since the

---

Beweismittel, and says that it was already a means of proof in the Burgundian law. For discussion of this distinction among German legal scholars, see Bartlett, *Trial*, p. 114. See also Lea, *Duel*, p. 103; Alexander Gal, 'Zweikampf,' p. 238, where he discusses the connection between a false oath and the judicial duel.   **17** See the *Kaiserchronik*, ll.

Points of Law at the Point of a Sword 39

breaking of a promise was equated with perjury, as is the case in the situation with Morolt. Because the issues surrounding a trial by battle were often major ones, the stakes were high, involving such considerations as the loss of property, a hand, legal protection or one's own life.[18] Consequently, these fights were often bestially ferocious, as is the case with Tristan's struggle. A vicious fight, in which each side took whatever advantage possible, should not be taken as a mark of a calculating and devious character, as critics of Tristan and chivalry have frequently assumed. Indeed, recent research has shown that medieval German literature of Gottfried's day contained such ruthless battles by aristocratic heroes whose conduct was never questioned.[19]

The ordeal by battle frequently led to death and certainly to bloodshed. A judicial duel involving treason in the twelfth century (1127) culminated in Herman the Iron, aptly named, seizing the genitalia of his opponent Guy of Steenvoorde and swinging the unfortunate traitor by them.[20] While God was expected to support the truthful combatant, no matter how strong his opponent,[21] there still was a certain amount of uneasiness. Those familiar with such struggles knew that there were many factors outside of divine intervention that could determine the course of a fight. Morolt gives us a good example, since he comes equipped with poison on his sword. For these reasons, the trial by battle attracted a lot of criticism at a relatively early date.[22] In contrast to the ordeal by fire, which involved the accused and the elements, the trial by battle demanded neither a direct response from the natural world nor an immediate sign of

---

15463–509, and Ebernand von Erfurt, *Heinrich und Kunegunde*, ll. 1490–616.   **18** Lea, *Duel*, pp 166–71.   **19** Haug, 'Gottfried', p. 111, criticizes Tristan for stooping to any means to win. See also Green, *Irony*, p. 88. Martin H. Jones, 'The Depiction of Military Combat in Gottfried's Tristan', in *Gottfried von Strassburg and the Medieval Tristan Legend* (Cambridge, 1990), pp 57–59, cites passages from Hartmann von Aue, Geoffrey of Monmouth, and Wace, that show that even in non-judicial combat, ruthlessness and fierceness were common and did not occasion criticism.   **20** *The Murder of Charles the Good, Count of Flanders*, trans. and ed. by James Bruce Ross (New York, 1967), pp 212–13.   **21** Ritschier expresses this belief in *Engelhard*, ll. 4034–38: 'Zewâre, waeret ir ein rise, ich wolte iu kampfes doch gestân, ûf den vil saeleclichen wân daz got die rehten wârheit mit sîner helfe nie vermeit'.   **22** See Dagmar Hüpper-Dröge, 'Der gerichtliche Zweikampf im Spiegel der Bezeichnungen für "Kämpf", "Kampfer" und "Waffen"', *Frühmittelalterliche Studien*, 18 (1959), pp 648–49, for a discussion of clerical criticism of the judicial ordeal in the Burgundian law codes, also pp 624, 627. Herbert Kolb, 'Himmlisches und irdisches Gericht in karolingischer Theologie und altdeutscher Dichtung', in *Althochdeutsch*, ed. by Rolf Bergmann (1987), pp 290–91, also mentions the constant criticism of the ordeal by battle from the early Middle Ages on. Such criticism centered on its judicial validity and its relation to Christian ethics. Theologians were against it and the secular courts were for it. Misgivings about the trial by battle were of long standing: for example, an eighth-century Langobard king, Liutprand, already expressed doubts about its validity, as did the Salian Franks (p. 270). See also Yvette Bongert, *Récherches sur les Courts laïques du Xe au XIIIe siècle* (Paris, 1949), pp 229–30, and Carbasse, 'Le duel judicaire', pp 385, 386–88, 393, 394, 396.

divine intervention.[23] Consequently, critics who fault Tristan for deviousness in this encounter cannot credibly maintain, as they try to do, that his prayers for assistance were an attempt to manipulate God, similar to Isolde's attempt.[24] There are two distinctive differences: in a battle, God is not asked to reply through the natural order of inanimate things. Secondly, there were no literally true but inherently false oaths, which are attempts to manipulate God.

The abundance of legal terminology and customs that appear with no elaboration in the speeches of Tristan and Morolt show that both Gottfried and his audience were familiar with the legal procedures surrounding a judicial duel. Gottfried seems to use this familiarity to shape his characterization of Tristan and Mark and indirectly give clues about his opinion of the two ordeals.

Since a judicial duel was the legal remedy of last resort, there were lengthy statements about the case beforehand. These took place in a courtroom setting, which included the peers of the realm, as well as the ruler, who usually functioned as judge, as Charlemagne did in Genelun's trial. The paradigmatic literary judicial duel, appearing in Priest Konrad's late twelfth-century work, with which Gottfried certainly could have been familiar, was the one relating to Genelun's guilt in the German versions of the *Song of Roland*. Medieval judges did not have to be neutral, as Charlemagne certainly was not.[25] While Mark functions nominally in this regard in the Morolt episode, he functions in a much less active way than the bishop of Thames, the presiding official, in the hot iron ordeal. Mark appears only on the sidelines, to wring his hands at the risk to his beloved nephew, and to help arm him. While both of these activities were based on the traditional responsibility of a brother for the safety of his sister's son,[26] the manner in which Mark carries them out causes Gottfried to note that the most timid of women could not have been more distraught (6524–25). Tristan does take center stage in the negotiations, causing Morolt to refer sarcastically to the newly knighted youth as the *voget* for Cornwall. As we hold this part of Gottfried's description of the courtroom scene up against contemporary legal practice, we might ask if Gottfried uses this apparent departure from normal procedure as a means to characterize the weakness and inferior ability of Mark over against Tristan. It would certainly fit with many other incidents that define Mark as an indecisive and insecure character.

In his formal challenge to Morolt, Gottfried's Tristan shows an intimate knowledge of legal procedures. He first makes all parties aware of what is at issue: whose interpretation of the law is correct (6450–54). As a gage of battle, he offers his glove. The rationale behind this gesture is to offer surety that the

---

23 Bartlett, *Trial*, p. 121. Edward Peters, Introduction to Lea, *Duel*, p. 7. See also Bongert, *Recherches*, p. 239.   **24** Green, *Irony*, p. 88. Stein, 'Schwertleite', p. 342.
25 See, for example, the portrayals of Charlemagne in Pfaffe Konrad's *Rolandslied* and Der Stricker's *Karl der Große*.   **26** Lambertus Okken, *Kommentar zum Tristan-Roman Gottfrieds von Strassburg* (Amsterdam, 1984), I, pp 186–87, 320.

duel will take place. Gloves, used since Franconian times as guarantees in cases of debt, signified in a duel that the participants owed each other a battle (6444, 6486–87).[27] Further indication of Gottfried's extensive understanding of courtroom procedure is Tristan's awareness that he can spoil his case by misspeaking: he asks the king and all present to listen to how he presents the case for a judicial duel so that he does not break any rules (6458–60).[28] There follows a clear and precise statement of what he intended to prove with the ordeal, a statement that could only have been produced by a writer with some sort of legal knowledge or experience: that neither Morolt, his lord, nor any other man has a right to exact tribute with force from Cornwall and England. The duel is to cover all eventualities and leave no opportunity for anyone to find a loophole later. Tristan's case will be proved before God and the world on the person of Morolt, who is responsible for the shame and misery that has befallen these two lands (6461–72).

Not only the larger legal issues but also the details of legal procedure appear in Gottfried's account. Judicial duels generally took place at a subsequent date; Tristan's and Morolt's is set for three days later (6494–95).[29] Negotiations also decided the site for the battle. In this case, an island so close to the mainland that everyone could see the battle was chosen (6721–26). Though otherwise unknown in other Middle High German literary descriptions of judicial ordeals, such a site was frequent in Old Norse saga accounts.[30] Because of the proximity of the island to the mainland, no one other than the combatants was allowed on the island (6727–30). Such firm rules, usually threatening the death penalty to interlopers, were common in order to avoid interference with justice.[31]

As the battle itself draws near, Gottfried paints a revealing picture in the approach of the two combatants, a picture that sums up their attitudes towards the encounter: Morolt, as we have previously seen in the court assembly, trusts in his strength and experience. This attitude, confidence in one's own ability instead of God's help, is characteristic of Pinabel in the Roland material as well,

---

27 Okken, *Kommentar*, I, pp 324–25.   **28** See Planck, *Gerichtsverfahren*, I, p. 795. **29** Such combats did not generally take place on the spot, but at a time in the future; a delay of 4–6 weeks was common in southern Germany; here we have three days. The protagonists had time to practice and to put their affairs in order, should the worst come to pass. They had to put up security for their reappearance; if the defendant did not show up, he was judged guilty. Generally, the battle stopped with the setting of the sun. See Lea, *Duel*, pp 173, 178, and Bongert, *Recherches*, pp 243, 246, for comments on the French situation.   **30** See Otto Holzapfel, 'Holmgangr', *HWBDR*, II, col. 219, who notes that sagas frequently describe duels on small islands according to definite rules. These duels often figured in legal questions. See also Beverly Kennedy, *Knighthood in the Morte D'Arthur* (Cambridge, 1992), p. 156. Holzhauer, 'Zweikampf', pp 272–73, in describing the origins of the judicial duel in the various Germanic legal codes and systems, discusses it in Old Norse society. He says it was often used in property matters. Planck, *Gerichtsverfahren*, pp 795–96, mentions the site in its legal context.   **31** See Planck, *Gerichtsverfahren*, p. 796.

which has much of the hagiographic legend in it. Morolt puts on an imposing display for the benefit of the spectators assembled on the mainland: he gallops his horse at full tilt, thrusting with his lance, as if he were engaged in courtly games. Tristan, meanwhile, stands before his boat and holds an earnest farewell with Mark and his subjects. He asks God to restore justice and go with him in the battle (6745–84).

Before the blows begin, both combatants go on the offensive in other ways: Tristan sets his boat adrift, because only one of them will survive the encounter. Morolt addresses him with the familiar form of the personal pronoun, either as a sign of lack of respect or as a signal that all social conventions are laid aside now that the battle is imminent.[32] The typical epic convention of the defendant's offer of a bribe appears here, as it does in Stricker's *Karl* during the duel to prove Genelun's guilt. In both of these cases, the defendants are much bigger and more experienced gladiators. Consequently, in each case, the refusal of this offer enhances the stature of the plaintiff.[33]

Emphasis on the uneven physical odds calls the David/Goliath comparison to mind and lends further support to the argument that God is on Tristan's side. Indeed, the parallels between David/Tristan, Saul/Mark, and Goliath/Morolt appear throughout the Morolt incident. The Hebrews, like the Britons, have the choice of settling the matter via a duel of two champions or a battle of the two armies. None of the other Hebrews or Britons is prepared to fight Goliath or Morolt individually. Both Tristan and David come from outside the country and both are accused of arrogance. Although both are inexperienced in such battles, both trust in God, knowing that the attack from the opponent is an attack on God as well. Saul and Mark both advise against the battle, but both arm their defender. David and Tristan both leave permanent reminders of their victory in their victims' foreheads and both behead their opponents.[34] These striking parallels reinforce the other indications in the narrative that God is on Tristan's side.

As the fight commences, Tristan, despite an energetic offensive, soon begins to get the worst of it at the hands of the experienced Morolt, who is described as one led by the Devil (6852). Later he appears as the condemned vassal of the Devil (6906). Such descriptions are a staple of these encounters, particularly in the language of legend and the Charlemagne material; we find them almost word for word describing Pinabel in the various versions of Genelun's trial. Like Pinabel, Morolt trusts in his own strength and is on the wrong side. Such a description only enhances the character of the protagonist, as do many other elements of Gottfried's characterization. The detailed account of the fierce battle that took place establishes the need for divine intervention.

---

[32] Okken, *Kommentar*, I, p. 74.   [33] In this particular case, Morolt offers a second bribe after he has wounded Tristan.   [34] See Okken, *Kommentar*, I, pp 304–06.

This course of events sets the stage for the allegorical elements that characterize the last decisive part of the battle. Against Morolt's strength, equivalent to that of four men, Gottfried sets God, Right, and Willing Heart as Tristan's companions in arms. As God and Right ride in to help, Tristan senses their presence and is able to spur his horse on to one last charge so that Morolt is overturned. Able to slice off Morolt's sword hand before he remounts, Tristan beheads Morolt.

In order to understand fully the significance of the presence of allegorical figures during this ordeal, it is necessary to examine briefly Gottfried's use of allegory and personification in other parts of the work. It appears most significantly in the knighting of Tristan and in the love grotto scene, crucial sections of the work that use allegorical devices to present a favorable portrayal or positive aspects of the event in question.[35] Of these two passages with allegorical trappings, the knighting ceremony has the most relevance for a comparison, since it, like the duel with Morolt, relies on the use of personification rather than on the extended allegorical composition of the love grotto scene.[36] Moreover, the duel with Morolt occurs not long after Tristan's knighting, and shows certain other parallels, such as the equipping of Tristan. In the knighting ceremony, Vulcan makes his armor; in the Morolt scene, Mark equips his nephew. In the knighting scene, four figures, Mettle, Means, Discretion and Courtesy, prepare Tristan to be a knight (4565–88; 4965–74). In the Morolt scene, Right and Willing Heart are his companions in arms. Their presence sets this battle apart from others used to settle disputes, such as the one with Morgan that immediately precedes the judicial duel. Another connection between the investiture and the judicial duel appears in the descriptions of Tristan's armor. In both sections, images of the Dart and the Boar, symbols of courage and love's torture, appear on his armor (4942–49, 6594–98, 6614–16).[37] Morgan has made slanderous remarks about Tristan's birth, which lead to his immediate dispatch by the alleged bastard. There are no elaborate descriptions of armor, of inner strengths, or of allegorical figures. The similarity with the knighting ceremony and the absence of such descriptions in the fight with Morgan, which stands between the two, show that for Gottfried, the ordeal by battle was a significant event that he treated with seriousness and a certain amount of approbation. The personification of Justice, making it a semi-divine being, provides Gottfried with another rhetorical technique to emphasize the rightness of Tristan's cause in this judicial duel.

[35] Gottfried changed the negative exile in the woods of his sources into a positive allegory of love. For comments on this point, see Hugo Kuhn, 'Allegorie und Erzaehlstruktur', in *Formen und Funktion der Allegorie: Symposion Wolfenbuettel, 1978*, ed. by Walter Haug (Stuttgart, 1979), pp 208–10. [36] For a discussion of the relationship between these two terms, see Jon Whitman, *Allegory: The Dynamics of an Ancient and Medieval Technique* (Oxford, 1987), pp 4–8, 263–72. [37] For a discussion of the symbolism of the boar in Gottfried's work, see Margaret Schleissner, 'Animal Images in Gottfried von Strassburg's *Tristan*: Structure and Meaning of Metaphor',

Brother Robert's translation of Thomas' *Tristan, Tristams saga ok Isöndar*, written in 1226,[38] is, as one might expect, much closer to Gottfried's account than other versions, since Gottfried names Thomas as his principal source. Although there are some differences in the two versions, Thomas, as presented to us via Brother Robert, also gives a lot of space to the legal obligations of the pact, as he does in the case of Isolde's trial by fire. While Brother Robert (and/or Thomas) does not present the detailed arguments about the treaty that Gottfried does, his choice of vocabulary throughout the text clearly shows that he understood the legal aspects of the situation very well. The Old Norse words *skatt*, tax or tribute, and *skattgilt* appear in the first mention of the arrangements, as does the Old Norse word for defendant, *verjandi*.[39] Both he and Gottfried begin the Morold section with a lengthy history of the origins of the treaty, though some of the details differ. For example, in Gottfried's version, details of the tribute were settled every fifth year in Rome (5979–6002), while in Brother Robert's version, the English kings and barons had to go to Ireland every fourth year to 'hear the laws, to dispense justice, and to fulfill the punishments of all men' (p. 37). This arrangement would seem to have some similarities with the tradition of the *thing*, the annual tribal meeting that, along with handling other business, settled legal disputes.[40]

The Old Norse version indicates that single combat can settle the issue: 'But if the tribute were to be denied him, he would engage in single combat to take it by force from the one who refused it, for one either had to pay the tribute or else face him in battle' (p. 37). However, Brother Robert uses different words for this fight; most striking when one compares his description with Gottfried's is the absence of the word *holmgangr*,[41] which was used for duels on islands, which is where the battle in *Tristan* took place. In Brother Robert, it occurs not on an island, but on the seashore. Words for battle or duel that appear in Brother Robert include *einvigi*, the most frequently used term, *bardaga*, *einn*

The Medieval World of Nature: A Book of Essays, ed. by Joyce E. Salisbury (New York and London, 1993), pp 81–82. She examines the positive and negative aspects of boar imagery. In her opinion, the use of the boar as a symbol during Tristan's knighting and the preparation for his duel with Morolt correspond to the positive side of boar symbolism, where the boar stands for the invincible warrior.   38 *Die nordische Version der Tristan Sage*, ed. by Eugen Kölbing (1878; repr., Hildesheim, 1978); *The Saga of Tristram and Isönd* (Lincoln, 1973), trans. by Paul Schach, are the editions used for this work. Page references to the English edition will be given within the text.   39 Kölbing, *Tristan*, p. 30, ll. 5, 7. See *An Icelandic-English Dictionary* (Oxford, 1982), Richard Cleasby, Gudbrand Vigfusson, and William Craigie, *skatt*, p. 540; *verjandi*, p. 697. (Hereafter referred to as CVC.) I would like to thank my colleague, Prof. Alice Sheppard, Department of English, Penn State, for helping me with Old Norse legal terminology.   40 William Ian Miller, *Bloodtaking and Peacemaking: Feud, Law, and Society in Saga Iceland* (Chicago, 1990), pp 16–19, and Ekkehard Kaufmann, 'Ding', *HWBDR*, I, cols 742–44.   41 CVC, 'a duel or wager of battle fought on an islet or holm, which with the ancients was a kind of last appeal or ordeal'.

móti einum gjarna berjast.[42] Why does Brother Robert avoid both the term for ordeal by battle on an island and the location? The answer may well lie in legal history. The *holmgangr* was condemned as heathen in Iceland about 1000–04 and was abolished through clerical influence in the Icelandic Allding at that time. Around 1012 it was also outlawed in Norway.[43] Therefore, it is not surprising that Brother Robert, whatever Thomas may have had in his source, does not use either the word *holmgangr* or its location for the judicial duel. If Thomas did portray the ordeal on a island, it probably would not have disturbed Gottfried, who would have been unaware of Icelandic and Norwegian society's concerns with pagan legal practices.

After this introductory section, Brother Robert's account stays very close to Gottfried's when he recounts Tristan's arrival in court. The Old Norse version differs slightly from the Middle High German version in its emphasis on the condition of thralldom in which the Irish have placed the Cornish and in its inclusion of a passage in which the women berate their husbands for allowing their children to be taken from them (pp 38–39). Tristam offers himself in single combat to settle the issue, for which his uncle promises to make him his heir (p. 39).[44] Mark's role in the Old Norse version differs strongly from Gottfried's description of it. The Old Norse Mark plays a much smaller but much more vigorous part. There is no weeping over his nephew's death and no arming of the young knight.

Tristram's offer of the glove introduces the scene in which he has a legal discussion with Morold, which contains some parallels with Gottfried's much more expansive treatment of this passage, though there are important differences. The situation with the tribute paid to Ireland offers two legal approaches to Cornwall: either the exact terms of the treaty are examined point by point from the Cornish point of view or the treaty is ignored, in the belief that mentioning treaties or oaths would undercut the Cornish position. Gottfried's Tristan takes the first approach; Thomas'/Brother Robert's, the second. In his speech before Mark, the barons, and Morold, Tristram concentrates on one major theme: the tribute has been exacted under duress and therefore should not be paid. Tristam bases his argument on the nature of tyranny:

> But tyranny is not justice, but lawlessness and an obvious shame and injustice. Therefore it is not right to pay the tribute, since it has always been exacted wrongfully, for it was always surrendered under duress and

---

42 CVC, *einvigi*, p. 123; *bardagi*, p. 52. For *einvigi* references, see Kölbling, *Tristan*, pp 31, l. 35; 32, l. 13; 34, l. 4; 35, l. 32; *bardaga*, p. 30, l. 25; *einn móti einum*, p. 31, ll. 24–25; *einn móti einum gjarna berjast*, pp 31, l. 37 to p.32, l. 1; *einn ydar móti mér einum*, p. 33, ll. 20–21. **43** Holzapfel, 'Holmgangr', *HWBDR*, II, col. 219. **44** In both versions, Tristan suggests a trial by battle, which, as our previous analysis has shown, would have been the expected legal remedy.

fear of pillage if this be justly judged. All goods that are seized with robbery everywhere are ill-gotten and since robbery is wrong, Morold shall not wrongly have anything from us. (p. 40)

By equating the demands of the Irish with robbery, he undercuts both the moral and legal validity of any argument that Morold could make. Examination of the Old Norse vocabulary used in Tristram's speech shows that Tristram combined legal expressions with more emotional ones relating to victimization. Such a rhetorical mixture produces a powerful effect: exploitation linked with legal words that imply or demand redress.[45]

Morold's speech that counters Tristan's arguments contains a similar combination of legal words linked with several with strong emotional content, but the vocabulary changes quite dramatically. Like his counterpart in Gottfried, Brother Robert's Morold seems to make an allusion to the concept of 'minne unde reht' enunciated in the MHG work. (See preceding discussion.) *Astsemd* (p. 33, l. 13), love or affection,[46] is what both Morolt figures expected on their arrival. Morold has as the center of his defense an issue that was prominent in Gottfried's version: the position of a perjurer among noblemen. The key word *eidrofar* can mean either the breaker of an oath or a perjurer.[47] In this section of Morold's accusation, he seems to equate the denial of tribute with breaking of oaths:

> [...] at ther *skyldut* mer skattinn *synja* of *eidrofar* vera ok mer *hafna*. (p. 33, ll. 18–19)
> ('[...] or that you would refuse me the tribute and break your oaths and repudiate my just claims'. [Schach, p. 40. Here and throughout, emphasis of legal terms is mine.])

Skyldut and *synja* both have definite legal usages: *skylda* meant 'to bind in duty, oblige, enjoin', while *synja* was an established legal word used in the meaning of denial.[48] The final word in this serious charge against the Cornish court is an emotional one: *hafna*, 'to forsake or abandon', is also a poetic word.[49] Only the trial by battle can clear Cornwall of this charge: Morold uses a word that would have been painful for noblemen to hear: *frjalsir* was a word that originally meant 'free-necked', pertaining to a ring round the neck, a condition of servitude from which one was released.[50] *Soemd*, 'honor', would indicate that their reputation

---

[45] Old Norse vocabulary in Tristram's speech that reflects the potent combination of emotion and legal terminology includes the following: p. 32, l. 23 *rani*, CVC, p. 487: 'any unlawful seizure or holding of property'. *Rani* appears in a series with *afli* (p. 32, l. 23), which means in this context violence (CVC, p. 7), and *ofriki* (p. 32, l. 24; CVC, p. 464, 'overbearing, sheer force'). Tristram thus stacks the legal deck against any treaty obligation that the Irish might defend. [46] CVC, p. 45. [47] CVC, p. 117. [48] CVC, pp 562, 614. [49] CVC, p. 231. [50] CVC, p. 174.

was restored.[51] Morold has put the issue of single combat in a context that is legally and socially just as serious as that which Tristram has adopted.

The gravity of Morold's charges forces Tristram to refer to a concept he seems to have deliberately avoided: oathbreaking. In accepting Morold's challenge, he uses the word *tryggrofar* (p. 33, l. 27), which refers to a treaty-breaker.[52] Both Tristam and Morold believe that single combat will settle the issue of who has right on his side. Morold's offer of his glove and Tristam's acceptance of the challenge set the actual battle in motion.

The battle scene proceeds in a manner similar to that found in Gottfried, though the allegorical parts are missing. Both works emphasize, to a larger extent than the Old French version, God's active role in giving victory to the just cause. This belief was of course central to the efficacy of the trial by battle. The conversation in which Morold offers Tristan help in exchange for defeat and healing parallels that in Gottfried.

Building on passages in Thomas' version as we have it, Gottfried expands the role of Tristan as the presenter of the legal case. This change gives added weight to Gottfried's portrayal of Tristan's intellectual gifts, but this particular section yields other insights as well. Not only Tristan's but also Morolt's speeches on the respective legal positions are more detailed than in Thomas, which suggests not only legal knowledge, but also intense interest in the law. (See preceding discussion.) The detailed discussion between Morolt and Tristan about the nature of the oath and Morolt's mention of *minne unde reht* show that both protagonists functioned within a mutually understood framework of legal custom and dispute settlement. The fact that Gottfried's source, Thomas, apparently approached the portrayal of this ordeal in the same manner as Gottfried did argues for the continued understanding of this legal procedure by the audience and against an interpretation that suggests manipulation of the law by a tricky character.

Written in the late 1460's, Sir Thomas Malory's *Book of Sir Tristram de Lyones* contains a lengthy account of the battle with Marhalt.[53] Based as it was on the longer version of the French prose *Tristan*, Malory's account lacks the tragic conception that was the heart of the Tristan material in the Thomas-Gottfried tradition. The French version tended towards a clear-cut delineation of the characters as entirely positive or entirely negative. This approach apparently appealed to Malory; added to the tendencies of his source was his own admiration for chivalry as the most worthy human institution.[54] Malory's

---

51 CVC, p. 618. **52** *Worterbuch zur altnordischen Prosaliteratur*, ed. by Walter Baetke, 2 vols (Berlin, 1965–68), II, p. 667. **53** Malory's version of the Tristan story bases itself on the second French Prose *Tristan*. See *The Works of Sir Thomas Malory*, 3rd edn (Oxford, 1990), ed. by Eugène Vinaver and revised by P.J.C. Field, III, p. 1443. (Textual references come from Volume I of this edition.) See also Bert Dillon, *A Malory Handbook* (Boston, 1978), p. 63, and Eugène Vinaver, *Le Roman Tristan et Iseut dans l'Oeuvre de Thomas Malory* (Paris, 1925). **54** Vinaver-Field, *Works*, III, pp 1445–46.

Tristan is an exemplar of the concept of the 'worshipful knight', a middle ground between the purely pugilistic warrior and the knight motivated by religious ideals.[55] In Malory's work, a prime motivation for Tristan to fight Marhalt is the amount of 'worship' he can gain with a victorious outcome:

> And also wete thou well, sir Marhalte, that this ys the gretteste cause that thou coragyst me to have ado with the, for thou arte called one of the moste renomed knyghtes of the worlde. And bycause of that noyse and fame that thou haste thou gevyst me corrayge to have ado with the, for never yett was I proved with good knyght. And sytthen I toke the Order of Knyghthode this day, I am ryght well pleased, and to me moste worshyp, that I may have ado wyth suche a knyght as thou arte. And now wete thou well, syr Marhalte, that I caste me to geete worshyp on thy body. (381)

This motive for the fight, to prove himself in battle immediately after his knighting, is present in other versions of the story, but Malory expands it and gives it greater emphasis, perhaps because of his tendency to portray Tristan as one of the most positive knightly figures in his work.[56]

Because Malory wants Tristan to enhance his knightly reputation as much as possible through this trial by battle, he must defeat an opponent of true distinction; in a work dedicated to King Arthur, that can only be a knight of the Round Table, as Malory's Marhalt is.[57] Marhalt's membership in the Round Table was an innovation of Malory,[58] which causes some narrative problems. Due to his membership in the Round Table, Marhalt therefore cannot appear as the negative, even sinister figure of Gottfried's work. This change perhaps also accounts for the change in Mark's role: in Malory, Mark announces that he will not pay the tribute. There is no mention of Marhalt being willing to take the children of noblemen into slavery, as there is in the Old French version.[59] The motif of the poisoned sword, necessary for the development of the plot, must have presented an awkward hurdle to Malory. There is no reference to the poison during the battle as there is in Gottfried's account. Only afterwards, as Tristram's condition worsens, does Malory give the reason: 'for, as the Frenshe booke seyth, the spere-hede was invenymed, that sir Trystrams might not be hole' (184). Malory effectively distances the motif from the positive picture of Marhalt he presents by using its presence in the source as a reason for mentioning it. Tristram's stature at the defeat of Marhalt has been foreshadowed by Malory's

---

Larry Benson, *Malory's Morte Darthur* (Cambridge, Massachusetts, 1976), p. 137. **55** Kennedy, *Knighthood*, pp 148–50, 154–55. Benson, *Malory*, pp 151–52. **56** Benson, *Malory*, pp 110, 116, says that Tristram was Malory's chivalric ideal. **57** Benson, *Malory*, p. 117, sees this judicial duel with Marhalt as a step in a series of challenges that lead Tristram eventually to membership in the Round Table. **58** Benson, *Malory*, p. 117. **59** Renee Curtis, *The Romance of Tristan* (Oxford, 1994), p. 30.

association of Tristram with Marhalt prior to the judicial combat.[60] This fact, plus Malory's preoccupation with the proof of one's mettle as a knight through combative encounters, ensures that the judicial battle with Marhalt has a different cast and context at the outset than the Middle High German and Old Norse versions do.

In moving from the literary context to the legal one, we must examine the position of trial by battle in Malory's England. While the jury had largely supplanted trial by battle in England during the course of the thirteenth century, trial by battle would certainly not have been totally unknown to Malory. As the closely related duel of chivalry, trial by battle had grown in popularity in late medieval England. While it was largely used for treason cases in which there was a fear of bribed juries, the gentry still favored it in some instances as a means to settle quarrels.[61] In Malory's portrayal of the Marhalt episode, treaty obligations still form the reason for the encounter and place the battle in a legal framework. A close examination of the vocabulary used makes this context clear. In the beginning of Malory's account, he uses the word *trwayge*, or tribute, to refer to Mark's obligation and states that it had not been paid for seven years. The meaning of this word places the situation firmly in a legal context. It was both the payment and the formal arrangement through which such a payment was made because of the subordinate status of the paying party.[62] The implication of inferiority that the word implies would not have been welcome to any king. Mark sends a delegation to Ireland, informing them that they had no intention of paying the tribute. If the Irish wanted it, they should send a knight that would 'fyght for his *ryght*' (380).[63] *Ryght* could mean a just claim, a legal right, including that of ownership.[64] The Irish king sends for Sir Marhalt, saying: 'go unto Cornewayle for my sake to *do batayle for oure trwayge* that we of *ryght* ought to have' (380). *Batyle* had a specific legal meaning:

---

[60] Kennedy, *Knighthood*, p. 150. [61] Bartlett, *Trial*, p. 138, indicates that, in England, during the course of the thirteenth century, the jury began to replace the ordeal as the impartial source of a verdict. Sir Frederick Pollock and Frederic Maitland, *The History of English Law before the Time of Edward I* (Cambridge, 1984), II, p. 632, notes that before the accession of Edward I, the defendant could ask for a verdict of his neighbors instead of a trial by battle. See this source, pp 600–01, for a description of trial by battle. Beverly Kennedy, *Knighthood*, pp 39–47, 160–61, discusses the position of trial by battle in late medieval England and in Malory. Benson, *Malory*, pp 176–77, makes distinctions between judicial duels and duels of chivalry, but notes that the two were closely related. On the subject of trial by battle in late medieval England, see J.G. Bellamy, *Public Order in England in the Later Middle Ages* (London/Toronto, 1973) pp 125–31, and J.G. Bellamy, *The Law of Treason in England in the Later Middle Ages* (Cambridge, 1970), p. 143. [62] *Middle English Dictionary* (Ann Arbor, 1996), T. 9, pp 1049–50. (Hereafter referred to as *MED*.) [63] Malory's Mark has a much stiffer backbone than either the Mark of Malory's Old French source or Gottfried's king. In both of the earlier works, Mark and his nobles impotently cringe at the prospect before them until Tristan arrives on the scene. See previous discussion of Gottfried and Curtis, *Romance of Tristan*, pp 30–31. [64] *MED*,

single combat as a legal device leading to a settlement.[65] Marhalt replies that he will '*do batyle in the ryght of you and your londe*' (380–01). While the lengthy discussion of the legal issues that is common to both Gottfried's and the Old Norse versions is absent, the usage of words with specific legal meanings without any explanation indicates that the audience still understood that the situation involved a legal matter.

Further legal references appear as Tristram goes out to meet the Irish knight. The young man fights for the '*ryght* of Cornwall' (383).[66] As in both Gottfried's and Brother Robert's versions, the battle takes place on an island (383). As in the Old Norse account, Marhalt must be satisfied as to the noble status of his opponent (383, 385). Judicial combat assumed a parity in rank between the participants; when Marhalt insists on this qualification in refusing to fight anyone but a king's son, Tristram reveals his identity.[67] The battle, according to Tristram, will affect legal obligations:

> And yf that I be nat *proved*, I truste to God to be worshypfully *proved* uppon thy body, and to deliver the contrey of Cornwayle for ever fro all maner of *trewayge* frome Irelonde for ever. (381)

Middle English *preven* has a legal meaning regarding the supplying of sufficient legal proof to settle a matter.[68] Tristram's statement is couched in the manner of a legal contract, with no exception either after passage of time or in the kind of tribute. This section contains the only direct reference to God as the guarantor of the results of the battle, contrasting to the frequent and explicit references in Gottfried's work to God's role.[69] The absence of an enveloping religious context as well as any formal prayers or commissions makes several telling indications. The loss of sanction by the Church for well over two centuries is reflected here,[70] as well as Malory's concentration on the development of Tristram as a chivalric model.

This consideration of Malory's version of the judicial duel between Tristram and Marhalt has brought us a very long way from the world of the thirteenth-century judicial duel in Gottfried's work. In Gottfried's work, the concept of right behavior, supported both by the frequent pleas for God's intercession and

---

Pt. R5 (Ann Arbor, 1985), p. 687. *Ryght* had other legal meanings as well, including a judgment or verdict, p. 686.　**65** *MED*, Pt. A-B (Ann Arbor, 1956), p. 665.　**66** Another reference to the people's *ryght* in this matter appears on p. 284.　**67** See also Felicity Riddy, *Sir Thomas Malory* (Leiden, 1987), p. 95, where she notes Malory's fondness for maintaining class distinctions.　**68** *MED*, Pt P6–R1 (Ann Arbor, 1983), p. 1278.　**69** Kennedy, *Knighthood*, p. 157, notes that Malory never portrays the religious aspects that customarily accompanied the ordeal.　**70** The thirteenth-century *Romance of Tristan* and Gottfried's *Tristan* both contain much more material about religious aspects concerning the trial by battle than Malory does. See the previous discussion about Gottfried and Curtis, *Romance of Tristan*, pp 30–38.

the allegorical warriors who aid Tristan, dominates over an opponent who appears as an accomplice of the Devil fighting with a poisoned sword. Brother Robert's version of Thomas casts the issue in terms of tyranny versus the rights of free men, a context that also places Morold in a negative light. Malory, however, seats Marhalt at the Round Table and thereby changes the function and character of this incident in a considerable way. Malory wants his Tristram to defeat a knight of the Round Table so Tristram can be a member of the Round Table, the highest goal of chivalry in Malory's terms. Nothing could be further from the ethos of Gottfried's work. The struggle between good and evil, which dominates so much of Gottfried's portrayal, is missing here, and with it, much of the mystery of Tristan's victory over Morolt, clearly due to the intervention of supernatural powers in Gottfried and to Tristram's own skill with arms in Malory.

Lydgate's *Troy Book* and the Confusion of Prudence[1]

ROBERT R. EDWARDS

For the high and late Middle Ages, the story of Troy performed a notable range of imaginative, political, and cultural work. Most important, of course, it offered a foundation myth for vernacular cultures. Though fallen Troy is a set topic of rhetorical lament, its loss is recuperated in the founding of Rome and the subsequent rise of other regions in Italy, thence the founding of France and Britain.[2] Even the legend of King Arthur's court, as the poet of *Sir Gawain and the Green Knight* suggests, is contained by Troy's fall.[3] Besides initiating a *translatio imperii*, the Troy story furnished an exemplary history, a mirror for princes, and a source for general moralizing, particularly on the mutable gifts of Fortune and more than occasionally on the wickedness of women.

The form of the story most suited to these multiple tasks was historical narrative, which claimed its origin in the supposedly authoritative accounts of Dares and Dictys. Rejecting Homer's poetic lies and their repetitions in Virgil and Ovid, medieval writers turned to prose history as an idealized discursive means. Such writing guaranteed both the accuracy of events and a faithful portrayal of the values and institutions that pagan antiquity bequeathed to Christian culture and that Christian culture distributed in turn from the Mediterranean to the North Sea world. Even when the story is rendered in verse, as in Benoît de Sainte-Maure, John Lydgate, and the *Gest Hystoriale* of Troy, the poets claim the warrant of prose. The poet of the *Gest* says, 'In this shall faithfully be founded to the fer ende, / Alle þe dedes by dene as þai done were' (Pro 78–9).[4] This double claim of transparency – the simultaneous insistence on historical fidelity and on the clarity of historical lessons – is an interesting, if problematic, facet of the medieval Troy story. For as the narratives show the

---

[1] I am grateful to Colin Fewer for his help in research for this essay. [2] An example of the elegiac treatment of Troy is 'Pergama flere volo'. See Hans Walther, *Initia carminum ac versuum medii aevi posterioris latinorum: Alphabetisches Verzeichnis der Versanfänge mittellateinischer Dichtungen* (Göttingen, 1959), no. 13985. An edition from Zurich Stadtbibliothek C.58 (s. xii) is printed by Jakob Werner, *Beiträge zur Kunde der lateinischen Literatur des Mittelalters* (Aarau, 1905; repr. Hildesheim, 1979), pp 8–12. [3] *Sir Gawain and the Green Knight*, ed. by J.R.R. Tolkien and E.V. Gordon, 2nd edn, rev. by Norman Davis (Oxford, 1972), l. 1–26 and 2522–30. [4] The '*Gest Hystoriale*' of the Destruction of

pattern of tragic action in history, they reveal as well the profound contradictions in the lessons that history conveys to succeeding ages.

Lydgate's *Troy Book* is one of the most highly contextualized versions of the story in the late Middle Ages. *Troy Book* is a poetic amplification of Guido delle Colonne's *Historia destructionis Troiae*, a thirteenth-century Latin prose rendering of Benoît's *Roman de Troie*. Like Guido, Lydgate begins his narrative with the story of Jason and Medea, and ends it with the disastrous return home of the Greek heroes and the death of Ulysses; the fall of Priam's Troy comprises the central action. Unlike Guido, though, poetic authority is imported as well as dismissed in *Troy Book*. Suffusing Lydgate's account, as a counter to prose history, are echoes and allusions to Chaucer, whom Lydgate praises as his poetic master and 'the noble Rethor that alle dide excelle' (3.553).[5] Moreover, if *Troy Book* consciously locates itself in an overdetermined literary context, it occupies at the same time a precise historical and political context. Henry, Prince of Wales, commissioned the poem in 1412 and, as Henry V, received it in 1420. In accepting Lydgate's poem, Henry probably felt no urgent need of lessons and princely advice; as Derek Pearsall suggests, he was more interested in being seen to accept wise counsel than in actually following it.[6]

The great lesson that Lydgate offers his prince is the importance of prudence. As C. David Benson has pointed out, prudence is 'Lydgate's principal moral concern in the poem'.[7] In his Prologue, Lydgate invokes first Mars and then Othea, the goddess of prudence, and he recommends prudence throughout *Troy Book*. The analysis I shall offer extends Benson's point in one crucial respect. I shall argue that *Troy Book* not only extols prudence but simultaneously charts its confusion. By confusion I mean both misunderstanding and undoing. My point is not that Lydgate is an ironist whose subtlety has thus far eluded detection. Rather, the virtue he celebrates so insistently is complicated by the movement from precept to narrative and by the competing meanings he seeks to hold in a coherent relation to each other as he expounds the lessons of pagan history to an aristocratic audience far removed in time and space.

To understand the role of prudence in Lydgate's poem, we must turn first to the history of the idea and the term. For medieval culture, prudence has Biblical, philosophical, and political resonance. In the Troy story, the last two are obviously the more important, though Lydgate invokes Solomon, the

---

Troy, ed. by G.A. Panton and D. Donaldson, EETS OS 39, 56 (1869, 1874; repr. London, 1968), p. 3. In *Troy Book*, Lydgate makes a similar claim about the substance of his text (5.3491–93), asserting the importance of historical accuracy over his poetic faults. **5** *Lydgate's Troy Book*, ed. by Henry Bergen, 3 vols, EETS ES 97, 103, 106, 126 (London, 1906–35), II, p. 410. See also *Troy Book: Selections*, ed. by Robert R. Edwards, Middle English Texts Series (Kalamazoo, 1998), p. 147 and n. **6** Derek Pearsall, 'Hoccleve's *Regement of Princes*: The Poetics of Royal Self-Representation', *Speculum*, 69 (1994), p. 386. **7** C. David Benson, 'Prudence, Othea and Lydgate's Death of Hector', *American Benedictine Review*, 26 (1975), p. 117.

Biblical exemplar of prudence, in his Envoy. The philosophical sense of prudence is succinctly defined in the Latin phrase 'recta ratio agibilium' – right reason directed toward what can be done.[8] In Book 6 of the *Nicomachean Ethics*, Aristotle lists prudence among the intellectual virtues. These virtues represent states of the soul and show the means by which right principles can be established. Intellectual virtues are engendered by instruction, while moral virtues arise from disposition and habit. A prudent man deliberates rightly about what is conducive to a good life. The things he considers are of necessity variable rather than true and stable. While wisdom, for example, studies universal truths and first principles, prudence is concerned with particular goods and the practical steps for achieving them. It thus addresses 'things about which deliberation is possible' (1141b8), which is to say, means rather than ends.[9] The spheres of prudence include individual conduct, domestic governance, and civic life. Aristotle insists that these are distinct species of prudence and not merely differences in degree (*Politics* 1.1.2; 1252a6). He thus disputes Socrates' claim that all virtues are forms of prudence, but he agrees that prudence implies the other virtues and so holds primacy among them.

Thomas Aquinas offers the most important explanation of Aristotle's theory of prudence for the Middle Ages. Aquinas' commentary on the *Ethics* explains that prudence deals with human goods and deliberation (*consiliari*).[10] It is 'a principle of doing' and therefore involves particulars (sec. 1194). In his treatise on prudence in the *Summa theologiae*, Aquinas accepts Aristotle's postulate that prudence has an 'imperative' role, directing the other virtues (*Ethics* 6.10; 1143a8); and he divides its activities into three phases: taking counsel, forming a judgment, and commanding action (2a2ae.47.8 resp.)[11] Elsewhere he extends the scope of prudence to include moral theology. So, for instance, prudence can be acquired or sent by divine grace ('prudentia vel eubilia, sive sit acquisita sive sit infusa' [2a2ae.52.1]). For the moral universe that Lydgate seeks to examine in Troy, the medieval tradition offers several important refinements of Aristotle. Aquinas opens up the possibility that prudence has not only a logical contrary (imprudence or recklessness) but also a negation, in the form of a vice simulating prudence (2a2ae.55). Stratagems such as cunning (*astutia*), guile (*dolus*), and

---

8 See *Summa* 2a2ae.47.2, translating *Ethics* 6.5; 1140b20. Lydgate's concern with other moral lessons is apparent, by contrast, in the *Siege of Thebes*, where the guiding principles are love and truth. See Robert W. Ayers, 'Medieval History, Moral Purpose, and the Structure of Lydgate's *Siege of Thebes*', *PMLA*, 73 (1958), pp 463–74. 9 Aristotle, *Ethics*, trans. by J.A.K. Thomson, rev. by Hugh Tredennick (London, 1976), p. 213. 10 Thomas Aquinas, *In decem libros Ethicorum Aristotelis ad Nicomachum Expositio*, ed. by Raymundo Spiazzi (Turin, 1949), pp 326–27. Further references to Aquinas' commentary will be by sections rather than pages. For convenience, I add the translations from *Commentary on Aristotle's 'Nicomachean Ethics'*, trans. by C.I. Litzinger (Detroit, 1964). 11 Thomas Aquinas, *Prudence* (2a2ae.47–56), ed. and trans. by Thomas Gilby, vol. 36 of *Summa Theologiae* (New York, 1964–81), p. 26.

cheating (*fraus*), which have their origin in avarice (2a2ae.55.8), forge a simulacrum of prudence. In addition, medieval thought connects prudence closely with providence, drawing on Cicero's etymologizing of Latin *prudentia* from *providens*, 'seeing forward or beforehand' (*De republica* 1.6 and *De natura deorum* 2.22.58). Thus Aristotle's emphasis on deliberation in the here and now is inflected by a concern for projecting forward in time.

In medieval political thought, which Lydgate maps onto his historical narrative of Troy, prudence is an omnipresent theme. John of Salisbury admonishes, 'without prudence and constant watchfulness not only will a commonwealth not progress, but even the humblest household will not rest on a secure foundation' (*Policraticus* 6.22).[12] Marsilius of Padua, citing both Aristotle's *Ethics* and the *Politics* (3.6), insists on the importance of prudence, allied with justice, for a 'perfect ruler' (*Defensor pacis* 1.14.2).[13] The *Secreta secretorum* numbers prudence immediately after piety in a list of attributes that a king should possess. An English translation roughly contemporary with Lydgate holds, 'it is nedfulle that the wijs kyng thinke oft of thingis that arne to come, so that he may wisely purveye and make contrary ordynaunce ayens hem, and þat he may the more lightly bere and susteyne þe contrarye aduersitees and aduentures' (ch. 13).[14] In Lydgate's imitation of the *Secreta*, written at the end of his life, prudence governs the others virtues needed for kingship. Lydgate has Aristotle admonish Alexander to follow imperial virtues, 'This to seyne first prudently discerne, / Twen vice and vertue his peple to governe' (657–58).[15] Thomas Hoccleve makes the same point in his *Regement of Princes*, written for Prince Henry at the same time that Lydgate began *Troy Book*. Prudence, says Hoccleve, governs the other three moral virtues (temperance, strength, and

---

12 John of Salisbury, *The Statesman's Book of John of Salisbury*, trans. by John Dickinson (New York, 1963), p. 246; *Policraticus*, ed. by Clement C.I. Webb (Oxford, 1909), p. 621a: 'Nam sine prudentia et sollicitudine non modo res publica non procedit sed nec minima consistit domus'. For John the monitory example regarding prudence is the story of Dido's reception of Aeneas (*Aeneid* 4), which disrupts the harmonious workings of her kingdom. The first citation in Denis Foulechat's Prologue to his 1342 translation of the *Policraticus* is to Proverbs 3:13: '"Beatus homo qui invenit sapienciam et qui affluit prudencia" Proverbiorum 30 capitulo. Ceste parole dit que l'omme est benoit qui treuve sapience et qui afflue largement de prudence'; Denis Foulechat, *Le Policratique de Jean de Salisbury*, ed. by Charles Bruckner (Geneva, 1994), p. 83. **13** Alan Gewirth, *Marsilius of Padua: The Defender of Peace*, 2 vols, Records of Civilization, Sources and Studies (New York, 1951), I, pp 178, 243–44. **14** *Three Prose Versions of the Secreta Secretorum*, ed. by Robert Steele, EETS ES 74 (London, 1898), p. 12. Cf. Bk. 2, ch. 13, p. 55. **15** *Lydgate and Burgh's Secrees of old Philisoffres*, ed. by Robert Steele, EETS ES 66 (London, 1894). The same connection between prudence and liberality reappears in lines 1030–36. In the *Fall of Princes* (8.1132–38), Boccaccio claims that vices exercise domination when the four cardinal virtues – prudence, temperance, righteousness, and fortitude – were abandoned; see *Lydgate's Fall of Princes*, ed. by Henry Bergen, 4 vols, EETS ES 121–24 (London, 1924), III, p. 806.

justice); it is 'vertu of entendement' (4761), governing man by reason, as it looks to past, present, and future.[16] He also places a faith in prudence that Lydgate's *Troy Book* unwittingly works to belie: 'There is no wight þat sche [prudence] schapiþ disceyue, / And, though men casten hem hire to begile, / Naght wole it be; by wit sche wole it weyue' (4768–70).

In Middle English usage, prudence appears in the mid-fourteenth century. The earliest citation in *MED* is from the *Ayenbite of Inwit*, describing the four cardinal virtues; but the term reaches currency in the 1380s and 1390s, and there is still much greater use in the fifteenth century.[17] One important semantic feature, which has, I think, a direct bearing on Lydgate's poem, is that late-medieval usage employs prudence to designate a range of meanings: wisdom, intelligence, discretion, foresight, shrewdness, knowledge, and words of wisdom. Aristotle's governing intellectual virtue is thus elided with moral virtue, various species of knowledge, and the resources of verbal expression. Thomas Usk's *Testament of Love* reflects the blurring of Aristotle's distinctions in its definition: 'Prudence is goodly wisdom in knowing of thinges'.[18] Usk's references to 'gubernatif' (Book 1) and 'reignatif' (Book 2) prudence make it clear that personal and political governance have intersected.

In John Gower's *Confessio Amantis*, prudence is connected to rhetorical eloquence (4.2652) as a form of practical judgment; prudence and wisdom together are said to govern all the theoretical sciences (7.65).[19] The most pervasive formulation in Gower's poem is between 'hih prudence' (5.2289, 5.3153, and 7.1787) and rulers who exercise their wits to pose and solve problems.[20] In Chaucer, the usage is more diverse and poetically rich. While Lydgate consistently shows prudence from a dominant position, Chaucer displays it operating in a subordinate position within 'a female science of actions' that Carolyn Collette associates with late medieval models for aristocratic women.[21] Dame Prudence is, of course, the source of wise counsel in the *Melibee* as well as the mother of wisdom. Griselde in the *Clerk's Tale* plays a similar role, complementing Walter's governance as an embodiment of natural reason; his people hold Walter '[a] prudent man' (IV.427) for recognizing the virtue hidden beneath her low degree.[22] Criseyde, when she is in the

---

16 Thomas Hoccleve, *The Regement of Princes*, in *Hoccleve's Works*, ed. by Frederick J. Furnivall, EETS ES 72 (London, 1897).   **17** *Middle English Dictionary*, ed. by Sherman M. Kuhn *et al.* (Ann Arbor, 1952–), *s. v.* prudence.   **18** Thomas Usk, *The Testament of Love*, in *Chaucerian and Other Pieces*, ed. by W.W. Skeat, vol. 7 of *The Complete Works of Geoffrey Chaucer* (Oxford, 1894), p. 103. See also *The Testament of Love*, ed. by R.A. Shoaf, Middle English Texts Series (Kalamazoo, 1998), p. 232.   **19** John Gower, *The English Works of John Gower*, ed. by G.C. Macaulay, 2 vols, EETS ES 81, 82 (London, 1901, 1903).   **20** Gower's examples are the king in the tale of the two coffers (5.2273–390), Ulysses discovering Achilles' identity (5.2961–3201), and Dares with his counselors (7.1783–883).   **21** Carolyn P. Collette, 'Heeding the Counsel of Prudence: A Context for the *Melibee*', *Chaucer Review*, 29 (1994–95), p. 421.   **22** Geoffrey Chaucer,

Greek camp, laments that she lacked one of prudence's three eyes (5.744) – the capacity for foresight; her reference may be to the famous image of three-eyed prudence on the chariot of the church in Dante's *Purgatorio* (29.130–32).[23] But if Chaucer offers conventional representations of prudence, he also complicates the virtue by showing its ambiguous applications. Placebo, the false counselor of the *Merchant's Tale*, cynically leaves old January to work by his own wisdom and prudence in choosing a wife. At the end of the *Clerk's Tale*, where the certainty of allegorical meaning progressively gives way, the Clerk addresses the 'noble wyves, ful of heigh prudence' (IV.1183) to warn them against Griselde and urge their resistance to her model of patience. In *Piers Plowman*, Langland shows the same ambivalence. Prudence holds its place among the four cardinal virtues, and as John Alford points out, Ymaginatif, an essential figure in Langland's conceptual and poetic enterprise, 'represents the exercise of prudence'.[24] Yet the virtues, prudence among them, are increasingly vulnerable to deceit. A curate complains, 'For *Spiritus Prudencie* among the peple is gyle, / And alle tho faire vertues, as vices thei semeth' (19.458–59).[25] Need admonishes Will before his final vision, '*Spiritus Prudencie* in many a point shal faille / Of that he weneth wolde falle if his wit ne weere. / Wenynge is no wysdom, ne wys ymaginacion' (20.31–33).

I have been rehearsing the doctrine of prudence and its formulations in late Middle English texts because these elements color the poetic representation of prudence in *Troy Book*. If Lydgate found in the Troy story a narrative that complicates prudence, he also found in his immediate intellectual and literary traditions a shifting field of meanings for the term. At various points, the capacity for foresight and nimble adjustment threatens to become indistinguishable from cold calculation and treachery. Language, in a repeated image, is poisoned by hidden venom. Though prudence offers the hope of outwitting Fortune by anticipating the consequences of action, the correlative problem is to escape the consequences of false and sham prudence. The confusion of prudence is perhaps most apparent in Lydgate's portrayals of chivalric heroism and political governance, where idealism stands alongside the failure and subversion of Lydgate's ethical precept. But the complications begin with the very start of Lydgate's poem.

Troy Book opens by invoking Mars and identifying him as not only the god of war but also the 'souereyn and patrown' (Pro 7) of chivalry. Lydgate then invokes Othea, the goddess of prudence, to advance his work, and he asks her

---

The Riverside Chaucer, ed. by Larry D. Benson, 3rd edn (Boston, 1987).   **23** Dante Alighieri, *The Divine Comedy*, trans. by Charles S. Singleton, 6 vols in 3 (Princeton, 1970–75). As Singleton notes (II, p. 723), in the *Convivio*, Dante equates prudence with wisdom.   **24** John A. Alford, *A Companion to* Piers Plowman (Berkeley and Los Angeles, 1988), p. 48.   **25** William Langland, *The Vision of Piers Plowman*, ed. by A.V.C. Schmidt (London, 1978).

specifically to make Clio his muse. Finally, he invokes Calliope, the mother of Orpheus and source of rhetoric and music, to foster the aesthetic dimensions of the poem. In the sequence of the poet's address, we find a careful articulation among poetic topic, meaning, and mode: war conducted through chivalry is seen through the lens of practical virtue and inscribed in history, while the poet's own discourse seeks to please through words and sound. Prudence stands as the middle term between epic material from pagan antiquity and Lydgate's encoding of the story for a medieval chivalric audience; it is the virtue that governs the lesson of history. Lydgate thus offers a paradigm and program for understanding the Troy story as a narrative of human judgments that alternately realize and fail the goals of practical wisdom, discretion, foresight, and good governance.

At first glance, this program of moral history would seem to offer few problems, but complications emerge on various levels when the poem turns from precepts to narrative. Book 1, which recounts the mythological origin of the Myrmidons, Jason's quest for the Golden Fleece, and the remote causes of the Trojan War, presents a rehearsal of the larger concerns that surface in the story. The myth, taken from Ovid's *Metamorphoses* (8: 501–660), explains the repopulation of Peleus' kingdom by ants transformed into men. Lydgate glosses the myth on the apocryphal authority of St Matthew and portrays the Myrmidons as exemplars of knighthood:

> Whiche for wisdam & prudent aduertence,
> Besy labour and wilful dilligence,
> By for-seynge and discrecioun,
> As I suppose in myn opinioun,
> That this fable of amptis was contreved […]. (1.71–75)

The virtues the Myrmidons demonstrate are not just the 'manly dedis' of war but hard work and, above all, the capacity for shrewd judgments in war and peace alike. The event that sets Jason's quest in motion is the loss of just this capacity. Jason's father, Eson, loses his wits to dotage, so that 'verrailly his discrecioun / Was hym birafte' (1.115–16), and the kingdom passes temporarily to his brother Peleus. With Peleus, the moral categories of the story lose their definition, and we enter the domain of ambiguity that comprises the history of Troy. In recounting the Myrmidon myth, Lydgate had described Peleus as 'Wys & discrete & also vertuous', but Peleus' scheme to deprive Jason of his heritage depends on the simultaneous failure and subversion of prudence. Jason lacks foresight and judgment, while Peleus operates with 'þe dirke deceyt, þe cloudy fals engyn, / I-gilt with-oute, but vnder was venym, / Wher-to Iason hath noon aduertence' (1.517–19).

The reciprocity of failure and guile in Jason and Peleus is restaged elsewhere in the episode. Cethes, Medea's father, counsels Jason to use prudence before undertaking the trials to gain the Fleece (1.1454–58, 1.3132–58); his motive is not so much to give wise counsel as to exonerate himself from potential blame, should the quest end in catastrophe. Yet Cethes himself fails to foresee the consequences of sitting Medea next to Jason, which reach far beyond the quest. Lydgate apostrophizes, 'But o, allas, þer lakked hiȝ prudence, / Discret avis of inward prouidence, / Wisdam also, with pereil caste a-fore' (1.1823–25). He chastises Cethes for failing to 'cast by discret purvyaunce' (1.1921); one late manuscript (Digby 230) reads, 'by prudent purvyaunce'. Set against Cethes' failure is the sham prudence of women, the structural counterpart of political deceit. Lydgate presents Medea as a creature of infatuated willfulness, and though she, too, eventually lacks foresight (1.3622), she is part of a sisterhood that uses fraud and betrayal to attain its purposes: 'þei ben so sliȝe, so prudent, and so wyse' (1.1943). The old woman who acts as an intermediary for Medea is a repository of Ovidian love lore, which in women simulates prudence in a way that recalls Chaucer's Wife of Bath: 'Of ȝeris passed olde experience / Hath ȝoue to hem so passyng hiȝe prudence, / Þat þei in loue alle þe sleiȝtes knowe' (1.2799–2801).

The misogyny of this passage is a feature of Guido's account that Lydgate struggles repeatedly to revoke, or at least displace from his responsibility.[26] What he cannot amend, however, is the metaphorical equivalence that follows from identifying prudence as a form of tactical advantage. If Medea is schooled in the tactics of love, she likewise possesses the technical knowledge that allows Jason to overcome the obstacles to the Fleece. The object of his quest, she tells him, lies beyond strength of arms or ingenuity, and only her 'counseil' (1.2362; cf. 1.2358) will permit him to prevail. The final part of Book 1 carries this functional sense of prudence one step further. As the Greeks lay their plans for attacking Lamedon's Troy, Peleus makes prudence a form of military tactics. His first concern is to avoid casualties by arranging the order of battle properly, and his language is the language of practical deliberation:

> First, be avis and gode discrescioun,
> For oure diffence and sauacioun,
> So prudently oure wardis for to make,
> Þat non of ours be at meschefe take,
> Þis ilke day, for lak of prouidence […]. (1.3997–4001)

The Greeks take the city by following Hercules' 'sleyȝt' (1.4280), which cuts Lamedon off from Troy by ambush and traps him between two forces. In a wonderful reversal of expectations, Lydgate inverts the trope of foresight to describe Lamedon's failure of prudence:

---

26 For discussion of Lydgate's effort to escape Guido's misogyny, see Gretchen Mieszkowski, 'The Reputation of Criseyde, 1155–1500,' *The Transactions of the Connecticut Academy of Arts and Sciences*, 43 (1971), pp 71–153; Anna Torti, 'From

> He was nat war of hem þat were behynde,
> He nat aduerteth nor casteþ in his mynde
> Þe grete slei3te nor þe trechery,
> Þat hym was schape, he koude it nat espie. (1.4077–80)

The confusion of prudence reaches perhaps its most profound level in Book 1 in the predicament that leads to Lamedon's undoing and sows the seeds of further conflict. The causal event is Jason's arrival in Lamedon's territory on his outward journey to Colchis. Though Jason intends only to refresh his crew, rumor and 'fals envy' (1.927) portray the Greeks as likely invaders who show no respect for Lamedon's authority, arriving as they have without his leave or safe-conduct. The central paradox is that Lamedon seeks to act prudently in ordering them to depart. Lydgate makes it clear that in one sense Lamedon acts rashly, '[w]ithoute counsail or avisenesse' (1.958). But in another sense, he acts reasonably to defend his land from potential aggression and to assert his royal control and prerogative; the Greeks arrive with 'no lycence / And hem purpose for to doon offence, / Be liklyhed, and his lond to greue' (1.931–33). In the so-called Scottish fragments of the poem, which reinscribe Guido within Lydgate's translation, the 'tythinge' that reaches Lamedon is that they have come 'for to spye ande see / The pryvateis of hys kynryk' (20–1). For his part, Jason is equally misguided in his understanding of Lamedon, controlling his rage when ordered to leave but construing the king's order as a transgression against 'fredam' and 'gentilnesse' (1.1044–45); in the Scottish fragments, the term is 'Iniquite' (line 126), translating Guido's 'iniuriam illatam' ('violence unlawfully inflicted').[27] Prudence thus becomes the ironic mechanism of tragedy rather than the remedy against unstable Fortune.

In the central narrative of *Troy Book*, Lydgate illustrates the lessons of prudence as they connect the public and private domains of chivalric culture. His focus here is preeminently on character – on the heroic subject's capacity to function coherently as a public figure and moral agent. To some extent, 'prudent' is an honorific title, applied almost formulaically to Nestor, Diomede, and Menelaus, and even to Cassandra in her role as a prophet. Yet in the principal antagonists of the story – Hector and Achilles, Priam and Agamemnon – prudence is the element of character that allows both didactic moralizing and an

---

"History" to "Tragedy": The Story of Troilus and Criseyde in Lydgate's *Troy Book* and Henryson's *Testament of Cresseid*', in *The European Tragedy of Troilus*, ed. by Piero Boitani (Oxford, 1989), pp 171–97; and Nicholas Watson, 'Outdoing Chaucer: Lydgate's *Troy Book* and Henryson's *Testament of Cresseid* as Comparative Imitations of *Troilus and Criseyde*', in *Shifts and Transpositions in Medieval Narrative: A Festschrift for Dr. Elspeth Kennedy*, ed. by Karen Pratt (Woodbridge, Suffolk, and Rochester, NY, 1994), pp 89–108.   27 'Die Fragmente des Trojanerkrieges von Barbour', in *Barbour's Des Schottischen Nationaldichters Legendensammlung*, ed. by C. Horstmann, 2 vols (Heilbronn, 1881), I, p. 218.

analysis of the complex motives behind human action and the larger pattern of destiny.

Hector's prudence is a key feature of the authorizing model of chivalric heroism. When Lydgate first presents him in the roster of Priam's sons at the start of Book 2, he explicitly connects the origins of chivalry to Hector's attributes of character:

> He was þe Rote and stok of cheualrie,
> And of kny3thod verray souereyn flour,
> Þe sowrs and welle of worschip & honour;
> And of manhod, I dar it wel expresse,
> Example and merour; & of hi3e prowesse,
> Gynyng & grounde; & with al þis I-fere,
> Wonder benigne & lawly of his chere,
> Discret also, prudent and vertuous. (2.244–51).

The identical formulation reappears in Lydgate's account of Dares' portraits, where Hector is 'of kny3thod spring & welle, / Flour of manhod, of strengþe pereles, / Sadde & discret & prudent neuere-þe-les' (2.4802–04). Both passages, which have no counterpart in Guido, present the same sequence of chivalric topics – exemplarity, might, and the qualities of deliberative character.[28]

The visible embodiment of Hector's virtue lies in his actions. Dispatched to subdue Panonia, he proves a thoughtful and restrained governor: 'so iust and so prudent, / So wel avised and so pacient / And so demenyd in his gouernaunce' (2.1129–31). As the Trojans prepare to face the Greeks in battle, 'prudent Hector' (3.312) oversees the careful disposition of Priam's troops, showing prudence in a tactical sense. He even admonishes Troilus, the second Hector, not to risk pursuing his advantage too far: 'late prudence kepe þe in a mene, / And wisdam eke holden a3en þe rene / Of þin hert & þi ferce corage' (3.211–13). In the moment before the first set-piece battle, Nature is said to have favored him with all the gifts of manhood, and Lydgate's description shows that these are preeminently qualities of intellectual judgment: 'He had in hym souereine excellence, / And gouernaunce medlid with prudence, / Þat nou3t asterte him, he was so wis & war' (3.489–91).[29]

The most compelling demonstration of Hector's prudence occurs in the Trojan debate over the prospect of war with the Greeks. Frustrated in his attempts to secure Hesione's return from Telamon, Priam convokes a parliament

---

28 For a review of Hector in high and late medieval literature, see Paul H.M. Oorts, 'The Reputation of the Trojan Prince Hector in the Middle Ages from Benoît de Sainte Maure to Jean Lemaire de Belges' (unpublished doctoral thesis, Pennsylvania State University, 1992). 29 When Hector first appears, in the battle at the Greeks' landing (2.8464–546), he is described for his physical prowess, not his attributes of character and

of his lords to discuss whether to wreak vengeance on the Greeks. He then assembles his sons, both legitimate and natural, to seek their counsel privately. After arguing for revenge, he turns to Hector to confirm his intention to prosecute the war. Hector's response is a speech that balances the claims of natural law with a sober calculation of risk. It is fitting, he says, for men to seek redress for wrongs and especially so for those exercising the office of knighthood, but his overriding concern is to forecast the full shape of action. He looks to the end as well as the beginning and rightly sees the middle as a ground of uncertainty and reversal:

> But first I rede, wysely in 3our mynde
> To cast aforn and leue nat be-hynde,
> Or 3e be-gynne, discretly to aduerte
> And prudently consyderen in 3our herte
> Al, only nat þe gynnyng but þe ende,
> And þe myddes, what weie þei wil wende,
> And to what fyn Fortune wil hem lede –
> 3if 3e þus don, amys 3e may nat spede. (2.2229–36)

In this passage, Lydgate's poetic technique reinforces Hector's exhortation, also in Guido (Book 6), to see the full scope of action. His run-on line, a comparative rarity in the balanced, parallel phrasing of *Troy Book*, stops on the word 'Al', and he marks it off with the trochaic pattern that fills out the line: 'Al, only nat þe gynnyng but þe ende'. Here more clearly than anywhere else in the poem, Hector addresses the temporal extension of prudence; he discerns a chain of causality that starts from known beginnings but vanishes before a determinate end. The resolution he offers is captured in the term 'dissymulacioun' (2.2294), which Lydgate relocates from its source in Guido and turns from its usual meaning of deceit and simulation.[30] Hector's 'dissymulacioun' is the ability to internalize suffering – 'oure wo endure' – and so to govern oneself and the state by discretion directed toward the past rather than commit the future to 'auenture' (2.2296).

Seen against the wisdom of his speech against the war, Hector's death is not only a tragic reversal but also a profound challenge to the ethic of prudence.

---

mind.   30 In Guido the source for Lydgate's term comes earlier in Hector's speech and in a different context: 'Conniuentibus igitur occulis non est incongruum Exione dissimulare fortunam, que iam tot annis suis est aptata dispendiis et quam mors in breui potest ab aura uiuaci diuellere, ut nobis omnibus sit parata causa quietis'. Text in Guido de Columnis, *Historia Destructionis Troiae*, ed. by Nathaniel Edward Griffin (Cambridge, Massachusetts, 1936), p. 60. The analysis I offer of 'dissymulacioun' varies from Bergen's glossing of the term, which he cites only in this passage of *Troy Book*. The *Middle English Dictionary* cites the line in Lydgate as an example illustrating 'concealment'.

The mechanism of his death is anticipated in his advice to Troilus and a later episode in which the Trojans fail to press their advantage and destroy the Greeks entirely. Lydgate explains that Fate intervenes through Fortune to dim the judgment of the Trojans: 'þei nat koude of neclygence se / Þe aftir-fal of her felicite' (3.1995–96). The effect of this blindness is particularly great on Hector; false judgment 'specially fordirked so þe siȝt / Of worþi Hector, þe prudent manly knyȝt / To sen a-forn what schuld after swe' (3.1987–89). Accordingly, he accedes to the request by his cousin, Ajax Telamon, that he withdraw from the field. It is this propensity for diversion, for losing sight of the end while in the middle, that subsequently proves his undoing. In battle, Hector wounds Achilles in the thigh and forces him to retire for treatment. He then by chance meets a Greek king whom he kills and begins to despoil of his handsome armor. Lydgate explains that Hector is distracted by covetousness, a vice contrary to his noble character. His focus on the prize leads him to put his shield behind his back and so leave his chest protected only by a breastplate.

Lydgate consciously glosses this act as an icon of imprudence. 'Reklesly', he says, 'He cast his shelde at his bak be-hynde' (3.5375–76). He laments, 'Allas, why was he þo so rek[e]les!' (3.5383). Achilles, returning to the field determined either to kill Hector or die in the effort, sees the advantage and slays Hector with a spear. Lydgate emphasizes the stealth of Achilles' attack, his falling on Hector '[a]ll vnwarly, or Hector myȝt aduerte' (3.5395). The overall effect of the episode is to illustrate the compounding of accident and remote causes that defined Fortune in the later Middle Ages.[31] Achilles returns by chance, while Hector's carelessness permits a Boethian catastrophe, which depends on the disparity between enormous consequences and an apparently trivial cause – 'Þoruȝ necligence only of his shelde' (3.5399). Hector falls victim to precisely the sudden mutability in chivalric heroism that prudence is supposed to forestall.

Hector's antagonist is also his foil in the realm of chivalric heroism. Achilles is described, on the authority of Dares, for his physical appearance and strength, but Lydgate adds no mention of his intellectual virtues (2.4548–59). Though he bears Apollo's prophecy about the downfall of Troy (2.5951–70), his actions are governed by the immediacy of his situations, as in his withdrawals from combat, his refusal to come to the aid of other Greeks, and his isolation from the principal Greek heroes. If in battle Hector acts out of heroic furor, Achilles devolves to brutishness. In his reproval of Achilles, which is simultaneously a remonstrance against Homer, Lydgate chides Achilles as 'so sleiȝty & so ful of fraude' (4.2789). Prudence as tactical skill is reduced to mere stealth in Achilles' plots to kill first Hector and then Troilus by ambush and trap. The capacity to recognize and press advantage becomes something verging

---

[31] For discussion of fortune, see Pierre Michaud-Quantin, *Études sur le vocabulaire philosophique du Moyen Age* (Rome, 1970).

on homicide, as Achilles attacks Hector from behind and dispatches a wounded Troilus 'falsly at þe bak' (4.2830), smiting off his head. Achilles commits a further transgression against honor itself when he drags Troilus' corpse through the field behind his horse. Lydgate amplifies Guido's claims that Achilles lacks nobility, vivacity, and compassion:

> For ȝif þat he had hadde his aduertence,
> Ouþer þe eye of his prouidence
> Vn-to knyȝthod or to worþines,
> Ouþer to manhod or to gentilnes,
> Or to þe renoun of his owne name,
> Or to þe report of his knyȝtly fame,
> In any wyse to haue taken hede,
> He hadde neuer don so foule a dede:
> So vengably [for] to haue y-drawe
> A kynges sone after he was slawe! (4.2841–50)

Here Lydgate offers a portrayal of Achilles as a chivalric antitype. The terms that most abuse him – and by association the poetic tradition celebrating his fame – are those expressing facets of prudence. Where Achilles fails as a hero, poetry fails as a mirror for princes (4.2834–40).

The contrast between Hector and Achilles is nowhere more dramatic than in the sphere of practical deliberation. Hector's counsel in Book 2 to weigh the means and ends of war has its ironic counterpart in Achilles' speech urging the Greeks to make peace after he has fallen in love with Polyxena. The irony is doubled, of course, because Achilles in love is only too reminiscent of Chaucer's Troilus. The main point, however, is that Achilles enacts a debased form of deliberation in addressing the Greek leaders. Following Hecuba's advice 'þat he wirke prudently and wel' (4.902), Achilles begins by directing the eye of prudence backward, arguing that no good reason for the war can be found: 'Ful fer abak wit was sette be-hynde, / Prudent lokynge, and avisenesse' (4.976–77). Helen alone, he claims, is the cause of the war and all they have risked in blood and treasure: 'And, in good feith, me semeth þat Eleyne, / Ȝif ȝe aduerte wysly in ȝour þouȝt, / With swiche a pris shulde nat be bouȝt' (4.1022–24). The benefit falls only to Menelaus, who already has other remedy, such as divorce and lawful remarriage. Rather than risk the uncertainty of Fortune and the still formidable might of the Trojans, Achilles proposes a simple expedient: honor can be served by leaving Helen in Troy, since Telamon already holds Hesione. Unwittingly, he argues the point made earlier by Paris to justify the abduction of Helen.

Achilles' motives are transparently self-serving, though he takes pains to hide them. What results is sham prudence, a simulation of reflection and deliberation in the political sphere. It reaches one extreme in Achilles' exhortation to put aside the public vice that in fact characterizes him privately:

> Wherfore, be wisdam lete vs voide pride
> And wilfulnes, only of prudence
> To han þe eye of oure aduertence
> To oure profyt more þan to veyn-glorie [...]. (4.1072–75)

He makes the political miscalculation of assuming beforehand that the Greeks will agree with him. It is this same blindness to other motives that brings about his death in a murder planned by Hecuba. Lydgate explains that Love blinds Achilles to the consequences of answering the summons to Apollo's temple, but the desire Achilles feels for Polyxena has no reality outside his intentions. The crucial element of the scene is the resemblance and difference with Hector. Just as Fortune darkens Hector's judgment when he allows the Greeks to escape destruction, desire obscures prudence for Achilles. He 'sette a-side wit and al resoun, / To caste a-forn by gode discrecioun / What was to do, with lokyng ful prudent' (4.3157–59). Hector suffers death through a momentary lapse; Achilles falls through a systematic collapse of the intellectual virtue that underwrites chivalric heroism.

Troy Book presents the confusion of prudence in governance through a second pairing of antagonists – Agamemnon and Priam. The contrasts between them are all the more remarkable for their similarities in practical virtues. Agamemnon is chosen leader by the Greeks to rule by his discretion (2.4442). As the ships gather to attack Troy, he reflects on the outcome of the war, 'reuoluyng of hiȝe discrecioun, / Þat he may so begynnen þat þe ende / Conclude wel' (2.5218–20). He reminds the Greeks of the uncertainty of war and of the opportunity for peace that was missed when they did not return Hesione: 'al had been vnwrouȝt / Ȝif we hadde seyn þis in oure þouȝt / Wisely aforn, and Exyoun restored' (2.6659–61). Besides deliberation, Agamemnon acts prudently to secure provisions, organize the defense of his camp on the plain before Troy, and prepare the order of battle. After Hector's death, he discerns the closing pattern of Fate – '[v]oide platly of ambiguyte' (4.79) – yet seeks a truce to allow Achilles to recover from his wounds and later to relieve the Greeks from Troilus' furious attacks (4.2112–21). When Palamides challenges his authority in open parliament, he recognizes the objectives but governs himself 'þoruȝ prudence & resoun, / With-Inne þe boundis of discrecioun' (4.135–36); events prove the wisdom of his judgment, for Palamides eventually dies in battle and Agamemnon is restored to power with the prospect of no further rivals.

Rhetorically, the best demonstration of Agamemnon's prudence is his consolatory speech to Menelaus after Helen's abduction. Menelaus is distraught over the plunder of the temple at Cytherea, the death of his men, and the loss of his wife to Paris. In an ironic echo of Hector's speech against the war, Agamemnon advises his brother, '3e schulde sli3ly dissymble 3oure offence' (2.4344), hiding his grief until he can exact vengeance in the future while in the meantime proving his 'manly herte' (2.4376):

> It is a doctrine of hem þat be prudent,
> Þat whan a man with furie is to-rent,
> To feyne chere til tyme he se leyser
> Þat he of vengaunce kyndle may þe fer;
> For sorwe oute-schewid, 3if I shal nat feine,
> Who-so take hede, it doth þinges tweyne:
> It causeth frendis for to si3e sore,
> And his enymyes to reioische more –
> Þi frende in hert is sory of nature,
> Þin enemy glad of þi mysaventure. (2.4351–60)

In his admonition, Agamemnon touches the diverse facets of Lydgate's representation of prudence. He offers wise practical counsel that sees beyond grievance into the future. Though duplicitous speech offers false prudence, he recuperates 'dissymulacioun' as a strategy for demonstrating patience and fortitude. Above all, he grasps the essential relation of the private and public spheres in urging Menelaus to contain his grief internally and present a regulated self to an unstable external world.

The prudence Agamemnon shows stands over and against his tragic fall to Fortune and Clytemnestra's dissembling. As with Hector's, Agamemnon's fate is an instance of structural irony. *Troy Book* devotes a more nuanced study of prudence to the figure of Priam. As a character, Priam struggles to balance passion and reason. Lydgate's metaphors, following Guido's, repeatedly portray him breaking the limits of containment and bursting forth. Prudence as an acquired, intellectual virtue must contend with his moral disposition toward recklessness. It is in the sphere of public action and governance that Priam achieves balance yet finally loses his capacity to negotiate changing circumstances. Lydgate's description of his rebuilding of Troy in Book 2 gives us a poetic emblem of Priam's foresight and judgment in organizing civic space as an expression of both magnificence and rational order. The astonishing formal craft of the city is a visible demonstration of powers of judgment at once architectural, political, and social. Priam oversees the artisans and the plans for building defensive walls, palaces, and avenues; and in the same way, he orchestrates the creation of a political community, repopulating Troy from the great multitude he has assembled: 'hem þat wern afore to hym foreyns, / He hath in Troye maked cite3eyns, / Ful discretly' (2.781–83). What stands behind the pragmatic exercise of building and statecraft is a calculation that Priam originally made when he beheld Lamedon's razed city.

> Wherfore þe kyng, after al this care,
> Hath souȝt a weye þe cite to repare;
> And cast hym fully, ȝif it wolde be,
> To make vertu of necessite. (2.461–64)

The echo of Chaucer is unmistakable, and the idea is Lydgate's addition to Guido. Like Theseus in the culminating speech of the *Knight's Tale* (I.3042), Priam intends to remedy catastrophe by pragmatic action. Lydgate goes further, though, to show the restorative effects on Priam, for whom the project of civic reconstruction is also the psychological antidote to grief.

In his magnificent city, Priam strives to show the political virtues required of a wise ruler. Lydgate makes it clear, however, that prudence must contend with the 'spark of old hatred' (2.1068). Hesione's captivity, Priam says, is an affront not merely to Trojans but 'ageynes gentilnes' (2.1177) generally; it threatens the wider social order that links Trojans and Greeks alike. But prudence cannot fully expel memory and malice. If Priam seeks to recover Hesione by diplomatic means, diplomacy can also serve to justify war. In dispatching Antenor as his peace emissary, Priam reveals in his language that prudence may separate the past from the future but it cannot fully resolve them: 'For þe surpluse of our mortal Ewre [Destiny] / We schal dissymvle, & prudently endure / Our harmys olde forþe in pacience' (2.1281–83). When the embassy fails and Priam decides to begin the war, Lydgate steps forward in his authorial role to reprove him for being overmastered by his passions and failing in reason, prudence, and providence (2.1810–12). Before convening the Trojan nobles in parliament, Priam has already decided to begin the war. Afterwards Lydgate chides him again for his 'þinne discreciou̅n' (2.2815) in allowing Paris' dream to carry the day in his sons' private debate over the war.

In the betrayal and downfall of Troy, prudence collapses as a means of judgment and action. The ability of heroic 'dissymulacioun' to contain contradictory motives gives way to the duplicitous speech of figures like Antenor and Aeneas. Priam foresees that they will betray him, but he fails in his own plot to trap the two. He is forced to accede publicly to the plan they announce for peace with the Greeks, which is a parody (4.5274–79) of his earlier decision to make virtue of necessity. Lydgate's description of Priam's predicament shows how far the sphere of prudence has been reduced and impoverished: 'He gan anoon dissymulen in þis cas; / For of prudence he clerly gan to se, / For þat tyme it may non oþer be' (4.5074–76). Amphymacus tries to preserve the integrity of deliberative speech by opposing Antenor and Aeneas, but he is exiled for his efforts. Lydgate's comments indicate that the arena of debate, hence deliberation, no longer exists: 'it is ful expedient, / Of prudence euery man to charge, / Þat his tonge be nat ouer-large' (4.5452–54). The final irony is that Priam participates in the downfall by accepting the horse the Greeks propose to leave behind. In a rare and therefore telling gesture of omission, Lydgate does not even try to name the virtue Priam lacks. He identifies it only by the locutions normally associated with prudence: 'Priam toke noon hede; / þe tresoun hidde he koude nat aduerte' (4.6186–87).

What, then, is the lesson that Lydgate tries to convey? If it is not to show that prudence is hopelessly contradictory – and there is no reason to think he regards it as such – what are we to make of the confusion of prudence in *Troy Book*? Has the truth of the story overrun the meaning Lydgate initially sets out for it, or has the narrative revealed another, unforeseen meaning in the complexities of history? The answer lies, I think, in the double lens through which Lydgate invites his contemporaries to view exemplary history. *Troy Book* depicts a pagan world constrained by a tragic pattern. Fate determines the destinies of characters and nations, and Fortune is the mechanism of change. Within such a world, prudence allows a measure of human choice and liberty, and shows the workings of natural reason. It suggests at various points that there were alternative histories available, as when the Greeks might have returned Hesione or Hector could have pressed his advantage to rout the Greeks completely. In other words, prudence preserves the appearance of free will against pagan destiny.

Lydgate's story nonetheless restricts this element of freedom. Each of the three large narrative movements depends on the confusion of prudence. In Book 1 prudence leads to the fall of Lamedon's Troy, as Lamedon acts out of mistaken judgment. In Books 2–4, as we have seen, prudence governs military strategy, chivalric heroism, and statecraft. At the same time, the pattern of tragedy follows the decay of prudence into cunning, ambush, and duplicitous speech. The epic antagonists Hector and Achilles are slain because they abandon prudence; and the chief political rivals, Priam and Agamemnon, cannot foresee their downfall. In Book 5, the catastrophes that befall the returning Greek heroes are exemplified by the fate of Ulysses, who tries to evade his prophesied death at the hands of his son. He seems to act prudently in imprisoning his son Telamon and immuring himself in a fortress. But the casual arrogance of his porter sets off the conflict that kills him when Telegonus, his son by Circe, arrives to see him. In all three parts of the story, prudence ironically hastens the disasters it is supposed to avert.

When we turn from pagan Troy to Lydgate's age, the perspective changes. *Troy Book* was commissioned by and addressed to a Christian prince. Lydgate recommends the lessons of prudence to Henry without irony or any evident sense of contradiction. He has set out 'Þe story pleyn, chefly in substaunce' (5.3543), and his book records '[c]haunge of Fortune, in hir cours mutable, / Selde or nat feithful ouþer stable' (5.3547–48). The lesson men must learn through prudence is to place no faith in transitory joy and worldly things. For Henry, prudence involves a further concern. Lydgate addresses him as a ruler whose works reflect prudence and finds in his character a latter-day embodiment of Solomon's discretion. Henry as a Christian prince has the chance to achieve directly what Trojan history finds only obliquely. The narrative of *Troy Book* ends with the reconciliation of rivals. In Thessaly, Achilles' grandson, Achilleidos, resigns the kingdom to Lamedonte, the son of Hector's widow Andromache. In Achaia, Ulysses' sons, Telamon and Telegonus, are bound to each other in mutual affection by their dying father. Henry, in turn, has conquered his heritage, contracted for marriage to Princess Katherine of France, and 'by his myȝti prudent gouernaunce' (5.3385) joined the two kingdoms. Lydgate suggests that the end hidden within the confusions of prudence is peace.

The Rider on the Sea-Monster.
'*Quid gloriaris in malitia ...*'

ROSEMARY MUIR WRIGHT

In the initials of early Irish manuscripts and in Viking carving in stone and wood, the beast head of the dragon is a recurrent symbol of evil, a warning against the snare of entrapment. However, this symbol may have a more specific meaning which relates to the sea, to the powers of darkness conjured up by the untamed ocean and which would be particularly appropriate to those whose home base lay in the lands skirting the North Sea and the Channel. If this beast head, for example, were to be identified as a sea dragon then the explanation of its ubiquitous presence in Northern imagery might find fruitful beginnings in the specific locations and needs of sea-going or sea-bound people.

My search began with a decorated psalter produced *c*.800 at the Abbey of Corbie in northern France in which the image of a rider on a sea monster in the opening initial to Psalm 51 (*Quid gloriaris*) caught my attention. Unusually, the opening initial of Psalm 51 in the Corbie Psalter, (Amiens, Bibliothèque Municipale, MS18, fol. 46ʳ), carries the image of a man riding backwards on a sea serpent (Figure 4.1). While the motif of riding in reverse is known to signify wickedness, the identity of the man of evil described in Psalm 51 is more usually that of Doeg, the captain of Saul who slaughtered the priests (I Samuel 22. 18).[1] The association of Doeg with this particular psalm was encouraged by the Hebrew caption which indicated that the psalm was composed when Doeg the Edomite warned Saul that David had sought refuge with the priests of the house of Ahimelech. The psalm is prophetic, pronouncing the destruction of the wicked and comparing this with the patience and trust of the servants of God. It is clear from the illustration of Psalm 51 in the ninth-century psalter now in Troyes Cathedral (MS 12, fol. 41*v*) that the link between David and Doeg's treachery was made explicit by the way in which the characters are identified for the reader by gold rustic capitals (Figure 4.2). In a sense this image is a visual denouncement before God of a particular type of man, a man of might who glories in iniquity and whose tongue devises injustice all day long.

---

[1] Ruth Mellinkoff, 'Riding Backwards. Theme of Humiliation and Symbol of Evil', *Viator*, 4 (1973), pp 153–76. The Corbie initials are analysed in Jean Desobry, *Le Manuscrit 18 de la Bibliothèque Municipale d'Amiens* (Paris, 1974), pp 73–118, esp. p. 97.

The Rider on the Sea-Monster

4.1 Initial 'Q' from the opening to Psalm 51. The Corbie Psalter: Amiens, Bibl. mun., MS 18 C, fol. 46

The gold labels on the painted ground highlight the textual indictment of the Psalmist's words.[2] The 'man of might' (*qui potens es in iniquitate*) of Psalm 51 appears to enshrine very specific evil qualities, through a set of values which are totally perverted and deliberately opposed to the will of God. In particular, the psalm appears to describe this type of wickedness, as being centred in speech; a lying tongue, a deceitful tongue, a wounding tongue. This catalogue of destructive voices, so boldly contrasted with the voice of praise of the Psalmist, is specifically meant to ensnare the servant(s) of God. By this specificity, Doeg the Edomite is comparable to the Antichrist who likewise killed the faithful, having ensured their destruction by deceptive words. He too is represented as a man of immense persuasive power which he wields even against the church itself.

Moreover, the psalm goes on to claim that the Psalmist is like a 'green olive tree in the house of God'. This echoes the words of Revelation in which the two witnesses who challenge the rule of Antichrist are described as the two olive trees. Has the more usual image of Doeg at the opening of this psalm (*Quid gloriaris*) been replaced in the Corbie Psalter by a figure of the Antichrist? If this is so, then we may have an early instance in psalter illustration of an image more usually associated with the Book of Revelation.

But why identify this figure as the Antichrist? Few extant examples in the Apocalypse illustrations provide comparable material, despite a developing iconography of the Antichrist in the latter part of the Middle Ages.[3] Visually, the Antichrist assumed one of two dominant forms, either that of a cosmocrator of cruel but seductive power or of a challenging beast arising from the sea. The Corbie Psalter of *c*.800 may be the earliest example of a composite image of these ideas. It is not alone. The closest referent to this conflation is the image of the Antichrist in the *Liber Floridus* of *c*.1120 (Ghent, University Library, MS 92, fol. 62ᵛ). It demonstrates how this particular combination of rider and sea monster had survived for three centuries suggesting that the iconography had been kept alive within the visual tradition (Figure 4.3). There is no doubt that the *Liber Floridus* image represents the Antichrist because the figure is clearly labelled and surrounded by texts from his life. The image appears in the bestiary section of this medieval encyclopedia where the visual accent would be on the biblical beast and the means of its recognition. Clearly the artist, Lambert of St Omer, understood that the clue to correct identification was the association of the monster with the Antichrist. Did the Corbie master use the same combination?

It has been proposed that this master came from an insular scriptorium, that he was a master who had direct access to visual formulae from Byzantine and

---

[2] Psalm 51. 1 in the Vulgate translation of the Hebraic version reads, 'Why glory in malice you that are mighty in iniquity, all day long thy tongue has devised injustice'.
[3] Rosemary Muir Wright, *Art and Antichrist in Medieval Europe* (Manchester, 1995), p.30 n. 33 and pp 60–77.

The Rider on the Sea-Monster 73

4.2 The opening to Psalm 51. Psalter: Troyes, Cathedral Treasury, MS 12, fol. 41v

classical sources but who used them in a manner which was distinctly anti-classical. The absorption of these sources into the insular tradition of scribal draughtsmanship which is so evident in the Corbie initials, rendered the Corbie master unique. Kuder's thesis claims that the initials are straightforward in their message and that there is no need for allegorical flights of fancy.[4] It is true that the imagery appears to speak directly to the audience however much the figures are bent into compliance with the shape of the letter. But this directness of approach need not invalidate Porcher's view that the figure on the sea beast could be understood allegorically as the Antichrist.[5] Inasmuch as the initial decoration prepared the monastic reader for the following text by picking up the opening words of the psalm, it is possible that the figure riding backwards on a sea dragon was immediately identifiable, given the exegetical link between Doeg as the murderer of the priests and the Antichrist. The Antichrist was equated with the Beast from the Sea described in the Book of Revelation. This Antichrist identification could be accommodated within the iconography of the sea rider, especially in combination with a sea monster and inset at that point where the reader would expect to see the evil man of Psalm 51. The allegorical reading of decorated initials pioneered by Heslop for the twelfth century could be applied to the Corbie initials.[6]

It does not seem as if the source of this image came from Apocalypse cycles in Carolingian circles, for the evidence of two related cycles in circulation at least by the first quarter of the ninth century offers no support for this combination of sea monster and human rider: the Trier Apocalypse (Trier, Stadtbibliothek, MS 31), which may have originated within the influence of the scriptorium of Tours, and the Valenciennes Apocalypse (Valenciennes, Bibliothèque Municipale, MS 99), produced at Liège. The Trier cycle is distinctive by the way in which it takes up satanic forms with an enthusiasm which is rarely found in the late-antique art on which it is dependent, but because of Trier's lack of commentary, the artist/designer was forced to rely on the textual account in the Book of Revelation which described the three harbingers of the End as three beasts. Effectively, this satanic trinity always appears in animal form, although on fol. 51[r], the third bestial emissary of Satan, the false prophet, appears in the form of a tiny man. By the substitution of the human form, the Trier artist may have been responding to an earlier tradition, perhaps shared by the Corbie artist, in which this form of evil tongue was given human guise. Otherwise Trier's

---

[4] Ulrich Kuder, *Die Initialen des Amienspsalters MS 18* (Munich, 1977), pp 235, 327. He sees the Corbie Psalter illustration as an isolated phenomenon, created by a master who may have been on pilgrimage to Corbie, 'war aller Wahrscheinlichkeit nach ein Peregrinus in Corbie'. [5] J. Hubert, J. Porcher and W.F. Volbach, *Europe in the Dark Ages* (London, 1957), p. 56. See also Desobry, *Le Manuscrit* 18 (1974), p. 97. [6] T.A. Heslop, 'Brief in words but heavy in the weight of its mysteries', *Art History*, 9 (1986), pp 1–11. See also J.J.G. Alexander, 'Ideological representations of military combat in Anglo-Norman art', *Anglo-Norman Studies*, 15 (1991/92), pp 1–24.

4.3 Antichrist on Leviathan. *Liber Floridus*: Ghent, University Library, MS 92, fol. 62

derivation from the Italian stem in the representation of the Apocalypse, emphasized the bestial nature of the forces of evil: 'And the beast which I saw was like unto a leopard, and his feet were as the feet of a bear, and his mouth as the mouth of a lion' (Revelation 13. 2). Valenciennes, on the other hand, had recourse to a different model, although ultimately derived from a seventh-century Italian prototype. The model for this northern French cycle was probably Insular, possibly a Northumbrian book of *c*.700, which may have reflected those '*imagines*' of the Book of Revelation brought back to Monk Wearmouth by Benedict Biscop.[7] Fol. 3^v of the Valenciennes cycle betrays Insular interlace and is also linked to fol. 172^v of the Durham Cassiodorus (Durham Cathedral Library, B.II.30). Valenciennes' strange sea monster may recall classical star-charts but its depiction of Satan is more like the naked giant of Anglo-Saxon illumination as in the Cotton Psalter (BL, Cotton MS Tiberius. C.VI, fol. 14). The designs of both the Valenciennes Apocalypse and the Corbie Psalter are similar in the way in which a key phrase from the text, rather than the main theme is chosen for the illustration. In the witness scene, for example, Valenciennes alone offers an image of the two witnesses, Enoch and Elias standing beside a cross. Normally this scene involves the murder of the witnesses who had preached against the evils of the Antichrist in the last days. Here however, the text refers to the eighth verse, 'and their Lord has been crucified' (*et dominus eorum crucifixus est*). The artist has picked up the phrase *crucifixus est* to present these standing figures as actual witnesses of the Crucifixion. In a similar way, the words '*quid gloriaris in malitia*' might have encouraged an imaginative substitution for the 'man of might' in the Corbie psalm illustration. It seems that in both cases, an evocative phrase, suggestive of pictures, is the motif force in shaping the illustration and that this tendency may be a feature of the Insular and Anglo-Saxon tradition on which both artists were dependent. The Corbie Psalter, like the Valenciennes Apocalypse, displays an apparent freedom from the literal narrative of the text which may be characteristic of the northern iconographic tradition. Even if this allegorical tradition encouraged the Corbie designer to conflate the 'son of perdition' described by Paul (II Thessalonians 2. 2–11) with 'the man of might' of the psalm, we still have to explain the conjunction of enthroned ruler and sea dragon.

A North African prototype, also dependent on a late-antique rendering, inspired the illustrated Beatus manuscripts of Spain.[8] Only in these Spanish manuscripts does the Antichrist appear in the illustrations to the text as a human protagonist against the Church, destroying its flock through false and seductive prophecy and killing all opposition.[9] The Corbie image involves a rider enthroned on the seat of a chariot. Despite the rich textual history of

---

[7] P. Meyvaert, 'Bede and the church paintings at Wearmouth-Yarrow', *Anglo-Saxon England*, 8 (1979), pp 63–77.   [8] G. Schiller, *Ikonographie der christichen Kunst*, V: *Die Apokalypse des Johannes* (Gütersloh, 1990), Texteil, p. 134, n. 400.   [9] John Williams,

The Rider on the Sea-Monster

Antichrist in the early Middle Ages from the fifth century onwards, outside Spain there is little evidence of the image of the Antichrist as a man before the Carolingian Apocalypses.[10] If the image in the Corbie Psalter does represent this evil force, it may be an early instance of this visual sign which has hitherto been overlooked.

One fruitful line of development lies in the association of this challenger with Leviathan, the terrible monster of the deep described in Job 40. 41, which exegesis interpreted as the devil tossed about on the rolling sea, like a serpent coiling across the undulations of the earth. Leviathan is described in the Vulgate translation as a sea serpent, 'Leviathan is to be made known as the serpent in the sea' (*Leviathan serpens in mari innotescitur*). Leviathan is also called King, ruler of all the children of Pride (Isaiah 33. 34). His Old Testament existence may find its ultimate source in the East in the Babylonian creation myth of the sea monster of chaos, Tiamat, who rebelled against the Canaanite Gods. This Babylonian creature may have some connection with the monsters of the Old Testament, like the seven-headed Lotan.[11] Wallace has pointed out that the words used to describe these beasts are identical in both Hebrew and Canaanite and are to be translated as 'gliding' and 'tortuous'. This would easily lend itself to the image of a serpent dragon. The Leviathan had been identified by God as part of his own creation, just as the Antichrist was allowed to exist by God's permission as part of his plan for salvation. The sea monster could not be overcome by man, only God could destroy its power, 'In that day Yahweh with his hard and great and strong sword will punish leviathan, the swift serpent, and leviathan the crooked serpent and he will slay the monster that is in the sea' (Isaiah 27. 1).

Leviathan ruled the waters of the deep where (presumably) it could do least damage to the earth. Leviathan is also connected to the Hebrew, *tannin*, of Isaiah 51. 9 which refers to dragons along with the word *rahaab* which means proud and insolent.[12] The references to Leviathan in the Old Testament are also linked to the general word for water or ocean, *tehom*. But a more specific meaning was that of primal chaos. In Job and in the Psalms this word is used to describe the dwelling place of Leviathan. In the Septuagint rendering of 'the bottomless pit' (*abyssos*) described in Revelation 11. 7, the word used is also

---

The Illustrated Beatus: a corpus of the illustrations of the Commentary on the Apocalypse, I (London, 1994), p. 134.   10 Adso Dervensis, *De Ortu et Tempore Antichristi*, ed. by D. Verhelst, Corpus Christianorum: Continuatio Mediaevalis, XLV (Turnhout, 1976), pp 22–30.   11 Howard Wallace, 'Leviathan and the Beast in Revelation', *The Biblical Archaeologist*, 11 (1948), pp 62–3.   12 I am grateful to Gregory Morris, St Deiniol's Library, Hawarden, Wales for the provision of all the Hebrew references and for the following notes: *Tannin* are probably great fish (Genesis 1. 2; Job 7. 12; Isaiah 27. 1) although on other occasions, they are serpents or dragons. Tehom is widely used in the Psalms (36. 7; 7. 4; 74. 15 and 107. 23). The *Tehom* was unleashed in the Flood of the Genesis narrative (Genesis 7. 11).

tehom. This restless force of chaos becomes in the New Testament the force of evil. In Revelation's great vision of the creation of the new heaven and the new earth, this symbol of the uncontrollable forces of the world is obliterated: 'for the first heaven and the first earth had passed away and the sea was no more' (Rev 21. 1).

The Septuagint tradition of the medieval Bible ensured the survival of this idea which would have been especially compelling for sea-bound communities. Likewise, the text of the Psalms also made frequent reference to the sea and to the monsters of the deep: 'So this is the great and wide sea, wherein are things creeping innumerable, both small and great beasts. There go the ships (or sea monsters): there is that leviathan, whom thou hast made to play therein' (Psalm 104. 25–26). These references were picked up in gloss and homily where the darkness and hidden power of the sea were evoked as a threat to man's security. In the early Middle Ages it would seem that the sea was identified with the realm of evil.

Gregory the Great's *Homilies on Ezekiel* draws parallels between the darkness of the waters and clouds and the ignorance of man: '*Dark waters were, and thickest clouds of the air*, because the wisdom of prophets is obscured' (Psalm 18. 11);[13] and goes on to expand this with quotations from the Gospels: 'What I tell you in darkness, that speak ye in light' (Matthew 10. 27). The imagery of a Romanesque initial from a French manuscript of the Homilies now in the Pierpont Morgan Library (New York, MS Glazier 6, fol. 39), shows the prophet struggling in the coils of the serpent, the visual equivalent of the phrase '*in quisbusdam locis obscurioribus*' which evokes him struggling in dark or concealed places to see his way through the darkness to the promise of enlightenment. This is assured by the adjoining text which promises that the glory of God is a mystery which the words of the text will uncover after great labour. The Homilies also make frequent references to the Apocalypse as in the opening of Homily VIII, where Gregory reminds the reader that 'the many waters' is to be understood as the people described in Revelation 17. 15 who have given their power and strength to the beast.[14] The illustration on fol. 39 presents a man, a man of might, seated on a throne above a monster (Figure 4.4). This aggressive

---

13 Gregorius Magnus, *Homiliae in Hiezechihelem Prophetam*, Corpus Christianorum: Series Latina, CXLII (Turnhout, 1971), *Homilia* vi, 1.1, line 7, p. 67: 'Tenebrosa, aqua in nubibus aeris, quia obscura est scientia in prophetis. Sed Salomonis voce attestante didicimus: Gloria regum celare verbum, et gloria Dei est investigare sermonem, quia et honor est hominum eorum secreta abscondere et gloria Dei est mysteria sermonis eius aperire. Ipsa autem per se Veritas discipulis dicit: Quae dico vobis in tenebris, dicite in lumine ... '
14 Ibid., *Homilia* viii, 1. 3, line 4, p. 101: 'Et audiebam sonum alarum, quasi sonum quarum multarum' (and I heard the sound of wings as it were the sound of many waters). Revelation uses *vox* (voice) not *sonus* (sound): Revelation 1. 15, 14. 2 and 19. 6. Ezekiel's use of *sonus* is a version of the cliché 'sound of many waters' which is found also in the psalms. However the association between the two may not have been lost on the medieval reader.

4.4 Illuminated Initial. St Gregory, *Homilies on Ezekiel*: The Pierpont Morgan Library, New York, MS G. 6, fol. 39. (Photo: David Loggie)

image encapsulates the section of text which explains John's vision of the heads of the Beast which bore the Whore of Babylon, 'And there are seven kings; five are fallen, and one is, and the other is not yet come; and when he cometh he must continue a short space. These have one mind and shall give their power and strength unto the beast'. The opening lines of the Homily *'tenebrosa aqua in nubibus aeris'*, encourage the reader to think allegorically. Here again, the reference to the waters of chaos and the beast of Revelation is given visual form in the conjunction of man and sea monster.

The various psalm commentaries, in a similar way, might have been a means of transmission for such images of the sea, the serpent and Leviathan itself. For example, in his commentary on Psalm 51, Cassiodorus immediately identifies the 'man of might' with the Antichrist: 'The roots will be those [people] of the same mind as the Antichrist and the ministers of the devil' (*Radices erunt Antichristi consentanei ministrique diaboli*). He goes on to make a clear connection between the prophecy of Enoch and Elias as the two witnesses of the Book of Revelation and their murder at the hands of the Antichrist with the murder of the priests at the hands of Doeg: 'For just as it was revealed by Elias and Enoch so is it declared by this pair of psalms that [the Antichrist] is to be destroyed by two most holy men at the end of the world, in order that he shall not be a secret cause of fear. Wherefore is this psalm suitably located after the fiftieth since the son of iniquity, of whom it speaks, is understood to have no pardon when stepping beyond the limit of redemption.'[15] Previously Augustine had also made the connection with the Antichrist at Psalm 51.[16] We know that the Corbie Psalter in particular was influenced by the commentaries of Cassiodorus, which encouraged the reader to explore a spiritual exposition of the text particularly pertinent in the context of a monastic community. In the northern tradition therefore, a man and a sea dragon might offer themselves as visual components in a symbol for the Antichrist.

But, even in combination, would they be sufficient elements to identify the subject? It seems likely that the idea of enthronement would have to be represented. As Antichrist was believed to rise to such power as to sit in the Temple of Solomon, the representation of a seated figure above the sea dragon might imply both enthronement and control over the sea beast itself. The

---

15 Cassiodorus, *Expositio Psalmorum*, Corpus Christianorum: Series Latina, XCVII (Turnhout, 1958), pp 473–77, lines 230–36: 'Nam sicut per Eliam et Enoch, duobus est viris sanctissimis in fine saeculi destruendus, ita et per hos geminos psalmos, ne occultus terreat Antichristus, indicatur. Unde convenienter post quinquagesimum hic psalmus est positus, quoniam filius iniquitatis de quo loquitur, terminum remissiones excedens, nullam veniam habere cognoscitur.'   16 St Augustin, *Expositions on the Book of Psalms*, A Select Library of the Nicene and Post-Nicene Fathers of the Christian Church, VIII, ed. by Philip Schaff (Grand Rapids, Michigan, reprint 1996), pp 197–202. Augustine notes a scribal confusion between Ahimelech and Abimelech in Psalm 51, Abimelech being regarded as a type of the Antichrist.

Antichrist, as a satanic parody, was said to ape Christ himself. Some images of the Lord enthroned may have responded to textual traditions which confused the Hebrew word for cherubim (*cereb*) with the word (*rekeb*) for chariot and may reflect a distant classical model of Apollo in his chariot. The Corbie image may also reflect that iconography but with a dramatic inversion of meaning. In this instance, which Kuder claims is original, the Antichrist is seated in a chair on the serpent's back.[17] The visual reference is the more precise because the rider of Corbie appears in a posture more associated with riding in a chariot than merely sitting on his dragon mount. The imagery of Psalm 29. 10 describes how the Lord is enthroned upon the flood, that is the sea. By riding on a sea dragon, the Antichrist figure presents a distinct challenge to God as the Antichrist is demonstrably enthroned on the waters which he literally sets below his feet. Later evidence in support of this idea comes from an inhabited initial D in a twelfth-century copy of Augustine's *Commentary on the Psalms* (Valenciennes, Bibliothèque Municipale, MS 39, fol. 8) in which the rider is clearly astride the sea dragon and represented as the satanic progeny of a writhing serpent which forms the frame of the initial and spews him forth, like Jonah from the mouth of the whale (Figure 4.5).

If these elements came to be necessary constituents of this Antichrist image, where then might the Corbie designer have found exemplars for his formula, trained as he was in the insular tradition yet exposed to classical models? Did this earthly protagonist lurk among the pages of insular art under another guise, especially under the guise of a sea serpent? We know that the combination of sea serpent and powerful ruler/rider was understood by the twelfth-century from the evidence of the illustrated Homilies of *c*.1110 produced in Toulouse in south-western France (New York, Pierpont Morgan Library, MS Glazier 6). Moreover, the connection between Leviathan and Antichrist was made explicit in the Bestiary image of the *Liber Floridus c*.1120 where the Leviathan texts from Job were directly inscribed in the visual field with the texts from the life of the Antichrist.[18] Scattered sections within the text of the *Liber Floridus* show that Lambert was following Gregory's *Moralia* but a visual source also must have been at hand, for the Antichrist formula appears to have been applied easily, even in a section like the Bestiary where such an image would not have been usual. Lambert must have seen an image of the mythical Leviathan perhaps in association with a seated figure of Antichrist. It has been suggested that Lambert had access to an illustrated *Moralia* not unlike that formerly at

---

17 Ulrich Kuder, *Die Initialen des Amienspsalters*, MS 18 (Munich, 1977), p. 236.   18 Jessie Poesch, 'The Beasts from Job in the *Liber Floridus*', *Journal of the Warburg and Courtauld Institutes*, 33 (1970), pp 41–51. See also Daniel Verhelst, 'Les Textes Eschatologiques dans le *Liber Floridus*', in *The Use and Abuse of Eschatology in the Middle Ages*, ed. by W. Verbeke, D. Verhelst and A. Welkenhuysen (Leuven, 1988), pp 299–305.

Cîteaux (Dijon, Bibliothèque Municipale, MS 168). Though the Wolfenbüttel copy (Herzog August Bibliothek, MS Guelf 1. Gud. lat. 2) of the Lambert image is faithful to the original, the fifteenth-century copy in Chantilly (Museé Condé, MS 724) misunderstood the hovering form of the Antichrist and made him ride the Leviathan. It is conceivable that in transmission the detail of the chair was omitted and the figure appeared to be floating just above the sea serpent.

If we could discover the visual sources for the twelfth-century image it might be possible to see whether such visual prompts could have been in circulation as early as 800. Jessie Poesch has suggested that the source of the image in the *Liber Floridus* is a Greek Septuagint.[19] She notes that the Septuagint version describes the Leviathan as 'king over all that are in the waters', a description which would evoke the image of Poseidon. In the examples which she cites, the descriptions in the Job text are illustrated by a variety of demons, one of which is clearly a merman. The particular manuscript of the Greek Septuagint text to which she refers, includes the Catena of Olympiodorus *c.*510 in which Leviathan is equated with the devil and described as king of every poisonous thing, the father of vile and ignoble sons. Byzantine Apocalypse literature recounts the ancient myth of a marine monster which had fought against God at the time of creation and would challenge him again at the end of time. In one of the Greek Apocalypse texts, the *Oracle of Baalbeck*, Antichrist is described in line 191 as the 'King with the changing shape': 'There will arise another emperor with a changing shape; and he will rule for thirty years.'[20] The *Pseudo-Ephraem* text warns of the *adventus mali*, the coming of the Evil One, signalling by the use of the word adventus that he would come with royal power, evoking the entry of the emperor riding in triumph. As the Antichrist was believed to be descended from the Jewish tribe of Dan, all major Byzantine Apocalypses made an interpretative connection with Jacob's blessing on Dan in Genesis 49. 17: 'Dan shall be a serpent in the way, a viper by the path, that bites the horse's heel, so that his rider falls backward.' These passages, cited by Irenaeus and Hippolytus, passed into the western tradition in which backward meant in the direction of sin.[21]

Did the Corbie artist arrive at his model from a similar conflation of sources? Kuder's thesis claims that the sources of the imagery of the Corbie Psalter lay in Byzantine and in Classical texts, a claim which is clearly supported by the formal appearance of the figures and their manner of dress. Though there were small bronzes of Taras or Arion riding a dolphin, the manner in which the manuscript figure is shaped into the body of the letter suggests a two-dimensional model such as a coin of antique origin. Taras was a son of Poseidon, God of the Sea, and identified with a pagan city, Tarent. Such a figuration could offer itself as a pagan counterpart to Antichrist on Leviathan. The visual potential of this

19 Poesch, 'The Beasts', p. 49. 20 Paul Alexander, *The Byzantine Apocalyptic Tradition* (Berkeley and London, 1985), p. 203 n. 44. 21 Mellinkoff, 'Riding Backwards', pp 154–55.

The Rider on the Sea-Monster

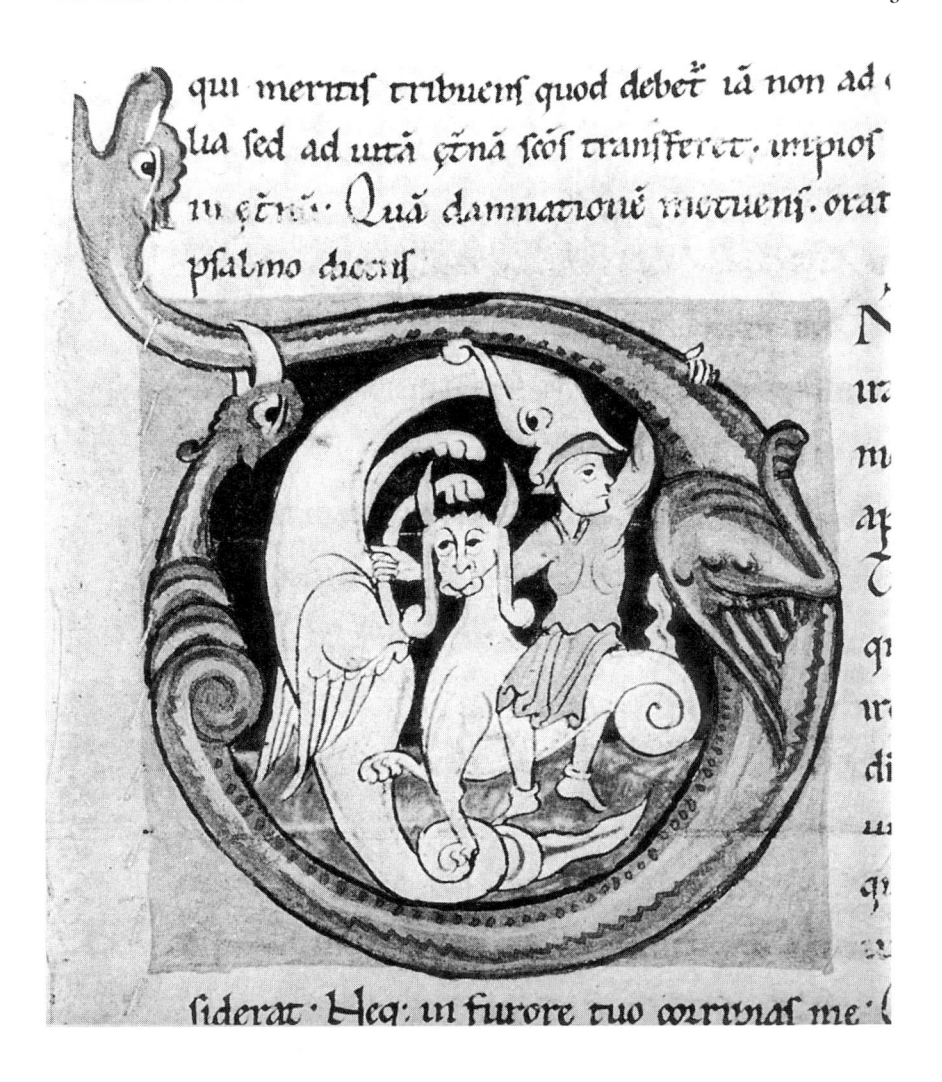

4.5 Initial 'D'. St Augustine, *Commentary upon the Psalms*: Valenciennes, Bibl. mun., MS 39, fol. 8. (Photo: G.P. Simon)

source of marine deities might be seen in the image of Poseidon riding a hippocampus (sea monster) on a Laconian cup from Cerveteri of about 550 BC (Cerveteri Museum, 90287). It is a reminder of the transmission of imagery on portable objects which find themselves in an alien culture.[22] Mosaic floors like those found at Herculaneum and Ostia also featured sea subjects of tritons riding sea monsters.[23] All the Corbie artist had to do was to turn the classically inspired figure riding a dolphin backward to suggest an evil rider. If the original had a scallop-shell throne, the artist of the Corbie initial also set his sea-rider on a throne. The Girona Beatus of Spain (975), carries an unusual set of figures at the foot of fol. 157^v, which may be linked to the preceding texts which describe the angel of the abyss, named in Revelation as Abaddon: 'Whose name in Hebrew is Abaddon, and in the Greek Apollyon'. John Williams speculates that the citation 'ruler of the Abyss' evoked the image of Poseidon which had been fused with that of Amphitrite in transmission. He stresses that the inclusion of the marginal figures of the sea riders is not the result of decorative caprice but 'is tied to some pictorial tradition'. Like the classical Atlantes which hold up the vision of Christ in Majesty on fol. 2 of the same manuscript, the Poseidon figure may be based on a Carolingian illustration possibly contemporary with the Corbie Psalter. A comparable sea monster decorates one of the canon tables in the Vivian Bible (BN, MS latin 1, fol. 327).[24]

The selection of a serpent motif for the Corbie initial to Psalm 51, must have been predicated on knowledge of the association between Antichrist and Leviathan. The Corbie artist appears to have used the traditional motif of a man disgorged by a sea monster, as in the Gellone Sacramentary (BN, MS latin 12048), in combination with the antique God of the Sea to suggest the man of iniquity who heralded the last days. If the compiler of the Corbie Psalter had been familiar with commentary of Cassiodorus, he would have understood the reference which the sixth-century patristic text offered. All that was required was to use the sea beast motif which signalled the monster of chaos in a new conjunction with a human rider.

The traditions of Antichrist literature which stem from Oriental and Late Jewish writings gave descriptions of Antichrist's physical features as a monster in human shape. But from the fifth century onward the Church Fathers had insisted that he was a human being. It would be interesting to speculate on the motives which brought together the separate elements of sea dragon and

---

22 Maria Pipili, *Laconian Iconography of the sixth century BC*, Oxford University Committee for Archaeology, no. 12 (Oxford, 1987), p. 49. See also the evidence of Roman mosaics from North Africa in Michele Blanchard-Lemee, *Mosaics of Roman Africa: Floor Mosaics from Tunisia*, trans. by Kenneth Whitehead (London, 1996), p. 130 and figure 89, illustrating Neptune in his chariot. 23 Alfonso de Franciscis, *The Buried Cities: Pompeii and Herculaneum* (London, 1978), p. 93 and fig. 132. 24 Williams, *Illustrated Beatus*, II, p. 58.

human autocrat given that the likely catalyst was a classical text depicting Poseidon as ruler of the waves. Just as the classical world offered models through the star charts for evil characters like the Whore of Babylon in the figure of Cassiopeia, so it provided a model for the Leviathan in the constellation of Cetus or Capricorn. This star sign was associated with the dark days of the winter solstice and in particular with the winter storms. The Latin version of the Greek poem by Aratus of Soloi, the *Phaenomena*, describes the fear of the sailors who had put to sea under that star sign, afraid to venture far from the shore and conscious of the thin planks which separated them from death:

> Beware of his months; you may be engulfed in waves
> if you sail the open sea. Dawn will not bring you
> a fair or far voyage, for day then is briefest
> nor will it come early though you row through the night
> trembling with fear. Only the South wind's painful sweep
> will assail you when the sun and capricorn join
> and the sailor is numbed by hard frost from Zeus.
> Yet all the long lonely year, the sea broods dark under keels
> and like flashing gulls that dive for their food
> We sit aboard ship staring at shoreline and sea.[25]

The distinctive feature of this sea monster is the curling tail often forked or split like that of a mermaid. The Leiden *Aratus* manuscript is an excellent example of what must have been a near-perfect Carolingian forgery. As the monster sent to devour the sacrificial Andromeda, the Cetus could be seen as the Leviathan of the Old Testament threatening the Church.

Many curling sea dragons in Romanesque initials seem to echo that composition, in particular when used to decorate the initial to Psalm 51. More needs to be done with the possibility that the dragons and monsters of the tanglewood initials are specific embodiments of evil rather than generalized enemies. From their mouths comes death in the form of ensnarement. Set in close relation to the text, these beast heads may function as a warning reminding the reader of the destruction wrought by evil speech. Just as everything that proceeds from the mouth of the Antichrist is evil, so is the emission of the dragon in the form of plant tendrils, like pliant tongues offering entrapment. These tendrils may themselves stand for the snares described in the psalms: 'The cords of Death encompassed me, the torrents of Perdition (Belial) assailed me; the cords of Sheol entangled me, the snares of death confronted me' (Psalm 18. 4–5). In the struggle to free themselves from that tendril interlace, animals, birds and mankind are depicted fighting for survival

[25] Aratus, 'Phaenomena', introduction and trans. by Stanley Lombardo (Austin, University of Texas, Ph.D. thesis, 1976)(Ann Arbor, 1987), II, pp 279–83.

by mutual destruction. Some, as *athlete dei*, even attempt to kill the serpent itself. This struggle has been most eloquently interpreted by the researches of Conrad Rudolph in the interpretation of the Cîteaux Moralia in Job.[26] I have no doubt that we are closer now to the spirit in which these images were created and to their reception than at first appeared. These initial letters were lingered over, ingested in the medieval sense. They acted as buttresses to the sacred text, as visual metaphors for their content and as receptive foci for the fears of the monastic reader.[27]

In this review of Antichrist evidence between the Corbie Psalter and the *Liber Floridus*, I have suggested that one strand in the complex warp of such imagery was laid by the association of the Antichrist with the 'man of might' of Psalm 51. Another was the identification of the Beast from the Sea with the Antichrist, once the Book of Revelation itself came to be illustrated. In this development, the Antichrist became identified as the murderer of the witnesses, Enoch and Elias, forming an analogy with Doeg in the psalm who had killed the priests of the Lord. I suspect that the imagery of the Antichrist has a much older history than the extant evidence provided by the Apocalypse cycles suggests. I propose that his sign as the rider on a sea monster is the contribution of the North Sea world in the widest sense of the northern European littoral. One wonders if this transmission of text and Antichrist image was also the business of the Irish monks. Conscious of their missionary role, their apprehension of the beast-headed prows that brought destruction, could they have infiltrated into their decorated beast initials the warning head of the toothed Leviathan? Eastern apocrypha were known early in Irish texts and the visionary voyage poems of the tenth century equate Ireland with the land of the witnesses, who preached to them of the coming of the Antichrist.[28] In the *Immram Snédgusa ocus Meic Riagla* (version I), Snédgus and Mac Ríagla of the community of St Columba make sea voyages, one of which is to an island where the king tells them that this is the island where Enoch and Elijah dwell. Elijah himself greets the clerics and preaches about the coming of the Antichrist, although their request to see Enoch is refused because he lives in secret until the final battle (Armageddon). On their visit to another island they warn of the forthcoming vengeance of God in the form of the Vikings:

> Men in ships, warriors with spears, without any faith whatsoever; ...

---

26 C. Rudolph, *Violence and Daily Life: Reading, Art and Polemics in the Cîteaux Moralia in Job* (Princeton, 1997). **27** D. Ganz, *Corbie in the Carolingian Renaissance* (Sigmaringen, 1990), provides evidence from the library at Corbie that a similar approach to the texts could have existed in the ninth century at the Abbey of Corbie. **28** Donncha Ó hAodha, 'The poetic version of the voyage of Snédgus and MacRíagla', in *Dán do Oide: Essays in memory of Conn R. O Cléirigh*, ed. by A. Ahlqvist and V.

The Rider on the Sea-Monster

> Thirteen months upon your travels – congregation of a vigorous
> one – since the storm of the joyous sea abounding in animals
> sent you forth.
> It will be better for us that what you tell should be our tales,
> with living words, with white hands, with swift feet.[29]

It is possible that the earliest human iconography of the Antichrist came from the North, arising from an identification of the evildoer of Psalm 51 (*Quid Gloriaris*) with the 'Son of Perdition' of the New Testament. For the North Sea World, his association with the great sea monster Leviathan must have stirred contemporary fears of the sea-borne raiders from across the North Sea.

Capková (Dublin, 1997), p. 429, vv. 72, 74, 75.   **29** I am indebted to Thomas O. Clancy, Department of Celtic, University of Glasgow, for this information. See his forthcoming article, 'Subversion at Sea: Style and Intent in the Immrama' in *The Otherworld Voyage in Early Irish Literature and History*, ed. by J. Wooding (Dublin, 2000).

North Sea Language Contacts in the Early Middle Ages: English and Norse

PAUL BIBIRE

Quite apart from any historical difficulties of definition in dealing with the Viking Age and its effects upon the British Isles, problems also arise in the terminology used for them. One of these is the word *Viking* itself. Whilst guaranteed to sell lurid picture-books in their tens of thousands, the modern word is a nineteenth-century loan-word from Scandinavian, not recorded before 1807 according to the *Oxford English Dictionary*, *s.v.* The native Old English word, *wicing*, does not survive. A derivative form of it was used as early as the Épinal-Erfurt Glossaries, the manuscripts and sources of which are earlier than the earliest Viking incursions into Britain, at latest early eighth century, possibly late seventh: *uuicingsceadan* glossing *piraticum*;[1] in the related Cleopatra Glossary the alternatives *wicingsceaþan*, *sæsceaðan* and *æscmen* are given.[2] Implications of violence and robbery are certainly expressed in the element *-sceaða* 'harmer; thief', and so it is not certain whether they were also implicit in *wicing*; the equivalence of *wicingsceaþan* and *sæsceaðan* might suggest that the primary semantic component of *wicing* was seafaring. The other equivalent, *æscmen*, simply seems to mean 'ship-men', where *æsc* is a rare word for 'ship',[3] subsequently apparently identified as 'Viking ship' as in *The Battle of Maldon*, presumably on (correct) identification with a poetic Norse word for (war-)ship, *askr*. The lemmata for these glosses are derivatives of Latin *pyrata*. This certainly included the sense 'pirate' in its rather wide semantic range, though it could just mean 'sea-man'.[4] The cognate Norse words certainly include piracy as one of their semantic components: there is a concrete masculine noun, *víkingr*, the person who carries out the activity of the abstract feminine noun *víking*. *Víking* implies, in the sources which describe it in any non-formulaic detail, something more organized than mere random piracy: a specific military expedition organized on a free-enterprise basis, with contributing partners, *félagar* 'fellows', who share the risks and proceeds. It could certainly involve trade but also certainly always implied and usually involved violence, and most

---

[1] *Old English Glosses in the Épinal-Erfurt Glossaries* (Oxford, 1974), ed. by J.D. Pheifer, p. 39, no. 736.   [2] Ibid. p. 39n.   [3] Ibid. p. 18, no. 321.   [4] For instance, *Revised Medieval Latin Word-List*, ed. by R.E. Latham (London, 1965), p. 352 (*s.v. pirata*).

of the indications, in contemporary poetry and later prose, are that it was undertaken for both profit and sport. The origins of the word, and also therefore its original or earlier meanings, are still much disputed, and none of the suggested etymologies is satisfactory, while several of them are impossible.

Another problem lies in the word actually used for the Scandinavians by Anglo-Saxons. The most usual term is *Dene*. This is almost always translated as 'Danes' by English historians, and also, unsurprisingly, by Danish scholars, and it can of course have that meaning. But it certainly had a wider meaning in English before and in the tenth century, and is applied to Scandinavians from Norway, most obviously in *The Anglo-Saxon Chronicle* entry for the year 787:

> A
> Her nom Beorhtric cyning Offan dohtor Eadburge; 7 on his dagum cuomon ærest .iii. scipu, 7 þa se gerefa þærto rad, 7 hie wolde drifan to þæs cyninges tune þy he nyste hwæt hie wæron; 7 hiene mon ofslog; þæt wæron þa ærestan scipu **Deniscra monna** þe Angel cynnes lond **gesohton**.
>
> E (and F)
> Her nam Breohtric cining Offan dohter Eadburge. 7 on his dagum comon | ærest .iii. scipu **Norðmanna** of Hereða lande. 7 þa se ge refa þær to rad. 7 he wolde drifan to ðes cininges tune þy he nyste hwæt hi wæron. 7 hine man of sloh þa. Ðæt wæron þa erestan scipu **Deniscra manna** þe Angel cynnes land **gesohton**.[5]

Æþelweard adds the detail that this occurred at Dorchester in Dorset.[6] Here *Deniscra manna* must be translated as 'of Norsemen', not 'of Danish men', since we are also told in E and F that they were *Norðmenn* who came from *Hereða lande*, most probably Hörðaland in south-western Norway. The cognate terms in Norse certainly also had wider senses: the second element of the name *Danmǫrk* is perhaps most likely to mean 'border' here, and the name should probably be translated as 'the borderland of the *Danir*'. And in Old Norse itself, the term *dǫnsk tunga* 'the tongue of the *Danir*', is used for the language of the Vikings, Norse, whether it be spoken in Denmark, Norway or Iceland. Clearly early OE *Dene*, Norse *Danir* could refer to Scandinavians in general. Again, the origin of the name is debatable, and its earliest senses cannot be securely recovered. Only once the royal campaigns organized by the Danish king Sveinn Haraldsson began, in the late tenth century, Old English prose sources must use the term *Dene* and its cognates only in the narrow, modern sense. Another rarer

---

5 *Two of the Saxon Chronicles Parallel*, ed. by C. Plummer (Oxford, 1892), remains the best synoptic edition. **6** *The Chronicle of Aethelweard*, ed. by A. Campbell (London, 1962), p. 27.

Old English term, also used in the EF Chronicle entry for 787, is *Norþmenn*. While this is frequently translated as 'Norwegians', it simply means 'men from the north', and could easily just mean 'Scandinavian'.

Other problems also arise from or are related to vocabulary. In the entries from the *Anglo-Saxon Chronicle* cited above, the chronicler concludes that these were the first ships of *Deniscra manna* which *gesohton* the land of the English. It is of course easiest to translate this as 'these were the first ships of Danish men which sought out the land of the English', and to conclude that, at least as far as the chronicler knew, there had been no prior contacts between English and Scandinavians in living memory. But the verb *gesecan*, past *gesohte*, Modern English *seek*, *sought*, does not necessarily only mean 'to seek out, visit'; it also has a very well attested secondary sense 'to attack', as does its Norse cognate *sækja*; this sense is therefore likely to be ancient. The sentence could well therefore mean that these were the first ships of Scandinavians which attacked the land of the English, and so would imply that the chronicler considered all earlier contact to have been peaceful. Given the increasingly powerful evidence for close early contact between Scandinavia and England in the sixth and seventh centuries, this latter interpretation must be preferable. To ride a hobbyhorse for a moment, any translator must of course choose between options such as these, even if he or she is aware of them. These examples demonstrate as clearly as possible that anyone, historian or otherwise, who wishes to work on this material must do so in the original languages with the primary sources, not in any modern translation, no matter how well-respected and scholarly it may be.

For the original places of origin of the English invaders who came to these islands in the fifth and sixth centuries, we are mostly dependent upon Bede, who describes them as Saxons, Angles and Jutes; Procopius adds Frisians to this list.[7] On this basis, the English may have come from the North Sea coastal regions either side of the Elbe as far south as the mouths of the Rhine, but also coming from somewhere which might be as far north as modern Jutland. This would mean that the English were descended from the most northerly peoples of the West Germanic tribes, those perhaps described by Tacitus as *Inguaeones*, and who were in closest contact with those peoples who were to be the ancestors of the Germanic Scandinavians. The linguistic distinction between West and North Germanic itself is unclear: there might not even have been sufficient differences in the fifth or sixth centuries to discriminate linguistically between them. Any existing linguistic differences could have been defined, then or later, along a single geographical and ethnographic, even political, boundary, quite

---

[7] *Venerabilis Baedae Historiam ecclesiasticam gentis Anglorum*, ed. by C. Plummer, I (Oxford, 1896), cap. 15, p. 31, this edition cited for the fulness of its notes; Procopius, *De bello Gotthico*, IV, 19.

possibly for instance the River Eider in Schleswig in the period of the legendary wars associated with Offa of Angeln,[8] though perhaps previously further north, before the westward expansion of the Danes to Jutland. Or quite possibly such existing linguistic boundaries, to the extent that they existed and were perceived, could subsequently have been explained and justified by the means of such legend. Alternatively or at different periods, the isoglosses might have been spread across a moderately broad area, within which communities might have used some features proper to West Germanic, and some proper to North Germanic.

Certainly Old English, as it subsequently developed, was by far the most similar of the West Germanic (Ingvaeonic) languages to Norse. This has led many scholars, most recently and importantly Hans Frede Nielsen,[9] to argue for a late pre-migration grouping around the North Sea coasts, so-called 'North Sea Germanic'. This included the ancestral dialects which gave rise to Old English, Old Frisian and Old Norse, which was a little more remotely related to Old Saxon, but excluded the other West Germanic language, Old High German, and of course also excluded Gothic, and any other East Germanic languages that might have existed. This is a plausible reconstruction, especially if it is seen as a late development, superimposed by geographical contact between the peoples around the North Sea, on an earlier possibly tripartite division of Germanic into East, West and North.

Plausibility is of course not proof. It is dependent upon the model employed. Thus for instance the tripartite division of Germanic implies the 'tree-diagram' of derivation, based upon the model of Darwinian evolution and employed at a time when that model was dominant; it is not without its uses in language-history, but by itself is very inadequate.[10] Many of the similarities between English and Norse must be due to later parallel developments, taking place almost certainly independently in the two languages. This phenomenon is usually called 'drift', and has continued to the present day within the Germanic languages. For instance, the Great Vowel Shift in fifteenth-century English is directly comparable with the simultaneous developments in early modern High German, but which did not take place in the geographically intervening dialects and languages of north Germany, Holland and the Frisian islands. Again, the eighteenth-century diphthongisations of long vowels in southern British English have similar and simultaneous parallels in modern Icelandic. So Old English had two sets of early sound-changes which produced diphthongs from original short front vowels, Breaking and Back Mutation, caused by different

8 See, for instance, *Widsith*, ed. by R.W. Chambers (London, 1912), pp 202–04 and references given there.   9 H.F. Nielsen, *The Germanic Languages. Origins and Early Dialectal Interrelations* (Tuscaloosa and London, 1989).   10 Cf. H.L. Kufner, 'The Grouping and Separation of the Germanic Languages', in *Toward a Grammar of Proto-Germanic*, ed. by F. van Coetsem and H.L. Kufner (Tübingen, 1972), pp 71–97.

phonological circumstances.[11] Old Norse had a similar (group of) sound-changes producing diphthongs from an original short front vowel, Breaking,[12] which seems to have taken place under the circumstances of both the Old English developments. Such developments are unknown in Old Saxon and Old High German; Frisian is recorded too late to give precise information. Such instances of 'drift' may indeed be relevant to the relationship between the languages concerned, because they seem usually to occur more frequently and in more similar ways between more closely related languages. But without precise and predictive explanations of their causes, they cannot be used for precise and reliable description of the relationships between these languages.

Most discussion of the actual relationship of Old English with Old Norse has assumed that both had been and remained unitary languages. This is a strange assumption, and in some particulars obviously untrue, but it is to some extent supported by the actual evidence. With only one obvious exception, all the developments which differentiate the different dialects of Old English are likely to have taken place within England, that is, after the Settlement, and their common source seems to have been a single, unitary language. The exception is the different products of First Fronting of North-West Germanic accented $\bar{a}$, to West Saxon $\bar{æ}$ but non-West Saxon and Old Frisian $\bar{e}$, where the non-West Saxon dialects seem to share a common development with Old Frisian: so much so that this development is sometimes called Anglo-Frisian Fronting. Similarly, the runic evidence from Scandinavia shows a single, common language used in the runic inscriptions up to the tenth century; only then do clear geographical differentiations appear in the epigraphic evidence. This is supported by analysis of the phonological system of the different Scandinavian languages, which all seem to share a common development up to and including the earlier part of the Viking Age.

This is rather striking and rather odd. In the case of the English, allegedly derived from a number of different Germanic tribes, dialectal diversity developed early. The attested Old English dialects are very different one from another, possibly already to the point of obscuring mutual intelligibility in the historical period. Early Scandinavian, spoken for a far longer period over a considerably larger geographic area within which land communication was considerably more difficult, would have been much more likely to have developed early diversity. In the case of the English, it has recently been argued (by Martin Syrett and David Parsons)[13] that possibly a *koine* developed at the

---

11 Old English developments are cited from A. Campbell, *Old English Grammar* (Oxford, 1959 and subsequent corrected reprints); also R.M. Hogg, *A Grammar of Old English*, I *Phonology* (Oxford, 1992); see the latter for further bibliographic references. 12 Old Norse developments are cited from A. Noreen, *Altnordische Grammatik* I, *Altisländische und altnorwegische Grammatik*, 4th edn (Halle, 1923). 13 Unhappily unpublished, and likely to remain so.

time of the Settlement, with a sort of cancellation effect eliminating any earlier dialectal diversity amongst the invaders. This would have created a new and uniform unitary language, which only after the Settlement could develop new dialects within England. Useful parallels can be drawn with modern Australian English and, at a further chronological remove, North American English, which only now is developing dialectal diversity. The Scandinavian problem is further obscured by lack of historical knowledge. It is possible that the runic inscriptions deliberately hide actual diversity behind an artificial, archaic and formal 'Runic North Germanic', a possibly ritual language used for runic inscriptions. The sources, in short, may deliberately mislead us. In the absence of evidence to support it, this view is reminiscent of the historical scepticism which disbelieves the sources because they exist, and Peter Sawyer's earlier views on the Viking invasions come to mind.[14] In any case, the great diversity of forms which actually appear in the earlier runic inscriptions certainly gives no impression of an artificial and formalized 'standard language', and this explanation is hardly credible on examination of the actual inscriptions. It is tempting to speculate that just such a *koine* as was suggested by Syrett and Parsons might have developed in early Scandinavia, and that the social and presumably political turmoil which had manifested itself further south during the Age of Migrations, and which is reflected in the body of Germanic heroic legend, had also affected Scandinavia, causing a levelling of earlier linguistic diversity. This may be reflected in some phonological developments, where Norse seems to show the reflexes of several disparate and incompatible earlier processes, for example, loss or assimilation in the *-mf-* consonant-group, where the m is lost before the voiceless fricative in e.g. *tofi* 'site of a ruined building', *fifl* 'idiot', but assimilates the *f* to itself in for example, *fimm* 'five'. Such inconsistencies could show that the later language had been produced by the fusion of several earlier dialects, and so inherited products of divergent developments. It is, however, quite possible that early Scandinavian shows a uniform and unitary language simply because it was a very conservative language which had not undergone significant change for some centuries prior to the seventh century: languages clearly do not develop at a uniform rate, despite the best endeavours of the glossochronologists.

It is generally accepted that Old English in general shows a fairly close 'family relationship' with Norse, certainly closer than that of any of the other ancient Germanic languages. But few scholars have looked within Old English, to its constituent dialects, for further signs of affinity. But these are there to be found, especially in Old Northumbrian. This is the group of dialects of English spoken between the Humber and the Forth, those of the two northernmost kingdoms of the English before the coming of the Vikings, Deira in the south, with its political and ecclesiastical centre at York, and Bernicia in the north,

---

14 P.H. Sawyer, *The Age of the Vikings* (London, 1962); a second edition (1971) was rather less controversial.

around the twin centres of Bamburgh and Lindisfarne. Bernicia was perhaps the last of the kingdoms of the English to be established, and probably came into existence towards the end of the sixth century. Northumbrian is known from a group of short texts from the early to mid eighth century,[15] and three large glosses from the second half of the tenth century. These tenth-century glosses are attributed in autograph colophons to two named glossators, Owun, the scribe of the gloss of the second and larger part of the Rushworth (MacRegol) Gospels, associated with Harewood near Leeds and now in the Bodleian Library, Oxford (MS Auct. D. II 19), and Aldred, the scribe of the glosses in the Lindisfarne Gospels and the Durham Ritual (BL, MS Cotton Nero D IV, and Durham Cathedral Library, MS A. IV. 19). Both the Lindisfarne Gospels and the Durham Ritual are associated with the community of St Cuthbert, which had fled from Lindisfarne and was at Chester-le-Street between 883 and 995. The Gospel glosses are textually related to each other, and certainly the Rushworth Gospels gloss was not composed in the manuscript but was copied into it. It is not clear how old the Gospel gloss itself may be; in particular it has been argued, on good but not incontestable grounds, that the Lindisfarne gloss was actually composed by Aldred, and so can be no older than the middle of the tenth century; if so, then the Rushworth glosses would be copied from Lindisfarne, probably indirectly.[16]

Northumbrian has many features which distinguish it from the more southerly dialects of Old English; it is in particular very different from West Saxon. It is perhaps subdivisible, at least in the tenth-century texts, into southern and northern subdialects, but we are at risk here of attributing dialect status to features which may simply indicate idiolects or idiographic peculiarities: the personal linguistic or orthographic habits of Owun or Aldred. However, there are pan-Northumbrian features, attested in both early and late Northumbrian, which show strong affinities with Norse. These include the form of the preposition *mið* 'together with', normal OE *mid*, ON *með*. The vowel shows that this cannot be a Norse loan, and indeed it is attested in the eighth-century texts. Equally, the preposition *til* 'to', normal OE *to*, ON *til*, is attested too early to be a Norse loan. There are also phonological parallels, most importantly the loss of unaccented word-final -*n*, which appears sporadically in the early texts, and is very frequent in Aldred's glosses (though it seems to be controlled by the quality of the preceding unaccented vowel: thus the loss is regular after *a* and *e*, but not after *u*). This loss takes place in all positions in Norse; it spreads southwards from Northumbrian in English during the Middle English period, reaching London and so standard English by about the fourteenth century. There are also morphological affinities between Northumbrian and Norse. In

---

15 Most easily available in H. Sweet, *The Oldest English Texts* (London, 1885 and later reprints). **16** P. Bibire and A.S.C. Ross, 'The Differences between Lindisfarne and Rushworth Two', *Notes and Queries* (April, 1981), pp 98–116.

particular, late Northumbrian ceases to distinguish between second and third person singular present indicative verb-endings: those which appear in West Saxon as -*st* and -*þ* and which survive in archaic modern English as -*st* and -*th*, 'thou dost, he doth'. In Aldred's tenth-century Northumbrian glosses, the second person singular ending -*s* appears in both second and third person singular forms, and by extension from the third person singular, it also appears in the plural. This seems to be a fairly exact parallel to the Norse development, first attested on the seventh century Björketorp stone, where the cognate ending -*r* (< *z* < *s*), originally second person singular, also appears in the third person singular form. Björketorp has the form **barutr**, 'he breaks', where the apparently contemporary Stentoften inscription, giving the same text, has the much more archaic form **bariutiþ**, which retains the original Germanic third person singular ending.[17] In both the Northumbrian and Norse developments, it is plausibly argued that the new ending has been extended from the second person into the third, so both outcome and development are likely to have been parallel. Yet because the endings are not identical, it is not possible to consider the Northumbrian development as a simple loan from Norse. In short, both early and late Northumbrian have features which associate that specific Old English dialect with Old Norse, and these are features which distinguish Old Northumbrian from all other attested dialects of Old English.

It is tempting to speculate that Northumbrian might show this affinity with Norse due to the nature and time of the English settlement in Northumbria. It may have been the last region to be affected by the English invasions, and the furthest from the likeliest point at which the invaders made the sea-crossing to England. All the obvious settlement areas nearer to the narrow seas were already occupied. Those invaders, perhaps, who came from furthest away, and so came last, maybe had to go furthest up the east coast of England to find land. Alternatively, if the direct crossing across the North Sea were attempted, those who lived furthest north might arrive furthest north. In other words, it might conceivably be argued that the settlers particularly of Bernicia might represent the invaders who had come from nearest to Scandinavia, and who might have shared some of the linguistic features of Norse. Arguments like these are grossly over-simple, even naïve, and certainly some of the correspondences between Northumbrian and Norse are due to post-settlement developments, but, as discussed above, even this may show a special affinity between two languages. That affinity certainly exists not merely between Norse and English, but between Norse and Northumbrian.

The early English were fully aware of their Scandinavian neighbours, and claimed a Scandinavian past. The dynastic legends and genealogies of most of

---

[17] Early Norse runic inscriptions are cited from W. Krause and H. Jankuhn, *Die Runeninschriften im älteren Futhark* (Göttingen, 1966).

the Anglo-Saxon royal houses claim Scandinavian ancestry as a matter of pride. Easily our most important surviving poem in Old English, and arguably one of the three or four finest long poems in English of any period is *Beowulf*,[18] which deals entirely and exclusively with Scandinavian material, and glorifies the legendary history of the North. This is supported by the sixth-century Swedish affiliation, perhaps even origin, of many of the artefacts at Sutton Hoo.[19] The case for early post-Settlement pre-Viking contact between England and Scandinavia seems now overwhelming. However, the nature, extent and duration of this contact remains wholly unclear, and thus few linguistic conclusions can be drawn from it. In particular, there is no certain evidence for borrowing between English and Norse at this period.

The vocabulary of early English was almost entirely inherited from West Germanic. This inheritance included a fairly small number of important words derived from Vulgar Latin, almost certainly borrowed in spoken form, for items of Roman trade, civil engineering and cookery, that must have been borrowed into West Germanic across the frontier of the Rhineland, perhaps by means of returning *foederati*. They include words such as *ceap* 'purchase' (Lat. *caupo* 'merchant'), *torr* 'tower' (Lat. *turris* 'tower'), *stræt* 'Roman road' (Lat. *strata (via)* 'paved (road)'), *piper* 'pepper'. This vocabulary is shared by the West Germanic languages, and not infrequently penetrated further into Germanic: thus Norse *kaupa* 'to buy', cognate with OE *ceap*, and *eyrir* 'ounce' are similarly early Latin loans. Old English subsequently acquired a second small but important group of loans, mostly from Latin, to do with the Christian church; these are generally accepted to have been borrowed at or after the Conversion during the early seventh century. These include words such as *mynstre* 'minster', *celc* 'chalice', *munuc* 'monk'. A few loans came from Greek, for instance *preost* 'priest', *deofol* 'devil', and most importantly *cirice* 'church'. This last is of very great importance, because the Greek word *kuriakos (oikos)* '(house) of the Lord' was not borrowed into Latin, which instead used another Greek loan, *ecclesia*, from which the Romance word, for example, French *église*, and Celtic words such as Welsh *eglwys*, are derived. The means whereby this Greek component reached English, and in particular the word 'church', have been much discussed. It has been suggested, for instance, that the medium of transmission was Gothic, since some of the Goths were converted to Christianity in the mid-fourth century, and were in contact with Greek as much as Latin Christendom. However, it is as probable that the word was borrowed directly from Greek into English, since Greek speakers, Archbishop Theodore of Tarsus and Abbot Hadrian of Naples, were at Canterbury from the early 670s onwards, and there is much evidence, direct and indirect, for the school or schools which they established there at that time; Bede claims that their pupils spoke Greek as easily as their

---

18 *Beowulf*, ed. by Fr. Klaeber, 3rd edn with supplements (Lexington, 1950).
19 R. Bruce-Mitford *et al.*, *The Sutton Hoo Ship-Burial*, 3 vols in 4 (London, 1975–83).

own native tongue. The spread of the word 'church' in the continental Germanic languages would on this basis be due to the English missionaries to the Continent in the early eighth century: figures such as St Willibrord and St Boniface. There is other possible linguistic evidence for the transmission of ecclesiastical vocabulary from Latin through English into Old Saxon and Old High German.

Apart from these components, Old English shows a remarkably pure West Germanic vocabulary. It has, for instance, very few Celtic loanwords at all: Max Förster reckoned only fourteen,[20] though interestingly the name *Crīst* probably passed through Irish (and hence acquired a long vowel) before reaching English: clearly the English spoke the name of Christ as they had heard it from the missionaries from Lindisfarne, not Canterbury. There is virtually no evidence for a North Germanic component to English vocabulary before the Viking invasions: I exclude here two debatable instances, both of which could have been inherited, the word *wicing* itself, and a word later used for Viking ships and cognate with Norse *askr*, *æsc*, both of which are rarely but fairly safely attested before the Viking period, and which are discussed above.

On first contact, it is very uncertain whether and to what degree the Scandinavian raiders and invaders and the English could communicate: to what extent contemporary English and Norse were mutually intelligible. Certainly some words were very similar if not identical, and some rules of sentence-structure were also very similar. Doubtless, with care, it would have been possible to construct simple sentences with carefully chosen vocabulary which would be intelligible to a naïve speaker of the other language. Whether such mutual intelligibility would have been sufficient for adequate communication is, of course, quite unknowable. But the question of mutual intelligibility is in practice far more complex. Doubtless there were many naïve speakers of English and early Norse who came into contact in the early Viking period: speakers of either language who had no knowledge of the other. But the pragmatics of the situation, gesture and manner, as well doubtless as a brandished weapon, could certainly convey much meaning that did not need direct and immediate mutual intelligibility of language. And even at the beginning of the Viking period, non-naïve speakers of both languages could probably be found, and indeed were likely to be on the Scandinavian ships and at the English ports or in the English monasteries: individuals who knew something of Germanic dialects other than their own, Frisian, Saxon and Frankish, if not Norse or English. Only one or two such non-naïve speakers would need to be present at an encounter for communication to be possible. Once Viking raids had begun with any seriousness, linguistic contact had also already begun: slaves taken by Vikings for ransom or sale would return with a speaking knowledge of Norse, and even those merely

---

[20] M. Förster, 'Keltisches Wortgut im Englischen', in *Festgabe für Felix Liebermann* (Halle, 1921).

threatened or blackmailed by Vikings would soon be acquainted with certain simple phrases. Even, therefore, in the piratical period of the early Viking Age, the problem of mutual intelligibility is compounded by probable understanding, if to an uncertain extent, of the other language.

Evidence of mutual Anglo-Norse linguistic understanding, or misunderstanding, at the period of the Viking conquests in the latter part of the ninth century may be derived from the personal names, recorded mostly in *The Anglo-Saxon Chronicle*, for Viking leaders. Ninth-century name-forms such as *Hingwar* or *Godrum* or *Hæsten*, as written in the Parker manuscript (CCCC 173), show little understanding of Norse names, and no serious attempt to reproduce them phonetically. This contrasts with the careful treatment of contemporary Frankish names. In particular *Godrum*, perhaps for ON *Guttormr*, seems to show disregard for the Norse name-form and a meaningless English folk-etymology. These forms show little more than personal contact, and in particular show no capability for translating from the sound-system of the one language into that of the other. As Gillian Fellows-Jensen points out,[21] the presentation of Norse-derived personal names in Old English sources changes later, and by the eleventh century some care and accuracy is shown, maybe indicating fairly wide-spread understanding of the name-forms. This development is already visible at the court of King Alfred, where Ohthere's name has been very accurately translated from Norse into its appropriate Old English form in the early tenth-century manuscripts of King Alfred's translation of the *Orosius*.[22] While the first element of a ninth-century form of Norse *Óttarr* is unlikely to have been very dissimilar to its English equivalent, the second element would not have been transparent, and its correct recognition implies care and understanding. Beyond that, the presence of this Norwegian at Alfred's court at the end of the ninth century does not give much further linguistic information: Ohthere might himself have learned English or used a bilingual interpreter, and it is even possible that Alfred might have acquired some knowledge of Norse in his long dealings with Viking opponents and allies. Certainly Ohthere and Alfred had no observable problems of communication.

At and after the Scandinavian settlements, the problem shifts from that of mutual intelligibility to possible bilingualism. Unfortunately there are few linguistic records from the Danelaw in the ninth century, at and after the period of initial conquest and settlement, and most of these are coin-legends, frequently very corrupt and of little linguistic content. However, bilingualism, at least in the Danelaw, is strongly suggested by some phonological evidence. Anglian Old English (Mercian and Northumbrian) in the middle and late Old English

---

21 G. Fellows-Jensen, *The Vikings and their Victims: The Verdict of the Names*, Dorothea Coke Memorial Lecture (London, 1995), p. 17. 22 *The Old English Orosius*, ed. by J. Bately (London, 1980), p. 13, printed from BL, Add. MSS, 47967 (the Lauderdale or Tollemache MS).

period, represents Germanic short accented *ă* before nasal consonants almost always as *o*, while Kentish and West Saxon increasingly consistently represent it as *a*. The only late Anglian exception to *o* is in Northumbrian in past singular forms of nasal-stemmed strong verbs Cl. 3, of the type *sang, swamm*, where all other verbs of this class in this dialect have *a*. Now, it is by no means certain that *o* of this origin fell together with earlier *o*, but certainly the scribes make no attempt to differentiate the two vowels, and hence coalescence seems the likeliest interpretation. But Old Norse had no such development, and always preserves *a* in such forms. In later Middle English, when the dialect-distribution of the vowels can again be mapped, the dialects of the midlands and north regularly have *a* for this vowel, other than in a fairly small region of the West Midlands stretching north through Worcestershire up to Cheshire and into Lancashire, which regularly retains *o*.[23] It is most striking that, apart from its northernmost extension, this is the only part of the Old English Anglian dialect-area which was not in the Danelaw. Middle English restoration of *a* before nasal consonants can most easily be seen as due to assimilation of English to Norse phonology in the Danelaw, that is, English spoken by people whose earlier language was Norse.

Similarly, Old English underwent an early palatalisation and assibilation of Germanic *k* before front vowels to a sound or sounds represented in Modern English as <ch>, very comparable to developments in the Romance languages and also in Proto-Indic. It also palatalised and assibilated the Germanic consonant-group *sk* in all positions to a sound or sounds represented in Modern English as <sh>. This second development also happened independently in High German, and has also happened independently in some of the later Scandinavian languages; neither development, however, had happened in Old Norse and they have still not taken place in modern Icelandic. Speakers of Old Norse therefore could not pronounce the Old English palatalised and assibilated sounds, and substituted the nearest available sounds in their own languages, *k* and *sk*. This appears rather entertainingly in place-names such as *Skipton*, West Yorkshire, which at first sight looks as though it should contain the Norse form of the element *skip* 'ship'. However, this is geographically quite impossible, given the position of Skipton in hilly country where there are no navigable streams and no ship could ever have sailed; the first element of this name must be the word *scēap*, 'sheep'. The sheep-word is peculiar to West Germanic, and is found nowhere else in Germanic or, for that matter, in Indo-European, and it must ultimately be related to the verb *scieppan*, Gmc *skapjan, 'to shape'. For a similar semantic development one may compare the modern Icelandic *skepna* '(farm-)animal'. The modern form of the place-name *Skipton* shows not only the sheep-word, but also probably an early Northumbrian development of the vowel undergoing Palatal Diphthongisation caused by the palatalised initial consonant-group: as,

---

[23] G. Kristensson, *A Survey of Middle English Dialects 1290–1350: The six northern counties and Lincolnshire* (Lund, 1967), pp 8–10, and references given there.

for example, *scilun* in Cædmon's Hymn (the Leningrad MS). But Norse-speaking settlers could not pronounce the initial cluster of the English form, and restored *sk*. This place-name is therefore English, but spoken with a Norse accent. Another interesting example is northern English *kirk*, Norse *kirkja*, 'church'. The word, as discussed above is a Greek loan-word, but in English both instances of *k* were palatalised and assibilated, giving normal English *church*. The Norse word is always and almost certainly correctly explained as a loan from English, due to the early English missionary and ecclesiastical influence in tenth- and eleventh-century Scandinavia. But the form *kirk* is often presented in English etymological dictionaries as if derived from Norse. It is, of course, a Danelaw form: an English word but spoken with a Norse accent. A number of other words which, it is sometimes claimed, show failure of palatalisation and assibilation in northern English, can equally properly be explained in these ways. It is important to note that these are not in any normal sense loanwords. They imply speakers of English who employed Norse phonological rules, that is, speakers of English whose native language was or had been Norse. They imply, in short, a bilingual population.

Bilingualism between Old English and Old Norse may also be implied by the so-called Grimston-hybrid placenames initially identified by Kenneth Cameron:[24] those place-names which have a Norse qualifier on an English base-element. The *ton* element could of course almost as easily be Norse *tún* as English *tūn* in an example such as this, and the first element, the personal name *Grim*, ON *Grímr* could well have been a current name in the Danelaw long after Norse ceased to be spoken there. A form such as *Grimston* therefore requires rather few necessary conclusions as to the language of the people who actually produced the place-name. But mixed-language names nonetheless may indicate a mixed population speaking more than one language. Certainly a place-name such as *Botham*, for a suburb of York, corresponding to Norse dat. pl. *búðum* 'at the booths', can only have retained its inflectional ending by identification with the English elements *-hām* or *-hamm*, and so this by definition is a mixed form. But in this example, of course, the Norse-derived word 'booth' is still current in English, and only the ending shows us that this form of the place-name must have already been formed early, most probably in Norse. Incidentally, the form *Botham* and the loan into English, *booth*, have been used as evidence for East Norse, and more particularly Danish, settlement in Yorkshire. While this may well have been the case, this evidence is not particularly strong support. It has been alleged that there is a dialectal distribution of Old West Norse *ú*, Old East Norse *ó*, in this root: thus Old Icelandic has *búð*, Old Danish has *bóð* 'booth'. But in actual fact, Old West Norse has both *ū* and *ō* in this root: beside *búa* 'to

---

24 K. Cameron, 'Scandinavian settlement in the territory of the Five Boroughs: the place-name evidence Part III, the Grimston-hybrids', in *England before the Conquest*, ed. by P. Clemoes and K. Hughes (Cambridge, 1971), pp 147–63.

dwell', *búð*, 'booth', Old Icelandic has *ból* 'dwelling' with *ō*, and *bǽli* 'lair' and *bǽr* 'farmstead', with *i*-mutation of *ō*. A geographical distribution of *ū* and *ō* in this root and words derived from it must therefore be regarded as very questionable, and it is far from certain that all varieties of Norse did not have both vowels in the ninth century.

Elsewhere in England, there is evidence for awareness of Norse technical vocabulary: in *The Battle of Brunanburh*, celebrating a battle in which the West Saxon king Æþelstan defeated an alliance of Picts, Strathclyde British and Vikings, the word (-)*cnearr* is twice used for Viking ships,[25] and this is almost certainly a loan of ON *knǫrr* 'ship', in particular 'ocean-going (cargo-)ship'. The battle occurred in the year 937, and the poem celebrating it survives only in the *Anglo-Saxon Chronicle* entry for that year; the gains won at Brunanburh were lost after Æþelstan's death two years later. This poem can therefore be dated very precisely, and is most unlikely ever to have existed outside the West Saxon dialect. The form of the word (-)*cnearr* is particularly interesting: no attempt is made to reproduce the *u*-mutation of the Norse word, but instead the vowel is diphthongised as it would have been before *rr* in early Old English. In other words, the word has been 'translated' from the sound-system of Norse into that of Old English, and is given the form that it would have had in English, had it been inherited rather than borrowed. This contrasts with the ninth-century failure to understand and interpret Norse personal names. It shows knowledge of Norse technical terms and a considerable degree of linguistic acuity in understanding them, in a high-status West Saxon text, which in content is hostile to Norsemen: a poem in praise of King Æþelstan.

Another potentially important example from tenth-century poetry must be discussed. The short poem *The Wanderer* is preserved in the Exeter Book, a manuscript written in the West Country at or just before 1000 AD, dated palaeographically. Its text is remarkably uncorrupt, and shows very few copying errors; it is therefore likely not to have undergone repeated copying before being written in the surviving manuscript. It contains one instance of the word *hrīð* (l. 102a), and another of the same word in an adjectival formation, *hrȳðge* (l. 77b).[26] This word occurs nowhere else in Old English; from its context in l. 102a it seems to mean 'storm (perhaps of hail)'. It must be related to ON *hríð*, meaning 'snow- or hail-storm'. The word could, of course, be inherited in Old English, and might only appear in these two instances in this poem by coincidence: the surviving 30,000 lines or so of Old English poetry contain a significant number of *hapax legomena*, words which are only recorded once. However, two instances within one hundred and fifteen lines, and no instances elsewhere, is an odd distribution for this word, and it is better explained as a

---

25 *The Battle of Brunanburh*, ed. by A. Campbell, (London, 1938), p. 94, ll. 35a and 53b; pp 108–09, n. 35.   26 *The Wanderer*, ed. by T.P. Dunning and A.J. Bliss (London, 1969), pp 122, 118.

Norse loan-word. Here, however, it is not a technical term for a Viking-derived concept, nor does it occur in a text with any overt Norse associations, and it is preserved in a manuscript from the south-west of England. It has also penetrated the exceedingly conservative poetic vocabulary. This must of course suggest that *The Wanderer* is a late poem: a conclusion which also on other grounds seems probable. It also strongly suggests high-status contact between English and Norse, so that the word could penetrate high-status vocabulary. In this context, it is noteworthy that *The Wanderer* may contain echoes of wisdom-poetry which we also know from the Norse pagan poem, *Hávamál*,[27] though in this respect it may not be unique, since such echoes seem also to appear in *The Seafarer*,[28] also found in the Exeter Book. Again, such wisdom-poetry is very likely to have been inherited by both English and Norsemen, but at the least acknowledgement of the relationship of content could have led to adoption of vocabulary. And it is of course possible that both content and vocabulary could have come directly from Norse into the Old English poems. In either scenario, high-status contact between Old Norse and Old English poetic traditions must be assumed, and this must in turn mean the performance of poetry in both English and Norse at high-status establishments in England. Norse skalds must have performed beside English scops at the courts of kings and noblemen, probably not only in the Danelaw. When *Gunnlaugs saga ormstunga* describes its hero as performing skaldic poetry for the English king Æþelræd the Unready at his court in London, the description may not be so improbable as is usually assumed.[29] Certainly, when the Icelandic poet Sighvatr Þórðarson is described as performing for Cnut in England a generation later, this may be accepted as historical.[30] Whether either king could have understood the poetry is another matter, but skaldic poetry was certainly not always intended to be immediately intelligible even to native speakers of Norse. Certainly the one person at the court who would be interested in understanding such poetry, other than the Norse poet himself and the object of his praise, would be his potential competitor, any English poet present. Competition between poets at the courts of great men is a common literary motif in Norse, for instance in *Gunnlaugs saga ormstunga*, and is also mentioned in Old English, in both *Widsiþ*[31] and *Deor*.[32] Thus the bi-cultural and bilingual court would provide an immediate context for possible mutual influence between court poets composing in different languages. That *Hǫfuðlausn*[33] is composed using end-rhyme, uniquely

---

27 *Hávamál*, ed. by D.A.H. Evans (London, 1986). **28** *The Seafarer*, ed. by I.L. Gordon (London, 1960). **29** *Gunnlaugs saga ormstungu*, ed. by Sigurður Nordal and Guðni Jónsson, Íslenzk fornrit III (Reykjavík, 1938). **30** In *Heimskringla, Óláfs saga helga*, cap. cxlvi, ed. by Bjarni Aðalbjarnarson in *Heimskringla* II, Íslenzk fornrit XXVII (Reykjavík, 1945), pp 271–74. **31** *Widsith*, ed. by R.W. Chambers (London, 1912). **32** *Deor*, ed. by K. Malone, 4th edn (London, 1966). **33** Finnur Jónsson, *Den norsk-islandske skjaldedigtning* A I–II, B I–II (København, 1912–15), A I pp 35–39;

for the period to which it is assigned, and is attributed to a Norse skaldic poet, the Icelander Egill Skalla-Grímsson, practising at the court of a Christian Viking monarch in York, Eiríkr blóðøx, *c.* 950, may show similar and immediate influence in the other direction, of (Latin) poetry on a Scandinavian poet. *Deor* is also important for its relationship of wording and content with the Norse poem *Vǫlundarkviða*:[34] a Norse poem which also shows English metrical features, as demonstrated by John McKinnell.[35]

Another Old English poem which may show Norse influence, on both its vocabulary and its semantics, is *The Battle* of *Maldon*.[36] This fragmentary text describes the beginning and part of a historical battle, fought by Ealdorman Byrhtnoþ of Essex against Vikings, just outside the modern town of Maldon, on the tenth or eleventh August 991; the poem itself must therefore be later than this date. How much later is debatable. Every personage mentioned on the English side is identified, either by name or by the name of a kinsman or (in the case of the Northumbrian hostage) also by status; no-one on the Viking side is identified other than an unnamed messenger. Presumably therefore the intended audience would have been interested in knowing who fought on the English side but not on the Norse side. This may indicate that this audience may have included either some of the participants in the battle, or their close acquaintance and kindred. So it is reasonable to assume, in the absence of evidence to the contrary, that the poem was composed fairly soon after the event. Interest in the battle, which had only local importance, is likely only to have been local to Essex and East Anglia; therefore the poem itself is also likely to have been local. In other words, it is probably a Danelaw text. The poem uses the word *æschere* (l. 69) for the Viking army, and this may well show identification of the rare OE word *æsc* 'ship' with Norse poetic *askr* 'warship', and may here specifically refer to Viking ships.[37] It has also been argued (in particular by Fred C. Robinson)[38] that the messenger's speech includes a number of phrases which in Norse would have specific legal implications, for example, *on hyra sylfra dom* (l.38b), perhaps for ON *sjálfdœmi*. This is plausible but unprovable. More strikingly, the word *eorl* is used several times (for example, ll. 6, 28, 51) for Ealdorman Byrhtnoþ, while the English word *ealdormonn* is not used at all. The word *eorl* is, in other and older English texts, simply a poetic word for 'man', and seems to have little wider significance in Old English; however, its cognate in Norse, *jarl*, had developed to a term of rank with the sense 'earl' by at latest the tenth century and probably earlier. Its early usage in Norse runic inscriptions

---

B I pp 30–33.   **34** *Edda: Die Lieder des Codex Regius*, ed. by G. Neckel and H. Kuhn, 4th edn (Heidelberg, 1962), pp 116–23.   **35** J.S. McKinnell, 'The Context of *Vǫlundarkviða*', *Saga-Book of the Viking Society*, 23:1 (1990), pp 1–27.   **36** *The Battle of Maldon*, ed. by D.G. Scragg (Manchester, 1981).   **37** See Scragg, *Maldon*, pp 72–3, l. 69.   **38** F.C. Robinson, 'Some Aspects of the *Maldon* Poet's Artistry', *JEGP*, 75 (1976), pp 25–40.

up to the seventh or eighth century, may also indicate that it was there a term of status, though then much less probably a term of rank. In ordinary English legal and historical texts from the reign of the Danish king Cnut onwards, the English word *eorl* is used with the sense of Norse *jarl*, as a specific term of rank for a nobleman lesser only than the king, and this seems to be the sense of the word in *The Battle of Maldon*, prompting John McKinnell's attempt to use this as a means of dating the composition of the poem.[39] However, this sense may have been used in the Anglo-Scandinavian kingdoms of the Danelaw much earlier, at any time from the late ninth century onwards, and it may be justifiable to see its use in *The Battle of Maldon* as indicating specific Danelaw usage, as well as showing high-status input into English. If this position is accepted, then Robinson's further arguments for Norse legal usage become more likely. Certainly Norse-derived legal terms such as *husbunda* 'householder, burgess', *husþing* 'town assembly', appear in the prose of *The Anglo-Saxon Chronicle* in descriptions of events of the eleventh century even outside the Danelaw.[40]

In this context it is necessary to mention Roberta Frank's proposition that *Beowulf* itself also derives its material from Viking sources, and that this poem, of any in Old English, should be seen as evidence for literary input into English from the Norsemen.[41] This suggestion cannot be entirely refuted, but on many grounds must be regarded as improbable. The material culture depicted in *Beowulf* can be confirmed in many specific details from sixth- and seventh-century English archaeology, but which are not available from Norse literary sources, for example, stone-paved roads. And the name-forms employed in *Beowulf* are entirely English, and could not have been reconstructed on the basis of Norse name-forms, even of the ninth century, without knowledge of the sound-changes which had affected both Old Norse and Old English. Name-forms such as *Hroþulf* could not be reconstructed from ON *Hrólfr*, where on runic evidence the medial consonant was lost before the ninth century, or *Onela* reconstructed from Norse *Áli*, where the *-n-* was lost in Norse probably in the seventh century; equally, it seems incredible that correct name-forms such as *Ongenþeow* could be re-created from *Angantyr*, *Hroþgar* from *Hróarr*, etc. Examples such as these contrast with (-)*cnearr* discussed above, since in that example the conditioning factor, the *-rr*, which would have produced a diphthong in Old English, is still present in the word-form. So an intelligent Anglo-Saxon has recognized that, in positions where Norse had ϱ / $a + rr$, he had $ea + rr$. No such translation-equivalences could be set up for many of the name-forms in *Beowulf*, and only with etymological knowledge can the modern scholar identify the disparate forms as being of the same origin. On the basis of such cultural and linguistic arguments it is possible to reject any probability of

[39] J.S. McKinnell, 'On the Date of *The Battle of Maldon*', *Medium Ævum*, 44 (1975), pp 121–36. [40] Dover, 1048. [41] For instance in R. Frank, 'Skaldic verse and the date of *Beowulf*', in *The Dating of Beowulf*, ed. by Colin Chase (Toronto, 1981), pp 123–39.

substantial late Scandinavian input into the composition of *Beowulf*. However, Roberta Frank's arguments may well be applicable to the reception of *Beowulf* in the tenth century up to and including the date of its unique manuscript, written at around the beginning of the eleventh century.[42]

In the latter part of the tenth century, the large tenth-century Northumbrian glosses give us direct access to two Northumbrian idiolects. Despite their many peculiarities, the dialects employed by Aldred and Owun show no certain loan-words from Norse. The texts are large enough to form statistically significant samples; also, they do not seem to be particularly conservative in vocabulary. They show no substantial influence in vocabulary or phonology from any other dialect of Old English. We can therefore take them as potentially representative of English vocabulary in Northumbria in the second half of the tenth century, providing always that we remember that we are dealing only with the language of two individuals. It is clear from the glosses written by Aldred and Owun that Norse vocabulary had hardly penetrated the sort of English that they were using, and it must therefore, in the absence of any evidence to the contrary, be assumed that, a century after the Scandinavian settlement in the Danelaw, the English spoken there had not absorbed many Norse words into its basic lexicon. E.G. Stanley's suggestion[43] that these glosses represent a standardized, even 'purified' earlier Northumbrian should probably be rejected because of the great variation between them, and in the case of Aldred's glosses, within them; Aldred's language also seems very innovative. The nature of these texts precludes, of course, use of the areas of technical vocabulary or of high-status vocabulary which elsewhere shows possible or actual Norse input into Old English. They are therefore useful in exemplifying the core vocabulary of late Old English, and showing beyond any reasonable doubt that even in late tenth-century Northumbria, almost as far removed as possible from the cultural centres of Wessex and in the heart of the Danelaw, the core vocabulary of English was entirely native and contained almost no Norse words. The northernmost forms of English, those of northern Bernicia, which developed into modern Scots, are of course completely without record in the Old and early Middle English periods: this is particularly unfortunate, given that the Firth of Forth and the Forth-Clyde valley may have been an important route of communication between the Viking kingdoms of York, Man and Dublin. Only coastal place-names, such as the Isle of May, indicate possible Norse input into the languages spoken there at these periods; the large amount of Norse vocabulary in Lowland Scots when that is finally recorded, in the fourteenth century, could

---

[42] D.N. Dumville, 'Beowulf Come Lately: Some Notes on the Palaeography of the Nowell Codex', *Archiv für das Studium der neueren Sprachen und Literaturen*, 225, pp 49–63. [43] E.G. Stanley, 'Karl Luick's "Man schrieb wie man sprach" and English historical philology', in D. Kastovsky and G. Bauer, *Luick Revisited* (Tübingen, 1988), pp 311–34, esp. p. 323, but cf. his discussion on p. 322.

simply reflect general northern English rather than any particular input into the form of English spoken in Lothian in the late Old English period.

With one exception, there seems to be little or no evidence for new Scandinavian settlement in the British Isles during the tenth century, and in particular during the period of royally-directed conquest of England under Sveinn Haraldsson during the last decade of the tenth century and up to the accession of his son Knútr (Cnut) in 1016. On the contrary, it is clear that the motivation and mechanism for the conquest was cash: the Danegeld. The exception to this was secondary Hiberno-Norse settlement in England and Scotland after the Battle of Clontarf and the expulsion of Scandinavians from Dublin. This secondary settlement seems to have taken place around the Solway Firth and the Dee estuary, and is marked by place-names where although the elements may be Norse, their ordering is Irish, for example, *Kirkpatrick*, *Kirkmichael*, where the qualifier follows the base-word. Clearly these settlers were linguistically somewhat mixed.

During Cnut's reign, although individuals bearing Scandinavian names bore high office, there is little to suggest any further settlement in England directly from Scandinavia, and it would seem that many of these individuals were drawn from the existing Scandinavian population of the Danelaw. Cnut seems to have maintained a fairly clear distinction between his roles as king of the English and king of the Danes. This contrasts with his treatment of Norway, subjugated under an earl. However, there is some evidence, summarized in part by Gillian Fellows-Jensen,[44] for some small movement, mostly of ecclesiastics and skilled artisans, to Scandinavia in and after the reign of Cnut. The ecclesiastical links which may go back to the reign of Cnut continue, of course, into at least the thirteenth century, as described long since by Leach.

Equally, following the reign of Cnut, and in particular during that of Edward the Confessor, English political links seem to have been stronger with Normandy than Scandinavia. There is little evidence for the survival of Norse as late as this in Normandy, and it is reasonable to assume that any Scandinavian influence mediated through the Normans, then or later, was only indirect and limited. In short, no serious political or personal influence from Scandinavia on the English people can reasonably be argued for any period after the late 1030s, and so it must be concluded that no further substantial Scandinavian input from abroad into the English language, at least as spoken in England, could have taken place after then.

English has long been recognized as the West Germanic language most similar to Norse, the language of the Vikings, and this similarity seems to be related to the origin of the English, but it is also shown in subsequent and apparently

---

44 In *The Vikings and their Victims*, cited above.

independent development of the two languages. Within English, however, its northernmost group of dialects, Northumbrian, shows far closer affinities with Norse, both in aspects which must be inherited, and also in its own further developments which are of the greatest importance for the subsequent history of English.

At and after the time of the major Viking assaults of the ninth century, the English sources, sparse though they are, nonetheless give evidence for a variety of attitudes towards Norse. The ninth-century sources do not bother to make sense of Norse names, and show no linguistic competence in their representation. In contrast, material from the tenth century and later sometimes shows great linguistic acuity in understanding and representing Norse vocabulary, even in texts such as *The Battle of Brunanburh*, which is both early and can only be associated with Wessex. Old English poetry also shows tenth-century penetration of Norse vocabulary into its otherwise archaic diction, perhaps associated with themes also represented in Norse poetry; such penetration, and indeed apparent mutual influence, must show very high-status contact between the languages, presumably at the aristocratic courts actually depicted in the literature. Such contact is not only demonstrated in the Danelaw, though it may have taken place more fully there. In contrast, however, the Northumbrian prose texts from the middle or latter part of the tenth century show very little effect of the impact of Norse, even though Northumbrian was the Old English dialect most similar to Norse, used in the areas where Middle English evidence shows very great Norse input, and written very far from any triumphalist West Saxon influence. On the evidence of the late Northumbrian glosses, ordinary English vocabulary even of the central and northern Danelaw in the latter part of the tenth century had not yet been much affected by Norse.

The subsequent development of the Scandinavian components in the English language is a matter of Middle English, supported by evidence from, for instance, dialect-studies and place-names, for it is not until the twelfth and thirteenth centuries that the huge numbers of Norse words, many of which survive in Modern English, start to appear. This is a vast subject, with its own intractable problems; these require their own detailed discussion. The history of language-contact between English and Norse in the early Middle Ages simply raises some of the problems which must be dealt with in the context of the entire subsequent history of English.

Hákon *Aðalsteins fóstri*: Aspects of Anglo-Saxon Kingship in Tenth-Century Norway[1]

GARETH WILLIAMS

The focus of this paper is Hákon Haraldsson, king of Norway *c*.935–*c*.961, known both as Hákon *inn góði* ('the Good') and as Hákon *Aðalsteins fóstri* ('Athelstan's foster-son'). The paper's subject matter, however, is as much twentieth-century scholarship as tenth-century kingship. Examination of the source material from which Hákon is known raises wider issues in the evaluation of saga literature as historical evidence, and in the current attitude to early medieval source material as a whole.

In the course of the last century, a major shift has taken place in historians' attitudes to the main documentary sources for the history of Norway in the early Middle Ages; the Icelandic sagas of the twelfth and thirteenth centuries. Saga literature can be divided into a number of categories, some of which are more obviously literary in tone, consisting in tales of a largely supernatural nature, and drawing on a variety of motifs from folklore and mythology, as well as on material from other European works of literature.[2] Other categories are more ostensibly historical, such as the Family Sagas, which purport to give accounts of actual events involving the early settlers of Iceland, and the Kings' Sagas, which as the name suggests purport to give accounts of the rulers of Norway and other neighbouring countries. Both Family Sagas and Kings' Sagas, however, also on occasion include supernatural events, together with other obviously 'literary' motifs.

Despite this, until the present century, the Kings' Sagas, and especially the greatest collection of these, *Heimskringla* (attributed to the Icelandic chieftain Snorri Sturluson)[3] were accepted as largely reliable accounts of historical fact, even where they concerned events several hundred years before the sagas were compiled. More recently this view has been condemned as uncritical, since such

---

[1] The author wishes to express thanks to Barbara Crawford, University of St Andrews, and James Barrett, University of York, for helpful comments on aspects of this paper, and especially to Paul Bibire, University of Cambridge, for helpful comments throughout the writing of this paper, and for reading through the paper in draft. Any mistakes which remain are, of course, entirely the responsibility of the author.   [2] For example, *Spesar þáttr*, a sub-section of *Grettis saga*, which is based on the Tristan legend.

texts often contain obviously unhistorical elements, as well as apparent anachronisms, with the saga writers of the twelfth and thirteenth centuries describing the society and political structure of the ninth and tenth centuries in the light of their own experience. There is a further question of authorial agenda, with the saga writers using 'historical' events to convey their own political messages. A recurrent example of this is the unification of Norway in the late ninth century under Harald *hárfagri* ('Finehair'), and the resistance of his power by free-minded individuals who fled from Norway, and settled in Iceland. This theme, and that of royal tyranny generally, can be linked with the Icelanders' struggle in the thirteenth century to maintain their independence from the growing power of King Hákon Hákonarson of Norway. A further problem is the distance in time between the events recorded and the writing of the sagas, and the difficulty of establishing the evidence on which the saga accounts were based.

Such textual problems rightly raise questions over the reliability of the sagas as historical sources. However, the reaction against the earlier 'uncritical' attitude has led, in some cases, to an equal lack of discrimination. A widespread attitude in recent years has been that since the sagas cannot be regarded as entirely reliable sources for the tenth century, they are therefore valueless as evidence for that period. At the most, according to this view, they can be used as evidence for the study of the period in which the sagas were actually written.[4] Such an approach is overly simplistic. The fact that a source is not reliable does not necessarily mean that it is valueless, but that it should be used with caution, and the evidence it contains evaluated in the light of the overall picture of the period presented by all the material available.

The aim of the current paper is to apply this cautious approach to the sources concerning Hákon, and to examine whether they may, while admittedly unreliable, contain any material which can plausibly be regarded as genuine historical tradition of the tenth century rather than literary invention of the late twelfth-thirteenth centuries. Before considering the five main sources for the reign of Hákon, a little further discussion of the genre of Kings' Sagas is necessary. All the sources of interest here can be considered within this genre, although two of them (the *Historia de Antiquitate Regum Norwagensium* and the

---

3 *Heimskringla*, ed. by B. Aðalbjarnarson, 3 vols, *Íslenzk fornrit*, 26–8 (Reykjavík, 1941–51). 4 For summaries and discussion of past and present attitudes to the Kings' Sagas, see T.M. Andersson, 'Kings' Sagas (*Konunga sögur*)', in *Old Norse-Icelandic Literature. A Critical Guide*, ed. by C.J. Clover and J. Lindow, *Islandica*, 45 (1985), pp 197–238; S. Bagge, 'From Sagas to Society: the Case of Heimskringla', in *From Sagas to Society: Comparative Approaches to Early Iceland*, ed. by G. Pálsson (Enfield Lock, 1992), pp 61–75; D. Whaley, 'The Kings' Sagas', in *Viking Revaluations (Viking Society Centenary Symposium, 1992)*, ed. by A. Faulkes and R. Perkins (London, 1993), pp 43–64. Entries on individual texts appear in the *Kulturhistorisk Leksikon for Nordiske Middelalder* (hereafter *KLNM*) and *Medieval Scandinavia: An Encyclopedia*, ed. by P. Pulsiano *et al.* (New York and London, 1993) (hereafter *MSE*).

Historia Norwegiae) are in Latin rather than Old Norse / Old Icelandic, and are therefore not technically sagas. However, they were written in a similar historical context and are textually and/or thematically linked with the sagas to an extent where they must be considered as part of the same group.

All five texts date from the late twelfth century to the early thirteenth century, apparently drawing to some extent on earlier material. It is customary to discuss this material in terms of two theories, generally distinguished as 'book prose' and 'free prose'. According to the book prose theory, the compilers of the sagas of the late twelfth century drew on earlier written texts which are now lost. According to the free prose theory, the sagas represent the earliest written version of the stories they contain, and drew only on a broad oral tradition, wherein the stories themselves were traditional, but the form in which the stories were passed on varied from one telling to the next. To a great extent, the question of whether sagas derived from written or oral tradition is immaterial to the evaluation of the historical accuracy of the sagas. Since we do not know precisely of what, if anything, earlier written and oral tradition consisted, and in any case have no reliable means of verifying either, it is impossible to argue with any certainty that one tradition was more reliable than the other. Furthermore, the authorities cited within the sagas themselves suggest that the saga compilers drew on both written and oral material (see below).

Two important earlier sources are known only from references in later compilations. These were compiled by Sæmund Sigfússon (1056–1133) and Ari Þorgilsson (*c.*1067–1148), both known as *inn fróði* ('the wise'). Sæmund is said to have written a chronicle of the Kings of Norway, probably in Latin, in the early twelfth century, while the first version of Ari's *Íslendingabók* ('Book of the Icelanders'), which was apparently written in the 1120s, is said to have contained *konunga ævi* ('kings' lives').[5] Although *Íslendingabók* only survives in a later, abbreviated redaction, which does not contain the relevant section, *Heimskringla* (which cites Ari as a source on more than one occasion) specifically refers to his reliability because

> he was wise, and so old that he was born the next winter after the death of king Harald Sigurðsson. He wrote, as he himself tells, lives of the kings of Norway according to the account of Odd son of Kol son of Hall of Siða, but Odd cites Þorgeir *afraðskoll*, that man who was wise and so old that he lived there at Niðarnes when Earl Hákon the Mighty was killed [that is, in 995].

Another cited source is Hall Þorarinsson, who remembered being baptized by Þangbrand as a child, a year before the conversion of Iceland (that is, in

---

5 *Heimskringla*, I, Prologus, p. 5; Andersson, 'Kings' Sagas', pp 199–201.

999).[6] Only one further generation would be required to stretch back to the mid-tenth century. In a period in which oral tradition seems to have been considered important, it is not unlikely that some genuine traditions might be passed down concerning major events, even though one may be sceptical over the details that accrue to the basic framework of the traditions. What does seem clear from such citations is that compilers such as Snorri Sturluson and, apparently, Ari Þorgilsson had some conception of historical methodology, since they thought it appropriate to validate their evidence in this way. Certainly the lost works of Ari and Sæmund provide some sort of bridge between the later compilations and earlier traditions, even if they themselves relied exclusively on oral tradition for their own work. While it cannot always be certain which elements in the later compilations are derived from these earlier works, it seems not unlikely that those elements common to the majority of sources derive from a common tradition, if not directly from a common source.

Probably the earliest surviving source concerning Hákon is the *Historia de Antiquitate Regum Norwagensium*, written by Theodricus Monachus.[7] Theodricus is thought to have been a monk at Niðarholm in Trondheim, and possibly to have been educated in Paris. The *Historia de Antiquitate* was written in Latin, probably between 1177 and 1188, and shows some awareness of non-Scandinavian material and sources. Interestingly, it cites an otherwise unknown *Catalogus Regum Norwagensium*. This indicates that like the saga compilations, it was drawing on earlier material. Although there is some overlap of content with the other relevant sources, the *Historia de Antiquitate* is textually independent of the others.

A second Latin source, the anonymous *Historia Norwegiae*, may be even earlier. It has been dated as early as the 1150s and as late as *c*.1220, but it is probably safe to describe it as late twelfth century. It shows textual similarities with the anonymous vernacular text, *Ágrip af Nóregs konunga sögum*, which probably dates from the 1190s. These similarities suggest either that one of the texts is partially derived from the other, or that both are derived from a common source, possibly the lost works of Sæmund or Ari. The compiler of *Ágrip* probably also used the *Historia de Antiquitate*, and, particularly importantly in the present instance, cites an existing saga of Hákon the Good. *Ágrip* also apparently draws on traditions from northern Norway.[8]

---

6 *Heimskringla*, I, Prologus, pp 5–7. Another similar passage appears later in *Heimskringla*, II (*Óláfs saga Helga*, ch. 179), p. 326 explaining the value of Ari's writings as a source on St Óláf. Andersson, 'Kings' Sagas', pp 200–01.   7 *Theodrici Monachi Historia de Antiquitate Regum Norwagensium*, in *Monumenta Historica Norvegiæ: Latinske Kildeskrifter til Norges Historie i Middelalderen*, ed. by G. Storm (Kristiania, 1880), pp 2–68; *Historia de Antiquitate Regum Norwagensium: an Account of the Ancient History of the Norwegian Kings*, by Theodoricus Monachus, trans. and annot. by D. and I. McDougall, with an introduction by Peter Foote (London, 1998); A. Holtsmark, '*Historia de antiquitate regum Norwagensium*' in *KLNM*, 6 (1961); Andersson, 'Kings' Sagas', pp 201–11; M. Cormack, '*Historia de antiquitate regum Norwagensium*' in *MSE*.

Fagrskinna, another anonymous vernacular compilation, probably written *c.*1220, draws amongst other things on *Ágrip*, and on the lost works of Ari and Sæmund, as well as on skaldic poetry. Because of rigid formal structures in the verse, skaldic poems are likely to have been more accurately preserved in oral tradition than prose, since the verse had to be remembered correctly to function properly as poetry, whereas a prose telling of the same story could be substantially reworked with each telling. *Fagrskinna* shows some textual similarities with *Heimskringla* (probably written *c.*1230–35), but there are also important differences, which suggests that the two drew on a common source, or sources, rather than that either derived directly from the other. *Heimskringla* cites Ari (who may represent the common source), and also draws on *Ágrip*, skaldic poetry, and oral tradition.[9]

The amount of detail on the life of Hákon presented in these five sources varies considerably. The *Historia de Antiquitate* is very brief, and very factual in tone, presenting little more than a catalogue of major events. The *Historia Norwegiae* is a rather longer work, in which the kings' lives form a single section, together with various geographical and antiquarian notes about the Scandinavian world as a whole. The section on the kings is more detailed than the *Historia de Antiquitate*, but still ostensibly factual in tone. *Ágrip* is somewhat longer, and more obviously literary in style. In addition to the reporting of major events, *Ágrip* includes a number of anecdotes, and introduces direct speech into the mouths of the protagonists, who are portrayed much more as characters than in the two Latin texts. *Fagrskinna* and *Heimskringla* are both considerably longer, containing much more detail, and incorporating passages of skaldic verse. The style of both is very literary, with the events portrayed more as stories than as history, and containing considerable amounts of direct speech. The two agree on some details, but disagree on others.

Some details seem obviously dismissable, or irrelevant. The intrusive story of the dog Saur (who became a king, and was bewitched with the wits of two men, so that he barked two words in three and spoke the third)[10] provides a good example of why one may justifiably be sceptical of the historical value of saga material. There are also several fairly clear anachronisms; the unification

---

8 *Historia Norwegiæ*, in Storm, *Monumenta*, pp 71–124; *Ágrip af Nóregs konunga sögum. Fagrskinna – Nóregs konunga tal*, ed. by B. Einarsson, *Íslenzk fornrit*, 29 (Reykjavík, 1984); T. Tobiassen, '*Ágrip af Nóregs konunga sögum*', in *KLNM*, 1 (1956); A. Holtsmark, '*Historia Norwegiae*', in *KLNM*, 6 (1961); Andersson, 'Kings' Sagas' pp 201–11; B. Einarsson, '*Ágrip af Nóregs konunga sögum*', in *MSE*; C. Santini, '*Historia Norwegiae*', in *MSE*. 9 *Heimskringla, passim*; *Ágrip af Nóregs konunga sögum. Fagrskinna – Nóregs konunga tal*, ed. by B. Einarsson, *Íslenzk fornrit*, 29 (Reykjavík, 1984); E.F. Halvorsen, '*Fagrskinna*', in *KLNM*, 4 (1959); H. Lie, '*Heimskringla*', in *KLNM*, 6 (1961); Andersson, 'Kings' Sagas', pp 216–27; Whaley, 'Kings' Sagas', pp 45–46, 53–54; B. Einarsson, '*Fagrskinna*', in *MSE*; D. Whaley, '*Heimskringla*', in *MSE*. 10 *Heimskringla*, I, *Hákonar saga góða* (hereafter *HSG*), ch. 12, p. 164.

of the country is portrayed as considerably more advanced than seems plausible for the tenth century, and *Heimskringla* portrays a very developed form of the *leiðangr* (naval levy), which is unlikely to have developed so fully across the whole country before the late twelfth century at the very earliest. Nevertheless, a number of key features can be identified in the sources which seem far more acceptable in the context of the tenth century.

All five texts agree that Hákon was fostered in England during the lifetime of his father Harald *hárfagri* ('Finehair'), hence his nickname of *Aðalsteins fóstri*.[11] They further agree that Hákon's brother Eirík *blóðöx* ('Bloodaxe') succeeded their father, but that he was so unpopular that when Hákon pressed his own claim to the throne, Eirík was unable to raise an army and was forced to flee the country, although they disagree about his subsequent fate.[12] Both *Fagrskinna* and *Heimskringla* add a story about the circumstances behind this fostering. According to this tradition, which clearly derives from a common source, Athelstan sent a fine sword as a gift to Harald *hárfagri*, and when Harald accepted it, Athelstan's ambassadors told him that in so doing he had accepted Athelstan's overlordship. In return, Harald sent the infant Hákon to England, where his ambassadors placed the child on Athelstan's knee, telling him that by accepting the child he was accepting Harald's lordship.[13] Both the *Fagrskinna* and *Heimskringla* versions draw on established literary genres,[14] but there is nothing inherently unlikely in the suggestion that Hákon should have been fostered at the court of Athelstan. Although there is no mention of this in English sources, William of Malmesbury (writing in the twelfth century) records in his *De Gestis Regum Anglorum* a tradition of diplomatic relations between Harald and Athelstan,[15] while R.I. Page has noted that a number of foreign princes are recorded as having been brought up at Athelstan's court, and subsequently installed in their own lands with Athelstan's help.[16] It is also consistent with the policy of the Wessex kings of standing as godfathers to Viking leaders as an attempt to bring them into alliance.[17] Despite the lack of

---

[11] *Historia de antiquitate*, ch. 2, p. 7; *Historia Norwegiae*, p. 104; *Ágrip*, ch. 2, p. 5; ch. 5, p.7; *Fagrskinna*, ch. 4, p. 73; ch. 6, pp 74–75; *Heimskringla*, I, *Haralds saga ins hárfagra* (hereafter *HSH*), ch. 39–40, pp 144–46. [12] *Historia de antiquitate*, ch. 2, p. 7; *Historia Norwegiae*, pp 105–06; *Ágrip*, ch. 5, pp 7–8; *Fagrskinna*, ch. 5–8, pp 73–79; *Heimskringla*, *HSH*, ch. 41–43, pp 146–49; *HSG*, ch. 1–4, pp 150–54. [13] *Fagrskinna*, ch. 4, pp 71–73; *Heimskringla*, I, *HSH*, ch. 38–39, pp 143–45. [14] R.I. Page, *Chronicles of the Vikings: Records, Memorials and Myths* (London, 1995), pp 30–34. Page makes the same point as the present paper (though focusing on different details), that Hákon makes a good case study in the problems of sorting fact from fiction when using saga material. However, Page's treatment of the subject was not intended to be exhaustive, leaving scope for the more extensive study presented here. [15] *Willelmi Malmesbiriensis monachi de gestis regum Anglorum libri quinque*, ed. by W. Stubbs, 2 vols (London, 1887–89), I, p. 149 (ch. 135). [16] R.I. Page, 'The Audience of Beowulf and the Vikings', *The Dating of Beowulf*, ed. by C. Chase (Toronto, 1981), pp 113–22, at p. 115. [17] *The Anglo-Saxon Chronicle* (*ASC*) contains a number of references to this, including Alfred standing godfather to Guðrum

contemporary evidence for Hákon's fostering, Page has pointed out that the nickname appears in the *Bersöglisvísur* of the skald Sigvat Þórðarson, quoted in *Heimskringla*, but supposedly composed in the 1030s. If the poem is correctly dated, this would bridge the gap between Hákon's own time and the lost writings of Sæmund and Ari in the early twelfth century. Furthermore, Page argues that the form in which the nickname appears (the words *Aðalsteins* and *fóstra* three lines apart in a verse about Hákon, presented without explanation) presupposes familiarity with the nickname on the part of the poem's audience, suggesting that the nickname was well established by the time the poem was written.[18]

This tradition of Hákon's English upbringing is extremely important, especially as it is almost the only detail common to all the sources, including the textually independent *Historia de Antiquitate*. If Hákon was brought up in England, and was familiar with English customs, then any study of his recorded actions as king of Norway must take this into account. Any suggestion that the details included in the sources are anachronistic must consider those details not only against the background of the development of Norwegian kingship, but also against the background of tenth-century Anglo-Saxon kingship. The *Historia de Antiquitate* specifically tells us that he was sent to Athelstan's court *ut nutriretur et discret morem gentis*[19] and, as will be shown below, the actions attributed to him by later texts are consistent with Anglo-Saxon *mores*.

A fundamental aspect of his English upbringing is that Hákon was apparently brought up a Christian at a time when Norway was basically still pagan. Only the *Historia de Antiquitate* fails to mention his Christianity explicitly. Even there, it may be implied as part of the general Anglo-Saxon *mores*, and the *Historia* further describes Hákon as *animi virtute praestans*. This is ambiguous, since it could refer to his manly courage, or to his virtuous soul. Both are consistent with other descriptions of Hákon, although the more spiritual interpretation is perhaps more plausible given that the author of the text was a monk. The other texts, however, are more explicit, although they vary in detail. By far the briefest is the *Historia Norwegiae*, which simply states that he was brought up a Christian, but became apostate.[20] All three of the vernacular texts confirm this. Both *Fagrskinna* and *Heimskringla* specifically mention that he was baptized in England,[21] and *Ágrip* mentions that he was a Christian, but abandoned many of his Christian customs for the sake of his pagan wife.[22] This latter point may conceivably represent a genuine tradition, but must be seen in the context of the saga topos of tenth-century wicked queens, as well as the

---

in 878, and Edmund standing godfather to Anlaf Sihtricsson and Rögnvald Guðröðsson in 942 (Text A) or 943 (Text D). Most directly analogous is the reference sub 894 [893](Text A) to Alfred as the godfather of the infant son of the Viking leader Hæsten.
18 *Heimskringla*, III, *Magnúss saga ins góða*, ch. 16, p. 27; Page, 'Audience', p. 114.
19 *Historia de Antiquitate*, ch. 2, p. 7.   20 *Historia Norwegiae*, p. 106.   21 *Fagrskinna*, ch. 6, p. 74; *Heimskringla*, I, *HSH*, ch. 39, p. 145.   22 *Ágrip*, ch. 5, p.8.

broader Christian tradition that behind every fallen man there is a corrupting woman.

A more plausible explanation for Hákon's apostasy is to be found in all three vernacular texts. While Hákon himself was Christian, and persuaded a number of his friends to convert (some even abandoned pagan sacrifices), the people of the þrœndalög refused to be converted, and forced Hákon to make pagan sacrifices, since this was expected of him as king.[23] This can be seen in the context of authority over religion as an aspect of political power. The people of the þrœndalög were acting in response to Hákon's attempts to persuade the whole law assembly to convert, and the saga accounts do not describe a wholly spontaneous uprising. Rather, they describe a group of pagan chieftains banding together against a perceived threat to their own authority.[24] Hákon's authority in the north rested heavily on his alliance with the powerful earls of Hlaðir, his namesake Hákon, and later his son Sigurð. *Heimskringla* tells us that Sigurð was 'the greatest man for sacrifices', as was his father before him,[25] and although the Hlaðir earls normally supported Hákon very actively, in this instance Sigurð may well have had an eye to his own political position, since he urged first compromise with, and then submission to, the demands of the northern chieftains.[26]

Hákon's own position after his enforced sacrifice is not entirely clear. Although he planned a punitive expedition against the northern chieftains, this was abandoned to face an invasion by his nephews, the sons of Eirík *blóðöx*. From then on the sagas concentrate on his conflict with the Eiríkssons, and the question of Hákon's religion only resurfaces with his death. Following his fatal arrow-wound at the battle of Fitjar (discussed in more detail below), the sagas give two slightly different accounts of Hákon's dying wishes. According to *Heimskringla*, Hákon stated that if he lived, he would leave the country and go amongst Christian men to make atonement for his sins against God, but that if he died in Norway as a pagan, then his friends should bury him there in the manner that seemed best. He then died, and was buried in a mound with his sword and armour, but no other treasure.[27] This burial seems to be a deliberate compromise between full pagan burial, and Christian burial without grave goods, as reflected in widespread archaeological evidence of the period. This suggests that his friends, apparently a mixture of pagans and Christians, recognized that he was in an ambivalent position. *Ágrip* also mentions that he was buried with no treasure apart from his sword and armour, but both *Ágrip* and *Fagrskinna* record that while Hákon was still alive, his friends offered to take his body to England and have it buried in a churchyard. However, Hákon

---

23 *Ágrip*, ch. 5, p. 8; *Fagrskinna*, ch. 9, p. 80; *Heimskringla*, I, *HSG*, ch. 13–18, pp 166–72. 24 *Heimskringla*, I, *HSG*, ch. 15–18, pp. 169–72. 25 *Heimskringla*, I, *HSG*, ch. 14, pp. 167–68. 26 *Heimskringla*, I, *HSG*, ch. 15–18, pp. 169–72. 27 *Heimskringla*, I, *HSG*, ch. 32, pp. 192–97.

refused, saying that he was unworthy of this because of his pagan acts, which he regretted, and insisted that as he had lived as a pagan, so he should be buried as one.[28] The two accounts are textually related, and the tone of this passage is suspiciously like a stock piece of hagiography, although it is obviously unusual for a saint's penitent quasi-humility to stretch quite so far as to deny himself the opportunity of redemption through proper Christian burial. To a lesser extent *Heimskringla's* account is also hagiographical, and one may justly be suspicious that both sets of dying words may be later interpolations. The account of the burial, however, seems more plausible in the light of archaeological evidence, although the burial rites may just as well represent the views of Hákon's friends as those of Hákon himself. This is even more true of a splendid skaldic verse, written in unequivocally pagan terms by Hákon's friend, Eyvind *skáldaspillir* Finnson. The poem, quoted extensively in both *Fagrskinna* and *Heimskringla*, describes Hákon in passing as protector of the sacred places of the Gods, but largely concentrates on Hákon's somewhat peevish translation to Válhalla. However, unlike many other skaldic verses, this one can hardly be regarded as an accurate eyewitness account, since Eyvind himself would have had to be dead (or a god) to witness most of what the poem describes.

From the perspective of Anglo-Saxon kingship, more important than Hákon's own state of grace are the saga accounts of his attempts to Christianize Norway. Both *Ágrip* and *Heimskringla* describe this in very similar terms. Hákon first apparently practised his religion in secret, although he fasted on Fridays and kept Sunday holy. He also tried quietly to Christianize the midwinter festival, and then began to convert his friends. Once Hákon thought that he had enough men in Norway to uphold Christianity, he sent to England for a bishop and other learned men. When they came to Norway, Hákon made it known that he wished to impose Christianity over the whole kingdom, and he had churches built and appointed priests to them. It was at this point that he came into conflict with the pagan chieftains of the Þrœndalög who, according to the sagas, burned his churches and slew the priests (or drove them away) shortly before forcing Hákon to make pagan sacrifices.[29]

This tradition of Hákon's attempts to Christianize Norway finds some support both from independent written sources and from archaeological evidence. The written evidence comes from two documents from Glastonbury Abbey, although neither is contemporary. The first is an obit-list preserved in a thirteenth-century customary. This commemorates amongst others a Bishop *Sigefridus*. This corresponds with a separate but overlapping obit list in the *De antiquitate Glastonie ecclesie* attributed to William of Malmesbury. This includes a commemoration of a *Sigefridus* described as *episcopus Norwegensis* and monk of Glastonbury, and seems to place his death around the end of the reign of

---

28 *Ágrip*, ch. 6, p. 11; *Fagrskinna*, ch. 13, pp 93–95.   29 *Ágrip*, ch. 5, p. 8; *Heimskringla*, I, *HSG*, ch. 13–18, pp 166–72.

Edgar (*d*.975) or slightly later.³⁰ This would be consistent with the career of a monk of Glastonbury who was brought over to Norway by Hákon to be bishop, and then driven out by the pagan reaction and forced to return to England, and thus seems to confirm the saga accounts of Hákon having an English bishop. One must note, however, that this interpretation of *Sigefridus* must be accepted with caution. While *Sigefridus* appears to be grouped in the *De antiquitate* with other figures of the reign of Edgar, it is possible that he may be later, and from the mid-990s to the middle of the following century, a number of Anglo-Saxon missionaries with similar names are recorded.³¹

Archaeological evidence also supports a partial Christianization of western Norway in the mid to late tenth century. B. Solli points to a number of possible Christian sites, and while the status of some of these is not wholly clear, Solli presents a convincing case for the existence of Christian graveyards on the small island of Veøy in Romsdal, on the west coast.³² Radiocarbon dates from these burials suggest that the churchyard was in use in the second half of the tenth century, or perhaps a little earlier.³³ Solli argues for a long and gradual conversion taking place throughout the Viking Age, rather than the sudden imposition of Christianity by royal authority, but concedes that the dating of the Veøy site fits the saga evidence of Hákon's activities.³⁴ Furthermore, there appears to be a broader pattern of few pagan burials along the western and southern coasts of Norway from *c*.950 compared with the rest of Scandinavia, suggesting that this area was one of the first to be Christianized.³⁵ This is not, of course, conclusive proof that the saga evidence is correct. Nevertheless, what evidence there is seems to support the saga tradition of Hákon's Christianization, and there is nothing within that tradition which seems inherently unlikely.

All sources apart from the *Historia de Antiquitate* record that Hákon passed laws. The *Historia Norwegiae* states that although he degenerated into paganism, he nevertheless passed diligent laws for his country; clearly bracketing lawgiving

---

30 F. Birkeli, 'The Earliest Missionary Activities from England to Norway', *Nottingham Medieval Studies*, 15 (1971), pp 27–37; M. Blows, 'A Glastonbury Obit-List', *The Archaeology and History of Glastonbury Abbey. Essays in honour of the Ninetieth Birthday of C.A. Ralegh Radford*, ed. by L. Abrams and J.P. Carley (Woodbridge, 1991), pp 257–69; L. Abrams, 'The Anglo-Saxons and the Christianisation of Scandinavia', *Anglo-Saxon England*, 24 (1995), pp 213–49. 31 P.H. Sawyer, 'Ethelred II, Olaf Tryggvason, and the Conversion of Norway', *Scandinavian Studies*, 59 (1987), pp 299–307; S. Edgington, 'Siward, Sigurd, Sigfrid? The Career of an English Missionary in Scandinavia', *Northern Studies*, 26 (1989), pp 56–59; Abrams, 'Christianisation of Scandinavia', pp 218–19, 221–23, 233–34. 32 B. Solli, 'Fra hedendom til kristendom. Religionsskiftet i Norge i arkeologisk belysning', *Viking*, 58 (1995), pp 23–48; B. Solli, 'Narratives of Encountering Religions: On the Christianisation of the Norse around AD 900–1000', *Norwegian Archaeological Review*, 29, no. 2 (1996), pp 89–114. 33 Solli, 'Fra hedendom', p. 39; 'Narratives', pp 103–07. 34 Solli, 'Fra hedendom', p. 39; 'Narratives', p. 105. 35 Abrams, 'Christianisation of Scandinavia', pp 219–20.

with Christian kingship.³⁶ *Ágrip* comments in more detail that he established the *Gulaþingslög* according to the advice of Þorleif the wise.³⁷ *Fagrskinna* states that he established law over the whole of Norway on the advice of Þorleif the wise and other learned men, and that of those laws the holy king Óláf made use of the greater part. *Heimskringla* is even more detailed, stating that he established the *Gulaþingslög* on the advice of Þorleif, and *Frostaþingslög* on the advice of Earl Hákon (of Hlaðir) and other wise men of the Þrœndalög.³⁸

Of these accounts, only *Fagrskinna's* is immediately anachronistic. It is unlikely that Hákon exercised any sort of control over the whole of Norway, and even more unlikely that he was in a position to establish laws over the whole country. The two areas in which Hákon is likely to have exercised authority, however, are Gulaþingslög and Frostaþingslög. His own power base was in the first, and the second was ruled by his ally and namesake, the powerful Earl Hákon of Hlaðir, whom *Heimskringla* credits with advising Hákon on the laws for that area. Unfortunately it is difficult to link Hákon reliably with the surviving lawcodes from these areas, since these survive only in redactions of the late twelfth-thirteenth centuries. Between the tenth and late twelfth centuries, several kings are credited with further introductions or modifications to the laws. Óláf Haraldsson (*c*.1015–30) was later regarded as a great law-giver, and introduced new laws concerning the Church, although otherwise he apparently 'made use of the greater part' of Hákon's laws, as noted above.³⁹ Further laws were introduced by Svein Álfífuson,⁴⁰ during the brief period of Danish rule between the expulsion of Óláf and the accession of his son Magnús, but these were supposedly repealed by Magnús, although similarities can be noted between one clause of the section in *Frostaþingslög* concerning the naval levy, and Heimskringla's account of the laws introduced by Svein.⁴¹ Magnús himself is credited with further laws, and the saga tradition particularly associates his lawmaking with an appeal by his advisers to the examples set by Hákon and Óláf.⁴² The laws as they survive contain a mixture of material, probably from a variety of periods, since the compilers of later redactions seem to have recorded old laws and new laws side by side, even when this led to direct contradictions within the text. Certain sections of *Gulaþingslög* contain dual entries for the laws of Óláf together with Magnús Erlingsson (1161–84),⁴³ but it is seldom possible to attribute sections of the laws directly to any of the kings whom tradition records as lawmakers.

36 *Historia Norwegiae*, p. 106.   37 *Ágrip*, ch. 5, pp 8–9.   38 *Fagrskinna*, ch. 9, p. 80; *Heimskringla*, I, *HSG*, ch. 11, p. 163.   39 *Heimskringla*, II, *ÓSH*, ch. 58, pp 73–74.   40 *Heimskringla*, II, *ÓSH*, ch. 23, pp 399–400; *Fagrskinna*, ch. 35, pp 201–02; *Ágrip*, ch. 28–30, pp 28–30.   41 E. Bull, *Leding. Militær- og finansforfatning I Norge in ældre tid* (Kristiania and København, 1920), p. 34.   42 *Heimskringla*, III, *MSG*, ch. 15–16, pp 25–31; *Fagrskinna*, ch. 48, pp 212–15; *Ágrip*, ch. 35, pp 33–34; *Morkinskinna*, ed. by F. Jónsson, Samfund til Udgivelse af Gammel Nordisk Litteratur, 53 (København, 1932), pp 26–31.   43 For example, *Gulaþingslög* §3, which specifies the number of delegates

What does seem clear, however, is the link between lawmaking, Christian kingship, and Anglo-Saxon influence. Hákon, as noted above, was apparently brought up a Christian in England, tried unsuccessfully to introduce Christianity to Norway, and introduced laws. Óláf Haraldsson was apparently converted to Christianity in England before taking the throne in Norway, and subsequently attempted to impose acceptance of Christianity in Norway by force, and introduced new laws. Svein Álfífuson was the son of Cnut, the Christian king of England and Denmark as well as of Norway. His mother Álfífa (OE Ælfgifu), whom saga tradition associates with him in his governance of Norway,[44] was also English, and Svein also introduced new laws. Magnús Óláfsson had no direct English upbringing (although he supposedly had diplomatic relations with Edward the Confessor)[45], but built on the Christian foundations established by his father.

By introducing such laws, Hákon, Óláf and Svein can be seen as acting in an established Christian pattern of the king as the just judge. While this pattern can be traced back to the model of kingship found in the Old Testament, this Old Testament tradition was consciously followed in Anglo-Saxon England. The earliest known Anglo-Saxon law codes followed the conversion of Æðelberht of Kent, while Alfred and his successors as kings of Wessex (and later England) introduced and reformed laws as symbols both of their Christian kingship and of their royal power. While it is impossible to state with certainty what laws, if any, may be attributed to Hákon and the other Norwegian kings, there is certainly nothing inherently unlikely in the suggestion that any of them, with English Christian influence behind them, should have attempted to introduce laws. Nor is it unlikely that Hákon should, as the sagas suggest, have introduced those laws on the advice of earl Hákon and other wise and learned men. It is not to be expected that the king would introduce such laws in complete disregard of existing customary law, and of the opinions of those familiar with the existing laws, even if he chose not to follow all their advice. This is particularly true where earl Hákon of Hlaðir is concerned since, as mentioned above, such sovereignty as king Hákon enjoyed in the north came by virtue of his alliance with the powerful earls of Hlaðir.

A further important tradition, which may to some extent be linked to the lawmaking, is that of the introduction of the naval defence system known as *leiðangr*. While the *Historia Norwegiae* states simply that Hákon strenuously defended his inherited lands,[46] both *Fagrskinna* and *Heimskringla* contain lengthy passages which describe his introduction of a moderately sophisticated defence system, with levies of ships and men, and warning beacons to summon

to be sent to the Gulaþing from each *fylki* under both rulers. **44** *Heimskringla*, II, *ÓSH*, ch. 23, pp 399–400; ch. 244, pp 403–05, ch. 247–49, pp 410–14; *Fagrskinna*, ch. 35, pp 201–02; *Ágrip*, ch. 28–30, pp 28–30. **45** *Heimskringla*, III, *MSG*, ch. 36–37, pp 65–67.

the levies.[47] The passages in the two texts show some textual affinities, but differ in quite significant details. Both texts claim that the system was introduced throughout the whole country, but while according to Heimskringla the system was introduced after the battle of Ögvaldsnes (in the Gulaþingslög), according to *Fagrskinna* it was introduced after the battle of Fræðarberg (in the Frostaþingslög). *Heimskringla* also mentions that the country was divided into units known as *skipreiður*; a unit which in the later law-codes was responsible for providing one ship, fully manned, equipped, and provisioned for the defence levy.[48] Again, it is difficult to accept all of this at face value, especially since *Fagrskinna* and *Heimskringla* disagree over the occasion on which the system was introduced.

This contradiction is less problematic than it seems, however. The introduction of any royal ordinance would have to be agreed separately with each of the regional law assemblies, and thus no new laws could have been introduced across the whole kingdom at exactly the same time. Since according to *Heimskringla* the ordinance was introduced after a battle which took place in the Gulaþingslög, while in *Fagrskinna* it was introduced after a battle in the Frostaþingslög, it is quite possible that the two texts are recording genuine traditions of the introduction or modification of the naval defence system in the two different law districts. Both texts, however, are likely to be mistaken in supposing that the system was introduced to cover the whole kingdom on either occasion. Whether Hákon had the authority to impose such a system over the whole of Norway is also questionable. Both *Fagrskinna* and *Heimskringla* specify that beacons (and by implication the rest of the system) were introduced from the north of Norway down to the Göta river, which in the thirteenth century and probably also the tenth formed the southern boundary of Norway. Historians have differed over the extent to which Hákon ever controlled the south-east around the Vík. According to *Heimskringla*, Hákon ruled the Vík briefly before making his nephew Tryggvi king over that area,[49] but the context of the grant suggests that Hákon was struggling to rule the combined kingdom and that he needed Tryggvi as an ally rather than as a subordinate. *Heimskringla* also tells us that the sons of Eirík Bloodaxe often attacked the Vík, but that Tryggvi had an army out to meet them,[50] which suggests that Tryggvi operated some sort of defence system. However, there is no evidence to suggest that such a system was introduced by Hákon rather than by Tryggvi, or that it necessarily took the same form as the system in the areas directly ruled by Hákon. A. Steinnes argued that it was probable that Hákon introduced some form of the *leiðangr* system in Gulaþingslög, likely that he introduced it in Frostaþingslög (where he relied on the support of Earl Sigurð), and possible that he introduced it in the Vík.[51] There has generally been agreement amongst historians that

46 *Historia Norwegiae*, p. 106.   47 *Fagrskinna*, ch. 12, pp 82–83; *Heimskringla, HSG*, ch. 22, pp 175–76.   48 *Gulaþingslög* §296; §300; §304; §310.   49 *Heimskringla, HSG*, ch. 9, pp 160–61.   50 *Heimskringla, HSG*, ch. 10, p. 163.   51 A. Steinnes, 'Kor gamal

there is unlikely to have been a single system throughout Norway before the late twelfth century at the earliest, and that a more firmly rooted system was likely in the Gulaþingslög than in other areas, since this was the heartland of Hákon's power. Chapter 315 of *Gulaþingslög*, which comes as a tailpiece to the section on the leiðangr, contains a list of the numbers and sizes of ships due from different areas of Norway, and E. Hertzberg argued that the heavier assessment listed for Gulaþingslög reflects the firmness of Hákon's control in this area,[52] while E. Bull also argued for an early system in the Gulaþingslög alone.[53]

While most historians have allowed for the possibility that Hákon introduced or modified some form of the *leiðangr* system in at least part of Norway, there is less agreement as to the form which the system took. The etymology of the word '*leiðangr*' itself suggests that some form of the institution existed by the mid-tenth century, but tells us nothing about that form.[54] Bull saw no reason to doubt *Heimskringla*'s statement that Hákon's system involved a division of Gulaþingslög into *fylki*, and these in turn into *skipreiður*, which according to the later *Gulaþingslög* were divided again into individual *manngerðar*, each responsible for providing one man for the levy.[55] Herzberg preferred to see the *manngerð* as the fundamental unit of the early system, but also accepted the *skipreiða* as part of the original system.[56] More recently, P.S. Andersen expressed doubts about the existence of such a rigid system at such an early date,[57] and H. Bjørkvik was also cautious on this point.[58] More recently still, N. Lund has been extremely sceptical about the existence of any sort of developed *leiðangr* system in Norway before the late twelfth century.[59] Lund's position is partly based on a healthy caution about the extent to which texts of the twelfth and thirteenth centuries may accurately reflect administrative systems of the tenth century, but his position on Norway is derived in part from his more extensive study of Denmark. Lund rejects the early introduction in Denmark of a structured *leiðangr* system along the lines of the later law codes. On comparative grounds, he suggests that such a system must also be late in Norway.

However, as part of the broader context of his study of the development of the Danish *leiðangr* system, Lund notes the development of an analogous

---

er den norske leidangskipnaden?', *Syn og Segn* (1929), pp 49–65, at p. 65. **52** E. Hertzberg, 'Ledingmandskabets størrelse in Norges middelalder', *Norsk Historisk Tidskrift*, 5 R. II (1914), pp 241–76, at pp 249–51. **53** Bull, *Leding*, pp 36–40. **54** D.G.E.. Williams, 'The Dating of the Norwegian *leiðangr* System: A Philological Approach', *NOWELE*, 30 (1997), pp 21–25. **55** Bull, *Leding*, p. 39. **56** Hertzberg, 'Ledingmandskabets størrelse', pp 245–47, 252–53. **57** P.S. Andersen, *Samlingen av Norge og Kristningen av landet, 800–1300* (Oslo, Bergen and Tromsø, 1977), pp 265–66. **58** H. Bjørkvik, 'Leidang', in *Kulturhistorik Leksikon for Nordisk Middelalder* (*KLNM*) 10 (1965); 'Manngjerd', in *KLNM*, 11 (1966); 'Skipreide', *KLNM*, 15 (1970). **59** N. Lund, *Lið, leding og landeværn* (Roskilde, 1996), pp 58–74. See also D.G.E. Williams, 'Land assessment and military organisation in the Norse settlements in Scotland, c.900–1266 AD', unpublished doctoral thesis (University of St Andrews, 1997).

system of military organization in England under the Wessex dynasty.[60] Military obligations had been linked with landholding in the Anglo-Saxon kingdoms at least as far back as the eighth century, but major developments took place under Alfred and his successors. According to the *Anglo-Saxon Chronicle* for 891, Alfred divided his troops so that half were on duty and half at home at any one time. As the entry for 893 shows, active service was limited both by time and by supplies. In that year, the part of the army commanded by Alfred's son Edward besieged a Viking army until 'they had completed their term of service and used up their provisions', whereupon they returned home.[61] This bears a marked resemblance to the terms of the Norwegian *leiðangr* system, which according to *Gulaþingslög* was limited both in time and provisions.[62] Alfred also introduced a system of military service based on the garrisoning of defensive settlements known as *burhs*. This system was expanded by Edward the Elder (899–924), and a document originally compiled during his reign, known as the 'Burghal Hidage', tells us how this was organized. For each *burh*, a set number of men owed duty from a set number of 'hides' of land.[63] While this was a system of territorial defence rather than of naval defence, it is nevertheless analogous with the *leiðangr* division into *skipreiður* and *manngerðar*. The Norwegian system replaced individual towns with individual ships, and garrisons with crews, but the basic concept is the same.

An even closer analogy may be seen in an Anglo-Saxon unit known as the 'ship-soke', which appears in the sources from the end of the tenth century. Like the Norwegian *skipreiða*, the 'ship-soke' was responsible for the provision of a ship with crew and provisions. The *Anglo-Saxon Chronicle* for 1008 mentions that Ethelred II summoned out one ship from every three hundred or three hundred and ten hides (the MS. versions differ on this point) across the whole kingdom, and Ethelred's law codes of the same year specify '*scipfyrdunga*' alongside other military obligations. However, the institution may well be older, since there is charter evidence of the Bishop of Sherborne owing a ship from three hundred hides of land some years earlier, while a dubious charter of Edgar also refers to ship-sokes.[64] The system could even date back as far as Alfred, who according to the Chronicle for 896 had a fleet of warships built. Given the apparent organization behind his *burh* system, and the structuring of

---

60 Lund, *Lið, leding og landeværn*, pp 51–57.   61 R.P. Abels, *Lordship and Military Obligation in Anglo-Saxon England* (London, 1988), pp 63–66.   62 *Gulaþingslög* §300; Bull, *Leding*, pp 16, 38. Provisioning in *Gulaþingslög* is limited to two months. There is no similar provision in *Frostaþingslög* but, as Bull points out, the Frostaþingslög was so far north that such a limitation would effectively exclude ships from the Frostaþingslög from active participation in *leiðangr* in those areas most likely to require defence. 63 For text and extensive discussion of the Burghal Hidage, see *The Defence of Wessex. The Burghal Hidage and Anglo-Saxon Fortifications*, ed. by D. Hill and A.R. Rumble (Manchester, 1996); Abels, *Lordship*, pp 68–81.

the fyrd, it is not unlikely that the burden of shipbuilding would also have been supported by some form of levy based on landholding. Some form of naval defence in the reign of Edward the Elder seems to be implied by the terms of the submission of the Danes in East Anglia, who agreed to defend all that Edward defended, by land and by sea.[65] Athelstan had a fleet with which to invade Scotland in 933 or 934,[66] and in 945 Malcolm, king of the Scots, agreed to be the fellow-worker of Athelstan's brother Edmund both by sea and land.[67]

Whether or not one accepts the existence of 'ship-sokes' in the early tenth century, there can be little doubt that the Wessex dynasty commanded a considerable degree of military organisation. Like Christianity and law-giving, this is certainly something with which Hákon could have become familiar at the court of Athelstan, and the repeated threat of invasion by his nephews provided a clear incentive for the introduction of an efficient coastal defence system. While the sagas are probably mistaken in suggesting that he was able to introduce such a system across the whole country, there is nothing implausible about the introduction of a naval defence system in those areas where his political authority was strong. Even the introduction of the *skipreiða* unit is not impossible, although it is extremely unlikely that this would have extended beyond the heart of the Gulaþingslög at this period.

One aspect of Anglo-Saxon kingship not mentioned by the sagas is the issuing of coinage. From the mid-eighth century onwards, virtually every Anglo-Saxon ruler issued coins in his own name. By the tenth century, the striking of coinage was tightly controlled by law, and Athelstan prescribed harsh punishments for those who struck coins without the king's permission.[68] He also used coins as a means to transmit political messages, such as his adoption of the title 'King of all Britain' on his later coins.[69] The development of mints in regional centres was part of the same extension of royal authority to be seen in the development of the *burhs*; many mints, indeed, were sited in *burhs*. However, neither historical nor numismatic evidence survives of any attempt by Hákon to introduce coinage. Although, one single coin carrying a somewhat mangled version of the name Hákon has in the past been attributed to Hákon the Good, it is now recognized that this coin post-dates Hákon by around half a century.[70] Obviously, it is not especially significant in terms of the accuracy of

---

64 Abels, *Lordship*, p. 93.   65 *ASC* (A), *sub* 921 [920].   66 *ASC* (A), *sub* 933; *ASC* (D, E, F), *sub* 934.   67 *ASC* (A, D), *sub* 945.   68 Athelstan, II; 14–14.2 in *English Historical Documents*, I, *c.500–1042*, ed. by D. Whitelock (London, 1955), p. 384.   69 M.M. Archibald and C.E. Blunt, *Sylloge of Coins of the British Isles*, 34: *British Museum, Anglo-Saxon Coins V, Athelstan to the Reform of Edgar, 924–c.973* (London, 1986), p. xix, and entries 43, 46–122, 174–98.   70 C. Ramus, 'Om nogle gamle mynter, der sandsynligen er at ansee som de ældste, der i de nordiske Riger, eller i nordiske Regenters Navne ere slagne', *Det Skandinaviske Litteraturselskabs Skrifter*, 21 (1826), pp 275–318, at pp 302–12; C. Holst, *om Norges ældste Myntvæsen* (Christiania, 1847), pp 8–19; K. Skaare, *Coins in Viking Age Norway* (Oslo, Bergen and Tromsø, 1976), pp 25–28.

the sagas that they fail to mention something which Hákon did not do. Like many other sources, the sagas frequently, though not invariably, fail to mention things which did not happen. Nevertheless, it is interesting in the light of the general point of Hákon's kingship made in this article, that he apparently made no attempt to introduce coinage. His successors Óláf Tryggvason and Óláf Haraldsson both introduced coinage on a small scale, and this has been interpreted as a manifestation of their desire to be seen to be acting like other Christian European rulers.[71] One might expect Hákon to have made the same attempt, as one aspect of his 'Anglo-Saxon kingship'.

However, Norway in the mid-tenth century had no coinage-based economy. This only developed gradually from the end of the century, and neither of the two Óláfs was particularly successful in this regard. It was only from the mid-eleventh century, after Scandinavia had seen a considerable influx of Anglo-Saxon, German and Byzantine coins, and after urban developments (all of which apparently post-date Hákon's reign) had begun to take place, that coinage was successfully introduced on a large scale.[72] It may be that Hákon and his advisers realized that this was one aspect of Anglo-Saxon kingship which simply could not be transferred to the less sophisticated economy of Norway. While law, religion, and military power all had precedents in tenth-century Norway, coinage did not. Its absence, while significant from the perspective of Anglo-Saxon kingship, is therefore not surprising.

A final point of interest in the saga tradition of Hákon, although one not directly relating to Anglo-Saxon kingship, is the account of Hákon's death given in all five of the major texts. All of them agree on the basic details, but the ways in which they differ are interesting, and perhaps revealing of the ways in which elaborations around central details developed in saga tradition. Hákon's deathbed attitude to Christianity has already been discussed, and needs no further mention here. Otherwise, all five texts agree that Hákon died as a result of an arrow wound received at the battle of Fitjar, in which he was otherwise victorious, and all but the *Historia de Antiquitate* note that after the battle the dying Hákon was taken to his nearby estate at Alreksstaðir. The *Historia Norwegiae*, *Ágrip* and *Heimskringla* all tell us that the place where he actually died was called Hákonarhella. All sources apart from the *Historia de Antiquitate* mention that Hákon was struck by the arrow in the muscles of the upper arm.[73] The interesting point is not so much the common ground (being struck by an arrow in the moment of victory is a detail which might plausibly be recalled

---

[71] Holst, *Norges ældste Myntvæsen*, pp 24–25; C.I. Schive, *Norges Mynter i Middelalderen* (Christiania, 1865), p. 3; Skaare, *Coins*, pp 28–29. [72] For the link between towns and minting in tenth-century England, see M.A.S. Blackburn, 'Mints, burhs and the Grately code, cap. 14.2', in *The Defence of Wessex*, ed. by Hill and Rumble, pp 160–75. [73] *Historia de Antiquitate*, ch. 4, p. 10; *Historia Norwegiae*, p. 107; *Ágrip*, ch. 6, p. 11; *Fagrskinna*, ch. 13, p. 93; *Heimskringla*, I, *HSG*, ch. 31–32, pp 190–92.

even in oral tradition, regardless of the relationship between the texts) as in the variations that are given on the origins of the arrow.

The *Historia de Antiquitate* states simply that this ill fortune was attributed to the malice of Gunnhild, widow of Hákon's brother Eirík (known in the Sagas of the Icelanders for her malicious witchcraft), while the *Historia Norwegiae* attributes the shot to 'a certain boy' amongst Hákon's defeated and fleeing enemies. *Ágrip* implicitly combines both stories, stating that nobody knows who fired the arrow, but that 'it is said' that Gunnhild's serving-boy shot the arrow, crying as he did so 'Make way for the king-killer'. Although it is not stated, given Gunnhild's reputation for witchcraft, it is not unreasonable to consider this to be a veiled reference to a charm, placed on the arrow. *Heimskringla*, as usual, elaborates even further, stating that 'many men say' that Gunnhild's serving boy (now named as Kisping) ran out from the throng, crying 'Make way for the king-killer', and fired the shot, but adding that it is also said that nobody knows who fired the shot. This account clearly derives either from *Ágrip* or from a common source, although it downplays the magical element, since the phrasing now suggests that the 'king-killer' refers to the boy himself, rather than to the charmed arrow. The emphasis has also shifted from saying that 'nobody knows, but there is a story' to 'many people tell the story, but it is also said that nobody knows'. However, despite elaborating the story and mentioning it before the less dramatic possibility that the story might not be true, even *Heimskringla* does not conceal this possibility. *Fagrskinna*, generally almost as prone to elaboration as *Heimskringla*, does not mention the story at all, although given the relationship between the various texts already established, the compiler of *Fagrskinna* almost certainly had access to *Ágrip's* version of events. This suggests that *Fagrskinna's* compiler actively chose not to include the story, perhaps because of its questionable authenticity. Thus, although it is possible to observe a gradual elaboration around the basic story, none of the texts accept the elaborated version uncritically, while one seems not to accept it at all. This is, of course, only a very minor detail in the overall tradition of Hákon's kingship, but it is a useful pointer to the attitudes of the sagas' compilers when dealing with traditions of dubious authenticity.

Saga evidence for the tenth century is not susceptible to proof or disproof in the manner of material sciences, or even of later, more heavily documented, periods of history. Any attempts to examine the evidence in such rigid terms will ultimately be fruitless. Nevertheless, it is possible to assess the plausibility of saga evidence in the light of whatever other sources are available. Examination of the saga traditions of Hákon *Aðalsteinsfóstri* suggests that, while not wholly reliable, the Kings' Sagas and the related Latin texts may well preserve an authentic tradition of Hákon's activities as king. Hákon's fostering by Athelstan is consistent with a known policy of Athelstan of fostering foreign princes, and a broader policy of the Wessex kings of standing as godfather to Viking leaders and their sons as a means of cementing alliance. In the light of this Anglo-Saxon upbringing, Hákon's activities as king are entirely plausible. The sagas probably overstate the extent of Hákon's authority throughout Norway as a whole, but his actions in attempting to Christianize Norway, to establish royal law throughout his kingdom, and to introduce a national system of defence, are very much what one would expect of a protégé of the Wessex dynasty of the mid-tenth century.

There are undoubtedly later accretions and anachronisms within the texts, but the key elements of Hákon's reign are as consistent with Anglo-Saxon kingship of the tenth century as they are with Norwegian kingship of the thirteenth century. Other documentary and archaeological evidence tends to support rather than to contradict the evidence of the sagas. It therefore seems unnecessarily pedantic and self-limiting to dismiss saga evidence of the tenth century as valueless because it is not susceptible to 'proof'. This is not to say that the sagas should be taken at face value; the evidence they supply must be carefully evaluated, and either accepted or rejected as seems appropriate for each particular instance. Simply dismissing the evidence of the sagas without qualification is just as uncritical as accepting them without reservations. While it is of course better to admit ignorance than to pretend to knowledge which we do not possess, it is better not to encourage that ignorance by ignoring evidence which may add to our knowledge and understanding.

Culture and Contacts in the Scottish Romanesque[*]

LORNA E.M. WALKER

In a paper entitled 'Architecture of the Anglo-Saxon Church 735 to 870' Richard Gem asked whether there was a conceptual model that could provide a key to understanding the architectural history of the period.[1] As he went on to say, 'If there has been a model it has been the wrong one: a picture of Viking destruction starting in 793 inhibiting the construction of new buildings for a century'. As he went on to prove, that picture is distorted, the argument flawed.

When we turn to the twelfth century and the Romanesque architecture and sculpture of Scotland we can begin with a similar comforting premiss: the devotion of the dynasty of Malcolm Canmore to St Cuthbert and the all-pervasive influence of Durham upon church building in the reigns of David I (1124–53) and Malcolm IV (1153–65). But how true is that image? How satisfactory is it in terms of the whole story?

Looking at the map of Romanesque sites in Scotland (Map 7.2),[2] our tour was bounded by St Andrews and Leuchars in Fife, where the circuit began and ended, and Dalmeny to the south of Abercorn in West Lothian. St Andrews

---

[*] This paper was written and presented with a specific end in view: to set the scene and provide a context for an excursion to some of the early medieval sites in Fife and Lothian on the following day. The aim was less to present the fruits of research in what, for the writer, was in several respects a new field than to provide an overview. As such, the discussion necessarily owes much to the work of others. In particular, I am indebted to Professor Geoffrey Barrow, Professor Robert Bartlett, Mr Neil Cameron, Dr Ronald Cant, Dr Barbara Crawford, Professor Judith Green and Dr Simon Taylor for their advice, references and help so kindly given while I was working on the paper. The picture that emerged, however, is my own. Subsequently, the research on Dalmeny and Tollevast has been taken a little further, and I wish to thank Dr Maylis Baylé and the Director of the Archives départementales de la Manche, Dr Jean-Paul Hervieu, for the careful consideration that each has given to my various queries: their comments and references have been invaluable. I am grateful also to Dr Kimberly LoPrete for discussing the French sources with me. Last, but not least, my thanks go to Bridget Henisch and Anna Ross for their encouragement and inspiration.

[1] R. Gem, *Journal of the British Archaeological Association* (hereafter *JBAA*), 146 (Leeds, 1993), p. 29. [2] I am most grateful to Jim Renny for his help with the maps.

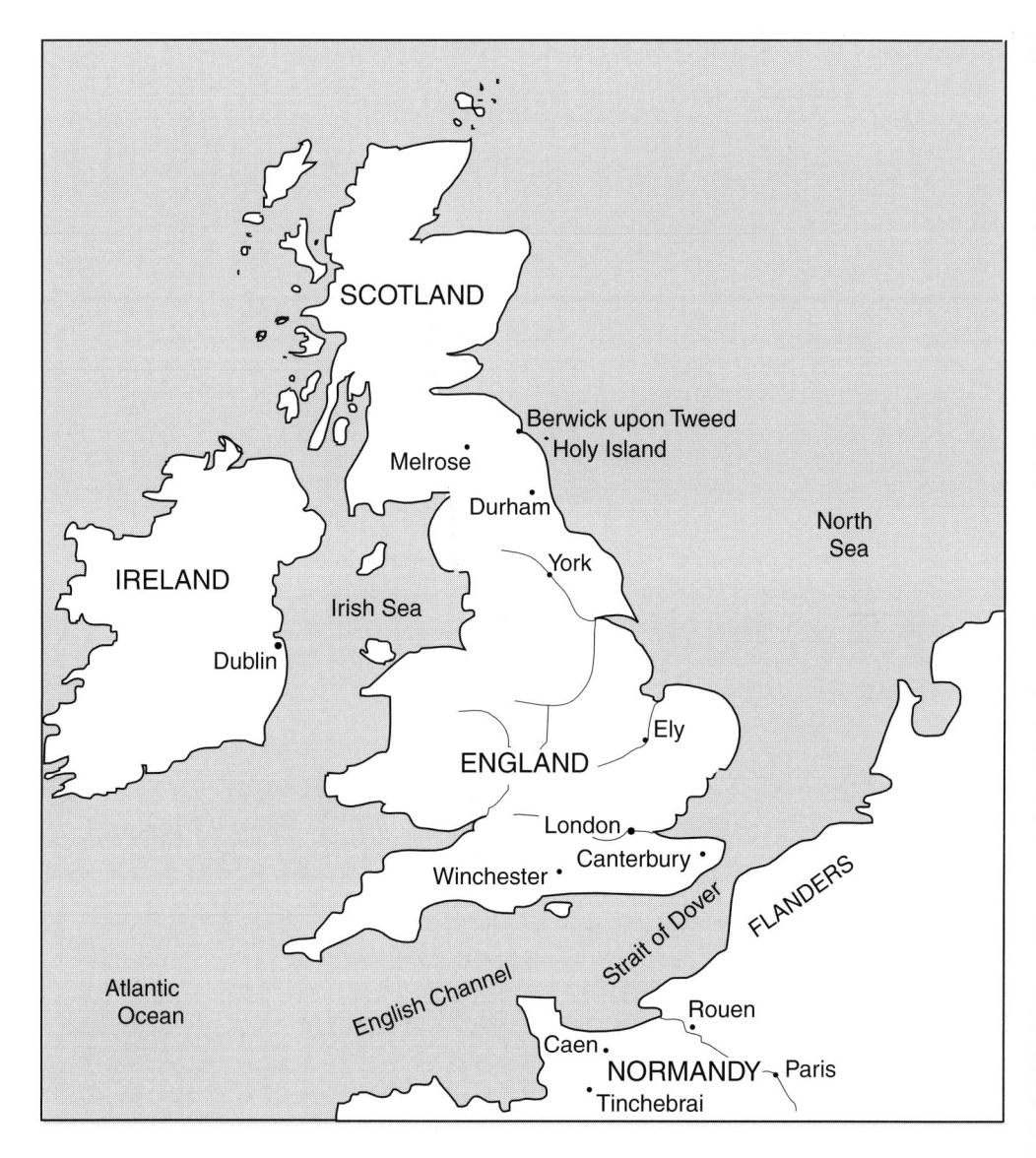

MAP 7.1 The British Isles and Normandy. (Drafted by L. Walker; drawn by J. Renny)

MAP 7.2 Selected sites in Scotland. (Drafted by L. Walker; drawn by J. Renny)

and Abercorn: appropriate points of reference for an enquiry that seeks to establish a background for the Scottish Romanesque within the context of the North Sea World. If it may seem far-fetched to compare so miniscule a site as Abercorn with St Andrews, the Compostela of the north, it is all, of course, a question of perspective. If St Andrews was unknown to Bede, Bede leaves us in no doubt about the earlier importance of Abercorn. The reference comes in his description of the state of Britain after the withdrawal of the Romans. Well-known though the passage is, and oft debated, it is worth recalling to mind:

> After that [withdrawal] Britain, or the British part of it ... was reduced to a state of terror and misery for many a long year because of two very fierce peoples from across the sea, the Scots from round about and the Picts from the north. We call these peoples 'from across the sea' not because they dwelt outside Britain but because they were separated from the territory of the Britons by two wide and long arms of the sea, one of which enters the land from the east, the other from the west, although they do not meet.[3]

3 *Bede's Ecclesiastical History of the English People*, ed. by B. Colgrave and R.A.B.

Then, with some rather erroneous chronology, Bede goes on to describe the Antonine Wall:

> It begins almost two miles west of the monastery at *Aebbercurnig* (Abercorn) in the place which the Picts call *Peanfahel* ('end of the wall'), while in English it is called Penneltun (Kinneil). It stretches westward as far as *Alcluith* ('the rock of the Clyde': Dumbarton).[4]

It is surely to a crossing of the Firth of Forth rather than an improbable sea journey via either the Solway or the Tweed that both the writer of the Anonymous *Life* and Bede refer when they describe St Cuthbert *navigans ad terram Pictorum*. And although 'the province of the Niud-' or 'Nith-folk' where he landed was almost certainly considerably further east than the later Queen's Ferry, it seems not unlikely that he would have made a little detour to Abercorn *en route*.[5] For by the date of Cuthbert's journey, between 651 and 664, while he was still a monk at Melrose, Abercorn, perhaps part of an even earlier diocesan system, had become a monastic centre of the post-Columban church closely associated with Lindisfarne.[6] A brief revival of Abercorn's episcopal authority in the 680s was ended by the battle of Nechtansmere. Abercorn does not figure in Geoffrey Barrow's useful map showing the principal religious houses within the medieval diocese of St Andrews.[7] But the fact that Abercorn is missing becomes less surprising when it is appreciated that Abercorn was a peculiar of the diocese of Dunkeld, one of the four enclaves of Dunkeld south of the Forth. It may not be too fanciful to suggest that this peculiarity had something to do with the strong Columban associations of Abercorn, remembering how, under Kenneth macAlpin, a part, at least, of St Columba's relics had been transferred from Iona to the king's new foundation at Dunkeld.[8]

Of Romanesque at Abercorn there is only one precious remnant: a blocked doorway on the south side, with a framing arch carved with shallow chevrons, a single order of shafts, block capitals, and a tympanum (Figure 7.1). With the exception of this doorway, the church as it stands today is of little relevance, for it is essentially a nineteenth-century restoration of a sixteenth-century

---

Mynors (Oxford, 1981), p. 41. 4 Ibid., p. 43. 5 *Two Lives of Saint Cuthbert*, ed. and trans. by B. Colgrave (Cambridge, 1940; repr. 1985), pp 83, 193. 6 I.B. Cowan, 'The Post-Columban Church', *Records of the Scottish Church History Society*, 18 (Edinburgh, 1974), pp 245–46. 7 G.W.S. Barrow, 'The Medieval Diocese of St Andrews', *Medieval Art and Architecture in the Diocese of St Andrews*, ed. by J. Higgitt, British Archaeological Association Conference Transactions (hereafter *BAA CT*), vol. 14 for 1986 (Leeds, 1994), facing p. 1. 8 A.O. Anderson, *Early Sources of Scottish History* AD 500–1286, 2 vols (Edinburgh, 1922; reprint. with Bibliog. Supplement and Corrigenda by M. Anderson, Stamford, 1990), I, p. 279 n. 4; p. 288. See G. Henderson, *From Durrow to Kells* (London, 1987), pp 189–91; J. Bannerman, '*Comarba Coluim Chille* and the Relics of Columba', *Innes Review*, 44 (1993), pp 14–47.

Culture and Contacts in the Scottish Romanesque　　　　　　　　　131

7.1 Abercorn Church: south doorway. (Photo: L. Walker)

reconstruction of a church that dates back to the twelfth century. But, in the context of the North Sea World, Abercorn provides some vital clues for the understanding of the Scottish Romanesque. These are to be found not in the fabric of the building itself but in a dusty basement room below the eighteenth-century Hopetoun aisle.[9] There, once one's eye has penetrated the gloom, are treasures indeed: fragments of two sandstone cross-shafts, two hogback monuments of white sandstone and a small piece of a third, two parts of a twelfth-century stone, two thirteenth-century coffin lids. Collectively they testify to the continuance of Christian worship on this site after 685 when King Ecgbert of Northumbria had been killed at Nechtansmere and Trumwine 'bishop of the Picts' was forced to flee south from his monastery and episcopal see at Abercorn back to Northumbria.[10]

The spiral designs, foliage, knotwork and key patterns on the cross-shafts from Abercorn display features common to all Celtic art, reminding one not only of the Lindisfarne Gospels and Hexham vine-scrolls, but also of the

---

9 Or so it was in 1996, adding to the excitement of the quest. But these sculptured stones are now more suitably housed in a small museum at the entrance to the Abercorn churchyard.　　10 *Bede's History*, p. 429.

7.2 Abercorn hogbacks and cross-shafts. (Photo: L. Walker)

Aberlemno stone, perhaps the best known of all the Pictish cross-slabs. Thought to be a product of the eighth or ninth centuries rather than the seventh, the eclecticism of the Abercorn crosses reflects the continued influence of Northumbrian art forms in the neighbourhood of 'the firth which divides the lands of the English from that of the Picts' – to quote Bede again.[11]

There is interesting variation in the two hogback monuments (Figure 7.2). I find this term somewhat misleading inasmuch as it is used to describe what are essentially grave covers in the shape of a house. But the name defines the strongly-marked curved ridge of the roof-line and refers also, perhaps, to the beasts which often, although not invariably, hold the ends of the roof in their grasp. It is a matter for debate whether these monuments derive from the vernacular architecture of the Viking Age or from house- or church-shaped shrines such as the Monymusk reliquary dating to c.700.[12] Most probably, as so

[11] Ibid. The Abercorn cross-shafts are illustrated in R. Cramp, *County Durham and Northumberland* in *Corpus of Anglo-Saxon Stone Sculpture*, I (Oxford, 1984), pt 2, plates 266–67; see also R. Cramp 'The Artistic Influence of Lindisfarne within Northumbria', *St Cuthbert, his cult and his community*, ed. by G. Bonner, D. Rollason, C. Stancliffe (Woodbridge, 1989), pp 225–26.   [12] *The Brecbennoch* of St Columba, now in the Royal Museum of Scotland. Described by J. Romilly Allen as being 'in the form of a small oratory' (*Celtic Art in Pagan and Christian Times* (London, 1904), p. 210), to G. Henderson and J. Bannerman, 'church-shaped' is a more appropriate term than 'house-shaped': see above, n. 7. Compare the church-shaped reliquary depicted on the thirteenth-century seal of Dunkeld Cathedral, 'presumably the up-to-date repository of all the relics committed to Dunkeld ... in 849': G. Henderson, *Durrow to Kells*, p. 190 and plate 260.

7.3 Inchcolm hogback with traces of end-beasts. (Photo: B.E. Crawford)

often, we should reckon with more than a single source. While one of the Abercorn hogbacks is steeply humped, the other has a very shallow convex curve towards the centre. The steeply pitched roof is carved with a fishscale pattern; the tiles of the other are oblong in shape. The earliest of these funerary monuments are to be found in north Yorkshire and date to the second quarter of the tenth century. As James Lang and Barbara Crawford have shown, they reflect patterns of Norse-Irish colonisation and trade along the waterways of northern England and southern Scotland.[13] A significant example, with the remains of end-beasts just discernible, is to be found on the island of Inchcolm in the Firth of Forth (Figure 7.3). This is dated to the mid-tenth century. Other variants are to be found at Brechin in Angus, at Meigle in Perthshire, and at Govan by Glasgow.[14] The two at Abercorn lack any trace of end-beasts. If prestigious and costly tombstones of this type are a mark of rank and wealth, they also bear witness to the continuing importance of Abercorn as a major ecclesiastical site in the tenth/eleventh century.

Three strands in our Scottish culture come together at Abercorn: Northumbrian (or Hiberno-Saxon – one still gropes for the most satisfactory terminology here), Scandinavian and Norman. There are only two examples of Norman tympana with sculptured decoration in Scotland, and Abercorn is one. The other, too weather-worn to photograph, is at West Linton in Roxburghshire. By contrast with Abercorn where the decoration consists of geometric ornament in a lozenge pattern, the Norman tympanum at West Linton has a figural hunting scene, *perhaps* Davidic in its connotations and, *if so*, reminiscent of the repertory of Davidic motifs which are a feature of Pictish and Scoto-Pictish art (I am being advisedly cautious here). Had the two tympana been transposed, we might have had a Scoto-Pictish reference at Abercorn as well, making the cultural tally there well-nigh complete. But this is too much to ask of serendipity. For me, the chance finds in the lumber-room at Abercorn were indeed serendipitous; I did not know of their existence before. It was the Romanesque doorway which first drew me to the site.

For the fourth cultural strand we have to retrace our steps across the water to the Pictish heartlands of Fife and Angus.[15] For what is arguably the most remarkable monument of Pictish art, we need look no further than the sarcophagus in the Cathedral Museum at St Andrews (Figure 7.4). This was found in 1833, buried deep in the ground close to the shrine church of St Regulus. Date, function and form have been hotly debated. Currently, however, a dating to the later eighth or early ninth century is generally accepted, and the

---

13 J.T. Lang, 'Hogback monuments in Scotland', *Proceedings of the Society of Antiquaries of Scotland* (hereafter *PSAS*), vol. 105 for 1972–74 (1975), pp 206–35; B.E. Crawford, *Scandinavian Scotland: Scotland in the Early Middle Ages*, 2 (Leicester, 1987), pp 172–74. See also, S. Taylor, 'The Scandinavians in Fife and Kinross', *Scandinavian settlement in Northern Britain*, ed. by B.E. Crawford (London, New York, 1995), p. 145; G. Fellows-Jensen, 'Scandinavian Settlement in Yorkshire', ibid., pp 184–85. For a full discussion of the various types of hogback monument see J.T. Lang, 'The Hogback: a Viking colonial monument', *Anglo-Saxon Studies in Archaeology and History*, 3 (Oxford, 1984), pp 85–176.   14 See B.E. Crawford, 'The "Norse" background to the Govan hogbacks', in *Govan and Its Early Medieval Sculpture*, ed. by A. Ritchie (Stroud, 1994), pp 103–12.
15 For the geographical distribution of Pictish sculptured stones, see E. Sutherland, *In Search of the Picts* (London, 1994), pp 70, 122, 124.

7.4 The St Andrews sarcophagus. (Photo: L. Walker)

sarcophagus is firmly placed within the context of Pictish art. Stress is laid upon the royal connotations of the iconography. These suggest that the sarcophagus is a monument to the secular patronage and 'retrospective sanctification' of one of the rulers to whom the foundation legends attribute the cult of St Andrew at Kinrymont – perhaps Onuist/Oengus son of Fergus (*c*.729–761). Whatever the date of the sarcophagus, and whatever its function, the panels which remain from this superb example are testimony to the quality and living presence of the sculptor's art in Scotland long before the advent of the Romanesque.[16]

From the relics of the Apostle we come to the building which contained them, 'the old church of St Andrew' as it was called in the fifteenth century, St

---

16 For the early history of St Andrews and the cult of the apostle, see M.O. Anderson, 'St Andrews before Alexander I', *The Scottish Tradition: Essays in Honour of R.G. Cant*, ed. by G.W.S. Barrow (Edinburgh, 1974), pp 1–13; *idem*, 'The Celtic Church in Kinrimund', in *The Medieval Church of St Andrews*, ed. by D. McRoberts (Glasgow, 1976), pp 1–10; U. Hall, *St Andrew and Scotland* (St Andrews, 1994). For the sarcophagus, see I. Henderson, *The Picts* (London, 1967); *idem*, 'The David Cycle in Pictish Art', in *Early Medieval Sculpture in Britain and Ireland*, ed. by J. Higgitt, BAR British Series, 152 (Oxford, 1986), pp 87–123; *idem*, 'The Insular and Continental Context of the St Andrews Sarcophagus', in *Scotland in Dark-Age Europe*, ed. by B.E. Crawford (1994), pp 71–102. Following upon its display at both the British Museum and the Royal Museum of Scotland, a day-conference on the St Andrews Sarcophagus was held in Edinburgh on 27 September 1997. For the papers presented at this conference, including I. Henderson, '*Primus inter pares:* the St Andrews Sarcophagus and Pictish Sculpture', see *The St Andrews Sarcophagus: a Pictish Masterpiece and its International Connections*, ed. by Sally M. Foster (Dublin, 1998).

7.5 St Rule's Church, St Andrews. (Photo: L. Walker)

Rule's Tower as it is known today (Figure 7.5). There is almost as much controversy about this as about the sarcophagus. When was it built, by whom, and for precisely what purpose? Without entering too far into the detailed technical arguments – every monument under discussion here could be the subject of a separate paper and of more than one – it is clear from the architectural evidence that the original building has been extended. Everything suggests that what began life essentially as a martyrium or shrine-church was subsequently enlarged. Never originally designed to meet congregational needs, the position of 'the old church' so close to the later cathedral is misleading, for St Rule's was 'not an undersized cathedral but a huge casket'.[17]

Stephen Heywood's reconstruction sketch indicates how the building might have looked after it had been enlarged by a westward extension.[18] That extension is attested by the marks of the roof line on the west face of the tower and by the western arch – now blocked up – which is clearly an insertion of the twelfth century.

Debate turns upon the chancel arch, the most easterly arch of the three that survive today, and upon the distinctive form of its decorative mouldings, which in points of detail are comparable to those of the blocked arch in the west wall of the tower (Figure 7.6). On stylistic grounds both these arches are dated to the first half of the twelfth century. An examination of the fabric of the building suggests that the eastern arch is all of a piece with the wall in which it stands – at least at the lower levels. It would seem, therefore, on the stylistic evidence of the mouldings, that if the eastern arch was an integral part of the original building and not an insertion, the building as a whole should be regarded as early- to mid-twelfth century in date. In this view the westward extension was added not long after the completion of the original building, both building campaigns being attributed to Bishop Robert (1123 x 1124–1159).

Recently, however, fresh evidence has been found to support the argument for a date earlier than the twelfth century for the original church of St Rule. Taking a sharp look at the upper courses of the eastern wall, Neil Cameron has drawn attention to the 'disrupted masonry' round the head of the eastern arch. He argues, convincingly, that the height of this arch has been raised and the arch itself rebuilt, noticing that while the capitals have been reused without alteration, the abaci have been recut. This recutting was necessitated by the new roll-and-hollow mouldings of the rebuilt arch – sculpted in keeping with current fashion.[19]

17 'First and foremost a shrine for St Andrew's relics': E. Fernie, 'Early Church Architecture in Scotland', *PSAS*, 116 (1986), p. 407, citing R.G. Cant, 'The building of St Andrews Cathedral', *Innes Review*, 25 (1974), pp 77–94. 18 S. Heywood, 'The Church of St Rule, St Andrews', *BAA CT*, 14 for 1986 (1994), *St Andrews*, p. 44, Fig. 3; the surviving fabric is fully discussed ibid., pp 38–46, and by E. Fernie, 'Early Church Architecture'. Both date all parts of the building to the twelfth century. 19 N. Cameron, 'St Rule's Church, St Andrews, and early stone-built churches in

7.6 St Rule's Church: chancel arch. (Photo: L. Walker)

To sum up: when we look at the east face of the building, what we see is the work of two separate campaigns. If the rich decoration of the mouldings dates one campaign to the early- to mid-twelfth century, the other may have been considerably earlier than this; Marjory Anderson's attribution of St Rule's to the episcopacy of Fothad II (*c*.1059 to 1093) – or even a little earlier – may well be nearer the mark.[20] The documentary evidence provides some support for this view. In the twelfth-century 'Legend of St Andrew' we are told that Robert, bishop of St Andrews from 1127 to 1159, 'set himself zealously to accomplish what he had much at heart – the *enlargement* of his church and its dedication to divine worship'. In a further telling passage the text goes on to say, 'But since funds were small, building was also carried out in a limited way.' On a close reading of the text, the attribution of the whole church to Bishop Robert seems less likely.[21]

There is little doubt that Bishop Robert's enlargement of St Rule's had much to do with his foundation in 1144 of a priory of Augustinian canons at St Andrews. But if there was need to accommodate the new community, there was also need to provide for an increasing number of pilgrims and to reconcile the competing claims of both. I very much like Neil Cameron's conclusion: that the eastern arch was raised to allow an unimpeded view from the new nave; a view right through all three arches – the two in the tower and the eastern or chancel arch – to the apostle's shrine raised high upon a feretory beyond. In this view Bishop Robert's rebuilding was in part, at least, an architectural response to pilgrimage, prompted both by the desire to provide 'a more elaborate setting for the shrine of the apostle' and the need to deal with the question of access – now becoming an urgent problem. In these preoccupations Bishop Robert was no different from the guardians of every major – and many a minor sanctuary of Western Europe in his time.

The dating of St Rule's is of some significance for our theme. All the experts are agreed that the building itself is of very high standard, pointing to the quality of its masonry and the careful proportions of the plan, 'a first-class piece of construction' in Eric Fernie's words. With it we may compare a group of related ecclesiastical buildings in east-central Scotland: a group which includes the square tower incorporated into the priory church at Restenneth and the round towers at Brechin and Abernethy. While Eric Fernie would position these 'to the late eleventh and early twelfth centuries and possibly

---

Scotland', *PSAS*, 124 (1994), pp 367–78, esp. pp 370–71. I am grateful to Mr Cameron for allowing me to see this article in page-proof. For discussion of the previous arguments for an earlier dating, see Gordon Donaldson, 'Scotland's Earliest Church Buildings', *Scottish Church History Society Records*, 18 (1972–74), pp 1–9; S. Cruden, *Scottish Medieval Churches* (Edinburgh, 1986), pp 14–20. 20 Anderson, 'Celtic Church', p. 6. 21 Cameron, 'St Rule's Church', pp 371–72, citing *Chronicles of the Picts: Chronicles of the Scots*, ed. by W. F. Skene (Edinburgh, 1867), p. 191. For the dating of this part of the text, more accurately described as a '*Historia Fundationis* of St Andrews Priory', see G.W.S. Barrow, *The Kingdom of the Scots* (London, 1973), p. 222 n. 57.

entirely into the twelfth', others would argue that by this time they would have appeared retrograde not only in England but in Scotland as well. Far from being anachronistic, these and other examples can be seen to support the view that Scotland had a tradition of church building in stone which dated back through the eleventh to the tenth century and perhaps beyond.

At Dunfermline Abbey, however, the first of the Romanesque monuments on our itinerary, the arguments for a Durham derivation are so strong that few would venture to dispute the case. They extend not only to the overall plan and individual features but to the very craftsmanship itself – the hands of the same master masons have been traced at work both in the cathedral and in the abbey.[22] And yet there are significant variations; Dunfermline is not just a pale reflection of Durham. Comparing the ground plan of Dunfermline Abbey with that of Durham Cathedral, one contrast is immediately apparent: the nave is narrower at Dunfermline than at Durham. For both the similarities and the differences the explanation lies – in part at least – in Dunfermline's history.[23]

When in 1128 David I converted his mother's foundation at Dunfermline from a Benedictine priory into an abbey and set about the rebuilding of the church, it was natural enough that he should look to Durham. In the eleventh and twelfth centuries St Cuthbert jostles for position with St Andrew as the cult most favoured and sought after by the Scottish royal house. It was to Edgar, king of Scots, that Durham owed Coldingham and a rich endowment in Berwickshire, in the south of the diocese of St Andrews. In the writ-notification of this grant, dated to 1097 (?c.1100) x 1107 and addressed *Omnibus suis hominibus Scottis et anglis*, Edgar refers to St Cuthbert as his lord.[24] If there were political advantages for both sides in a bond of confraternity between the community of St Cuthbert at Durham and the Scottish royal house, the spiritual dimension is no less significant.[25] Nor should we forget that as far north as the banks of the Forth Abercorn had been, for a time at least, a daughter house of Lindisfarne and part of St Cuthbert's patrimony. There seems little doubt that the extension of the diocese of St Andrews into Lothian had followed swiftly upon

---

22 Cruden, *op. cit.*, pp 26–35; Neil Cameron, 'The Romanesque Sculpture of Dunfermline Abbey: Durham versus the Vicinal', *BAA CT*, 14 for 1986 (1994), *St Andrews*, pp 118–23. **23** For a detailed analysis of the successive stages of building at Dunfermline, see E. Fernie, 'The Romanesque Churches of Dunfermline Abbey', *BAA CT*, 14 for 1986 (1994), *St Andrews*, pp 25–37. **24** *Early Scottish Charters* (hereafter *ESC*), ed. by A.C. Lawrie, no. xix, p. 16: 'Sciatis quod ego do ... Deo omnipotenti et Sancto Cuthberto domino meo et ecclesie Dunelmensi et monachis in eadem ecclesia Deo servientibus ... mansionem de Goldingaham ... '. For discussion of the authenticity of this writ and related documents, see A.A.M. Duncan, 'The Earliest Scottish Charters', *Scottish Historical Review* (hereafter *SHR*), 37 (1958), pp 103–35, esp. pp 107–08; J. Donnelly, 'The Earliest Scottish Charters', *SHR*, 68 (1989), pp 1–22; A.A.M. Duncan, 'Yes, The Earliest Scottish Charters', *SHR*, 78 (1999), pp 1–35. **25** For relations between the kings of Scotland and Durham in the period covered by

the extension of the authority of the king of Scots into those parts in the tenth and eleventh centuries. But, as Marinell Ash reminded us long ago, the creation of the medieval diocese of St Andrews – the largest and wealthiest in Scotland – 'had to take account of an ancient church and its continuing traditions' – both north and south of the Forth.[26] Edgar's brother, Alexander, was at Durham on 29 August 1104 when the relics of St Cuthbert were translated to their new shrine behind the high altar in the newly-built choir. In this he was but following in his parents' footsteps: Malcolm III was the only layman whose presence at Durham is recorded when the foundation stone of the new cathedral was laid on 11 August 1093.[27] St Cuthbert's journey into the land of the Picts comes sharply into focus at this point, as also the significance of his cult for members of the House of Wessex. Reginald of Durham leaves us in no doubt about the devotion of Queen Margaret, sister of Edgar the Ætheling, to St Cuthbert. It was a devotion in which David shared – at least in the earlier years of his life, visiting Durham with his bride shortly after their marriage in 1113–14.[28] By that date building at Durham had progressed well into the nave, and most, if not all, of the great cylindrical columns, which are such a prominent feature both at Durham and at Dunfermline, would have been in *situ*.

The plan printed by Eric Fernie illustrates the relationship of David's building, the third church at Dunfermline, to its predecessors, Dunfermline I and II.[29] The arguments over the dating of Dunfermline I need not be elaborated here. Over Dunfermline II there is no dispute: Turgot's biography makes it clear that at her death Margaret was buried as she had requested 'in the church of the Holy Trinity which she herself had built, over against the altar and the venerable sign of the Holy Cross'.[30] Writing in the early fifteenth century, Wyntoun locates Margaret's tomb in the nave of Dunfermline III:

---

this paper, see G.W.S. Barrow, 'The Kings of Scotland and Durham', *Anglo-Norman Durham 1093–1193*, ed. by D. Rollason, M. Harvey and M. Prestwich (Woodbridge, 1994), pp 311–23; V. Wall, 'Malcolm III and the Foundation of Durham Cathedral', ibid., pp 325–37; P. Dalton, 'Scottish Influence on Durham 1066–1214', ibid., pp 339–52; J.A. Green, 'Henry I and David I', *SHR*, 75 (1996), pp 1–19.   **26** M. Ash, 'The diocese of St Andrews under its 'Norman' bishops', *SHR*, 55 (1976), pp 106–26. **27** Symeon of Durham, *Historia Regum in Opera omnia*, ed. by T. Arnold, 2 vols, Rolls Series (London, 1882–85), II, p. 220.   **28** For David's visit to Durham late in 1113 or early in 1114, see Reginald of Durham, *Libellus de admirandis Beati Cuthberti virtutibus quae novellis patratae sunt temporibus*, ed. by J. Raine, Surtees Society, I (London, 1835), cap. 74, pp 151–52; on this passage and its dating see V. Tudor, 'The Cult of St Cuthbert in the Twelfth Century: the Evidence of Reginald of Durham', *St Cuthbert: His Cult and His Community to AD 1200*, ed. by G. Bonner, D. Rollason and C. Stancliffe (Woodbridge, 1989), p. 465 and n.160. That relations between Durham and the Scots deteriorated during David's reign is argued by Barrow, 'Kings of Scotland and Durham', pp 311–23. **29** E. Fernie, 'Romanesque Churches of Dunfermline', p. 29, Fig. 5.   **30** *Vita S. Margaretae Scotorum Reginae*, ed. by H. Hinde, Surtees Society, 51 (Durham, 1868), cap. 13, p. 254: *ibique, sicut ipsa jusserat, contra altare et sanctae crucis (quod ibidem*

'Before the Rwde awtare'.[31] Excavations in 1916 revealed the existence of five graves in Dunfermline II. Eric Fernie's research indicates that in Margaret's church the main altar was situated west of the arch into the apse. Surviving remains show that in Dunfermline III the rood screen stood on the chord of the apse of Margaret's church. If, as is most likely, the nave altar in David's church stood before the rood screen, it lay immediately above the main altar of Dunfermline II. Of the five graves discovered at the excavations in 1916, the evidence strongly suggests that the one found immediately to the west of this position was Margaret's own. It would have faced the main altar, situated west of the apse, and be an appropriate burial place for the founder of the church.

What becomes evident when comparing the third church at Dunfermline with Durham Cathedral is David's concern that his new church should reflect as much as possible of the old, and in particular give due honour to his mother's tomb and to the sacred space in which it lay. The wish was easier than the fulfilment. The lie of the land at Dunfermline, the fact that the ground drops away so steeply to the west of the church, made it impossible to position the new chancel immediately above the old and extend the nave much further to the west. As David was seeking to build a larger church in keeping with the monastery's new status and with its role as the dynastic burial place of the royal house, the only solution was to expand eastwards and to build a new eastern arm. Of this eastern arm, the crossing which formed the link with churches I and II, and the two transept arms, nothing is visible today. While we know something of the transept of David's church from eighteenth- and early nineteenth-century drawings, the ground plan lies buried beneath the present parish church which was erected in 1818. Of this, built in the style of the Gothic Revival, perhaps the less said the better. Of greater interest are the remnants of the chapel built on at the east end of David's church to receive the bodies of Malcolm Canmore and his wife, translated there after Queen Margaret's canonisation in 1250. Walking round the exterior of the parish church to-day, one can still see part of the lower courses of this chapel. In the centre lie the base plinths of Margaret's shrine, pieces of the fashionable and expensive Frosterley marble imported from county Durham.

Resuming our stance in the second bay of the nave of David's church, Dunfermline III, looking towards the east, we need to visualise the nave altar in front of us, the rood cross above our heads. The site is that of the eastern end of Dunfermline II. As Eric Fernie explained in a paper published in 1994,[32] if David could not build the main sanctuary of his new church immediately above the old, he did the next best thing. He built the nave sanctuary above the site of

erexerat) *venerabile signum*.... **31** Andrew of Wyntoun, *Orygynale Cronykil of Scotland*, VII. 3 (*The Historians of Scotland*: Edinburgh, 1872), III, p. 165. **32** See above, n. 19. I am much indebted to this paper for my understanding of the architecture of Dunfermline Abbey.

the principal altar in his mother's church. In this way the continuity of the sacred space was preserved. Whether his mother's tomb remained undisturbed at this time, or whether – as has been suggested – it may have been elevated when David's church was consecrated in 1150 is very much an open question.

As we stand in the centre of the nave, two pairs of decorated columns, one to the north and one to the south, serve to delineate the sacred space. The columns act as markers: the spirals to either side of the choir screen signal the divide between choir and nave, and, together with the zig-zags, define the bay containing the nave altar, the rood, and the site of Margaret's tomb (Figure 7.7). At Durham spiral columns are found both in the choir and before the bays with altars in the transepts. Again they act as markers, identifying the sacred space. At Dunfermline the vocabulary is the same, but the fact that all the other columns in the nave are plain – apart from the two pairs discussed – makes the language even more emphatic. A language of signs and symbols. This is certainly one key to Romanesque. For the origins of the spiral column as a sacred sign and symbol, Eric Fernie looks south to Rome and the spiral columns of St Peter's shrine.[33] Attempting to contextualize, and thinking of the spirals on the Abercorn cross-shaft, the St Andrews sarcophagus and the Pictish cross-slabs at Aberlemno, Cossans, Elgin, Shandwick and Nigg, is it too fanciful to suggest that the symbolism may have had even subtler shades of meaning in David's kingdom than at Durham itself?[34]

The narrowness of David's church is explained by his resolve to retain as much as possible of his mother's church, a resolve which indicates that Margaret's church had already assumed a relic character. His further desire to respect her tomb helps to explain another puzzle at Dunfermline: the location and decoration of the three surviving twelfth-century doorways. Of one of these, the entrance for the laity, which led into the seventh bay on the north side of the church, there is less to be said. Obscured by a fifteenth-century porch, it lacks decoration – the chevron arches apart. Of greater interest is the south-east processional doorway leading from the cloister into the nave. The positioning of this entrance in the second bay of the nave-aisle rather than the first, and west of the twelfth-century rood screen, may again have to do with the site of Queen Margaret's tomb. It must always be remembered that it was not until after her canonisation in 1250 that her relics were translated to their new resting place east of the high altar in the enlarged choir. Looking through the doorway across the nave, the spiral columns are clearly visible. What is striking, in contrast to the north-west doorway, is the rich ornamentation of the capitals

[33] See E. Fernie, 'The Spiral Piers of Durham Cathedral', *BAA CT*, 3 for 1977 (1980), *Durham Cathedral*, pp 49–58. [34] Here the spiral breast-plate on the Elgin slab seems especially significant. See I. Henderson's reconstruction, 'The Insular and Continental Context of the St Andrews Sarcophagus', in *Scotland in Dark-Age Europe*, ed. by B.E. Crawford (1994), fig. 5.7.

7.7 Dunfermline Abbey: north nave arcade. (Crown Copyright: RCAHMS)

and abaci. In its detail this ornament may be compared with that of the south-west nave doorway at Durham, as also with the capitals of the caryatids in the Durham Chapter House, a reference which I owe, once again, to a recently published article by Neil Cameron. As Neil Cameron has also shown, there is a relationship between the sculptural style at both Durham and Dunfermline and the style of illuminated initials in contemporary Durham manuscripts.[35]

It is when we turn to the principal entrance at Dunfermline, the west doorway, the latest of the three surviving twelfth-century entrances, that the trail becomes more exciting in terms of the search for the Scottish Romanesque (Figure 7.8). For if, again, there are Durham resonances, there is much for which an explanation must be sought elsewhere: an overall design, iconography and style that is not explicable in terms of Durham alone.

It is in the outer order that the principal interest of the Dunfermline west doorway lies. This carries an arch carved with an alternating design of protuberant grotesque heads and decoration in lower relief: foliage, interlace and knot patterns, a bird, triquetras and other ornamental motifs too weather-worn to decipher. Here the comparison is not with Durham but with Dalmeny, and also with those arches carved with human and animal heads which formed the subject of joint research by George Zarnecki and Françoise Henry some years back. As their enquiry showed, it is to the early twelfth century and to the district between the valleys of the Loire and the Gironde that the earliest concentration of arches with such motifs belongs.[36] As there is nothing to indicate that David's church, contrary to normal practice, was built from west to east rather than east to west, a date as late as the third quarter of the twelfth century has been suggested for the west doorway at Dunfermline. The fact that the new church was dedicated in 1150 means little, of course, in terms of the final completion of the nave. Indeed the building itself, the contrast between the richness of the nave and wall arcades at ground level and the plainness of the triforium and clerestory above, is an argument for a decline in the level of funding following upon David's death in 1153.

When we turn from the royal abbey at Dunfermline to the parish church at Dalmeny there is much greater uncertainty in terms of patronage, provenance and date. There is virtually no written documentation for Dalmeny. That there was at least a church there by the later twelfth century, we know from mention of a parson of Dalmeny in a charter in the Dunfermline Register (1165 x 1182).[37]

[35] Cameron, 'Romanesque Sculpture of Dunfermline Abbey', see n. 22 above; both the south-east and the west doorways are discussed in this article. [36] F. Henry and G. Zarnecki, 'Romanesque Arches Decorated with Human and Animal Heads', *JBAA*, 3rd ser., 20–21 (1957–58), pp 1–34 (reprinted in G. Zarnecki, *Studies in Romanesque Sculpture* (London, 1979), pt. vi, pp 1–35). As F. and P. Sharratt pointed out (*Écosse Romane* (La Pierre-qui-Vire, 1985), p. 204), the west doorway at Dunfermline may also be compared with the (destroyed) north doorway of the cathedral of St Giles in Edinburgh (illustration in Cameron, 'Romanesque Sculpture of Dunfermline', pl. XXIIID). [37] *Registrum de Dunfermelyn*, Bannatyne Club, 74 (Edinburgh, 1842), no. 165. The

7.8 Dunfermline Abbey: west doorway. (Photo: L. Walker)

Another important piece of evidence is the confirmation by Roger de Moubray in 1238 x 1245 of his grandfather's grant of the church of Dalmeny to Jedburgh Abbey.[38] This grandfather was Waltheof son of Cospatric, lord of Inverkeithing, a descendant of Waldeve or Waltheof, lord of Allerdale, whose elder brother, Cospatric II, earl of Lothian and Dunbar, was killed at the Battle of the Standard in 1138. Before I had assembled the evidence, I was happy with the view, generally accepted, that the patrons of Dalmeny were the earls of Lothian/Dunbar, the senior line in descent from Cospatric Maldredson, earl of Northumberland (1067–1072, d.1074 or 1075), and that the building of the Romanesque church at Dalmeny should be attributed either to Earl Cospatric II who died in 1138, or to his son Earl Cospatric III who lived until 1166, or perhaps to both.[39] So exalted a patronage would fit in well with so resplendent a church as Dalmeny. Unfortunately there is no evidence to suggest that the lordship of Dalmeny and its church was ever held by the earls of Lothian/Dunbar.

Waltheof son of Cospatric, the descendant of the junior branch of the family of Cospatric earl of Northumberland, was dead by 1199. Before that date, as his grant to Jedburgh shows, the lordship of Dalmeny and its church was in his hands. How long had his family held it and how did they come by it? Here we enter the realm of conjecture. But a writ of Malcolm IV granting free passage across the Forth to the prior of St Andrews and his demesne tenants throws some light upon the question.[40] Dated to between 1153 and 1160, the writ is addressed to the abbot of Dunfermline and Cospatric son of Waltheof as controllers of the ferries at Queensferry. As Dalmeny kirk is just one and three-quarter miles south-east of the old harbour of South Queensferry, it seems very likely that it was as lord of Dalmeny that Cospatric had a controlling interest in the ferries. In view of the fact that the Queen's Ferry lay in Dalmeny parish, it is arguable that

---

reference to two parsons in the text is perhaps a mistake. I am grateful to Simon Taylor for giving me a date for this document and discussing these charters with me, as also for much other kindly help.   **38** Scottish Record Office (RH. 6/34). See also ibid., no. 37 and *Liber cartarum prioratus Sancti Andree in Scotia*, Bannatyne Club, 69 (Edinburgh, 1841), p. xxviii; I.B. Cowan, *Parishes of Medieval Scotland*, Scottish Record Society, 93 (Edinburgh, 1967), p. 44. For the dating of Roger de Moubray's charter, see D.E.R. Watt, *A Biographical Dictionary of Scottish Graduates to AD 1410* (Oxford, 1977), p. 354, col. 2.   **39** So C. McWilliam, *The Buildings of Scotland: Lothian* (Penguin Books, 1978), p. 168. While a death-date of *c.*1147 is there suggested for Earl Cospatric II, the identification of the earl with 'the chief commander of the men of Lothian' struck down by an arrow at the Battle of the Standard in 1138 (*Henry, Archdeacon of Huntingdon, Historia Anglorum: the History of the English People*, ed. by D. Greenway (Oxford, 1996), p. 717) is generally accepted. There is helpful discussion of the earls of Lothian and their kin in W. Percy Hedley's account of the Serjeanty of Beanley, *Northumberland Families*, 2 vols (Newcastle upon Tyne, 1968), I, pp 235–41.   **40** *The Acts of Malcolm IV 1153–65*, ed. by G.W.S. Barrow, *Regesta Regum Scottorum*, I (Edinburgh, 1960), no. 126, p. 189.

the pilgrimage to St Andrews may have contributed to the development of the site, remembering Turgot's description of the provision made by Queen Margaret for 'dwellings upon either shore of the sea that separates Lothian and Scotland; so that pilgrims and poor might turn aside there to rest, after the labour of their journey.'[41] Dedicated to St Cuthbert, Dalmeny itself would not have been without important relics, but of these there is no trace in the sources.

It is this same Cospatric who as 'brother of Alan son of Waltheof' is found, together with Alan, witnessing a charter of David I in 1139.[42] This joint attestation comes as no surprise when we remember that in 1136 the king of Scots had captured Carlisle and, by the Treaty of Durham made with Stephen, had regained control over Cumberland and Westmoreland. For Alan son of Waltheof was lord of Allerdale below Derwent in Cumbria, inheriting from his father an enfeoffment owed to Malcolm III and confirmed by Henry I. It would seem that under David I and Malcolm IV the connections between this branch of the family and the court of the king of Scots were almost as close as those of the earls of Lothian/Dunbar. Hedley, in his study of Northumbrian families, states that Alan son of Waltheof had been in the wardship of David I. If so, then Cospatric may well have been a royal ward too. The evidence suggests that Cospatric, Alan's brother or half-brother, was a younger son or – perhaps – a bastard.[43] It seems likely that Dalmeny, a lordship created from the royal demesne, was conferred upon Cospatric as a comparatively landless younger or illegitimate son by David I. 'Culture and Contacts': the one is as important as the other when seeking to identify and interpret the Romanesque.

When we confront Dalmeny, approaching from the south, the impact of the sculptured doorway is immediate (Figure 7.9). It is this emphasis upon the portal that brings Dalmeny to the forefront of architectural and sculptural development in Scotland in the first half of the twelfth century. The dating of Romanesque monuments is notoriously problematic, but it would seem that at Dalmeny the building campaign should be dated to the middle rather than the third quarter of the twelfth century or later, as some authorities have suggested.[44] If this is correct, then Dalmeny may be earlier than Alne and other churches in Yorkshire with which it has often been compared. While the monumental doorway, the chef d'oeuvre, was probably the finishing touch, it is

[41] Anderson, *Sources*, II, p. 77.   [42] Lawrie, *ESC*, no. cxxi, p. 93.   [43] Hedley, *op. cit.*, p. 236; see the 'Distributio Cumberlandiae ad Conquestum Anglie', *Register of the Priory of Wetheral*, ed. by J.E. Prescott (London, 1897), p. 387, and compare the 'Chronicon Cumbriae', printed and discussed by T.H.B. Graham, 'Allerdale', *Transactions of the Cumberland and Westmorland Antiquarian and Archaeological Society*, ns. XXXII (Kendal, 1932), pp 28–37; I.J. Sanders, *English Baronies* (Oxford, 1960), p. 134.   [44] For the later dating, see C.A. Ralegh Radford, *Archaeological Jnl*, 121 (1964), pp 186–87; Cruden, *Scottish Medieval Churches*, p. 132. At the conference in 1996 I referred to the force raised by Malcolm IV for the Toulouse expedition of 1159, and suggested that the impact of southern French examples such as Cahors and Moissac might have acted as a

7.9 Dalmeny Church: south doorway. (Photo: L. Walker)

7.10 (a) Dalmeny Church: apse. (Photo: L. Walker)

Culture and Contacts in the Scottish Romanesque 151

(b) Corbels nos. 4 and 5 at the head of the apse, shown together

(c) no. 4 (left)   (d) no. 5 (right)   (e) no. 6 (apse south)

7.10 (b)–(e) Dalmeny Church: corbels in the apse. (Photo: L. Walker)

contemporary with the church as a whole. The iconography of the Dalmeny portal still awaits its historian.[45] Points to notice are the elaborate sophistication of the total composition, which, in the originality and complexity of its design, goes beyond that of either the south or the west doorways at Dunfermline. If the blind arcading recalls the interior decoration of the nave walls at Durham and Kirkwall, a decoration which we find replicated on the exterior of the church at Leuchars and at the cathedral at St Andrews, at Dalmeny this device is used in a novel way to give a vertical impulse to the portal as a whole.[46] Notable also in the outer archivolt, as at the west doorway of Dunfermline, is the alternation of protuberant mask-head voussoires with those carved in lower relief. As for the subject matter, weather-worn though the stones are and difficult to read, there is much in the bestiary illustration that suggests Cistercian influence, *inter alia*. Stylistically, there is also, as Maylis Baylé has pointed out, 'a strongly Scandinavian flavour', especially noticeable in the grotesque heads and in the figures of animals ending in an irregular thread-like interlace. Just one more observation before we cross the threshold: in the projection of the portal at Dalmeny there is an echo of the Roman triumphal arch. Notice also the little human figures standing sentinel on either side of the hood-mould. Here, several examples in French Romanesque sculpture spring to mind. But this might well have struck a more familiar chord: is there not something of a parallel in the Evangelist symbols that flank the Canon Table in the Book of Kells (fol. 5^r)?

Step inside the church at Dalmeny and the resonances are quite different. In the richness of the Anglo-Norman chevron decoration, the sophisticated elegance of the arches into the chancel and the apse is comparable to that found at Leuchars and at Tyninghame. But most striking of all are the corbels which support the ribs of the vaults in the chancel and the apse (Figure 7.10).[47] Again similar examples are to be found at Leuchars.[48] A familiar feature of the repertory of Romanesque art when discovered on the exterior of buildings, tucked under the eaves of the roof, such sculptured corbels have few prototypes

catalyst for the Dalmeny portal. The argument is not vitiated by the fact that models were to be found nearer home – in both England and Normandy – inasmuch as I was thinking primarily of the initiatives taken by the patron. But since then I have revised my views on the date of Dalmeny, largely as a result of correspondence with Dr Maylis Baylé. The careful consideration that Dr Baylé has given to my queries is much appreciated.   **45** There is some discussion of the iconography in J.S. Richardson, *The Medieval Stone Carver in Scotland* (Edinburgh, 1964), pp 19–25; *Écosse Romane*, pp 170ff.   **46** A scheme followed in the north portal of the western transept at Kelso Abbey (?*c*.1160).   **47** I am grateful to the Session Clerk, Mr W. Ross, for his endless patience and courtesy during my numerous visits to take photographs.   **48** A little later than Dalmeny, see Cruden, *Scottish Medieval Churches*, p. 132. At Leuchars the four surviving interior corbels encircle the apse in a sequence of alternating beast- and horse-heads. At Dalmeny, five of the eight corbels in the chancel and apse are all of the same

on the interior. The roof-truss heads at Værnes and Mære in Trøndelag, dated to *c*.1150, are one exception but, in both instances, while the heads protrude into the interior space, they decorate the beam ends on either side of the nave and are distanced from the spectator.[49] The cat masks at Durham are remote, puny and tame by comparison with the Dalmeny corbels, so too, are the examples in the nave of the church of St Étienne at Caen (Figures 7.11 & 7.12). At Dalmeny, as at Leuchars, the proximity of these frightening heads to the spectator and their prominence within the sacred space contained by the chancel and the apse is quite extraordinary. What was the inspiration for such a terrifying ensemble? There is surely more than the sculptor's pattern book at issue here.

Culture *and* contacts. Somewhere between 1154 and 1159 Cospatric son of Waltheof is found attesting Malcolm IV's confirmation charter to Dunfermline Abbey.[50] He rubs shoulders there with some familiar names from the king's entourage, including those of Earl Cospatric III of Dunbar, Hugh de Morville, the royal constable, and Philip de Colville. Exceptionally, Robert de Brus does not seem to have been present on this occasion. As Professor Barrow long ago pointed out, it was from Lower or Western Normandy, and particularly the Cotentin, a region to which 'Henry I's lordships and friends belonged', that Scotland's 'Norman' families hailed in the first period of immigration under David I.[51] These were the families who formed the 'west Norman mafia' in the early years of Henry's reign in Judith Green's apt phrase.[52] Kappelle's research has revealed a similar pattern of settlement in 'English' Cumbria.[53] Whether David himself, before he became king, had held land or office in Western Normandy is debatable. Geoffrey Barrow has suggested that David may have been rewarded 'with a small lordship in the Cotentin' in return for his services to his patron, Henry I. If so, the confirmation by David, when he was earl of

type: a monstrous beast-head, more elaborate than those at Leuchars. There is one horse-head, similar to those at Leuchars, and two grotesque face-masks, one a mouth-puller. For comparable examples of the latter see N. Kenaan-Kedar, *Marginal Sculpture in Medieval France* (Scolar Press,1995), pp 16, 18. **49** M. Blindheim, *Norwegian Romanesque Decorative Sculpture 1090–1210* (London, 1965), pp 15–18, figs 33–47. For the suggestion that the idea may have been introduced from abroad and, perhaps, from England, see M. Blindheim, 'The Roof-Truss Heads of the Nave of Vaernes Church in Trondelag, Norway', *Romanesque and Gothic: Essays for George Zarnecki*, ed. by N. Stratford, 2 vols (Woodbridge, 1987), I, p. 17 and n. 12. **50** *Acts of Malcolm IV*, no. 118, p. 185. For the Scandinavian origins of the personal name Waldeve or Waltheof, see S. Taylor, 'The Scandinavians in Fife and Kinross', *Scandinavian Settlement in Northern Britain*, ed. by B.E. Crawford (1995), pp 150–51. **51** G.W.S. Barrow, *The Kingdom of the Scots* (London, 1973), p. 321; see also idem, *The Anglo-Norman Era in Scottish History* (Oxford, 1980), esp. chapter iii, and pp 91, 94–97, 99. **52** J.A. Green, 'Henry I and David I', *SHR*, 75 (1996), p. 2. I am grateful to Professor Green for allowing me to read a copy of this paper before it appeared in print. **53** W.E. Kappelle, *The Norman Conquest of the North* (London, 1979), chapter 7.

7.11 Church of St Étienne, Caen: corbels in the nave. (Photo: Courtauld Institute of Art)

7.12 Durham Cathedral: corbels in the nave. (Photo: The Conway Library, Courtauld Institute of Art)

Huntingdon, of Robert de Brus's grant of Querqueville to St Mary's York becomes more explicable.

Looking at the map of Romanesque monuments in this part of Normandy, the following place name stands out, Scandinavian in its derivation: Tollevast (Map 7.3).[54] First mentioned in Duke Richard II's grant of dower to his wife, Judith of Brittany, c.996–1008,[55] a donation by Robert son of Humphrey of Tollevast to the abbey of Marmoutier in c.1090 suggests that by the late eleventh century Tollevast had passed out of the ducal demesne into the hands of a local lord. Charter evidence shows that the vill and church of Tollevast remained under seigneurial control throughout the twelfth century.[56] Not until

---

54 For the derivation, see J. Adigard des Gautries, *Les noms de personnes scandinaves en Normandie de 911 à 1066* (Lund, 1954), pp 420–21.   55 M. Fauroux, *Recueil des actes des ducs de Normandie de* 911 à 1066, Mémoires de la Société des Antiquaires de Normandie, 36 (Caen, 1961), pp 82–85.   56 Suggested by a charter of Robert son of Humphrey of Tollevast granting the land of one Turgis de Toutfresville to the Abbey of Marmoutier. Undated, and surviving only in seventeenth-century copies, this charter has been published by L. Couppey, 'Encore Héauville. Supplément aux notes historiques sur le prieuré conventuel d'Héauville à la Hague', *Révue catholique de*

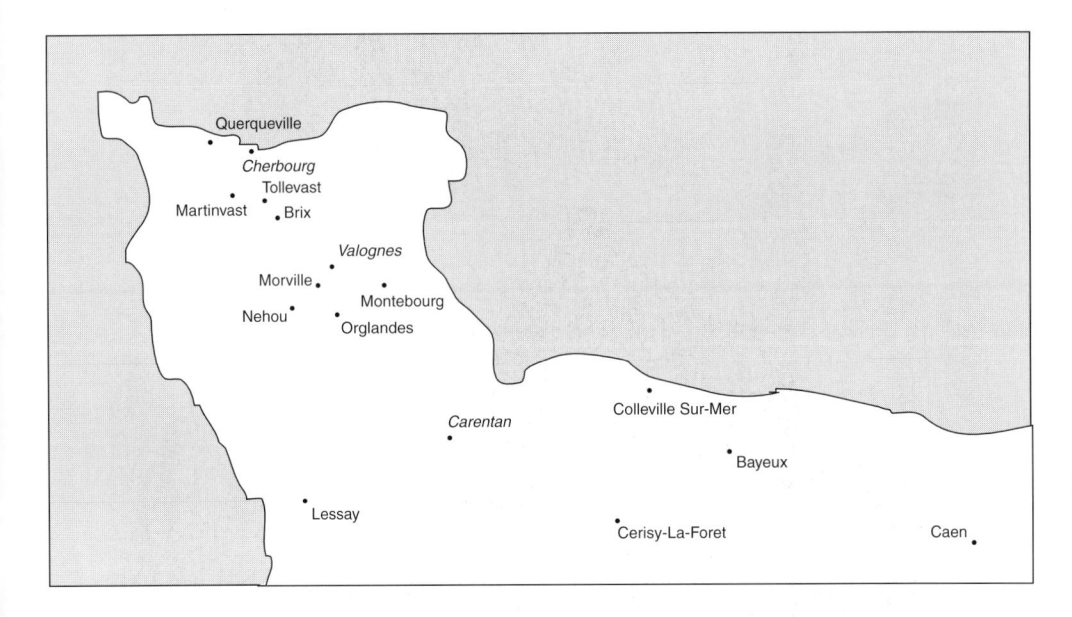

MAP 7.3 Selected sites in the Cotentin. (Drafted by L. Walker; drawn by J. Renny)

1219 was the patronage of the church of Tollevast gifted to the canons of the abbey of Voeu at Cherbourg by Thomas de Tollevast.[57] At Tollevast the church, dated to the first quarter of the twelfth century, is almost as exotic a creation as Dalmeny.[58] In its elevation, seen from the south-east, Tollevast, with its extraordinarily tall central tower, is also reminiscent of St Rule's (Figure 7.13). While, as a toponymic surname, Tollevast has not been found in English sources before the thirteenth century, the village of Tollevast lies less than ten miles south of Querqueville, and it would seem that Querqueville was a place in which both Robert de Brus and David, before he became king, may have had an interest.[59] Tollevast is also only three miles north of Brix from whence the Brus

Normandie, 10 (1900–1901), pp 439–40. A date of *c.*1090 for this gift is supported by J. Adigard des Gautries, *op. cit.*, p. 420 n. 31. I am grateful to M. Jean-Paul Hervieu for sending me a photocopy of the relevant pages from Abbot Couppey's article. **57** Thomas reserved the patronage of his manorial chapel for himself (Archives de la Manche H 3717). The original charter was destroyed in 1944, but a summary of its contents is to be found in the inventory: *Département de la Manche, Archives écclesiastiques*, ser. H, pt. ii (Abbaye de Cherbourg, Saint-Lô, n.d.), p. 620. The grant was confirmed by Hugh de Morville, bishop of Coutances, in 1219 (H 3718). I am indebted to M. Jean Paul Hervieu and M. Claude Pithois for supplying this information. **58** Illustrated in *Normandie Romane*, 2 vols (La Pierre-Qui-Vire, 1967), I, pls. 65–75. **59** See the confirmation by Earl David of Robert de Brus's grant of

7.13 Tollevast Church: view from the south-east (Photo: L. Walker)

family came, and about eight miles north-west of Morville. Coleville-sur-Mer is a little further afield to the south-east, but still in the department of the Manche. Significantly, while Reviers is further to the west in Calvados, the de Redvers' lordship in Normandy centred upon Néhou in the Cotentin, some ten miles south of Tollevast (as the crow flies), and (by 1098, at least) Vernon in the Vexin. Richard de Redvers I (d. 1107) is described by Orderic Vitalis as one of the 'barons of the Cotentin' (*Constantinienses*) who supported Prince Henry in the troubled years of the 1090s.[60] After his accession Henry I rewarded Richard with extensive lands in England, the principal holdings being in Devon, Dorset, Hampshire, and the Isle of Wight.[61] Men with links to the English west country formed a significant element in David's following, and Judith Green has suggested that the de Redvers' lordships in England may have played a pivotal role in this recruitment. Common cross-Channel origins imply that this incursion 'reflected not so much [English] west country recruitment as west Norman recruitment'.[62] While as yet no-one with the name of Tollevast can be shown to have made their way to Scotland, it is in the context of the de Redvers family and the Isle of Wight that the name occurs in English thirteenth-century sources.[63] Interestingly, in the 1220s a Richard de Tolewast is found attesting a confirmation by William de Redvers to the abbey of Montebourg.[64] While

Karkarevil to St Mary's York (1114–24), Lawrie, ESC, no. 52. If we accept the identification of *Karkarevil* as Querqueville (Barrow, *Kingdom of the Scots*, p. 322–23), there remains the question of the capacity in which David confirmed this grant of land in Normandy. As Professor Barrow says, this is 'one of the minor mysteries in the career of David I' (for the suggestion that David may have received a lordship in the Cotentin from Henry I, see Barrow, *Kingdom*, p. 322, also Barrow, *Kingship and Unity* (London, 1981), p. 35). The point is discussed by J.A. Green, 'Henry I and David I', p. 10 n. 49; cf. *The Charters of King David I*, ed. by G.W.S. Barrow (Woodbridge, 1999), p. 53. According to Geoffrey the Fat, David was in Normandy in *c*.1116, visiting the abbey of Tiron, mother house of his foundation at Selkirk, 'Life of Bernard of Tiron', Migne, *Patrologia Latina*, CLXXII, cols 1426–27, cited by J.A. Green, *op. cit.*, p. 8 n. 41.
60 *The Ecclesiastical History of Orderic Vitalis* (hereafter *OV*), ed. by M. Chibnall, 6 vols (Oxford, 1973), IV, p. 220; see further ibid., V, pp 298, 314; compare William of Malmesbury, *De Gestis Regum Anglorum*, ed. by W. Stubbs, 2 vols, Rolls Series (London, 1887–89), II, p. 471.   **61** The later baronies of Plympton, Christchurch and Carisbrooke. For a full discussion of the de Redvers family and its estates in England and Normandy, see *Charters of the de Redvers Family and the Earldom of Devon, 1090–1217*, ed. by R. Bearman, Devon and Cornwall Record Society, n.s. 37 (Exeter, 1994), Introduction, pp 1–51; see also, Barrow, *Anglo-Norman Era*, pp 70–71.
62 'Henry I and David I', p. 13; and see Barrow, *Anglo-Norman Era*, pp 99–105. Alexander de Néhou figures as a witness to two of Alan of Galloway's charters in the early thirteenth century: K.J. Stringer, 'Periphery and Core in Thirteenth-Century Scotland: Alan son of Roland, Lord of Galloway and Constable of Scotland', in *Medieval Scotland: Crown, Lordship and Community*, ed. by A. Grant and K. Stringer (Edinburgh, 1993), pp 99, 108–09, 111; cf. Barrow, *Anglo-Norman Era*, pp 79–80 n. 105.
63 *Book of Fees*, II, 1306.   **64** Cartulary of Montebourg no. 213, Paris BN, lat. 10087,

Richard de Redvers I was not the founder of Montebourg, he was a generous benefactor to the abbey and was buried there.[65] These are facts from which some inferences may be made. Dr Baylé has suggested that the English possessions of the abbey of Montebourg – at Axmouth (Devon), Loders (Dorset) and Weeke (Isle of Wight) – may provide the key to the pronounced Anglo-Norman flavour of the sculptural decoration at Tollevast and Martinvast.[66] I am not implying that we should necessarily look for direct links between Tollevast and Dalmeny, although if we had more information about marriage alliances in this period, such links might be found; rather is it a question of inherited and shared taste and traditions, of milieu and mentalité.[67] Set against this background, the achievements of patrons and artists are better understood; the similarities and differences – one of the fascinations and delights of Romanesque art – thrown into sharp relief.

Anyone who knows Dalmeny and has stood in the nave of the little church at Tollevast, cannot but be struck by the correspondence between the two.[68] Ignoring the rood and the unfortunate furnishings of the high altar at Tollevast, the immediate experience is almost identical. Almost, but not quite. Most importantly, at Tollevast the apse is covered by a semi-dome; in the absence of ribs there are no corbels to encircle the most sacred space. And at Tollevast the eight great corbel heads which carry the ribs of the choir vaults are less homogeneous than at Dalmeny. As a result of this variation in locus and subject matter the effect is less dramatic; to my mind it also spells a difference in function; a difference too in the predominant cultural strands, and perhaps in forms of patronage as well. There is a moralising tendency at Tollevast, which culminates in the last of the series of corbels on the right at the entrance to the apse: an aureoled figure rescuing a giant-sized human enmeshed like Laocoon in the toils of a serpent (Figure 7.14). For this there is no counterpart at Dalmeny, although a beast-head from Tollevast would be a little more at home there (Figure 7.15).

In this comparison between Dalmeny and Tollevast the wheel has come full circle. Even as Abercorn provided the starting point for this discussion, so with the ideas sparked off by those monuments first seen in that dusty crypt at

p. 89: kindly communicated by Dr K.S.B. Keats-Rohan.   65 *OV*, VI, p. 146 and n. 2.
66 M. Baylé, 'Remarques sur les ateliers de sculpture dans le Cotentin 1100–1150', *Romanesque and Gothic*, I, p. 12.   67 A question also of the distinction between concept and realisation. Compare T. Garton, 'The Transitional Sculpture of Jedburgh Abbey', *Romanesque and Gothic*, I, p. 81: 'Other influences [upon the sculptural decoration at Jedburgh] from the south of England are chiefly a matter of ideas and iconography rather than style, and do not imply the presence of masons or sculptors from the south of England, but rather a patron or sculptor who had seen work in the south of England.' A similar argument may be applied to the work of the 'Herefordshire School' of sculpture.
68 Whilst I have long been interested in Dalmeny, it was the late Professor R.J. Adam who first pointed my footsteps in the direction of Tollevast in a review (n.d.) of S. Cruden,

7.14, 7.15 Tollevast Church: interior corbels. (Photo: L. Walker)

Culture and Contacts in the Scottish Romanesque

7.16 Pictish grave-marker: Meigle Museum, Perthshire, no. 26. (See J. Romilly Allen, *The Early Christian Monuments of Scotland* (Edinburgh, 1903), Pt. III, Fig.318A, facing p. 304.)

Abercorn does my paper end: hogbacks, that legacy of Viking colonialism again. While, sadly, the Abercorn hogbacks do not have the heads of animals as supporters, those on the island of Inchcolm and at Brechin do. So, also, does the Pictish grave marker from Meigle in Perthshire where the slot – perhaps containing a relic or a cross – is held between the jaws of two wild beasts (Figure 7.16). What are such frightening heads doing in these examples? What is their role? Much the same, I would suggest, as that of their counterparts on the Dalmeny corbels. At Dalmeny the various elements in our Scottish culture surface once again. There is much in the Oseberg find that would seem relevant

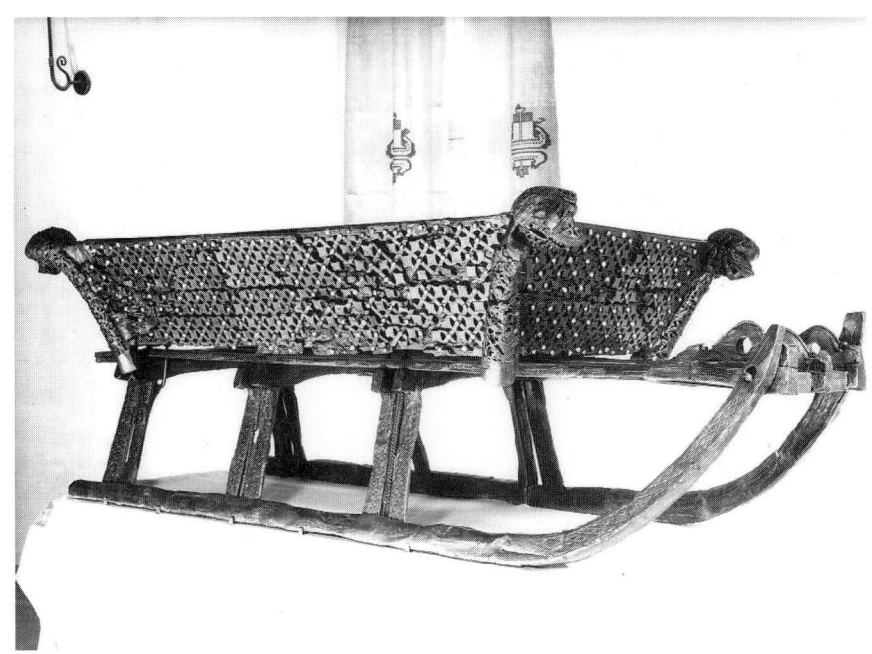

7.17, 7.18 Carved animal-head posts from the Oseberg ship burial. (Photo: University Museum of Cultural Heritage, Oslo)

here: in particular, the fearsome animal-head posts, so superbly carved (Figures 7.17 & 7.18). If grave furniture from a ninth-century burial ship seems too far a cry from Dalmeny and Tollevast, the hogbacks, together with ties of kinship and affinity may provide a link. The region round Tollevast is replete with Scandinavian place names. Bizarre although the Dalmeny corbels may seem to us, and out of place in a Christian setting, their function would seem not dissimilar from that of the spiral columns at Dunfermline, Durham – and at Rome: to define and to protect the sacred space.[69]

Scottish Medieval Churches (Edinburgh, 1986), citing *Écosse Romane* (1985). **69** I should like to add a post-script. After I had completed my paper, I came across an article by Siv Kristoffersen which seemed to me to reinforce the argument ('Transformation in Migration Period Animal Art', *Norwegian Archaeological Review*, 28 (1995), pp 1–15). At the risk of seeming to flirt with the structural anthropologists, I would cite one passage. Comparing the Germanic animal art of the Migration Period with that of the art of the Northwest Coast Indians in the eighteenth and nineteenth centuries, Kristoffersen gives this quotation from Lévi-Strauss, *Structural Anthropology* (1963), p. 261: 'The painted chests of Northwest Coast art are not merely containers embellished with a painted or carved animal. They are the animal itself, keeping an active watch over the ceremonial ornaments which have been entrusted to its care.' In the same way, Kristoffersen suggests, within the Germanic modes of thought, the brooch decorated with animals, or animals with human heads, was transformed and given superhuman strength and ability to watch over the wearer. To those versed in the literature of the sagas such metamorphosis is a familiar concept.

Seafaring and Trade in East Fife

COLIN J.M. MARTIN

Since remote prehistory the inhabitants of what is now Fife, that triangular peninsula poised between the great estuaries of Forth and Tay on Scotland's east coast, have been mariners. Perhaps as many as eight thousand years ago mesolithic hunter-gatherers were venturing into the unpredictable waters of the North Sea, for the remains of a seasonal camp-site at Morton, encapsulated in wind-blown dunes to the north of St Andrews, have yielded to archaeologists the bones of fish which could only have been caught in deep water.[1]

The craft they used were almost certainly dug-outs or skin boats. Such vessels have been widely used by traditional maritime societies from the earliest times, and are found in many places today. Dug-out vessels (in their basic form no more than hollowed-out logs) are not well suited to the open sea, and were probably confined to estuaries and inland waters. An example found at Friarton, on the Tay Estuary near Perth, has been dated by its geological context to *c.*8,000 bp.[2] Skin boats, on the other hand, can be wonderfully seaworthy vessels, as their still-functioning descendants, the tarred-canvas *curraghs* of western Ireland, amply testify. There are several early historical references to such craft in Scottish waters, and it was in a skin-covered *curragh* that St Columba sailed from Ireland to Iona. Though their fragile nature militates against preservation in archaeological contexts the 'ghost' of what may have been one has been recognized in a Bronze Age burial at Dalgety Bay, Fife.[3] Vessels of this kind were still in use on the River Spey in the late eighteenth century, the last one now being preserved in the Elgin Museum.[4]

Between the late first and early third centuries AD Roman shipping was active in this area.[5] Tacitus' account of campaigning against the tribes north of the Forth by his father-in-law, Julius Agricola, lays special stress on the efficacy of the fleet:

---

1 J.M. Coles, 'The Early Settlement of Scotland', *Proceedings of the Prehistoric Society*, 37.2 (1971), pp 284–366.   2 I.A. Morrison, *Landscape with Lake Dwellings* (Edinburgh, 1985), p. 56.   3 T. Watkins, 'A Prehistoric Coracle in Fife', *International Journal of Nautical Archaeology*, 9.4 (1980), pp 277–86.   4 J. Hornell, 'British Coracles', *Mariners' Mirror*, 22 (1936), p. 299 and pl. I, fig. 2.   5 C.J.M. Martin, 'Water Transport and the

The war was pushed forwards simultaneously by land and sea; and infantry, cavalry, and marines, often meeting in the same camp, would meet and make merry together. They would boast, as soldiers will, of victories on land against the conquest of the ocean. The Britons, for their part, were stupefied by the appearance of the fleet. The mystery of their sea was divulged, their last retreat cut off.[6]

This pattern was evidently repeated by the campaigns of the emperor Septimius Severus from 208 to 211, in which massive armies roamed destructively across Fife and along north-east Scotland's fertile coastlands as far as the Moray Firth. They appear to have been provisioned almost entirely by sea.[7] Given the scale of these activities it is inconceivable that no Roman ships were wrecked in Scottish waters. None has yet been found, though the remains of Spanish amphorae of second century date found in a cave near Fife Ness are perhaps best explained as recoveries from a shipwreck on the nearby Carr Rocks.[8]

By the medieval period trade between eastern Scotland and continental Europe was flourishing, with activity centred on ports such as Berwick, Leith, Perth, Dundee, and Aberdeen.[9] The exported commodities were mainly raw materials – sheepskins, raw wool, hides, and fish. Imports included textiles, wine, and manufactured goods. Continental pottery provides an indelible marker of such contacts, and a wide range of ceramics from the Baltic to western France characterizes many Scottish urban archaeological sites.[10] We have little direct evidence of the ships by which this trade was conducted, but the excavation of medieval levels in Perth have yielded fragments of clinker-built boats, some of them quite large,[11] while a fine example of the ubiquitous cog which dominated North Sea trade in the later medieval period has been recovered almost intact from the River Weser outside Bremen.[12]

Pilgrimage was another major plank in the region's economy, just as tourism is today. Ecclesiastical centres like St Andrews, or the shrine of St Margaret at Dunfermline, were perennially popular, but so too were less well-known destinations such as the Isle of May, close to the mouth of the Forth. Here recent excavations have uncovered the remains of the Benedictine priory founded in the 1140s by David I to commemorate the martyrdom of a local

---

Roman Occupations of North Britain', in *Scotland and the Sea*, ed. by T.C. Smout (Edinburgh, 1992), pp 1–34.   6 Tacitus, *Agricola*, 25, trans. by H. Mattingly, *Tacitus on Britain and Germany* (London, 1948), p. 75.   7 Martin, 'Water Transport', pp 25–28.   8 A.J.B. Wace and Professor Jehu, 'Cave Excavations in East Fife', *Proceedings of the Society of Antiquaries of Scotland* (hereafter *PSAS*), 49 (1915), pp 233–55.   9 P. Yeoman, *Medieval Scotland* (London, 1995), pp 69–71.   10 Ibid. p. 70.   11 C.J.M. Martin, *Scotland's Historic Shipwrecks* (London, 1998), pp 110–11.   12 D. Elmers, 'The Cog as a Cargo Carrier', in *Cogs, Caravels and Galleons: the sailing ship 1000–1650*, ed. by R.W. Unger (London, 1994), pp 29–35.

saint and his followers, reputedly slain by Vikings in the ninth century.[13] Among the discoveries there was the fifteenth-century grave of a young man who had been buried with a scallop shell in his mouth, indicating that he had made the pilgrimage to Santiago de Compostella.

During the sixteenth and seventeenth centuries the mercantile burghs of Fife, poised between the trade routes of the North Sea and the firths which gave access to the great seaports of Leith and Dundee, were flourishing centres of international commerce.[14] These dynamic little towns, nestling along the northern shores of the Forth, were once described by James VI as the 'fringe of gold' which surrounded the 'beggar's mantle' of Fife's dour interior. Some, like Crail (Figure 8.1), enjoyed trading privileges rooted in royal charters issued in medieval times while others, such as Pittenweem and Anstruther, had obtained their royal burghal status more recently. Yet others – Elie is a good example – enjoyed no royal patronage, but still produced resourceful merchant adventurers whose seafaring endeavours took them deep into the Baltic and as far south as Bordeaux.

Such was the volume of traffic entering the Forth by the 1620s and 30s that a coal-burning lighthouse was erected on the Isle of May in 1636 (Figure 8.2) to provide a leading light for vessels approaching the firth.[15] A toll was levied on shipping to maintain it. The beacon was replaced by the present light in 1816, and would have been demolished altogether had not one of the Commissioners of the Northern Lighthouse Board been Sir Walter Scott, who insisted that its lower storey be preserved. Happily this part still survives, albeit capped by a romantic crenellated roof which was added in 1886.

Crail's ascendancy as a seaport was eclipsed in the seventeenth century by its great rival Pittenweem. This harbour town is on record as a seaport in 1228, and was erected as a royal burgh in 1541. A confirmation charter was issued by Charles I in 1633.[16] The burgh's main activity was continental trade, based on exporting the products of its agricultural hinterland and of the coal and salt industries along its coastal fringe. Because the market potential of its own sparsely populated hinterland was slight, most of the return cargoes of timber, ironwork, wine and manufactured goods found their way to Dundee or Leith. Pittenweem thus enjoyed dynamic trading links with continental Europe and with its own national capital. Throughout the later sixteenth century and for the first four decades of the seventeenth the town was extremely prosperous.

The diversity of trading contacts enjoyed by Pittenweem skippers during this period has been demonstrated recently by archaeological excavation in a

---

13 Yeoman, pp 21–28.   **14** T.C. Smout, *Scottish Trade on the Eve of Union, 1660–1707* (Edinburgh and London, 1963), pp 136–42.   **15** W.J. Eggeling, *The Isle of May* (Edinburgh and London, 1960), pp 33–37.   **16** A. Graham, 'Archaeological Notes on Some Harbours in Eastern Scotland' *PSAS*, 101 (1971), pp 263–64.

Seafaring and Trade in East Fife

8.1 The modern town of Crail retains much of its medieval character. It focuses on the harbour, behind which (centre right) stood the castle, now demolished. The parish church can be seen top left. At centre-left is the High Street, with its triangular marketplace now filled with a central spine of houses. Beyond the High Street the road broadens into the Marketgate, with the Tolbooth at its lower right-hand corner. A second market place is evident above the site of the castle. The Nethergate extends beyond it. Much of the pattern of the medieval property strips, or rigs, can still be discerned in the garden boundaries. (Photo: Colin Martin)

8.2 The surviving lower storey of the original coal-burning lighthouse on the Isle of May, built in 1636. The crenellated roof is a nineteenth-century addition. (Photo: Colin Martin)

garden immediately behind the crescent of houses fringing the harbour.[17] Here a rich deposit of broken crockery was revealed, tipped onto the surface of an abandoned roadway. Material associated with the deposit, including three coins of Charles I, suggested that it had been dumped around 1635–40. Much of the pottery is exotic, and the origins of the varied types span most of Europe's western seaboard. There are north German and Scandinavian cooking wares, salt-glazed stonewares from the Rhineland, decorated delftwares, and pottery from northern, central, and western France. The latter includes polychromes from the workshops at Saintes, near Bordeaux, associated with the famous mid-sixteenth-century potter Bernard Pallissy.[18] Iberian sources are represented too, with fragments of olive jars made at Seville and a couple of sherds of Hispano-Moresque lustreware from Valencia on the Mediterranean coast of Spain.

17 C.J.M. Martin, 'A Group of Pipes from Mid Shore, Pittenweem', in *The Archaeology of the Clay Tobacco Pipe. X. Scotland*, ed. by P. Davey, BAR British Series 178 (Oxford, 1987), pp 183–209.   18 J.G. Hurst, 'Sixteenth- and Seventeenth-century Imported Pottery from the Saintonge', in *Medieval Pottery from Excavations*, ed. by V.I. Evison,

The character of this material suggests that it was derived from a collection built up over a century or more, and that it came from a household whose members enjoyed extensive continental trading links. It is not unreasonable to suppose that its sudden deposition followed a major clear-out, perhaps connected with the development of housing along the shore which the circumstances of the roadway's abandonment implies.

Amongst the deposit were large numbers of clay tobacco pipes. Smoking had gained currency in Scotland during the reign of James VI and I, whose *Counterblasts to Tobacco* of 1604 represent the first recorded government warning against smoking, in which the king rails at the evils of 'ane weade soe infective as all young and ydill personis are in a manner bewitchit thairwith, the taking whereof being a special motive to their often meitingis in tavernis and alehousis'. All the pipes found in the deposit of imported continental pottery at Pittenweem appear to be Dutch, with one exception. This bears the mark 'W B', which can be identified as that of William Banks, who was probably Scotland's first licensed pipemaker. He was active in Edinburgh from 1622.[19] In spite of his self-proclaimed monopoly, cargoes of Dutch pipes were still coming into the Forth as late as 1635, when a Dundee barque freighting goods bought in Holland and Zeeland was wrecked near Dunbar. Among the goods plundered by local people were 'one thousand pound weight of tobacco and seven barrell pypes'.[20] During the same decade, however, there is evidence of a growing domestic industry, manifested by a challenge to the Banks monopoly which reached its climax in 1642.[21] Dutch imports are unlikely to have continued far into the 1640s, when political and economic pressures must finally have killed them off. This is reinforced by the dominance of Scottish pipes in the upper levels of the Pittenweem deposit, and by the generally poor standard of manufacture and finish which they display.[22]

This evidence reinforces the conclusion that the imported pottery and Dutch pipes were tipped onto the abandoned road surface at Pittenweem towards the end of the decade 1630–40. That the event was related to structural development along the foreshore seems beyond question, and it is tempting to suggest that Charles I's charter of 1633, which alludes to the burgh's 'reid, port, heavin and harberie', provided an impetus for these changes. Social habits were changing too, and for all the crown's strictures against smoking the habit was certainly a popular one in Pittenweem by 1634. In that year John MacFarlane was granted a licence to trade as a tobacconist in the town.[23] By then his business was already well established, and may indeed have been functioning for

H. Hodges and J.G. Hurst (London, 1974), pp 221–55. **19** *Register of the Privy Council of Scotland* (hereafter *RPCS*), xiv, Addenda, 1545–1625 (Edinburgh, 1898), p. 589. **20** Ibid. Second series, vi, 1635–1637 (Edinburgh, 1905), pp 241–41. **21** Ibid. Second series vii, 1644–1680 (Edinburgh, 1906), pp 324–25. **22** Martin, 'A Group of Pipes'. **23** D. Cook, *Annals of Pittenweem* (Anstruther, 1867), pp 21–22.

some time, since the application was a response to Charles I's Act of 19 April 1634, which introduced controls on the existing tobacco trade, including licensing.[24]

Pittenweem's prosperity was abruptly curtailed by the effects of the Covenant and the Civil War. In 1637 the burgh and harbour were fortified.[25] Trade ceased abruptly, and by 1640 the town's merchant fleet lay 'wrackit at the full sea'.[26] Five years later more than fifty Pittenweem men, most of them mariners, perished in the battle of Kilsyth.[27] Economic decline was exacerbated by failed crops and the outbreak of plague.

The brief period of Commonwealth government imposed on Scotland in the 1650s did little to reverse the decline. Thomas Tucker, an English official sent by Cromwell to assess Scotland's customs revenue in 1656, recorded only two ships at Pittenweem, though at 80 and 100 tons these were relatively large. In the same report Crail musters only one vessel, while Anstruther's merchant fleet of ten small vessels had an average size of only 23 tons apiece.[28]

Following the Restoration in 1660 (Charles II had visited the East Neuk in 1651, and had been feasted with 'some great buns') much of the area's former prosperity returned. Pittenweem remained the dominant harbour, and in 1667 John Cook, who almost certainly lived in the Gyles, a fine merchant's house which still stands at the harbour head (Figure 8.3), took his ship the *James of Pittenweem* as far afield as Tangiers. Five years later he voyaged to Cadiz, as did another Pittenweem skipper, James Acheson of the *Anna*.

Our knowledge of the individuals who made these voyages, and the commercial mechanisms by which they operated, is largely fragmentary, based as it is on the few administrative records which have survived.[29] An exception is the mercantile career of Alexander Gillespie of Elie, whose *Journal* of trading voyages between 1662 and 1685 has recently come to light. This important document, of which no contemporary parallel is known, runs to seventy-four closely written manuscript pages, and is now in the archives of St Andrews University Library (MS 38352). It provides a unique account of a working seventeenth century merchant skipper's career.

Gillespie was born into a seafaring family, and in his early years (we may presume) he was bound to a master – almost certainly a close relative – to learn seafaring skills and the business of commerce 'as weel without as within the country', as the indentures of Thomas Russell, a merchant apprentice from Alloa, were to put it a few years later.[30] This no doubt involved voyaging to

---

24 *RPCS*, Second series, v, 1633–1635 (Edinburgh, 1904), pp 271–73.   25 Cook, *Annals*, pp 31 and 35.   26 Ibid. p. 53.   27 Ibid. pp 54–55.   28 'Report by Thomas Tucker upon the Settlement of the Revenues of Excise and customs in Scotland, AD MDCLVI', in *Miscellany of the Scottish Burgh Records Society* (Edinburgh, 1881).   29 Smout, *Scottish Trade on the Eve of Union*.   30 T.C. Smout, *A History of the Scottish People* (London, 1969), p. 154.

8.3 Seventeenth-century merchants' houses on the Pittenweem waterfront. The property on the right, known as the Gyles, probably belonged to John Cook, who traded as far as Tangiers in the 1660s. (Photo: Colin Martin)

Norway, the Baltic, London, Holland, and Bordeaux, learning to navigate the routes he would follow in later life and fitting himself into the complex web of contacts and personal relationships upon which a successful mercantile career depended.

In 1663, by which time he appears to have been a well-established skipper, he married into another Elie merchant family. Christian Small was the heiress to a local estate, and it seems likely that it was for her benefit that the *Journal*, which Alexander began while off the Texel on 19 April 1662, was written. Christian was almost certainly an equal partner in the business, running its affairs ashore. Two centuries later women were to take part in managing the burgeoning fishing industry of the East Neuk ports, for it was they who stayed at home to look after the businesses while their menfolk were at sea. It seems likely that the merchants' wives of the seventeenth century played a similar role. Gillespie frequently refers to letters he sent back to Elie from ports along his routes, and if the dour and unimaginative writing style which characterizes the *Journal* is anything to go by these are unlikely to have been of a romantic or trivial nature. Much more probably they concerned the couple's extensive and wide-ranging business affairs. The *Journal* may itself be seen as a running account of Alexander's contribution to their joint partnership.

His voyages, though apparently driven by opportunistic tramping, show evidence of seasonal patterns and of response to wider political and economic influences. From 1662 to 1667 his activities were largely confined to the North Sea, though there was one trip in 1663 to Bordeaux and another in 1667 to Nantes. Both were timed for late in the year to catch the first vintage. The other voyages traversed the North Sea rim touching Norway, London, and the Netherlands. Trips to Holland were curtailed between 1665 and 1667 by the Second Dutch War, when he wisely stuck to home waters with trips to Orkney and the west coast of Scotland. Outward cargoes to the continent included grain, salt, and coal, while his return loads usually consisted of timber and iron.

Although no details are given about the size of Gillespie's ship, the *Anna of Elie*, she was able to deliver 85 tuns of Dysart coal to London in 1668. The same year saw his first recorded venture into the Baltic, when he passed through the Danish Sound on 25 March bound for Danzig and Konigsberg. Most of the voyages ended at Leith, Edinburgh's great *entrepôt*, where details of some of Gillespie's return cargoes survive in the customs records. On a later trip from Danzig, for instance, he brought back lint, skins, wax, barrel-staves, steel, and linen-making equipment. Another entry records a cargo from London in 1674, which included silk, fine fabrics, falconry equipment, gum arabic, indigo, pewter, barrel hoops, tobacco, cheeses, raisins, figs, ginger, dates, glass beads, shovels, aniseed, Brazil wood, galls, garden seeds, grey paper, hops, and wool cards.

After 1668 his incursions into the Baltic are frequent, and the wine run to Bordeaux becomes an almost annual event. Gillespie usually arrived there by the end of September, and spent a month or so assembling his cargo. This was evidently a protracted though doubtless agreeable business which involved first-hand negotiations with the wine producers. The wine was normally unloaded at Leith before the end of the year, in time to cash in on Scotland's traditional festive season. On three occasions he was able to make a further trip for the second vintage, leaving early in the New Year and returning to Leith in March or April. This evidently lucrative routine was broken only by the Third Dutch War, in 1672–4.

In June 1676 Gillespie took passage to Rotterdam in a brother skipper's vessel, and stayed there for six months to supervise the building of his new ship, the *James*. This was evidently larger than her predecessor, and cargoes upwards of 118 tuns are later recorded in her hold. No evidence of her type is on record, but she was almost certainly of *fluit* build. This ubiquitous Dutch cargo ship, with its round-tucked stern and steep tumblehome (supposedly to minimize the Danish Sound tolls at Elsinore, which were based on the beam at deck level), was the workhorse of North Sea trading throughout the century.[31] *Fluits*

---

31 R.W. Unger, 'The *Fluit*: Specialist Cargo Vessels 1500 to 1650', in *Cogs, Caravels and Galleons*, pp 115–30.

Seafaring and Trade in East Fife

8.4 A Fife merchant ship, depicted on the tombstone of Robert Ford of Kilrenny (d. 1672). The vessel shows the distinctive characteristics of a Dutch *fluit*, and is apparently unarmed. A navigational cross-staff is shown on the right, while the circle on the left probably represents a mariner's compass. (Photo: Colin Martin)

combined seaworthiness and reliability with a capacious hold and the ability to operate with a small crew – typically five or six men. Just such a ship is represented on the tombstone in Kilrenny churchyard of the East Neuk skipper Robert Ford, who died in 1672 (Figure 8.4).

During the final nine years recorded by his *Journal* Alexander Gillespie made a trip to Rotterdam almost every spring, usually followed by a run to the Emmies Islands on the southern coast of Norway. This triangular trip was probably extremely profitable, for he would have been able to convert the raw materials brought as outward cargo from Scotland into low-bulk manufactured goods from Holland which could be sold at high mark-ups in Norway and Scotland. Any spare capacity for the final leg of the voyage, from the Emmies Islands back to Scotland, could be taken up by a load of Norwegian timber. Gillespie was normally home by late summer, in good time for the wine run to Bordeaux.

Specific cargoes carried by the *James* are listed in a number of customs returns. At Leith in 1674/5, for example, she landed goods from Bordeaux which included, in addition to her staple cargo of wine, chestnuts, brandy, vinegar, prunes, tobacco, walnuts, soap, confections, hams, and paper. Rotterdam (and to a lesser extent London) provided manufactured items such as furniture, brushes, pottery, glassware, playing cards, fashionable clothing, and paintings.

Much of Gillespie's *Journal* records pilotage observations, clearly with the intention of expanding and updating his already intimate knowledge of the waters in which he navigated. He makes no mention of charts, while the only instruments to which he refers are the compass, lead-line, and sand-glass. Apparently working from nothing more than personal experience and these basic aids, Gillespie's achievements seem little short of miraculous. During twenty-one years of intensive sailing in some of the world's most difficult coastal waters he never suffered a serious mishap, and always seems to have reached his intended destinations. His method, as revealed in the *Journal*, was to minimize sea time and maximize safety by staying in harbour – for weeks if need be – until optimum conditions for the next leg prevailed. It was a canny blend of caution and determined enterprise, and it brought profitable returns.

For all that, his life at sea was not without danger. The weather could not always be predicted, landmarks might be missed or mistakenly identified, and pilotage in unfamiliar waters sometimes led to groundings. Human predation was also endemic in the seventeenth century North Sea, and on three occasions Gillespie was accosted by pirates. The first instance was in September 1674, when an Ostend privateer intercepted him off Ushant and demanded a hogshead of beer. A year later, near Jersey, the ship was 'plondered with ane caper', while in 1676, off the east coast of England, Gillespie and two fellow-skippers were forced to pay £5 scots (one-twelfth of the sterling equivalent) to another pirate. These modest demands, though no doubt irritating enough to the victims at the time, sound more like those of a well-established protection racket than the ruthless buccaneering of popular legend.

How far beyond 1685 Alexander Gillespie's seafaring career may have continued, if at all, is not known, for in that year the *Journal* ends. But in 1682 he built a substantial town house in the heart of Elie, and around its front door he erected a monumental edifice with doric columns and a scrolled pediment which contained his family crest, a sundial, the date, and the initials of himself and Christian Small. Though the house was demolished long ago Gillespie's doorway was incorporated into the more modest residence which replaced it, and still survives as a local curiosity called the 'Muckle Yett'. It is a fitting monument to a formidable and successful maritime partnership which ended more than three centuries ago, and it is to be hoped that behind it Alexander and Christian enjoyed the fruits of a well-earned retirement.

The Cult of St Fillan in Scotland[1]

SIMON TAYLOR

No age in Scotland has probably ever had more than its fair share of men and women of exceptional virtue or high moral stature who within Christendom are usually referred to as saints. However, if we were to judge by traditions, commemorations and place-names alone, we would be forgiven for thinking that in one age more than in any other saints had abounded. Such a golden age is often described by that much abused and overworked adjective 'Celtic', not only because it was a period when Celtic languages were spoken throughout much of what constitutes modern Scotland, but also because many of the saints bear Celtic (Gaelic, Pictish or Cumbric) names, and are therefore of insular origin, as opposed to the saints' cults which were imported from the Continent and the Near East.

The period in question, when most of the men and women flourished who have left their commemorative traces throughout Scotland, is an extension of the so-called 'Age of Saints' in Ireland: from the early sixth to the early eighth century AD. It is not the remit of this chapter to explore what lay behind the social, political and religious circumstances of this period. It is of course necessary to distinguish between the actual lives and activities of these saints on the one hand and on the other their invocation in the form of commemorations and place-names, which can arise many centuries after they lived, and many miles from the lands they saw while alive. However, as a general rule, it can be said that the less important or famous a saint, the more likely it is that

---

[1] Many people have contributed helpful ideas and suggestions to the following piece of work: the longer it lay unpublished, the longer the list grew! I would like to express my thanks to Dr Marjorie Anderson, Dr Steven Boardman, Rev. James Bruce, Dr Thomas Clancy, Dr Barbara Crawford, Mr Mark Hall, Dr Alan Macquarrie, Dr Michael Penman, Ms Morag Redford and Professor Richard Sharpe. All errors are, needless to say, entirely my responsibility. Thanks are due also to Mr Niall Robertson for permission to print Figure 3; to Mr Jim Renny for his valuable work on the maps; and to Sue and John Wyllie, formerly of Kirkton of Strath Fillan, now of Killin, for their hospitality and encouragement. Finally I would like to thank the Anderson Research Fellowship, which has supported me during the writing of this chapter.

dedications or place-names containing that saint's name point to genuine early association.[2]

This exploration of the cult of St Fáelán (or Fillan as he is known in Scots and English, Faolàn in modern Scottish Gaelic), as expressed in dedications and place-names, as well as in medieval martyrologies and legend, is offered as an example of the complexities, and frustrations, involved in the study of saints' cults in Scotland. The tenuous nature of the evidence, and therefore of the general conclusions, will be obvious throughout, and this situation is typical of saints' commemorations in every part of the country.

Map (9.1) shows the distribution of all those places in Scotland which point to a local cult of Fillan, expressed as a place-name, a church dedication, or a fair-day. The map is accompanied by a Key which gives full historical information about each of these commemorations (Appendix 2).

The most notable feature of this distribution is the complete absence of any trace of Fillan's cult in the North-East, as well as in the old province of Moray. The only one north of the Great Glen is Killilan, Kintail ROS. As I will argue later, this dearth of Fillan-commemorations in the north may reflect later medieval power politics more than any activities of the early medieval Church.

The next type of evidence is derived from liturgical texts such as martyrologies, calendars and breviaries. By far the most important is the *Aberdeen Breviary*, the first book printed in Scotland (1509 and 1510). It was compiled under the supervision of William Elphinstone, bishop of Aberdeen 1483–1514, and contains the lives of many Scottish saints, in the form of *Lectiones* ('readings') for their feast-days. It drew on various sources, both written and oral, from many parts of Scotland. The written sources it used consisted mainly of *Vitae* ('Lives') or *Legenda* of saints, scarcely any of which have survived.[3] However, preliminary research into sources by Alan Macquarrie suggests tentatively that where the *Breviary* compilers had earlier materials on which to draw, these are often as early as the twelfth century or even earlier.[4] No consistent attempt was made to harmonize different legends, as the following study of Fillan and the two related saints, Kentigerna and Conganus (Comgán), will show. Before looking more closely at the story of St Fillan as told by the *Aberdeen Breviary*, however, I want to survey the written evidence which existed in both Scotland and Ireland before 1500.

[2] See S. Taylor, 'Seventh-century Iona abbots in Scottish place-names', in *Spes Scotorum Hope of the Scots*, ed. by D. Broun and T.O. Clancy (Edinburgh, 1999), pp 35–70, at p. 35; also M.O. Anderson, 'Columba and other Irish Saints in Scotland', in *Historical Studies*, 5, ed. by J.L. McCracken (London, 1965), pp 26–36, at p. 27.   [3] For a good discussion of the sources and of the methods of compilation of the *Aberdeen Breviary* (*Breviarium Aberdonense*, Bannatyne, Maitland and Spalding Clubs, 1854), see D. McRoberts, 'A Legendary-Fragment in the Scottish Record Office', *Innes Review*, 19 (1968), pp 82–83; A. Macquarrie, *The Saints of Scotland* (Edinburgh, 1997), pp 6–9.
[4] Macquarrie, *Saints*, p. 9.

The Cult of St Fillan in Scotland 177

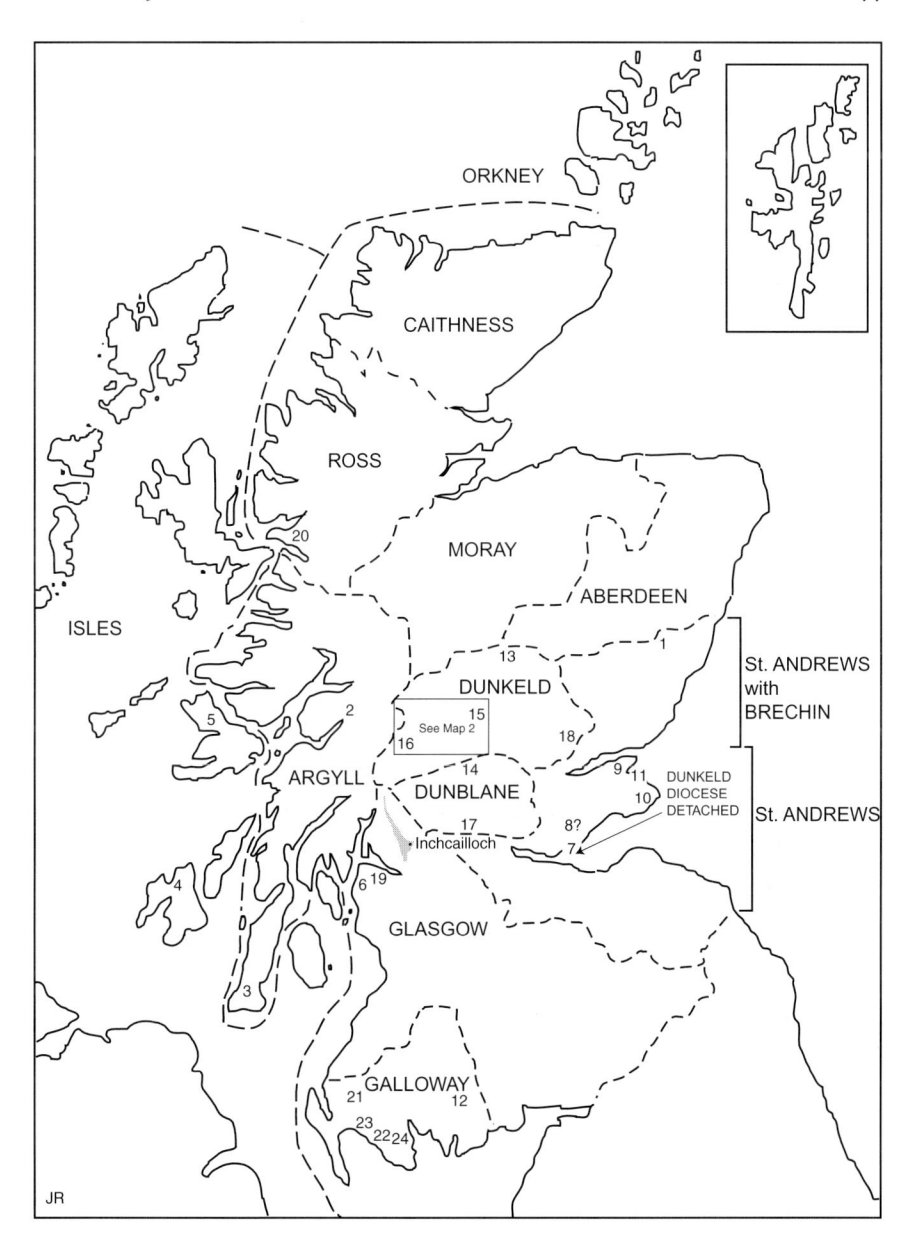

MAP 9.1 (Showing the dioceses of Scotland *c.*1300.) Each number represents a place or cluster of places indicating a local cult of Fillan, expressed as a place-name, a church dedication, or a fair-day. A full key to these numbers can be found in Appendix 2 Note that no. 18 (the medieval parish of Luncarty) lay in the diocese of St Andrews. (Drafted by S. Taylor; drawn by J. Renny)

Our earliest reference to the seventeen or eighteen Irish saints called Fáelán is found in the Martyrology of Tallaght (hereafter M.T.), the best version of which is preserved in the Book of Leinster, a codex copied in the late twelfth century.[5] In their 1931 edition of M.T. Best and Lawlor state that the Book of Leinster recension represents 'in substance the original compilation',[6] which itself can be dated to 828x33.[7] In fact, Best and Lawlor, followed by Ó Riain, see nothing to contradict Máel Muire Ó Gormáin's statement (1166x74) that it was from M.T. that Óengus derived his own martyrology, itself written in verse 828x33, the *Félire Óengussa* or Martyrology of Óengus (hereafter M.O.).[8]

Two of these saints called Fáelán were later particularly commemorated in Scotland, one on 9 January, one on 20 June. Under 9 January M.T. has (heading the list of Irish saints): Fáelán of Clúain Móescna. This same saint is also commemorated in M.T. under 26 August, where a marginal note adds that Clúain Móescna (Kylmisken) is in Meath, in Fartullagh (now in Co. Westmeath).[9] The notes on M.O.[10] contain similar information, adding that his church was Calue in Huí Tortain, which cannot be further identified, but the Uí Tortain are located near Ardbraccan, Meath, two miles west of Navan.[11] Apart from the date of his commemoration (9 January), there is nothing to connect this Fillan with Scotland.

Under 20 June M.T. has the feast of 'Faelain amlabair i Sraith Eret[12] i n Albain' (Fillan the dumb in Strathearn in Scotland), while Óengus at the same date calls him 'Fáelán ... in t-amlabar ánsin' (Fillan that splendid mute).[13] M.T. explicitly links him with Scotland, and this same statement is repeated in various forms in the notes on M.O., as well as in several other later martyrologies. The source of this information would seem to have originated in M.T., and therefore

---

5 The MS text of M.T. is included in vol. 6 of the *Book of Leinster*, the final volume of the Bergin and Best edition, ed. by A. O'Sullivan (Dublin,1983), pp 1596–1648; on the *Book of Leinster* see *The Martyrology of Tallaght*, ed. by R.I. Best and H.J. Lawlor, Henry Bradshaw Society 68 (London, 1931), pp xii–xiii; J.F. Kenney, *The Sources for the Early History of Ireland: Ecclesiastical* (New York, 1929; repr. 1966), pp 15, 65. 6 Best and Lawlor, p. xx. 7 P. Ó Riain, 'The Tallaght Martyrologies, Redated', *Cambridge Medieval Celtic Studies*, 20 (1990), p. 38 et passim. 8 Best and Lawlor, p. xx; P. Ó Riain, 'Martyrologies', p. 22 and n. 8. 9 Kylmisken (now obsolete) lay in the parish of Lynn, barony of Fartullagh (*Fir Tulach*), Co. Westmeath (see *Corpus Genealogiarum Sanctorum Hiberniae* (hereafter *CGSH*), ed. by P. Ó Riain (Dublin, 1985), note on 670.33, p. 211); here and elsewhere the place is mentioned in connection with Brigit. 10 These notes are in Irish and Latin, sometimes a mixture of both. Of their sources nothing certain is known, but they would appear to date from the eleventh century or later (*The Martyrology of Oengus*, ed. by W. Stokes, Henry Bradshaw Society, 29 (London, 1905; repr. Dublin, 1984), pp xlvii–xlviii; Kenney, *Sources*, p. 481). 11 See E. Hogan, *Onomasticon Goedelicum* (Dublin and London, 1910) under Ui Dortain and Ui Tortain. 12 For *Eren[n]*. 13 This early reference to some kind of speech impediment has been skilfully worked into the dramatic opening miracle in the Fillan and Kentigerna *Lectiones* in the *Aberdeen Breviary*. See Appendix 1 below.

The Cult of St Fillan in Scotland

to be at least as old as the first half quarter of the ninth century. The note on M.O. in the Laud 610 manuscript gives us the additional information that *Ráith Érenn* (note the different generic element) in Scotland is near *Glen Drochta* in the west.[14] The earliest manuscript witness of M.O., the *Leabhar Breac*, notes at 20 June that he was from Rath Erenn in Alba and from 'chill Foelan i Laigis' ('the church of Fillan [Kilfillan] in Leix [Co. Leix, Munster]').[15] This same note describes him as the son of Óengus (killed 483x512 AD), son of Natfraoch, and therefore of the Eoghanacht, the ruling dynasty of Munster. Watson states that he was quite possibly the Fillan who is said to have been trained by Ailbe of Emly (Co. Tipperary), who died in 534 (A.U.),[16] a statement which I have been unable to trace further back than Bishop Forbes, who writes: '[Fillan of 20 June] was a disciple of S. Ailbe, who, wishing to go to Tyle (Thule), sent out instead twenty-two disciples, one of whom was Faolan of Ratherran'.[17]

From the above material, therefore, a tentative picture emerges of a saint who flourished in the first half of the sixth century, who was originally of royal descent from north Munster in Ireland, and who settled somewhere in central Scotland (west Perthshire).[18] However, this picture is composed of evidence of very varied reliability. The most reliable part is the west-Perthshire context, the least reliable is the Munster connection and the early date.[19]

Whatever the historical reality which lies behind the west-Perthshire Fillan, the later medieval Scottish calendars seem to have confused the two Fillans mentioned in M.O., so that the information we find attached to the Fillan commemorated in M.O. on 20 June becomes attached to the Fillan commemorated on 9 January. The Drummond Missal, written in the eleventh-century in Ireland, still has them as separate saints. It is in Latin, but the forms of many of the personal names show that it was translated from an Irish original.[20] At 9 January we find:

---

14 The question as to the exact identity of the Scottish places mentioned in these entries is discussed below p. 184. **15** On p. 90; the *Leabhar Breac* was a compilation made in north Munster in the early fifteenth century, and was published in facsimile by the Royal Irish Academy in 1876. See Kenney, *Sources*, p. 25 and Ó Riain, 'Martyrologies', p. 23. The notes to M.O. in the *Leabhar Breac* are published in *On the Calendar of Oengus*, ed. by W. Stokes, Transactions of the Royal Irish Academy, Irish Manuscript Series, 1 (Dublin, 1880). **16** 'Quies Ailbe Imlecha Ibuir' *s.a.* 533; see W.J. Watson, *The History of the Celtic Place-Names of Scotland* (Edinburgh and London, 1926), p. 164. **17** A.P. Forbes, *Kalendars of Scottish Saints* (Edinburgh, 1872), p. 340. **18** It may also be significant that the medieval Irish and Scottish genealogists point to a close relation between this Fáelán and the earls of Lennox, all of whom they allege are descended from Corc son of Lughaidh, king of Munster (see Anderson, 'Columba', p. 34, and Watson, *Celtic Place-Names*, pp 219–20). The medieval parish of Killin/Glendochart lay along the Lennox's north-east border. **19** Not too much can be made of the Munster connection, as Oengus son of Natfraoch was a popular figure to whom later genealogists and hagiographers assigned otherwise unknown or doubtful figures in need of a royal connection. I am grateful to Dr Thomas Clancy for this observation. Furthermore the *Leabhar Breac*, the source of this Fillan-Munster connection, was itself a Munster compilation (see n. 15 above). **20** That a vernacular

> Vitalis quoque sanctus hoc die et apud Hiberniam Felan ad Christum migraverunt ('Also on this day St Vitalis died ('went to Christ'), as did Felan in Ireland').[21]

On 20 June the Drummond calendar has:

> Rome natale sancti Silverii qui anno uno Romanam cathedram rexit; et apud Hiberniam Faelani ('In Rome the death of St Silverius who was pope for a year, and in Ireland [the death of] Faelanus').[22]

'Natale' means literally 'birthday', but in saints' calendars means 'heavenly birthday', that is 'day of death'. It is possible that a later tradition misinterpreted this as 'birthday', thus reducing two Fillans to one by assigning one date to his birth (20 June) and one to his death (9 January). A saint's date of death was the more important, which explains the later transfer of information from 20 June (perhaps considered his birthday) to 9 January. I have found no later medieval Scottish calendar which commemorates Fillan on 20 June.[23]

However, this 'reduction' of Fillan does not end here. As already mentioned, seventeen or eighteen men of the name of Fillan (Fáelán) are commemorated in M.T. A further two of these commemorations, that at 21 October and that at 31 October, although showing no connection with Scotland, have contributed to the fully-fledged legend of St Fillan as found in the *Aberdeen Breviary*. The fact that three, possibly four, of the 233 monks of St Fintan or Mundu, almost all of whom are painstakingly listed in M.T. under 21 October, are called Fillan has no doubt led to the later medieval association of the 'Scottish' St Fillan with St Mundu in the *Aberdeen Breviary*; while the commemoration of another Fillan at 31 October has supplied the Scottish Fillan with two brothers, mentioned in the *Aberdeen Breviary's Lectio* on St Conganus.[24]

The *Aberdeen Breviary* contains three accounts which feature St Fillan: that of Fillan himself at 9 January, that of his mother Kentigerna at 7 January, and that of his maternal uncle Conganus (Comgán) at 13 October. A full text and translation of the first can be found in Appendix 1, collated with the other two. Although they share some basic features such as their familial relationship, and the fact that they moved from Ireland to Scotland, there are also some important differences. While the Fillan and Kentigerna *Lectiones* locate their

---

original underlay at least part of the Drummond Calendar can be seen by genitive forms of personal names such as 'Fintain' or 'Faelain et Aeda' (Forbes, *Kalendars*, pp 5, 26, 27). For more on the Drummond Calendar, see Ó Riain, 'Martyrologies', pp 22–23. **21** Forbes, *Kalendars*, p. 1. **22** Ibid. p. 16. **23** For a full catalogue of these calendars, see D. McRoberts, *Catalogue of Scottish Medieval Liturgical Books and Fragments* (Glasgow, 1953). For several examples of defective calendar tradition, see Anderson, 'Columba', pp 26–27, one of which is Fillan himself (ibid. p. 26). **24** See Appendix 1 below, n. 105.

activities in western Perthshire and the northern Lennox, the Conganus *Lectio* locates Comgán, and by implication Fillan and Kentigerna, firmly in the Loch Alsh area, Wester Ross, formerly northern Argyll, *c*.130 km to the north. Furthermore, the Comgán *Lectio* brings on board yet another Fillan to eke out its material: Fillan the brother of Fursu (Fursey) and Ultán, who in the early to mid-seventh century were active first in East Anglia, then in the Low Country, whose story is told at some length by Bede in his *Historia Ecclesiastica* (III. 19), and whose feast-day was 31 October. Forbes is the first to remark on this 'confusion'.[25] Forbes further points out that certain aspects of the legend of Comgán seem to be genuinely early, since Lochalsh is described as being in 'northern Argyll' rather than in Ross, a description which, Forbes claims, could not be later than the reign of Alexander II. 'Northern Argyll', however, retained its identity well into the later middle ages.[26]

To summarize the evidence so far: the cult of a holy man called Fáelán was so well established in western Perthshire by the early ninth century that it is noted in Irish sources, and the note in the *Leabhar Breac* associated him with the royal kin of Munster in the first half of the sixth century. Through a common enough confusion of calendar dates, the feast day of this saint was moved from 20 June to 9 January, where it remained throughout the medieval period in Scotland. Furthermore, other details, sparse enough, from Irish martyrologies, concerning other saints called Fillan, were used in later medieval Scotland to fill out his story and those of associated saints with more detail. Through these associated saints he becomes linked, not with sixth-century Munster, but with eighth-century Leinster, thus confusing the picture even more.

One of these associated saints is Kentigerna, Irish Caintigern, claimed by the *Aberdeen Breviary* to have been the mother of St Fillan and sister of St Conganus. There is nothing earlier than this to associate these three figures. Her name appears in the Annals of Ulster *s.a.* 733 (true date 734):

> Caintigernd ingen Ceallaig Cualann moritur ('Caintigern, daughter of Cellach Cualann, dies').[27]

Cellach Cualann, her father, was the last Uí Máile king of Leinster, who died in 715 (A.U.).[28] He himself is mentioned in A.U. three times (704, 709 and 715),

---

25 Forbes, *Kalendars*, p. 346. 26 Northern Argyll was not included in the earldom of Ross until the later fourteenth century, although it was held by the earl of Ross in 1293 ('terra comitis de *Ros* in *Nort Argail*', *The Acts of the Parliaments of Scotland* (hereafter *APS*), ed. by T. Thomson and C. Innes (Edinburgh, 1814–75), i, p. 447). See also A. Grant, 'The Province of Ross and the Kingdom of Alba' in *Alba: Celtic Scotland in the Middle Ages*, ed. by E.J. Cowan and R.A. McDonald (East Linton, 2000), p. 88. 27 *Annals of Ulster* (to 1131) (hereafter A.U.), ed. by S. Mac Airt and G. Mac Niocaill (Dublin, 1983), item 4. 28 For more on him, see A. P. Smyth, *Celtic Leinster* (Dublin, 1982), pp 65, 67, 81; Cualann is the genitive of Cualu, a district covering the foothills of

which also record the deaths of eight of his children, from 709 to 748: four sons and four daughters, including Caintigern in 734. There is nothing to suggest that any of Cellach's children had a connection with Scotland, or that any of the daughters were especially religious. And finally, there is no record of a son of Cellach Cualann called Comgán. On the other hand, Cellach did have a grandson called Fáelán, not through Caintigern, however, but through another daughter, Conchenn.[29]

Caintigern is also the name of the queen of Fiachnae, king of the main Cruthin tribe, Dál nAraide, in the later sixth century. Described as faithful and modest (*fidelis et pudica*), she appears in the Latin life of St Comgall, founder of Bangor Abbey (died 602), who cures her of poison and reveals the poisoner. The *Life* locates this miracle at Rathmore of Moylinny, Co. Antrim, the chief seat of the Dál nAraide.[30]

Comgán is found in the M.T. at 13 October (his feast-day in the *Aberdeen Breviary*), as well as 2 August, with the epithet *Céle Dé* (Culdee).[31] In the *Aberdeen Breviary* all three, Kentigerna, Conganus and Feolanus, are brought together and given eventful biographies which begin in Leinster and end in various parts of western Scotland: Kentigerna on Inchcailloch in Loch Lomond, Conganus on Loch Alsh, and Feolanus in Strath Fillan. The link between this disparate group may be geographical rather than historical, having its origin around the shores of the three splendid interconnected sea lochs in Wester Ross, Loch Duich, Loch Alsh and Loch Long (see Map (9.1) and Key no. 20): less than 1km from the east end of Loch Duich, on the south bank of the River Shiel, is the old chapel site of *Cill-Chaointeort*,[32] a chapel within the medieval parish of Kintail ROS,[33] last used as a burial place *c*.1870, and containing the female name Latinized as Kentigerna.[34] On the north side of Loch Alsh the parish kirk of the medieval and modern parish of that name was also known as *Kilchoan* 'the church of Comgán'.[35] It is no doubt this church

---

the Dublin Mountains (ibid. p. 52). 'Fillan' was a popular name amongst the Leinster royal kin, including King Fáelán (died 738), son of Conchenn, daughter of Cellach Cualann; see ibid. pp 57, 123. Kentigerna's father in the *Aberdeen Breviary* is called Tyrennus, which might in fact represent Latin *tyrannus* 'tyrant, king, etc.'. For an early seventh-century king of Leinster called Fáelán, see note 113 below.   **29** See previous note.   **30** C. Plummer, *Vita Sanctorum Hiberniae*, 2 vols (Oxford, 1910), ii, 'Comgall' §52. I am grateful to Mr Henry Gough-Cooper for bringing this reference to my attention.   **31** He is identified by Reeves as Comgán Fota (Comgán the tall), anchorite of Tallaght, who died in 870 (W. Reeves, *The Culdees of the British Islands* (Dublin, 1864; reprinted Felinfach, 1994), pp x–xi, 9; and A.U. *s.a.* 869). However, this is impossible, given a date for the composition of M.T. no later than 833 (Ó Riain,'Martyrologies', p. 38 et passim). **32** *Kilkinterne* 1543, *Registrum Magni Sigilli Regum Scottorum* (hereafter *RMS*), ed. by J.M. Thomson *et al*. (Edinburgh, 1882–1914), iii, no. 2903.   **33** Nearby is the parish kirk of Glenshiel, a parish created *c*.1750 out of Kintail (*Origines Parochiales Scotiae* (hereafter *OPS*), Bannatyne Club (1851–55), ii (2), p. 391).   **34** W.J. Watson, *Place-Names of Ross and Cromarty* (Inverness, 1904; reprinted Evanton, 1996), p. 172.   **35** It appears as

which is referred to in the *Aberdeen Breviary's* Comgán *Lectio* as having been built by Fillan, and where, according to the same source, a Comgán cult still flourished in the early sixteenth century.[36] And finally, at the northern tip of Loch Long, also in Kintail parish, is Killilan, 'the church of Fillan', for early forms of which see Key no. 20. Since there are no commemorations in this area to Fursu or Ultán, who Comgán's *Lectio* tells us accompanied him from Ireland, we can assume that the local cults of Comgán, Fillan and Kentigerna were not the result of a 'back-reading' from the legend which found its way into the Comgán *Lectio* in the *Aberdeen Breviary*. It is possible, rather, that the legend which interwove the lives of these three saints had its source in Kintail and Loch Alsh, and was current at the cathedral chapter of Ross at Fortrose, which held both the parishes as common churches.[37] Either directly from Wester Ross, or from Fortrose, the legend could have been collected by the compilers of the *Aberdeen Breviary*, who then further elaborated it with the extraneous figures of Fursu and Ultán. It may have been this geographical juxtaposition of dedications to Kentigerna, Fillan and Comgán which suggested a familial relationship, which was then transferred to Fillan of Strath Fillan, who may or may not have had anything to do with the Fillan commemorated in Kintail. There are no dedications to Comgán near Strath Fillan,[38] and traditions current in the church of Glasgow in the fifteenth century associate Kentigerna the patron saint of the parish kirk of Inchcailloch, now Buchanan parish STL, with Kentigern, not Fillan.[39] Inchcailloch, although *c*.38 km south of Strath Fillan, is linked to it by an almost direct route up Loch Lomond and Glen Falloch, and the northern boundary of the parish of Inchcailloch (Buchanan) comes within two kilometres of the parish of Killin.[40] Although there is no documentary evidence of a nunnery on the island, the name (*innis cailleach* 'island of nuns') strongly suggests that there was some such foundation (*pace* Cowan and Easson),[41] and

---

Kilchoan on R. Gordon's map of northern Scotland, in the county of Ross, printed by Blaeu in 1654 (J. Stone, *Illustrated Maps of Scotland, from Blaeu's Atlas Novus of the 17th Century* (London, 1991), Plate 33). 36 See also Appendix 1, n. 105. 37 I.B. Cowan, *The Parishes of Medieval Scotland*, Scottish Record Society, 93 (1967) s.n. 38 The nearest is in fact on Seil Island in Lorn, on the Argyll coast. Note, however, that immediately north of Strath Fillan, around Loch Rannoch, there was a flourishing cult of St Con(n)án, which through misidentification with Comgán might have contributed to a Fillan-Comgán link. See Watson, *Celtic Place-Names*, pp 257, 282. 39 The fifteenth-century Book of Devotion associated with Robert Blackadder (bishop of Glasgow from 1483, archbishop from 1492 to 1508) calls Kentigerna the patron of the church of Inchcailloch and sister of Kentigern. The Book of Devotion adds that in Gaelic Kentigerna is called *Machquha*. This hypocoristic of Kentigerna (as well as of Kentigern) is found in the place-name Balmaha, also in Buchanan parish, on the mainland opposite Inchcailloch. See J. Durkan, 'The place-name Balmaha', *Innes Review*, 50 (1999), p. 88. 40 Strath Fillan was originally a chapel of Killin, and, after 1318, was treated as a conjoint parish with Killin. It was united with Killin in 1617 (Cowan, *Parishes*, pp 191, 102; W.A. Gillies, *In Famed Breadalbane* (Perth, 1938), p. 296). 41 I.B. Cowan, and D.E.

the siting of the parish kirk there till 1621 points to important early religious connections. Whatever the origin of the link between Kentigerna and Fillan, it is not surprising to find the Kentigerna-cult centred on Inchcailloch drawn into the force-field of the flourishing cult immediately to the north. The fact that around the same time as the *Aberdeen Breviary* was linking Inchcailloch with Fillan, Glasgow was linking it with Kentigern shows just how much these traditions were susceptible to manipulation.[42]

The next stage in this enquiry is to look at other evidence for the cult of St Fillan in Scotland apart from that provided by place-names containing his name, dedications and fairs, as shown on Map (9.1) and Key, and to underline the importance of western Perthshire as the centre of that cult. As already mentioned above, early Irish sources locate a Fillan in Scotland with some precision. M.O.'s 'Glenn Drochta' must be Glen Dochart, the glen which runs west from Killin, and which continues to the north-west as Strath Fillan.[43] Watson would identify Rath Erenn with Rottearns, Ardoch, north-east of Dunblane PER (1926, 227).[44] MacDonald on the other hand argues that Rath Erenn is in fact Dundurn, the important hill-fort which lies in the uppermost reaches of Strathearn, about one mile to the east of the village of St Fillan.[45] It is much more likely, however, that Rath Erenn is represented more correctly in M.T. as 'i Sraith Eret',[46] as well as in the Rawlinson B.505 note[47] as 'Srath hErenn' that is, Strathearn, and refers to the general area of central Scotland, from Strath Fillan to Dundurn, in which we find so many later traces of a Fillan-cult, despite the fact that Strathearn proper goes no further west than Loch Earn (see Map (9.2)). The place-name element *srath*, which in Ireland means 'low-lying land by a river, haugh-land', rather than 'broad valley', its meaning so widely attested in Scotland, is relatively uncommon in Irish place-names, in contrast to the very common element *ráth* 'fort, enclosure'. It is therefore much more likely, in an Irish context, for a scribe to miscopy *ráth* for *srath* than *vice versa*. In other words, the form with *srath* is the *lectio difficilior* and is therefore more likely to be the original.

Our earliest securely dateable evidence of Scottish provenance for the cult of St Fillan in this area comes from the reign of Robert I (1306–29). In February 1318 the king granted to the Augustinian abbey of Inchaffray the right of patronage of the church of Killin on condition that the abbot and convent should find a canon to celebrate divine service in the church of Strath Fillan

---

Easson, *Medieval Religious Houses Scotland*, 2nd edn (London and New York, 1976), p. 156.   **42** See above, n. 39.   **43** A. MacDonald, '*Ràth* in Scotland', *Bulletin of the Ulster Place-name Society*, series 2, vol.4 (1982), p. 54. For early forms of the name Strath Fillan, see Appendix 2. Note that Glen Dochart in medieval and early modern record applies to the whole of this area. Today it is restricted to the glen between Killin and Crianlarich. See Map (9.2).   **44** Celtic *Place-Names*, p. 227.   **45** '*Ràth*', pp 55–56.   **46** For 'i Sraith Eren'.   **47** Rawlinson B 505 is a good copy of M. O. I am grateful to Professor Richard Sharpe for pointing this out.

9.1 View across Strath Fillan, showing the Kirkton, looking towards the west. The present main road from Fort William to Glasgow (A82) can be seen running along the far-side of the strath from right to left. (Photo: S. Taylor)

(*Strathfulane*);[48] while later in the same year (in October) there appeared the first mention of a priory of Strath Fillan, dependent on Inchaffray Abbey.[49] As Cowan and Easson rightly point out, this sudden development from a single canon to a priory within a few months is misleading. There is evidence from King David's time (1124–53) for an abbot of Glendochart, and his monastery would no doubt have been situated where the later priory arose.[50]

48 *Regesta Regum Scottorum* (hereafter *RRS*), v (*Acts of Robert I*) ed. by A.A.M. Duncan (Edinburgh, 1988), no. 134. For 'church' (*ecclesia*) read 'chapel' (*capella*). It did not develop parochial status until after this date (Cowan, *Parishes*, p. 191). Note also that Glendochart was an alternative name for the parish of Killin (see for example the 1428 charter), by which time Strath Fillan had obviously still not developed independent parochial status. See also next note. 49 The confirmation charters of the bishop and the dean and chapter of Dunkeld, later in 1318, speak of the 'chapel of St Fillan ('Sancti Felani') in *[G]lendochred*', at which there is a prior and canons (*Charters, Bulls and other Documents relating to the Abbey of Inchaffrey* (hereafter *Inchaff. Chrs.*), Scottish History Society (1908), nos. 126–27). 50 Cowan and Easson, p. 52. The reference is *APS*, i, p. 372, quoted in J. Stuart, 'Historical notices of St Fillan's Crozier, and of the devotion

There would seem, however, to be important adjuncts of this earlier monastery which did not pass directly to its Augustinian successor, but remained in hereditary hands in various families in the parish until comparatively recent times. These are St Fillan's Bell (Key no. 16.d), some kind of a shrine (Key no. 16.c), perhaps his hand or arm (Key no. 16.b), a portable altar or manuscript, or wooden bowl (Key no. 16.a)[51] and, most famously, his crosier (Key no. 16.e), all of which are discussed in detail in Anderson, with important additions in Watson.[52] The crosier itself is the subject of a long and detailed article by the important nineteenth-century historian John Stuart, the last he wrote.[53] There is little that can be added to these analyses. Suffice it to say that the hereditary keepers or dewars (*dèoraidhean*, singular *dèoradh*) of these relics of St Fillan were scattered over a wide area, from near Killin in the east to Strath Fillan in the north-west (see Map (9.2)), all within the medieval parish of Killin or Glendochart. It is as if the whole of this glen, which was at the same time one of the main thoroughfares between the western highlands and the central belt, was under the protection of St Fillan, a protection realized by the physical presence of his relics at different places along the route. Furthermore, the dewar of the crosier, who held the lands of Ewich about 1km south of Kirkton of Strath Fillan, was in 1428 confirmed in his special rights of pursuing anywhere in Scotland goods or cattle stolen from anyone in the parish of Killin/ Glendochart. As Stuart points out this special privilege, which carried with it important revenues meticulously set out in the 1428 document, seems to date only from the time of Robert I. It paints a picture of a figure who combines ancient hereditary religious office with later medieval trouble-shooting, perhaps reflecting a growing lawlessness in the region.[54]

It is no co-incidence that the name of Robert I should be invoked in the 1428 charter in connection with rights and relics of St Fillan, since we have abundant

---

of King Robert Bruce to St Fillan', *PSAS*, 12 (1878), p. 140, and in full in W. J. Watson, 'The Place-Names of Breadalbane', *Transactions of the Gaelic Society of Inverness*, 34 (1928), p. 252. **51** The *Meser*, mentioned only once in 1468 (*The Black Book of Taymouth*, Bannatyne Club 1855 (reprinted by Kilchurn Heritage n.d.), p. xxxvi); for various interpretations see J. Anderson, 'Notice of the Quigrich or Crosier and other relics of St Fillan, in the possession of their hereditary keepers, or dewars, in Glendochart, in 1549–50', *PSAS*, 23 (1889), p. 118 and Gillies, *Famed Breadalbane*, p. 80. **52** Watson, *Celtic Place-Names*, p. 265; 'Place-Names of Breadalbane', pp 253–54. **53** See above, n. 50. The article itself was a direct result of the acquisition of St Fillan's Crosier by the Society of Antiquaries from its hereditary keepers, the Dewars, who in the early nineteenth century had emigrated, lock, stock and crosier, from Glen Dochart to Canada. The amazing details of this story are fully set out in the two pieces which immediately precede Stuart's article (*PSAS*, 12, pp 122–33). **54** Ibid. p. 157. The (lay) abbot of Glen Dochart, mentioned in an assise of King David I (see above, p. 185) is also linked to proceedings regarding stolen cattle. There will doubtless be a direct, formal connection between the legal duties of the abbot in the twelfth century and of the dewar in the fourteenth, kept alive and relevant by the fact that Glen Dochart (including

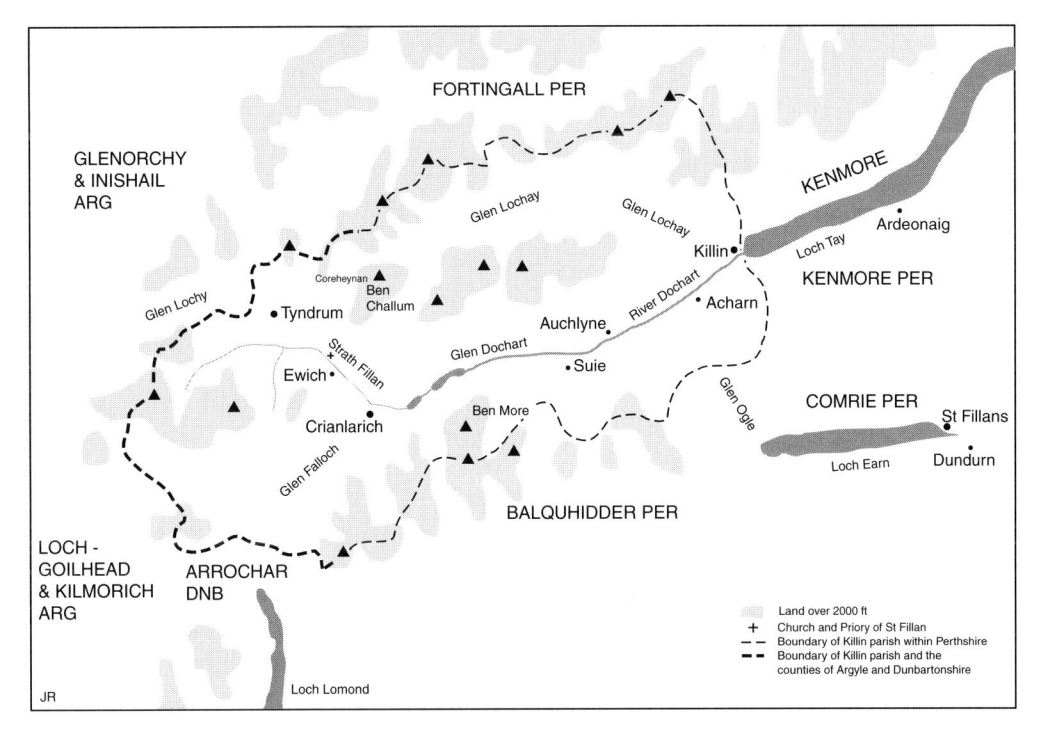

MAP 9.2 The medieval parish of Killin PER, including Strath Fillan, showing the places mentioned in the text and in Appendix 2, nos. 14–16. From Killin to Crianlarich is approximately 20 kilometres. (Drafted by S. Taylor; drawn by J. Renny)

other evidence of that king's personal devotion to the saint. It is this personal devotion, fully discussed by John Stuart and more recently by Geoffrey Barrow, which led to an upsurge of interest in Fillan in the later middle ages.[55] The exact details of the support which St Fillan and his contemporary representatives afforded a beleaguered Robert I in the Strath Fillan area in 1306, and at Bannockburn in 1314, must remain a matter of speculation, but of his special devotion to the saint there can be no doubt.[56] As already mentioned, he (re-)endowed a priory at Kirkton of Strath Fillan in 1318, the remains of which still exist, and gave its staffing and maintenance into the care of Inchaffray Abbey.[57]

This devotion was shared by the king's immediate family: in the year of the king's death (1329) the Exchequer Rolls record that Sir Robert Bruce of

Strath Fillan) was the chief conduit for cattle moving between the western Highlands to the central belt.　**55** Stuart, op. cit. pp 144–47; G.W.S. Barrow, *Robert Bruce*, 2nd edn (Edinburgh, 1976), pp 226–27.　**56** Barrow, *Bruce*, p. 437.　**57** *Inchaff. Chrs.*, no. 12.

Liddesdale, the king's illegitimate son, gave £20 to the church of St Fillan in Strathfillan.[58]

Many of the dedications to St Fillan in central eastern Scotland can be interpreted as a reflex of this royal Brucian devotion. The most obvious one is the St Fillan dedication in Aberdour FIF. Aberdour parish contains the monastery of Inchcolm, a major centre of the cult of Columba in eastern Scotland.[59] That a church which is so closely associated with Inchcolm should have a dedication to a non-Columban saint requires some explanation. The first mention of St Fillan as patron of Aberdour church is from 1390 (see Key no. 7). In 1325 Robert I granted the barony of Aberdour to the closest and most loyal of all his followers, Thomas Randolph earl of Moray, in whose family it remained until 1342, when it was granted by Randolph's son John to his friend William Douglas.[60] We need look no further than the Randolph connection to explain the Aberdour dedication.

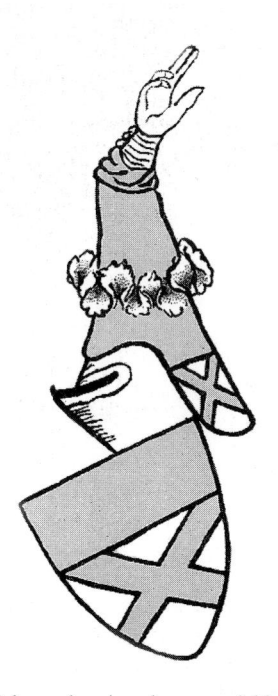

9.2 Helmet showing the armorial bearing of the family of Bruce of Annandale, probably representing the arm-reliquary of St Fillan. From the late 14th-century Flemish Armorial De Gelres. Illustration taken from *PSAS* 25, Plate 50; printed also in S. Boardman, *The Early Stewart Kings*, opposite p. 143. See also footnote 58.

The famous healing well near the church, which is first mentioned in 1479 as the Pilgrims' Well ('le pilgramyswell')[61] is traditionally linked with St Fillan. In 1474 the Hospital of St Martha was founded in Aberdour for the support and

---

58 'ad fabricam ecclesie Sancti Felani': *The Exchequer Rolls of Scotland* (hereafter *ER*), ed. by J. Stuart *et al.* (Edinburgh, 1878–1908), i, p. 214. Note that the family of Bruce of Annandale has as part of its armorial bearings an arm on the helmet which, from the position of the fingers (two held aloft in a gesture of benediction) must be an arm reliquary (see Figure 9.2). In the light of the strong Fillan cult within the Bruce family, it is probable that this represents the reliquary of St Fillan's arm. I am grateful to Dr Steve Boardman for drawing this to my attention.   59 S. Taylor, 'Columba east of Drumalban: some aspects of the cult of Columba in eastern Scotland', *Innes Review* 51 (2), 109–30.   60 *RRS*, v, no. 263; *Registrum Honoris de Morton*, hereafter *Mort. Reg.* (Bannatyne Club, 1853), ii, no. 64.   61 *Mort Reg.* ii, no. 232.

9.3 Carving of an arm with open hand, attached to a ringed equal-armed cross found at Kirkton of Strath Fillan. It may have marked the grave of one of the dewars of St Fillan's arm-reliquary, as suggested by Peter Yeoman, *Pilgrimage in Scotland* (1999), p. 92, where this photograph first appeared. Total length: 33.5 inches (Photo: N. Robertson)

entertainment of the 'poor and the pilgrims'[62] and from the 1479 charter it is clear that it is the Pilgrims' Well which is the chief attraction. There is, however, no explicit link between this well and St Fillan until the nineteenth century, and it must remain a moot point as to whether the well was earlier associated with a different saint, gaining its fame through association with St Fillan from the fourteenth century onwards.[63]

There are other Fillan-associated places in Fife. Pittenweem, with its famous cave (for which see Key no. 10), is not specifically associated with Fillan until Chambers, writing in the early seventeenth century, informs us that Fillan was abbot of the Fife monastery of Pittenweem.[64] We should not, however, assume that this is merely seventeenth-century fiction. Pittenweem was the land-base of the priory of the Isle of May, whose saint was Ethernan, the focus of an important

---

[62] 'pauperibus et peregrinis'; *Mort. Reg.* ii, no. 231. [63] The pilgrims' hospital was given over to the care of the Sisters of the Third Order of St Francis in 1486. For a full account of this, see W.M. Bryce *Scottish Grey Friars* (Edinburgh and London, 1909), pp 267–72, 391–95; see also W. Ross, *Aberdour and Inchcolme* (Edinburgh,1885), pp 44–52. The local reverence for the saint is reflected in the name of a tenant in Aberdour in 1479 viz Fulanus Roberti (Felanus Roberti in 1486) i.e. Fillan Roberts (*Mort. Reg.* ii, nos. 232 and 233). [64] D. Chambers (Camerarius), *De Scotorum Fortitudine Doctrina et Pietate* (Paris, 1631), p. 76.

cult, and himself the victim of hagiographic confusion, thus spawning a 'ghost saint', Adrian. The history of his monastery is as complex as that of his cult.[65] The important point for the Fillan-association is that, from being a cell of the abbey of Reading (England), May/Pittenweem became closely linked to the priory of St Andrews in the early fourteenth century, and it was another close associate of Robert I, Bishop William Lamberton of St Andrews, who was responsible for the transference of rights and revenues of May/Pittenweem from Reading to St Andrews. This was in the year 1318, co-incidentally the same year in which Robert I established canons at Strath Fillan, and the year in which, in the presence of Robert I, Bishop William consecrated the finally completed cathedral at St Andrews.[66] The inclusion of the monastery of May/Pittenweem into the body of the Scottish Kirk at the height of the popularity of the new Fillan cult in Scotland, and by one of the king's inner circle of advisors, is explanation enough of a Fillan tradition, reflected not just in Chambers' statement, but also in local toponymy and legend.

The Lamberton-St Andrews connection may well explain the special veneration in which Fillan was held in St Andrews, a feature hitherto unnoticed by writers on the saint. To quote W.E.K. Rankin, from his fine book on the parish kirk of the Holy Trinity of St Andews:

> There is no indication why an altar in [Fillan's] name should have been erected in Holy Trinity. It was one of the oldest altars and the Inventory does not preserve the name of its founder.[67]

It is first mentioned in 1449, when the priest was Mr Robert Pantre. Rankin further notes that the family of Bishop Kennedy (bishop of St Andrews 1440–65) took a special interest in it.

The church of Forgan in north-east Fife was also known as St Fillan's (see Key no. 9). It had belonged to the priory of St Andrews since 1198x1202, and the priory also held lands in the parish.[68] This St Andrews link alone could have accounted for the placing of the church under the patronage of St Fillan after the revival, or rather introduction, of his cult to St Andrews in the early fourteenth century.

There is in Fife only one commemoration of Fillan which would, if interpreted correctly, testify to his cult there in the early medieval period: this is the place-name Lumphinnans, Ballingry parish in west Fife. The early forms of this name (for which see Key no. 8) are problematical. The first element is Gaelic *lann*, 'enclosure, field; church' (cognate with Welsh *llan*, 'enclosure;

---

65 Discussed in Cowan and Easson, pp 59–60, 94–95. 66 Barrow, *Bruce*, p. 374.
67 W.E.K. Rankin, *The Parish Church of the Holy Trinity of St Andrews* (Edinburgh, 1955), p. 80. 68 See *Liber Cartarum Prioratus Sancti Andree in Scotia* (hereafter *St A. Lib.*), Bannatyne Club (1841), pp 260, 274.

church'). Where the second element represents the name of a saint, it is best translated 'church'.[69] In 'Lumphinnans' it seems to have lost any ecclesiastical association by the time the name is first recorded in the mid-thirteenth century, and the place plays no obvious part in the parochial structure established in the twelfth.[70] This is further testimony to the antiquity of the site. The earliest forms point to a Fillan- rather than a Finán-dedication, although the phonetic changes known as assimilation and dissimilation make it impossible to be certain. This phenomenon is also responsible for the fact that the earliest form of Kilellan, Houston RNF (Key no.19), which has every appearance of being a genuine Fillan dedication, is *Kelenan* (1205 x 1207), while Kilfinan in Cowal ARG (a Finán-dedication) appears as *Kylfelan* and *Kilelan* in 1362, and as *Kyllellan* in 1491.[71]

The dedication of the chapels at Doune Castle to St Fillan (Key no.17) reflects an even later period than that of Robert I. Robert duke of Albany, responsible as earl of Menteith for most of the building work at Doune Castle in the late fourteenth century, seems also to have had a special relationship with St Fillan. Bower tells the story of how he swore by God and St Fillan that he would relieve Cavers Castle, besieged by the English, in 1403 'even if no one else comes with me except my boy Patrick as rider of my warhorse'.[72] By evoking St Fillan, Duke Robert is at the same time quite consciously evoking the spirit of Robert I at a moment of crisis in Anglo-Scottish relations. However, Albany had other reasons for cultivating the saint. He had acquired Glen Dochart by 1375, a key territory in his strategy of accumulating lands stretching from western Perthshire to Fife, and therefore was in especial need of the favour of the powerful local saint into whose territory he had intruded himself.[73]

Regarding Luncarty (Key no. 18) I can offer no explanation beyond the general popularity of the saint in central eastern Scotland in the later medieval period.

Something different was happening in the Scottish North-East. As Map (9.1) makes clear, there is a total absence of Fillan commemorations in this area. Again an explanation can be found in the secular politics of the fourteenth century. During the thirteenth century the Comyns had developed into the most powerful family in the north and north-east of Scotland, dominating as

---

69 For a discussion of this element, see S. Taylor, 'Place-names and the early church in Scotland', *Records of Scottish Church History Society*, 28 (1998), pp 8–10, 16–22. 70 Cowan, *Parishes*, pp 10 and 12, under Auchterderran and Ballingry. 71 *Registrum Monasterii de Passelet* (hereafter *Pais. Reg.*), pp 113, 146, 154. 72 *Scotichronicon by Walter Bower in Latin and English*, ed. by D.E.R. Watt (hereafter *Chron. Bower* (Watt)), 9 vols (Aberdeen/Edinburgh, 1987–98), viii, p. 55 (Bk. 15, c.16). 73 S. Boardman, *The Early Stewart Kings, Robert II and Robert III* (East Linton, 1996), p. 271. I am grateful to Drs Michael Penman and Steve Boardman for their very helpful insights and comments on the importance of the relationship between saints' cults and secular politics in later medieval Scotland.

they did large tracts of Aberdeenshire and Moray.[74] However, their entrenched opposition to Robert Bruce, later Robert I, brought down bitter retribution not only on their own heads, but also on the heads of many of the inhabitants of the lands under their sway: the most extreme example of this was the so-called harrying of Buchan by Robert I in 1308, which would have adversely affected the development of a saint's cult so closely bound up with the new dynasty. Robert I's attempt to win back popularity from major ecclesiastical land-holders who had suffered in his Comyn-campaigns, such as the monastery of Deer in Buchan, seems not enough to have endeared the new royal cult of St Fillan to people of Aberdeenshire, or of any of the former Comyn territories.[75]

The commemorations in the rest of Scotland are almost exclusively from a Gaelic-speaking milieu, and several of them considerably pre-date the fourteenth century (see Key nos. 6, 12, 19, 21–4). Kilellan (Key no. 19) in Renfrewshire, a Cumbric-speaking area until perhaps as late as the eleventh century, is first recorded in the twelfth century, but it is more difficult to set a *terminus a quo* for its formation. It could be as early as the eighth century, when place-names containing the Gaelic element *cill* ('church') were being coined in non-Gaelic-speaking areas of Pictland.[76] Although the element seems to have ceased to generate place-names by the time Gaelic was imported into Pictland on a large scale in the late ninth century, it remained active as a place-name element in western and south-western Scotland until much later.[77] The cult of Fillan in Renfrewshire, as evidenced by Kilellan, could be as late as the eleventh century, when Scottish cults would have been introduced into British Strathclyde along with Gaelic, following the final annexation of Strathclyde to the kingdom of the Scots in the early eleventh century.[78]

I would like to conclude with some observations, and speculations, on the St Fillan cult in Scotland. Its focus was Glen Dochart, especially the upper part of the glen, which by the early fourteenth century was also known as Strath Fillan, and his association with this general area was known in Tallaght near Dublin by the early ninth century. If this Irish information contains the place-name 'Strathearn', as I have argued above that it does, and if this is not simply the result of the imprecise geographical knowledge of a non-local, then we can assume that his cult was even wider than Glen Dochart at this early date, and

---

[74] See A. Young, 'The Earls and Earldom of Buchan in the Thirteenth Century', in *Medieval Scotland, Crown, Lordship and Community*, ed. by A. Grant and K.J. Stringer (Edinburgh, 1993), passim.   [75] See Stuart, 'Historical notices', pp 177–78.   [76] See S. Taylor, 'Place-names and the Early Church in Eastern Scotland', in *Scotland in Dark Age Britain*, ed. by B.E. Crawford (Aberdeen, 1996), p. 103.   [77] See W.F.H. Nicolaisen, *Scottish Place-Names* (London, 1976; second impression with additional information, 1979), pp 142–44 and Taylor, op. cit. (1996), p. 99.   [78] For a good summary of the various arguments regarding the complex history of the last centuries of independent Strathclyde, see Macquarrie, *Saints*, pp 191–92.

included at least the upper part of Strathearn. It is therefore probably no coincidence that we find strong Fillan traditions, albeit late, attached to upper Strathearn around the east end of Loch Earn (at St Fillan's) and the important neighbouring hill-fort of Dundurn. However old these traditions are, there can be little doubt that they relate to the same Fillan as the saint of Glen Dochart. In other words, Fillan is the saint who dominates the most important, in fact the only, route-way from Fortrenn (lowland Strathearn, and the heartland of southern Pictland) to northern Dál Riata (Lorn, Mull and Iona). This route must have played a vital role in communications between the Gaels of Dál Riata and the Picts of Fortrenn and Fife, communications of both a secular and an ecclesiastical nature. Whatever the details of the spread of the Columban church from Dál Riata into Pictland, whether this was accomplished during the latter half of the sixth century under Columba himself (died 597) or under his immediate successors, there can be no doubt the route which the Iona churchmen took to southern Pictland passed along Strath Fillan, down Glen Ogle and into Strathearn (see Map 9.2). In the later seventh-century, under Adomnán, abbot of Iona and writer of the famous *Life* of Columba, we have evidence, in the form of place-names and other commemorations, for intense Columban activity in Atholl,[79] and even for this more northerly destination Strath Fillan and Glen Dochart represent one of only two possible routes into Atholl from Iona. I have argued elsewhere that place-names and other commemorations along important route-ways taken by the clerics of Iona could date back as far as the seventh century.[80] The question therefore arises as to why the pass which must have been most frequently used by them stood under the invocation of a saint who had no obvious Columban connections. One answer might be that his cult was already so well established that it could not be displaced. If this analysis is correct, it is a further piece of evidence that Fillan was indeed a figure of the early sixth century, as already suggested by the late and fragmentary written evidence discussed above.[81] If this is true, then it might even be suggested that the limits of the cult of St Fillan in western Perthshire, that is, Killin on Loch Tay and Dundurn near the east end of Loch Earn, represent the limits of Dál Riatan eastern expansion in the very poorly documented early sixth century. Dundurn was certainly a key fortification, the possession of which must have been keenly contested, since whoever controlled

---

79 See Taylor, 'Iona abbots', pp 57–60, 68–69 and 39 (map). For a map of the route-ways from Dál Riata to Atholl, see ibid. p. 50. **80** Taylor, ibid. and Taylor, 'Columba'. **81** An alternative explanation would be that the Fillan-cult *superseded* traces of the Columban church in these important passes in the eighth or early ninth century, with the saint in question belonging to the early eighth-century royal Leinster context as indicated by the *Aberdeen Breviary*. For more on the links between Leinster and Pictland, see A.P. Smyth, *Warlords and Holy Men* (Edinburgh, 1984), pp 82–83. See also S. Taylor, 'Place-Names of Abernethy [Perthshire]' in *Pictish Reflections* [to be published by the Pictish Arts Society].

it would control access to and from Fortrenn.[82] If this key-fortress stood under the invocation and protection of Fillan, as it appears to have done, then, along with his undisputed presence in Glen Dochart, this would make him a figure of immense significance for the Gaels of Dál Riata, and would explain why he may have been outshone by Columba and his successors, but could not be completely displaced by them.

There is certainly no doubt that Fillan reigned supreme in Glen Dochart,[83] and the profusion of his relics spread along the thirty km of the glen, together with the rights accorded to the dewars of at least one of these relics, the crosier, presents a picture of a saintly *dominium* unique in Scotland. Perhaps if Robert I had never entered that *dominium* and experienced the power of the saint in such a positive way, Fillan's grip on the glen might have gradually faded away, and his cult may not have spread into the eastern lowlands. As it was, the cult was promoted by the king and those close to him at a national level, to such an extent that churches were re-dedicated to him, and his bell was carried at one coronation at least (that of James IV in 1488),[84] while in the saint's glen the status of his relics and their keepers was royally confirmed and re-defined.

We are thus left with what is for Scotland an extraordinarily vivid picture of a later medieval saint's cult, the origins of which are as obscure as the many saints' cults who have left us little more than their name. Given the large number of saints called Fillan in the Irish martyrologies, we cannot be sure that all the commemorations to Fillan in Scotland are to the same saint: it is probable, but not provable. It is more certain that the two saints who are often mentioned in modern writings as being at the core of the Fillan cult – Fillan of 9 January and Fillan of 20 June – are in fact one person.[85] Many of the accretions to the Fillan story found in the *Aberdeen Breviary* under 9 January (Fillan), 7 January (Kentigerna) and 13 October (Comgán) may derive from genuine tradition; however, it is just as likely that they are the result of misinterpretation both of early sources such as martyrologies, as well as of geographical and toponymic data. Robert I, whose devotion to Fillan was so strong and so influential, probably knew as little as we do today about the true identity of Fáelán the splendid mute.

---

[82] It was besieged in 683, but we are not told who was besieging whom (A.U.). [83] That is, 'Greater Glen Dochart', including Strath Fillan. [84] *Accounts of the Lord High Treasurer of Scotland*, ed. by T. Dickson and Sir J. Balfour Paul (Edinburgh, 1877–1916), i, 88: 18 shillings were paid 'til a man that beyris Sanct Fyllanis bell, at the Kingis commande'. [85] This was first suggested by M.O. Anderson in 1965 ('Columba', p. 26).

APPENDIX I

The text of the Fillan *Legenda* in the *Aberdeen Breviary* for 9 January given below is taken from the microfilm of the printed original NLS Mf.Pres. 9 (1–2), hereafter Mf. There are minor variations between it and the edition printed in 1854 (*Aberdeen Breviary*), hereafter AB. These are noted below. The punctuation and capitalisation, as well as the use of *i* and *u*, are of the printed original. Abbreviations have been silently expanded, except where there is doubt as to the form intended, when the abbreviated letter(s) have been put in square brackets. Emendations to Mf have been put in angled brackets. I am indebted to Alan Macquarrie for help with translating and explaining the rubrics.

Januarius fo.xxvi *verso*

Sancti Foelani abbatis et confessoris. oracio
Deus qui beatum foelanum confessorem tuum atque abbatem in profundum fluminis deiectum a morte saluasti; et in eodem per anni curriculum uisitacione angelica confouisti concede quesumus ut eiusdem intercedente suffragio efficaciter subleuemur optato.[86]

[The feast of] St Fillan abbot and confessor. Prayer.
God who saved from death the blessed Fillan your confessor and abbot after he had been thrown into the depth of the river, and who in that same river cared for him for a whole year through the visitation of an angel, grant, we beseech you, that by the intercession of his prayer we may be raised up efficaciously according to his will.

---

86 'per dominum' omitted.

Ad matutinas ix lectiones fiant cum memoria et medie lectiones de epyphania et de sancta maria. Lectio i.
Foelanus ex scotorum nobili familia sanguinis propagine: patre quidem feriach nomine et kentigerna matre mulierum deuotissima originem duxit. Natus sicut de eodem uaticinatus est lapidem in ore habens propter quod a patre in tantum contemptui dabatur eu[n]dem iam natum in lacu quodam seu stangno eisdem proximiori precipitari et demergi iussit. In quo sub anno integro per angelos dei ministros diuinitus enutritus est: sed anno elapso reuelacione diuina per ybarum episcopum inuentus inter angelos iocundantem eu[n]dem de lacu incolumem leuauit et secum baptizatum diuinis litteris insigniuit.[87]

At Matins there are to be nine lessons, with the commemoration and the middle lessons of the Epiphany and of St Mary. Lesson 1.[88]
Fillan originated from a noble family of *Scoti*[89] by race, his father being called Feriach,[90] and his mother Kentigerna, the most devout of women. He was born, as had been prophesied of him, with a stone in his mouth, on account of which he was held in such contempt by his father that at his birth he ordered him to be thrown into a near-by loch or pond. Here for a whole year he was divinely looked after by angels, the ministers of God; but after a year through divine revelation he was found playing amongst the angels by Bishop Ibar,[91] who lifted him safely out of the loch, baptized him and, keeping him with him, instructed him in the knowledge of God.[92]

87 'Tu autem.' omitted.　　88 This means that of the nine lessons (*lectiones*) at Matins on 9 January, the first three and the last three are proper to Fillan i.e. are specifically about Fillan, and read only on his day, while the middle three are of the Epiphany, since the feast of Fillan falls within the octave of the Epiphany. St Mary is also included probably because the Epiphany was regarded as a Marian feast.　　89 *Scoti* is probably used here to mean 'Irish', as in Kentigerna's own lesson or *lectio* [hereafter Kent. *Lect.*] (7 January, vol.1, fol.xxivv to xxvr), where she is called 'ex Scotorum propagine regali' ('from the royal race of the *Scoti*'), but is at the same time firmly located in Ireland, with a Leinster father (a subking, Tyrennus) and a Munster husband. In Congan's lesson [hereafter Cong. *Lect.*] (13 October, vol. 2, fol.cxxvi[r] to[v]) Comgán, Kentigerna's brother, is said to be descended from a family of subkings of the *Scoti*, the Irish (*Ybernences*) and the Leinstermen (*Laynenses*).　　90 *Feriatus*, Kent. *Lect.* (Mf; *Feriacus*, AB). Note the similarity with the name 'Feradach', father of Leamhain (a back-formation from Lennox), who allegedly married the first member of the Munster royal house of Eoghanacht to settle in Scotland. He is described as king of Pictland (*Cruithentuath*) in a Munster genealogical tale (Watson 1926, 119, 220), and seems also to be included in a Pictish king-list (Anderson 1980, 90, 246). This may be of significance for two reasons: firstly there are the alleged genealogical connections between the Eoghanacht and Fillan (for which see above p. 179); and secondly Kentigerna according to Kent. *Lect.* ends her days on an island in Loch Lomond, in the heart of Lennox.　　91 'Ybarus episcopus'

Lectio ii.

Sed iuuenilibus cum eodem transactis annis ad <monasterium> sancti mundi abbatis deuotissimi se contulit a quo sacre religionis regulam et habitum suscepit monachalem In eius monasterio non longe a claustro seorsum cellulam ut diuine contemplacioni facilius insudaret secreto construxit. In qua nocte quadam dum illius monasterii fratres per seruulum que[m]dem cenam sibi paratam nunciarent: seruo uero percuntante per dicte cellule rimulam inspiciendo quod ageret. Uidit beatum foelanum in tenebris scribentem senistram eius manum lumen clarum prebentem manui dextre. At seruus ille factum admirans con /fo.xxuii *recte*/ tinuo reuersus fratribus retulit.[93]

Lesson 2.

But when he had passed his youth with Ibar he went to [the monastery of][94] the most devout abbot Saint Mundu,[95] from whom he received the rule of holy religion and the monastic habit. In his monastery, so that he might more easily labour in divine contemplation, he secretly built a cell not far away from the cloister, in which, one night, when the brothers of the monastery sent a little servant to tell him that dinner was ready for him, the servant investigating by looking through a small crack in the above-mentioned cell to find out what was going on, saw the blessed Fillan writing in the darkness, his left hand emitting bright light for his right hand.[96] But the servant, amazed at this, immediately went back and told the brothers.

---

appears also in Kent. *Lect.* in the same role. 'Sancti Ibari episcopi' M.T. 23 April. 'bishop Ibar ... in Becc-ériu/Beggary Island [Co. Wexford] ('in Hérinn Bicc') he departed' M.O. 23 April, which also has a lengthy note on him, including a genealogy which links him to the Uí Echach of Ulster, adding that he had a conflict with Patrick, which resulted in Ibar's exile to Beggary Island ('little Ireland'). Chambers (1631) 118, asserts that there was another Bishop Ibar, whom he associates with St Fillan (no doubt because of the *Aberdeen Breviary* account), and who died in *Tifedalia* (Teviotdale), and this is followed by Forbes, *Kalendars* 359. He is not mentioned as a Scottish saint by Watson (1926). **92** According to Kent. *Lect.* Ibar restores Fillan, cured of his deformity, to his mother, then baptizes him. This underwater interlude is likely to be connected with the famous *Poll Fhaolain* 'St Fillan's Pool', in Strath Fillan, in which those suffering from mental illness were immersed before being tied up and left all night in St Fillan's church nearby. For a full account of this see Carmichael 1941, vol. 4, 202. **93** 'Tu autem.' omitted. **94** The Latin is ungrammatical here, and requires some such noun. **95** Mundu is a hypocoristic form of Fintán, for whom see Watson 1926, 304, 307 and Reford 1988, 211–12. The link between Fillan and Mundu, based on a (?deliberate) misunderstanding of Irish martyrologies such as M.T., is discussed above p. 180. **96** Through Boece's story of the miracle of St Fillan's arm just before the battle of Bannockburn in 1314, this has become St Fillan's most famous attribute. The original account of this miracle, along with Bellenden's translation of it, can be found in Stuart 1878, 172–5. Boece was part of the circle of those who compiled and published the *Aberdeen Breviary*. The importance of St Fillan's arm is eloquently

Lectio tercia.
Beatus uero foelanus de huiusmodi facto diuinitus cercioratus in seruum indignatus quod fratribus sua secreta reuelasse<t>[97] quare superna disposicione grus quidam eiusdem monasterii domesticus illius serui oculum extrahendo cecauit: sed et ipse beatus foelanus pietate motus suorumque fratrum supplicacione et instancia oculum serui denuo incolumem restituit.

Third lesson.
So the blessed Fillan, apprised of this by divine inspiration, was angry at the servant for having revealed his secret to the brothers, on account of which by divine permission a pet crane of the monastery blinded the servant by pecking out his eye. But the blessed Fillan, moved by pity and by the pleas and entreaties of his brothers completely restored the servant's eye.[98]

attested by the carving of an arm attached to a ringed equal-armed cross found at Kirkton of Strath Fillan. I am grateful to Niall Robertson, who found this carving, for drawing my attention to this. See Figure 9.3 [photo of carving]. See also Figure 9.2 and n. 58 above [arm-reliquary on 14th-century helmet]. 97 AB, which is grammatically correct; *reuelasse*, Mf. 98 The pilgrims' well in Aberdour, associated with St Fillan, for which see above pp 188–89, was traditionally sought out by people with eye-diseases (Ross 1885, 52), while the water in a bason 'made by the saint [Fillan]' at *Dun-Fhaolain* (Dundurn, by St Fillan's, Comrie PER) was resorted to by 'all who are distressed with sore eyes' (*OSA* (Comrie), 271, note). The connection between Fillan and eyes is no doubt bound up with this story, and may well derive from it. A very similar story is told of St Columba, including a luminous hand, in Manus O'Donnell's *Betha Coluimb Chille* (O'Kelleher and Schoepperle 1918, §168). Although slightly later than the *Aberdeen Breviary* account (O'Donnell wrote his life in Ireland in 1532), the story there is more integrated into the wider story, and is more tightly told, with the crane pecking out the eye of the spying servant through the hole in the door.

Tres medie lectiones de epyphanian domini cum Responsoriis de nocturnis secundum ordinem. Lectio uii.

Interea uero dum ipsius foelani fama ubique predicaretur beato patre mundo uita reddito illius monasterii cui prefuit unan<i>mi[99] fratrum consensu beatus foelanus in abbatem inuitus tamen eligitur ubi traditum sibi regimen uirtutibus et optimis morum exemplis quam feliciter gubernauit fratresque suos cum omni sanctitate casti<t>ate[100] et humilitate instruxit et informauit illos quosque in christum credentes reperit ut suos carissimos et speciales amicos in caritate dei et dilectione tractauit eisdem super omnia hospitalitatem obseruando.[101]

Three middle lessons of the Lord's Epiphany, with the responsories of the Nocturns according to the Ordinal.

Lesson 7.

Meanwhile Fillan's fame was broadcast on all sides and, the blessed father Mundu having died, the blessed Fillan, though reluctant, was by the unanimous consent of the brothers elected abbot of the monastery of which he [Mundu] had been in charge. When its government had been handed over to him, he ruled it happily by his virtues and best examples of his ways, and with all sanctity, chastity and humility he instructed and taught his brothers; and he sought out those who believed in Christ, and treated them as his own very dear and special friends in the love of God and in charity, above all by showing them hospitality.

---

[99] AB; *unanmi*, Mf.   [100] AB; *castiiate*, Mf.   [101] 'Tu autem domine miserere nostri.' omitted.

Lectio uiii.
Sed angelica monicione relicta sancta matre kentigerna auunculo suo congano uiro sanctissimo ad locum qui siracht dicitur in superioribus partibus de glendeochquhy[102] peruenit in quo loco eidem cum septem seruis clericis locus basilice edificande diuinitus ostensus est ubi paululum moratus cum suo caniculo ferocissimum aprum qui antea totum populum suis minatibus[103] deuastauerat penitus fugauit uariosque de eodem loco a gentilitatis et ydolatrie errore atque perfidia ad christi fidem conuertebat.[104]

Lesson 8.
But on the advice of an angel he left his holy mother Kentigerna and came to his uncle Conganus,[105] a most saintly man, to a place called *Siracht*[106] in the upper part of Glendochart,[107] where a site for building a church was divinely shown to him and the seven serving clerics with him.[108] After staying there a little while he completely drove away with his little dog[109] a very ferocious boar which had been devastating all the people with its threats, and he converted many locals from the error and falsehood of paganism and idolatry to faith in Christ.

---

102 Although obviously representing Glendochart, the form of this name is almost identical with contemporary spellings of Glenduckie, Flisk parish FIF (NO283188) (e.g. *Glendooquhy* 1499 *RSS*, i, no. 340). There was a chapel of Glenduckie first recorded in 1450 (see Millar 1895, ii, 325). It would seem therefore that the text has passed through the hands of someone more familiar with Fife and the diocese of St Andrews than with western Perthshire and the diocese of Dunkeld. This lack of familiarity probably also accounts for the garbled place-name *Siracht* (see n. 106 below).   **103** In classical Latin this would be 'minacibus', from 'minax' 'threatening'.   **104** 'Tu autem.' omitted.   **105** According to Kent. *Lect.* Kentigerna leaves her home and with Fillan and Conganus comes to a hermitage ('ad heremum') as far as Strath Fillan (*Straphilane*), where she lives the contemplative life with them for some time. According to Cong. *Lect.* Conganus, after ruling his kingdom [in Ireland] as a good Christian ruler, was attacked by neighbouring subkings, wounded in the foot, and took up the religious life. He then sailed with his sister Kentigerna, her sons Felanus, Furseus and Ulcanus (=Ultán), and seven other clerics to Scotland to Loch Alsh (*Lochelch*) in northern Argyll ('in *Erchadia Boriali*'). A short time after this Fillan built a church in his honour, where Conganus is still venerated, and when Conganus died he was buried on Iona.   **106** This is presumably a scribal or typographic corruption of *Strath*, later Strath Fillan, and refers to a place at or near the medieval priory of Strath Fillan. For further evidence that the text has passed through the hands of someone unfamiliar with the place-names of this area, see n. 102 above.   **107** This describes exactly the position of Strath Fillan.   **108** Note that in Cong. *Lect.* Conganus and company crosses to Scotland with seven clerics (see n. 105 above).   **109** This is the only mention of Fillan's dog, and may have been suggested at some point in the development of the legend by the name Fáelán itself, which means 'little wolf'. 'Caniculus' might even have been used at some stage as a Latin version of his name. See also n. 113 below.

Lectio nona.
Edificante autem eo ecclesiam in loco celitus sibi ostenso cum de curribus eiusdem boues relaxati fuissent lupus uorax et ferus unum de bobus nocte interfecit et commedit: atque mane cum bouem non haberet qui bouis interfecti locum suppleret oracione fusa ad deum idem lupus ut domesticus reuersus cum ceteris bobus se sub iugo aratri subiugauit qui eciam perseuerans usque ad dicte ecclesie consummacionem cum reliquis trahendo permansit quo facto ad solitam suam naturam rediit nulli lesionem faciendo beatus uero foelanus post plurima et uaria alia miraculorum gesta dierum fe-/fo. xxiii *uerso*/licium plenus quinto Idus Januarii migrauit ad christum et in dicta ecclesia que inter <populos>[110] straphillane dicitur honorifice <t>raditus[111] sepulture. Atque ibidem requiescit.[112]

Cetera omnia de communi unius abbatis cum oracione ut supra cum memoria epyphanie et sancte marie.

Ninth Lesson.
While he was building the church in the place shown him by heavenly inspiration, when his oxen were unyoked from the wagons, a fierce and greedy wolf one night killed one of the oxen and ate it; and in the morning when he did not have an ox which could take the place of the one which had been killed, he poured out a prayer to God and that very wolf came back as if tame and submitted itself to the yoke of the plough along with the other oxen. And it remained until the said church had been completed, pulling with the rest of them, after which it returned to its usual nature, doing harm to no-one.[113] The blessed Fillan, after many and various other miraculous deeds, full of happy days, went to Christ on the 9 January, and was honourably buried in the said church which is called Strath Fillan amongst [the (local) people], and there he rests.[114]

All the rest [is] from the common of a single abbot with the prayer as above, with the commemoration of the Epiphany and St Mary.

---

110 Some such noun would seem to be missing here. I owe this emendation to Alan Macquarrie.   111 AB; *eraditus*, Mf.   112 'Tu autem domine.' omitted.   113 As with Fillan's dog, for which see n. 109 above, this story about the wolf may have been suggested by the name Fáelán ('little wolf'). It is reminiscent of the story told about Fáelán mac Colmáin, king of Leinster (fl. 628), when he was a boy with Saints Coemgen and Berach. See Plummer 1922, 'Berach' §§33–4; 'Coemgen (I)' §§27–8; 'Coemgen (II)' §18; 'Coemgen (III)' §§32–4.   114 Kent. *Lect*. recounts that Kentigerna, deprived of the company of her son and brother (either because they have died or because they have withdrawn from the world, the text is unclear), withdraws to live the simple life of an anchorite on Inchcailloch in Loch Lomond, Lennox ('ad insulam *Inchcailzeoch* in *Louchloumont* in *Leuenax*'), where she finally dies, on 7 January, and in her honour the parish church now stands on the island, dedicated to her. See also above pp 183–84.

APPENDIX 2

Key to Map (i): each number refers to a *locus* of the Fillan cult as witnessed by place-names or dedications. They are organized alphabetically by county (pre-1975), then by parish, which is given after each name.

ANGUS
1. **St Fillan's Well**, Lochlee c.NO45 78
Mentioned in Jervise (1882, 115) as being beside the burn of Gleneffock (O.S. Landranger 'Water of Effock'), a tributary of the North Esk.

ARGYLL
2. **Allt Fhaolàin**, Ardchattan & Muckairn NN153518
Gaelic 'Fillan's burn'. See Gleann Fhaolàin below.

Gleann Fhaolàin, Ardchattan & Muckairn NN152520
'Fillan's glen'. This shares the same specific element as Allt Fhaolàin, Inbhir Fhaolàin and Làirg Fhaolàin, all of which form an interconnected system in Glen Etive: the Allt Fhaolàin flows through Gleann Fhaolàin and meets the River Etive at Inbhir Fhaolàin, while Làirg Fhaolàin is at Allt Fhaolàin's upper end. It would appear that there was some kind of an ecclesiastical foundation somewhere in this glen.

Inbhir Fhaolàin, Ardchattan & Muckairn NN160506
   Invereoland Thomson's map [quoted in Beveridge 1923, 68]
   Inverellan Dorret's map [quoted in Beveridge 1923, 68]
Gaelic 'Fillan's burn-mouth'. See Gleann Fhaolàin above.

Làirg Fhaolàin, Ardchattan & Muckairn NN137536
'Fillan's pass'. See Gleann Fhaolàin above.

3. **Kilellan**, Campbeltown NR684148
Killelan 1499 *RSS* iv fol.148
Gaelic 'church of Fillan'; a farm, and the site of a ruined chapel. It lay in the medieval parish of Kilkerran. Watson 1926, 285.

4. **Killinallan (Cillean Ailean)**, Kilmarrow and Kilmeny (Islay) NR315723
Gaelic *cillean* 'small church'. It is identified as a Fillan-commemoration by Thomas (1882, 267). MacEacherna states that local tradition associates it with a St Allan, otherwise unknown, but points out that it could also be interpreted as *Cill an àilein* 'church of the green' (1976, 52). He says it occurs also as the name of a chapel at Kildalton, in the south-east corner of Islay (ibid.).

Kilellan, (Islay)
Mentioned as a Fillan-commemoration by MacEacherna (1976, 53), but otherwise unlocated.

5. **Kilenaillan**, Kilninian and Kilmore (Mull)　　　　　　　NM546455
　　Killane 1509 *ER* xiii, 213
　　Killenaillan 1654 Blaeu's *Atlas Novus*
The site of a ruined chapel is still shown on the O.S. Landranger map. Listed as a Fillan-dedication in Redford 1988, 198, it is uncertain whether it does in fact contain the saint's name. See Killinallan, Islay ARG for a discussion of other possible interpretations.

AYRSHIRE
6. **St Fillan's Well**, Largs　　　　　　　　　　　　　　　NS195675
[lands of] *Sanct-Phillanis-well* 1615 *RMS* vii no. 1183 [on lands of Skelmorlie-Cunningham]
Grid reference from Redford 1988, 198. According to *OPS* there was a chapel nearby dedicated to St Fillan (i, 89).

FIFE
7. **St Fillan's Kirk**, Aberdour　　　　　　　　　　　　　　NT194855
　　ecclesia sancti Fulani de Aberdouer 1390 *Morton Reg.* ii, 174
The parish kirk is dedicated to St Fillan, the earliest reference to this being in 1390. For more details, see above pp 188–89.

St Fillan's Well, Aberdour
The well lay near the parish kirk, which was dedicated to St Fillan (see above under **St Fillan's Kirk**). It is first mentioned in 1474, simply as the pilgrims' well, and is not explicitly connected with St Fillan until the late nineteenth century, by the local historian William Ross (1885, 44, 52). For more details see above pp 188–89 and Appendix 1 n. 98.

8. **Lumphinnans**, Ballingry　　　　　　　　　　　　　　NT174934
　　Lumfilan 1242 and 1245 *Pitfirrane Writs* nos. 1 and 2
　　Lumphenen 1393 *Pitfirrane Writs* no. 8
　　Lumphenane 1415 *Pitfirrane Writs* no. 12
　　Lu[m]fennen 1437 *Dunf. Reg.* no. 406
　　[L]umfulan 1468 *Pitfirrane Writs* no. 38
　　Lumfillans 1496 *Pitfirrane Writs* no. 43
　　Lumphinnanis 1501 *Pitfirrane Writs* no. 44
For a discussion of this name, see above pp 190–91

9. **St Fillan's Kirk**, Forgan   NO446259
This parish was originally called Naughton (*Adnacthen* etc.: Nechtan's Ford), and included the estate of that name, now in Balmerino parish. It is first mentioned as being dedicated to St Fillan in the late sixteenth century, when the parish is referred to as the 'parochin of *Sanct Fillan*'. Two centuries later the local minister called the parish 'Forgan alias St Phillans' (*OSA* 10, 381). He also connected Fillan with the estate of St Fort, about a mile to the west of the old kirk of St Fillan's, in the belief that it meant the fort of a saint: 'This was probably in ancient times the dwelling of the saint.' (*OSA* 10, 381–2). In fact St Fort derives from Sandford, referring to a sandy ford over the Motray Water!

10. **St Fillan's Cave**, Pittenweem   NO550026
The extensive cave lies below the ruins of the priory of Pittenweem, which developed out of the mainland base of the priory of St Ethernan, Isle of May, which lies *c*.10 km offshore. The upper part of the cave is vaulted, and was obviously part of the complex of medieval priory buildings. Both Pittenweem and the Isle of May lay in the medieval parish of Anstruther. See above pp 189–90.

11. **St Andrews**   NO509167
Altar of St Fillan in the parish kirk of the Holy Trinity, St Andrews, first mentioned in 1449. See p. 190 above.

KIRKCUDBRIGHTSHIRE
12. **Ernfillan**, Crossmichael   NX75 65
The first element is probably Gaelic *earrann* 'share, portion' (Watson 1926, 147, 170). On the O.S. Pathfinder map the name survives in Ernfillan Hill and Ernfillan Glen.

PERTHSHIRE
13. **Struan**, Blair Atholl   NN808654
The medieval parish of Struan is now part of Blair Atholl. At the parish kirk, dedicated to St Fillan, there was an early iron hand-bell associated with the saint and known as *Buidhean* 'little yellow one';[115] it had a fair day called *Féill Fhaolàin*, held beside the kirk on the first Friday in the new year (Old Style), about 20 January (New Style); and a near-by well was called *Tobair Fhaolàin* or St Fillan's Well. A wooden image of the saint survived the Reformation and was kept in the kirk. In times of drought its feet were dipped in St Fillan's Well to bring on rain, a practice which persisted until about 1720, when the local

---

[115] Now in Perth Museum and Art Gallery (accession number 3–1939).

minister smashed it and flung the broken pieces into the River Garry (MacKinlay 1914, 169 and Kerr 1998, 43–4).[116]

14. **Dùn Fhaolàin**, Comrie NN708232
This is another name for the hill-fort of Dundurn (for which see above pp 193–94). The remains of St Fillan's Chapel are to be seen near the base of the hill, while St Fillan's Well and St Fillan's Seat are on the hill itself. Dùn Fhaolàin is first mentioned in the Comrie account in *OSA*, which is the first certain reference to St Fillan in this area.

St Fillan's, Comrie NN692244
Only so called since 1817, when the first feus were granted along the edge of Loch Earn. The earlier name of the settlement was Port of Lochearn (Porteous 1912, 6).

St Fillan's Chapel, Comrie
See **Dùn Fhaolàin** above. An old chapel-of-ease and burial place near the foot of Dundurn.

15. **Killin** (parish) NN572332
Féill Fhaolàin (St Fillan's Fair) was held in Killin on 9 January, and until about 100 years ago the mill at Killin was idle on that day (MacKinlay 1914, 168). For the Healing Stones of St Fillan, associated with this mill, and other local traditions connected with the saint at Killin, see Gillies 1938, 80–2.

16. **Strath Fillan**, Killin NN359285
    church of *Strathfulane* 1318 *Inchaffray Chrs.* no.123
    chapel of 'Sancti Felani' in *[G]lendochred* 1318 *Inchaffray Chrs.* no. 126
    monastery or chapel of *Straithfulane* 1498 RMS ii no. 2458
See above pp 182–88.

Lands in Strath Fillan and Glen Dochart (Killin parish) associated with the relics of St Fillan:
a. **Coreheynan** NN370335
    lands of *Coreheynan* 1468 *Taymouth Bk.* xxxvi
Coire Sheanain, probably Seanan's Corrie, from a man's name (Watson 1928, 263). This remote corrie lay at the head of Gleann a' Chlachain, west of Strath Fillan. In 1468 it was held by a MacGregor who is described as dewar of the *Meser* ('Deore de Meser'). Watson would derive 'meser' from *meise* 'portable

---

[116] Local tradition tells that the minister paid dearly for this act. Kerr 1998 (43–5) has a good summary of the sources and traditions relating to Struan and St Fillan. I am grateful to Mark Hall for bringing this to my attention.

altar' (see Gillies 1938, 80). Alternatively, might it be derived from the Scots *mazer* or *macer* 'wooden bowl'? See also Croftindewar (16b).

b. **Croftindewar** † (at Acharn) c.NN56 31
Cryetindowar in Auchincarn [Acharn] 1551 *RMS* iv no.682 [one of the lands which Queen Mary feued to Malicius Deware and heirs]
Gaelic *croit an dèoraidh* 'croft of the dewar'.
'Croftindewar: a triangular piece of land *c.*80 acres in extent, which belonged to the family of Dewars ... It is now merged with the farm of Acharn.' Gillies 1938, 389. Acharn is a farm *c.*1 km south-west of Killin. This is probably the croft in Killin called *Dewar-Namais* (one of the relics of St Fillan), mentioned in 1632 (*RMS* viii no. 1981). It appears also as *Dewarnamanscroft* in 1640 and *Dewarnamaynescroft* in 1670 (Watson 1926, 265). Watson also suggests that the relic in question may have been the saint's arm (1928, 254).[117]

c. **Dewarnafargs Croft** † (at Auchlyne) c.NN51 29
crofta in *Auchlyne* nuncupata *Dewar-Nafargs-croft* 1632 *RMS* viii no. 1981
Gaelic *croit dèoraidh na Fairg(e)* 'croft of the dewar of the shrine'; the old chapel at Auchlyne in Glen Dochart was known as *Caibeal na Fairg(e)* in the early twentieth century; see Watson 1926, 265.

d. **Dewarvernan's Croft** † (at Suie) c.NN48 27
lie *Dewaris-croft* in lie *Suy* called *Dewar-Vernans-croft* 1632 *RMS* viii no. 1981
Gaelic *croit dèoraidh a'Bhearnàin* 'croft of the dewar of the bell' [literally 'gapped one']. This is no doubt the bell which was carried at the coronation of James IV (see above p. 194; see also Watson 1926, 265).

It was at Suie in Glen Dochart, where, according to Watson, there are a cemetery and the remains of a chapel (1928, 254). Suie is Gaelic *suidhe* 'seat', in place-names usually referring to a natural chair-shaped feature closely associated with a saint (Watson 1926, 260–3). The saint in question here must be Fillan (Watson 1928, 254).

e. **Ewich** (or **Iuich**) NN363274
Eyich in *Glendochart* 1336 Stuart 1878, 155 [sixteenth-century summary of a charter of Alexander Menzies lord of *Glendoquhart* to Donald M'Sobrell dewar Cogerach]

---

117 He does not give a reason for this assumption, but it seems he would derive *man(s)* and *mayne(s)* from French *main* 'hand'. If this is the case, then the assumption is highly implausible. The earliest form of the word describing the relic in question is *mais* (1632), which may be compared to the *meser* of Coreheynan, at the opposite end of Killin parish (16a above). The *na* in all three cases represents the Gaelic definite article (feminine genitive singular).

Eicht 1551 *RMS* iv no.682 [feued to Malicius Deware and heirs by Queen Mary]

Probably derived from Middle Irish *eo* 'yew' (modern Scottish Gaelic *iubhar*), meaning 'place of yew-tree or yews' (Watson 1928, 262).

The lands of Ewich belonged to the dewar of the *coigreach*, the staff or crozier of St Fillan, by 1336 (Stuart 1878, 155).

17. **St Fillan's Chapels** at Doune Castle, Kilmadock   NN728011
    capella Sancti Fulani propre castrum de *Downe* 1505 *ER* xii, 323
    capellanus capelle Sancti Phillani 1536 *RMS* iii no.1574
    capellania de Sanct Phillane infra castrum de *Doune* et capellania Sancti Phillane extra idem castrum situata 1602 *Retours* (Perth) [quoted Watson 1926, 285, footnote]

Two chapels dedicated to St Fillan at Doune Castle, one inside the castle, the other beside it, on the banks of the River Teith. See above p. 191.

18. **St Fillan's Burn** †, Redgorton   NO094295
    Sanct-Phillanis-burn 1596 *RMS* vi no.586.

This is one of the marches given in Scots defining the vill and lands of Halton of Luncarty in the medieval parish of Luncarty (diocese of St Andrews, now part of Redgorton). It may point to the fact that Luncarty kirk was dedicated to Fillan, as assumed by Mackinlay 1914, 168–9, an asumption based apparently on the burn-name. It is also mentioned in the early twelfth century (as *Lonfortin*) as one of the churches founded by the largely mythical St Modwenna (Forbes *Kalendars*, 406, where *Lonfortin* wrongly identified with Longforgan PER).

RENFREWSHIRE

19. **Kilellan**, Houston   NS383689
    ecclesia de *Kelenan* 1205x1207 *Pais. Reg.* 113
    ecclesia de *Kilhelan* 1225 *Pais. Reg.* 372–3
    ecclesia de *Kylhelan* 1227x1229 *Pais. Reg.* 114
    ecclesia de *Kilhelan* 1227x1229 *Pais. Reg.* 115

A medieval parish, now part of Houston parish RNF. A fair was held here in January (see *OPS* i, 81). According to the same source there was near the church a rock called St Fillan's Chair and a St Fillan's Well, to which 'until lately' the country people used to bring their sickly children.

Note the confusion in the index of the *Pais. Reg.* between this Kilellan and Kilfinan in Cowal ARG, for which see above p. 191. This mistake was repeated by Watson 1926, 285, but corrected by him in a note on p. 518. This tendency to assimilate *n* to *l* after *l* is the exact counterpart to the dissimilation of *l* to *n* after *l* seen in the earliest occurrence of Kilellan in 1205 x 1207. See also the discussion on Lumphinnans above pp 190–91.

Barfillan, Houston   NS393680
A farm c.1.2 km south-east of Kilellan kirk, it contains Gaelic *bàrr* 'summit, top' (or its Cumbric cognate).

St Fillan's Chair, Houston; see Kilellan RNF above.

St Fillan's Well, Houston; see Kilellan RNF above.

ROSS AND CROMARTY
20. **Killilan**, Kintail   NG947303
    Killewlan 1749 *Geog. Coll.* ii, 541
See the discussion of the churches of the Loch Alsh/Loch Long/Loch Duich complex pp 182–83 above. See also Watson, 1926, 284 and 1904, 181.

WIGTOWNSHIRE
21. **Airyolland**, New Luce   NX15 62 and 16 62
    On the OS Pathfinder map, the farms of High and Low Airyolland farms are shown, along with Airyolland Moss (NX14 61), Fell, Loch and Wood. See also Kilfillan, Old Luce and Sorbie, below.

22. **Airyolland**, Mochrum   NX309476
See Kilfillan, Sorbie, below. On the OS Pathfinder map shows, besides Airyolland, Clays of Airyolland (NX31 48).

23. **Kilfillan**, Old Luce   NX20 55
    Kilphillen 1654 Blaeu's *Atlas Novus*
Note also **Ardfillan** in same parish (NX21 55). Also Airyolland, New Luce, lay in the same medieval parish of Luce.

24. **Kilfillan**, Sorbie   NX46 46
In a charter of 1282, the parish of Sorbie (or at least a division of it) is referred to as *Kirkfolan* (*Dryb. Lib.* no.238). MacQueen (1973, 19) mentions two àirigh-names ('sheiling, cattle-station') containing the saint's name, attached to one or both of the Wigtonshire Kilfillans: **Airyolland** (*Arewlene* 1498, *Arehullen* 1561). Note also the parish of Balmaclellan KCB, which contains the personal name Gille Fáelàin (*loc. cit.*).

On the O.S. Pathfinder map, this name survives in Kilfillan Bridge, Kilfillan Burn and Kilfillan Hill.

BIBLIOGRAPHY AND ABBREVIATIONS[118]

The following abbreviations of pre-1975 counties are used:

ARG	Argyll	PER	Perthshire
AYR	Ayrshire	RNF	Renfrewshire
FIF	Fife	ROS	Ross and Cromarty
INV	Inverness-shire	STL	Stirlingshire
KCB	Kirkcudbrightshire	WIG	Wigtownshire

Aberdeen Breviary Breviarium Aberdonense, Bannatyne, Maitland and Spalding Clubs 1854.
Anderson, M.O. 1980, *Kings and Kingship in Early Scotland* (revised edition, Edinburgh).
Beveridge, E. 1923, *The Abers and Invers of Scotland* (Edinburgh).
Carmichael, A. 1941, *Carmina Gadelica* (Edinburgh).
Chambers (Camerarius), D. 1631, *De Scotorum Fortitudine Doctrina et Pietate* (Paris).
Dryb. Lib. Liber S. Marie de Dryburgh, Bannatyne Club 1847.
Dunf. Reg. Registrum de Dunfermelyn, Bannatyne Club 1842.
ER The Exchequer Rolls of Scotland, eds J.Stuart *et al.* (Edinburgh, 1878–1908).
Forbes, *Kalendars* A.P. Forbes, *Kalendars of Scottish Saints* (Edinburgh, 1872).
Geog. Coll. Geographical Collections relating to Scotland made by Walter Macfarlane, SHS 1906–8.
Gillies, W.A. 1938, *In Famed Breadalbane* (Perth).
Jervise A. (and Gammack, J.) 1882, *Land of the Lindsays* (2nd edn Edinburgh).
Kerr, J. 1998, *Church and Social History of Atholl* (Perth).
MacEacharna, D. 1976, *The Lands of the Lordship* (Port Charlotte, Islay).
MacKinlay, J.M. 1914, *Ancient Church Dedications in Scotland: Non-scriptural* (Edinburgh).
MacQueen, J. 1973, 'The Gaelic Speakers of Galloway and Carrick', *Scottish Studies* 17, 17–33.
Millar, A.H. 1895, *Fife: Pictorial and Historical* (2 vols) (Cupar).
O'Kelleher, A. and Schoepperle, G. 1918 (eds) *Betha Colaim Chille: Life of Columcille (Compiled by Manus O'Donnell in 1532)* (Urbana, Illinois) [facsimile reprint Dublin 1994].
OPS Origines Parochiales Scotiae, Bannatyne Club, 1851–5.
O.S. Ordnance Survey.

---

[118] The references found here are to works cited only in the appendices/captions or both in the appendices/captions and in the main text. For those occurring in the main text alone, full details are given in the footnotes.

OSA The [Old] Statistical Account of Scotland 1791–99 (Edinburgh; reissued county by county in twenty volumes, with new introductions, 1978).

Pais. Reg. Registrum Monasterii de Passelet, Maitland Club 1832; New Club 1877.

Pitfirrane Writs Inventory of Pitfirrane Writs 1230–1794 ed. W. Angus, Scottish Record Society 1932.

Plummer, C. 1922, *Bethada Náem nÉrenn/Lives of Irish Saints* (Oxford).

Porteous, A. 1912, *Annals of St Fillans* (Crieff).

PSAS Proceedings of the Society of Antiquaries of Scotland

Redford, M. 1988, 'Commemorations of Saints of the Celtic Church in Scotland', unpublished MLit. thesis, University of Edinburgh.

Reeves, W. 1864, *The Culdees of the British Islands* (Dublin, reprinted Felinfach 1994).

Retours Inquisitionum ad capellam domini regis retornatarum ... abbreviatio, Rec. Com. (3 vols, 1811–16)

RMS Registrum Magni Sigilli Regum Scottorum eds J.M. Thomson et al. (Edinburgh, 1882–1914).

Ross, W. 1885, *Aberdour and Inchcolme* (Edinburgh).

RSS Registrum Secreti Sigilli Regum Scottorum, eds M. Livingstone *et al.* (Edinburgh, 1908–).

Stuart, J. 1878, 'Historical notices of St Fillan's Crozier, and of the devotion of King Robert Bruce to St Fillan', *PSAS* 12 (1876–78), 134–82.

Taymouth Bk. The Black Book of Taymouth, Bannatyne Club 1855 (reprinted by Kilchurn Heritage n.d.).

Thomas, F.W.L. 1882, 'On Islay Place-Names', *PSAS* 16 (1881–82), 241–76.

Watson, W.J. 1926, *The History of the Celtic Place-Names of Scotland* (Edinburgh and London).

Watson, W.J. 1928, 'The Place-Names of Breadalbane', *Transactions of the Gaelic Society of Inverness* 34 (1927–28), 248–79.

Yeoman, P. 1999, *Pilgrimage in Medieval Scotland* (London).

Brendan the Navigator: a Twelfth-Century View

C.R. SNEDDON

The aim of this essay is to consider why a sixth-century Irish saint should have become the subject of a poem written for a queen of the Anglo-Norman King of England Henry I, and what light this choice of subject can shed on the geopolitical concerns of a twelfth-century ruler governing a state bordering on the North Sea. This question will be approached through the legend of St Brendan, whose reputation as a navigator made him a plausible hero for the tenth-century *Navigatio sancti Brendani*.[1] This work reveals, if we are to believe the claims of Geoffrey Ashe,[2] enough maritime knowledge of the Atlantic to make it possible to wonder whether or not the Irish might have reached Newfoundland before the Vikings. Even if this speculation is so far unconfirmed, Ashe has the merit of drawing together the information available to the Irish geographer Dicuil in his 825 treatise,[3] and material on curragh boats' construction and seaworthiness,[4] which apparently inspired Tim Severin to replicate in the late 1970s, Kon-Tiki style, Brendan's supposed route to America.[5]

---

1 *Navigatio sancti Brendani abbatis. From early Latin Manuscripts*, ed. by Carl Selmer, University of Notre Dame Publications in Medieval Studies, 16 (Notre Dame, Indiana, 1959); *The Voyage of St Brendan. Journey to the Promised Land*, trans. by John J. O'Meara (Dublin, 1978).   2 Geoffrey Ashe, *Land to the West. St Brendan's Voyage to America* (London, 1962), esp. pp 19–119.   3 For a modern edition, see *Dicuili Liber de Mensura Orbis Terrae*, ed. by J.J. Tierney, Scriptores Latini Hiberniae, 6 (Dublin, 1967). For a more recent study of Dicuil, see Werner Bergmann, 'Dicuils *De mensura orbis terrae*', in *Science in Western and Eastern Civilization in Carolingian Times*, ed. by Paul Leo Butzer and Dietrich Lohrmann (Basel and Boston, 1993), pp 525–37. For the use made of Dicuil's information by Ashe, see *Land to the West*, ch. 4, esp. pp 126, 129 and 131; Ashe also refers to geographers from Antiquity, whose information he suggests was also available to the author of the *Navigatio* (*Land to the West*, pp 157–92). Hogetoorn points out that the Hereford Mappa Mundi of *c*.1300 places Brendan's paradise off the coast of Morocco (Corry Hogetoorn, 'Le Voyage de Saint Brandan par Benedeit', *Rapports. Het Franse Boek*, 55 (1985), pp 110–24, esp. p. 121); this is not inconsistent with the more southerly regions of the Atlantic discussed by Ashe on the basis of the geographers of Antiquity.   4 See Ashe, esp. pp 67–71, for the curragh boats, and pp 73–119 for the places in the text of the *Navigatio* for which he suggests identifications.   5 See Tim Severin, *The Brendan Voyage* (London, 1978), and the brief discussion in

What is known about the historical Brendan, the founding Abbot of Clonfert in Galway, suggests that, as well as visiting St Columba on the island of Hinba in Argyll some time after AD 563, he may have travelled to Wales, Brittany, Orkney and the Shetlands, and may have founded other monasteries in Ireland.[6] These activities make him a significant figure in the context of the saints and seamen of the North Sea World of the sixth century, though one who appears only in the second rank of Irish saints. However, after his death, a distinctly wider significance came to be attached to his name. The ninth-century *Vita Sancti Brendani* and in particular the tenth-century *Navigatio* show that his role has become that of the model abbot leading his flock, and that his travels and leadership qualities have made him the hero of a journey into the Western Ocean to paradise.[7] The *Navigatio* is a religious text, which may perhaps as Ashe has claimed recall both the Irish 'immrama' tradition of a hero's journey seeking the Isle of the Blest[8] and the knowledge of actual Irish explorations by monks and others of the North Atlantic, but whose avowed purpose of describing Abbot Brendan's journey to paradise is unambiguously edifying; the text's numerous references to the monastic life confirm this edifying role.[9]

The principal focus of this article is, however, neither the tenth-century *Navigatio* nor twentieth-century interpretations of it, but rather one particular twelfth-century vernacular adaptation of the *Navigatio*,[10] namely the Anglo-Norman poem devoted to Brendan.[11] This poem is well known to students of

---

Hogetoorn, pp 121–22. The possibility of the Irish being precursors of the Vikings is left open by the remarks in Henry Loyn, *The Vikings in Britain* (Oxford, England, and Cambridge, Massachusetts, 1994), pp 11, 17–18, which suggest that by and large most Celts in the settlement of Iceland were brought there as slaves of the Vikings, though Ashe, pp 128–29, claims Dicuil's authority for the view that some Irish people had already settled in Iceland.   6 See David Hugh Farmer, *The Oxford Dictionary of Saints* (Oxford, 1978), pp 54–55, for a summary biography, which suggests Brendan lived *c*.486–*c*. 575; see also Selmer, *Navigatio*, pp xvii–xix, and Peter Harbison, *Pilgrimage in Ireland. The monuments and the people* (London, 1991), pp 37–48.   7 For information on the *Vita*, see Selmer, *Navigatio*, pp xx and xxvi, and Hogetoorn, p. 111. A possibly related ninth-century text, the *Vita anonyma brevis sancti Machutis*, is discussed in Jean-Claude Poulin, 'Sources hagiographiques de la Gaule, ii: Les Dossiers de S. Magloire de Dol et de S. Malo d'Alet (Province de Bretagne)', *Francia*, 17/1 (1990), pp 159–209, esp. pp 160–68.   8 See for the 'immrama' Ashe, pp 53–63, and Hogetoorn, pp 112–13. 9 See Selmer, *Navigatio*, pp xx–xxv.   10 See Carl Selmer, 'The Vernacular Translations of the *Navigatio Sancti Brendani*: A Bibliographical Study', *Mediaeval Studies*, 18 (1956), pp 145–57 for an overview of the vernacular versions of the *Navigatio*; cf. Hogetoorn, pp 114–15 for an account of the Germanic versions.   11 The most recent critical edition, based on the four manuscripts and one fragment then known, is by E.G.R. Waters, *The Anglo-Norman Voyage of St Brendan. A poem of the Early Twelfth Century by Benedeit* (Oxford, 1928; repr. Slatkine, Genève, 1974) (hereafter Waters). This is the edition from which Benedeit's poem is cited in this article. Waters' text, with an introduction and facing translation in Modern German was reprinted in *Benedeit. Le Voyage de Saint Brendan*, ed. by Ernstpeter Ruhe, Klassische Texte des Romanischen

Brendan the Navigator: a Twelfth-Century View

French literature in England,[12] but it stands apart from other works of the period in several respects which will now be discussed, in order to see whether the information we have about it allows us to understand what its original purpose may have been, and thus clarify why the legend of an Irish saint should have been of interest to the royal patron who commissioned this particular translation of the *Navigatio sancti Brendani*. In order to achieve this aim, the Anglo-Norman *Brendan* will be studied as a work of literature in its own right, and then compared to its source, of which it claims to be merely a translation.[13]

Studied as literature, the Anglo-Norman *Brendan* is unusual both in poetic form and in genre. As far as its form is concerned, it seems to be one of the earliest texts to use the octosyllabic couplet,[14] which was later in the twelfth

---

Mittelalters in zweisprachigen Ausgaben, 16 (München, 1977) (hereafter Ruhe). The poem has since twice been published from the 'best' manuscript (London, British Library, MS Cotton Vespasian B. X, fos. 1–11) by Ian Short and Brian Merrilees, *Benedeit. The Anglo-Norman Voyage of St Brendan* (Manchester, 1979) (hereafter Short and Merrilees, *Anglo-Norman Voyage*) and by the same editors in *Le Voyage de Saint Brandan par Benedeit*, 10/18, 1652 (Paris, 1984), on the second occasion with a French translation; the differences in lineation between the Short and Merrilees text and the Waters text are given on p. 23 of Short and Merrilees (1979). The manuscripts are described in Waters, pp ix–xxii, and, with the addition of a second fragment, in Short and Merrilees, *Anglo-Norman Voyage*, pp 6–8; the published transcription of the second fragment should be checked, and the variants taken into account, in any future critical edition.   **12** See M. Dominica Legge, *Anglo-Norman Literature and its Background* (Oxford, 1963), esp. pp 8–18.   **13** *Brendan*, ll. 9–13. Legge, p. 10, claims, on the basis of the repeated word 'letre' in ll. 10–11 and of the association of 'litteratus' with the ability to read Latin, that Benedeit first wrote a text in Latin and then translated his Latin into French; since the comparison undertaken in Waters, pp lxxxiii–xcix, clearly shows that the ultimate source of Benedeit's poem is the *Navigatio*, Legge's interpretation of 'letre' involves Benedeit in the cumbersome process of first producing a Latin paraphrase before writing his French poem. It seems simpler to take 'letre' in its literal meaning of 'letter', but used as a form of synecdoche with the part standing for the whole, so that 'letter' stands for 'writing' without reference to any particular language; l. 11 would then be construed as showing deferred coordination, a common construction in Old French which could be used to avoid ambiguity as well as for stylistic variation, i.e. 'put into writing and into French', which means that Benedeit wrote only one text, namely the French poem from which this line is taken; for a complementary discussion of Brendan ll. 9–13, see Robin F. Jones, 'The Precocity of Anglo-Norman and the *Voyage of Saint Brendan*', in *The Nature of Medieval Narrative*, ed. by Minette Grunmann-Gaudet and Robin F. Jones, French Forum Monographs, 22 (Lexington, Kentucky, 1980), pp 145–58, esp. pp 148–49. The corollary of this conclusion is that the Latin prose text printed by Waters is not by Benedeit; Hogetoorn, p. 115, refers to Waters and Selmer for the two other hypotheses so far put forward to explain the relationship of the surviving texts, neither of which assumes that Benedeit used a Latin intermediary source instead of the *Navigatio*.   **14** Legge, p. 14, says 'perhaps the oldest', which may indeed be the case, even if Benedeit is writing in or after 1121 as the present article proposes, and not in or before 1118 as Legge, p. 8, Jones, 'Precocity', pp 146–47, and Ruhe, *Benedeit*, p. 18 n. 23, assume. Paul Meyer, 'Le couplet de deux vers', *Romania*, 23 (1894), pp 1–35, used Benedeit's poem as an example of the

century to become the normal medium for courtly narrative, as can be seen in the romances based on classical subjects, such as the *Roman d'Énée*, or based on allegedly Celtic subjects such as Chrétien de Troyes' *Li Contes del Graal*; the use of the octosyllabic couplet also for shorter narrative forms, such as the *Lais* of Marie de France, or the numerous and often anonymous *fabliaux*, confirms this general acceptance of the octosyllabic couplet as the medium *par excellence* for literary storytelling in French.[15] Before 1100, octosyllabic lines were certainly known, as for that matter were decasyllabic and dodecasyllabic, but the normal poetic unit was the stanza or the *laisse*, probably with accompanying music in both cases. The choice of the couplet as the basic unit of expression thus seems to be linked with the emergence of poetic texts without music,[16] and the significance of this may well be that the texts in which the couplet was used were no longer intended for the lord's great hall or for public performance, but rather for a more intimate recitation in the lady's chamber to the lady and her household.[17]

As far as its genre is concerned, the Anglo-Norman *Brendan* is not easy to situate. The two classic genres of the period before 1100 are the *chanson de geste* and the saint's life, which were lyric rather than narrative forms with their use of stanza or laisse as their basic unit. In content, they dealt with major issues affecting society as a whole; in the case of the *chansons de geste*, issues of the secular world are raised, such as loyalty to one's lord even against one's own private interest. In the case of saints' lives, it is clear that the passion and miracles of a saint demonstrated the power of Christian faith, and both types of text thus have in common a concern for reinforcing a positive morality which will benefit society, and through society the individual within it.[18] In contrast, despite the

---

early use of the couplet in Old French, though both Waters, pp l–lii, and Jones ('Precocity', p.153, and Robin F. Jones, 'The Mechanics of Meaning in the Anglo-Norman *Voyage of Saint Brendan*', *Romanic Review*, 71 (1980) pp 105–13, esp. p. 106 n. 6) see greater liberty of enjambement and greater syntactic freedom in the text than Meyer.   15 For an overview of the romances and the shorter narrative forms, see John Fox, *The Middle Ages. A Literary History of France*, i (London and New York, 1974), pp 134–67, 167–71, 225–39.   16 See Legge, pp 16, 244, for an alternative suggestion that Benedeit's strict use of eight syllables to the line, even for feminine lines, may reflect composition for a hymn tune; whatever merit this argument might have for an octosyllabic text composed in stanzas, there is no suggestion that any analogue has been identified with any other work written in couplets.   17 See Legge, p. 3, esp. n. 2. Jones, 'Precocity', pp 145–46, stresses the originality of the text as one intended to be read rather than sung. R.N. Illingworth, 'The Structure of the Anglo-Norman *Voyage of St Brendan* by Benedeit', *Medium Aevum*, 55 (1986), pp 217–29, esp. pp 227–28, sees the poem's structure as a work of craftsmanship using interlace and at the same time reflecting oral performance to a listening audience; the question of session length which he raises is clearly appropriate to a text which is to be publicly performed, but seems less relevant to a text for private recitation, unless Illingworth intends to imply that Benedeit had not yet seen the full implications of the change to private performance.   18 See, for evidence of church approval of these two traditional genres, the Penitential of Thomas of Chobham, quoted by Edmond Faral, *Les jongleurs en France au moyen âge*.

risk of oversimplifying, the narrative texts of the twelfth century may be said to proceed through testing individual heroes via the mechanism of the *aventure*; social expectations here provide the more or less firm foundation against which the hero can be judged, but in the end the focus of attention is on the achievement or otherwise of the individual rather than on the preservation or reinforcement of a particular social or religious world order.

The Anglo-Norman *Brendan* deals, not with the passion and miracles of a saint, as might have been expected from a conventional saint's life, but rather with a series of tests which certify the worthiness of Brendan and his chosen crew to achieve their goal, which is to reach paradise and see it before they die. If one could treat this in terms of later twelfth-century literature, the *Brendan* poem is a courtly romance, which through a series of *aventures* confirms the worth of the hero. However, how does one treat a saint like Brendan as needing to have his worth proved? Far from Brendan needing to be tested through a series of *aventures*, it is Brendan's own inner certainty that guides the crew successfully to their destination, so that the model of later twelfth-century literature hardly seems applicable to an understanding of this text.[19]

A detailed comparison of the *Navigatio* and Benedeit's poem is likely to cast some light on both Benedeit's intentions and his originality by identifying the nature of the changes he has made to his source. In the introduction to his critical edition of the Anglo-Norman *Brendan*, Waters has undertaken a full comparison which establishes a certain number of changes, and these confirm that the poem provides a tauter narrative than its Latin source, and is thus an adaptation rather than the translation it purports to be.[20] The principal differences will be highlighted as they arise in the course of the poem. The first difference is in the motivation of the journey. In the Latin text, Brendan receives a chance visit from Barintus, who tells him about his journey to paradise and thus inspires Brendan's curiosity. From a dramatic point of view,

---

Bibliothèque de l'École des Hautes Études, IVe section – Sciences historiques et philologiques, 187e fasc. (Paris, 1910), pp 44 and 67 n. 1. For his part, Jean Larmat, 'L'eau dans la *Navigation de saint Brendan* de Benedeit', in *L'Eau au Moyen Age*, Senefiance, no. 15 (1985), pp 233–46, esp. p. 243, sees the Anglo-Norman *Brendan* combining hagiography and the epic.   **19** Illingworth, 'Structure', pp 225–26, discusses what has been called the 'ambiguous nature' of Brendan's character, agreeing that Brendan is normally presented as confident and self-assured, but that at other times he seems to need reassurance. Illingworth concludes that there is no ambiguity in Brendan's character, but that his role is sometimes that of the abbot, and sometimes that of the individual on his own personal quest for which he himself needs guidance. However, Brendan's role may also be understood as part of the typological structure of the text discussed below, in which Brendan is, like Moses, unable to do more than see the promised land, and therefore human and fallible; see Ruhe, pp 21–25. A possible parallel among later courtly heroes would be Galahad, achieving the Grail quest through a series of other worldly adventures; Brendan as a humanised figure of power may be an early role-model.   **20** Waters, pp lxxxiii–xcix.

this has the disadvantage of giving us a description of paradise at the beginning of the work, and of depriving Brendan's journey of its unique quality. The Anglo-Norman text tells us that Brendan, as a good feudal saint, wishes to assert his right as the son of Adam to see his patrimony for himself.[21] His journey is thus not an act of simple curiosity, but one which reflects a determination to learn about what is rightfully a human possession, and the execution of this project places Brendan in the role of champion and missionary. The description of paradise when it comes can then be seen as the culmination of the journey, and its links with the account of the New Jerusalem in Revelation ch. 21 become all the more pointed.[22] Meantime, Barintus's role is reduced to that of the wise hermit, whom Brendan seeks out for confession and advice before setting out on his own journey.[23]

The second difference concerns the use made of the liturgy, whose symbolic and spiritual significance is retained, while having a less obtrusive role in the daily life of Brendan and his monks. The story as it unfolds is in detail often more dramatic and relevant to a courtly audience than the Latin, but follows the same general liturgical pattern of a journey that must be repeated annually for seven years until the crew is fully tested, and in particular, until the three monks who at the beginning of the journey insisted on adding themselves to the ship's company have been removed from the scene.[24] After consulting Barintus, Brendan chose a crew of fourteen monks, constructed and provisioned their boat, and then accepted reluctantly the three additional monks when they were on the point of setting sail.[25] The first stage of the journey sees them enthusiastically rowing, although the wind is favourable, until Brendan advises them to save their strength; when they do need to row, they can then keep going, just, until forty days have passed and they make their first landfall, where they find an uninhabited city, and more than enough food and drink for the next stage of their journey. On this island, the first of the supernumerary monks is tempted to steal a golden goblet, despite an express warning from Brendan. Brendan sees the theft taking place in the spiritual and physical darkness, the sinner

[21] *Brendan*, ll. 39–70, esp. ll. 47–58. Surprisingly Ruhe, pp 20–22, sees no explicit motivation for the journey in Benedeit's text, though he rightly argues against the idea of simple curiosity as a motive for Brendan's journey in the *Navigatio*. Jones, 'Mechanics', p. 107 and 'Precocity', p. 147, still accepts the idea of curiosity, but goes beyond this by asserting the aim of being reunited with God, 'Mechanics', p. 108. [22] *Brendan*, ll. 1673–1808, which is not only based on Revelation 21.11–20, but contains also allusions to Genesis 3.24, Exodus 3.8 and Deuteronomy 34.4. Compare the notes in Waters, pp 130–33 with Ruhe, p. 23 and n. 32. [23] *Brendan*, ll. 71–102. [24] *Brendan*, ll. 547–54 and ll. 877–84, the latter passage being preceded at ll. 831–32 by an explicit reminder of Jesus's command to commemorate him through the Last Supper on Maundy Thursday in Luke 22.19, and of the commandment to love one another and to wash one another's feet in John 13.34 and 13.14; the three additional monks leave the company at respectively ll. 333–54, ll. 1199–1214 and ll. 1499–1510. [25] Respectively *Brendan*, ll. 103–56, ll. 157–84 and ll. 185–202.

confesses, and after absolution dies and goes to paradise. This episode seems designed to encourage belief in Brendan's power, and his ability to secure salvation even in unpromising circumstances.[26] As in the *Navigatio*, Brendan then sails to the Island of Sheep, and thereafter to an island which is not identified in the Anglo-Norman text until after the monks have lit a fire and the island begins to move; they then discover they have landed on a whale. The whale is the island on which the voyagers spend the three days of Easter each year for the seven years of their journey, prompting the whale to be identified with the whale in which Jonah spent three days, prefiguring the three days of Jesus's crucifixion, harrowing of hell and resurrection.[27] After the whale, the travellers reach the paradise of birds, where one of the birds tells Brendan of the fall of Satan, the birds being those angels who fell with Satan, but who, because they had simply followed Satan, were deprived of God's glory and now pass their time singing the canonical hours. This episode implies the mercy of God is very great if the fallen angels can be redeemed in their own paradise, or perhaps purgatory, of song. The detail of the canonical hours sung by the birds is not reproduced in the Anglo-Norman poem, which continues to concentrate on the dramatic and spiritual implications of the events.[28] For his part, Ernstpeter Ruhe saw the *Navigatio* as embodying a specifically Irish conception of the pilgrimage, seen as the ideal form of monastic existence, with each stage on the journey seen as a station on the way to true life in the hereafter.[29] Benedeit's text, with its focus on Easter, seems rather a reenactment of the liturgical cycle, culminating in the resurrection of the earthly Christ and his arrival in paradise. However, it may be fair to add that if the concept of the test is added to that of a journey from one station to the next, then Waters is correct in saying that the story becomes a pilgrim's progress;[30] this concept is not far removed from the notion of the *aventure* as it emerged later in the twelfth century. Jones goes beyond the text when he implies that Benedeit's poem is already a romance, though his discussion elsewhere is more nuanced, and makes

---

26 *Brendan*, ll. 281–354. A straightforward demonstration of his power can be seen in *Brendan*, ll. 1035–66, where Brendan's call to the monks to repent is followed by the fish whose fighting had scared Brendan's monks forming up into an escort for the boat, to celebrate St Peter's day. **27** *Brendan*, ll. 423–80. The second visit to the whale at *Brendan*, ll. 831–50, includes in ll. 837–40 the recovery of the cauldron lost on their first visit, which confirms that nothing no matter how insignificant has been abandoned to hell. *Brendan*, ll. 787–822, contains the episode of the intoxicating spring, which Ruhe, p. 14, treats as an example of the punishment of the monks for disobedience, who are saved only by the efficacy of Brendan's prayer; it seems however preferable to treat this as a demonstration that Brendan himself can harrow hell and bring out of it after three days those souls who should not have entered it. **28** See for the detail of Benedeit's simplification of liturgical detail Waters, pp lxxxiii–xcix passim. However, enough liturgical detail is retained to remind us of the monastic way of life of Brendan and his monks, as for example on the Isle of Ailbe, in *Brendan*, ll. 695–715. **29** Ruhe, *Benedeit*, p. 13. **30** Waters, p. civ.

the very reasonable point that the nature of a text destined to be read by the author to an aristocratic public affects the nature of narrative discourse and the meaning it can convey.[31]

The third difference is Benedeit's willingness to reduce the number of episodes which comprise the journey to paradise, apparently as Waters believes for dramatic reasons to eliminate two of the less interesting episodes and to focus on the approach to hell, but more probably as at least one later critic has implied for structural reasons.[32] After leaving the paradise of birds, Brendan travels on for a considerable time until reaching the Isle of Ailbe, where they spend Christmas.[33] Other episodes include the visit to the intoxicating spring, which in *Brendan* follows the section where they are becalmed in the coagulated sea.[34] These various experiences are then repeated as part of the annual cycle of events.[35] However, the cycle is perhaps more accurately imagined as a spiral[36] since they seem slowly to be approaching hell; they see a fight between two sea-serpents, and then after a storm take refuge on another island where they are miraculously fed.[37] At this point, two episodes from the *Navigatio* are omitted, namely the Isle of Three Choirs and the Isle of Grapes.[38] In narrow plot terms, this omission has the advantage, as Waters has already indicated, of tightening the narrative structure while reducing the detail of the monastic life, but has the disadvantage of omitting the moment when one of the supernumerary monks is left behind to join a choir.[39] A further fight is witnessed between griffin and dragon, they pass a pillar of blue jacinth (clear crystal in the *Navigatio* and perhaps intended as an iceberg there),[40] and are then attacked by the smith of the smithy of hell.[41] Having survived this attack, they then pass a volcanic mountain where in the Anglo-Norman text the second of the supernumerary

---

[31] See R.F. Jones, 'Mechanics', p. 105 n. 2; 'Precocity', pp 156–57.   [32] See Waters, pp xcii–xciii. Illingworth, pp 217–19, describes a structure which would require some sort of compression of the narrative; Jones, 'Mechanics', does not require a similar compression, since his structure is in terms of dialectic oppositions, such as those created by earth and water.   [33] *Brendan*, ll. 611–786.   [34] *Brendan*, ll. 787–822.   [35] *Brendan*, ll. 823–96.   [36] See Janet Hillier Caulkins, 'Les notations numériques et temporelles dans la *Navigation de saint Brendan* de Benedeit', *Le Moyen Âge*, 80 (1974), pp 245–60, esp. p. 255, for a diagram of the complete journey, though island G on the diagram implies that they landed on hell, when in fact they sailed past hell but stopped to talk to Judas on his rock.   [37] *Brendan*, ll. 897–1004; the latter episode, *Brendan*, ll. 969–1004, shows a storm turned to the travellers' advantage by forcing fish onto the shore. Ruhe, pp 24–25, sees these various miracles, which he lists on p. 24 n. 33, as part of the pattern of Brendan acting typologically, since Brendan, like Moses, receives his instructions from God through a series of messengers rather than face to face; this comparison seems to overlook the fact that in Exodus 3.6 Moses did not dare to look at God when he appeared in the burning bush in Exodus 3.2, and that God on the mountain speaks directly to Moses, for example, in Exodus 19.3.   [38] These episodes are chs. 17 and 18 in Selmer, *Navigatio*, pp 49–55.   [39] See *Brendan*, ll. 1499–1510, for the equivalent passage in Benedeit's poem.   [40] See Ashe, pp 91–93.   [41] *Brendan*, ll. 1005–34, and ll. 1067–1186.

monks is snatched away to hell on account of his sins, and come to the place where Judas is kept in torment.[42]

The fourth difference concerns the treatment of the Judas episode, which is considerably expanded in the Anglo-Norman text.[43] Judas describes at length the repeated torments that he suffers, but also says that Brendan is seeing him on the sabbath, his day of rest from torment. Brendan is sufficiently moved by this to command the devils who come, apparently on Sunday for the first day of the week of torture, to give Judas a further day's rest and only return on Monday.[44] The sight of Brendan acting, apparently with divine authority, to ensure that Judas does not get more than his due punishment, shows Brendan's increased stature, acting like Jesus and the prophets directly on behalf of God. It also shows this God to be the merciful God of Jesus and the New Testament, rather than the Old Testament God of vengeance. Brendan's increased spiritual understanding provides confirmation that their journey is now nearly over, and that they are approaching paradise. Before they arrive, a brief mention is made of the disappearance of the third and last of the supernumerary monks, who will have been judged by God; this disappearance replaces the account in the *Navigatio* of the monk who stayed on the Isle of the Three Choirs.[45] In the Anglo-Norman poem, one of the supernumerary monks goes to paradise, and another to hell, and this even-handedness is preserved by Brendan not knowing where the third and last monk has disappeared to, whether heaven or hell.[46] Now that the crew is reduced to the fourteen monks chosen by Brendan, they reach Paul the Hermit, who tells them that their journey is now complete at the end of the seventh year.[47] They return for a final time to the whale to celebrate Easter, and then reach paradise, where they are given a guided tour of those parts which they are permitted to see while still alive; the description here given of paradise is based more on the account of the New Jerusalem in Revelation and on reminiscences of the terrestrial paradise described in Genesis than on the details given in the *Navigatio*. They then return directly home, where their story produces many converts. At the end of his life, Brendan goes directly to paradise.[48]

To summarize the differences between the Anglo-Norman poem and its Latin source, the *Navigatio*, the poem is dramatically much tighter and the descriptions of the journey more realistic than in the Latin text. This is partly because the monastic life is described in much less detail in the French, but also for two other reasons, firstly because the Anglo-Norman poem encourages a typological interpretation of Brendan's role, and secondly because of the structure of Benedeit's work. As was pointed out by Ernstpeter Ruhe in his 1977 edition,[49]

---

42 *Brendan*, ll. 1187–1220. **43** See Waters, pp xcv–xcvi. **44** Hogetoorn, p. 120, notes the emotion of Brendan in his response to Judas as one of the significant differences between the *Navigatio* and the *Brendan* poem. **45** *Brendan*, ll. 1499–1510.
46 *Brendan*, ll. 1509–10. **47** *Brendan*, ll. 1511–1612. **48** *Brendan*, ll. 1613–1840.
49 Ruhe, pp 21–25, where he discusses the motivation for Brendan's journey supplied

the account early in the poem of the future fate of the three supernumerary monks seems to cast Brendan in the role of Moses; one of the monks will be sustained by God, but the other two will be given over to Satan with Abiron and Dathan, two opponents of Moses whom the earth swallowed up in the story told in Numbers 16, 1–33. If this is to be taken at face value, Brendan has the role of Moses in leading his crew to the promised land, which he sees in part only during his lifetime. But Moses is a type of Jesus, and this function of Brendan as a type of Jesus seems clear not only from the arrival on the whale every Easter, but also from the mercy shown by Brendan to Judas, and his unwillingness to declare damned the supernumerary monk who disappeared. It is as if the Old Testament type of Moses has been replaced by the forgiving Jesus of the New Testament.[50]

As far as the structure of Benedeit's work is concerned, it will be clear by now that the Anglo-Norman poem is a complex text, with an innovative narrative form, a feudal but therefore universally valid motive for Brendan to reclaim the inheritance of Adam, and a factual mode of presentation which, like the Bible, is to be interpreted spiritually[51] as well as literally.[52] The style of the poem shares with many Old French texts a syntactic progression from psychological subject to psychological predicate, which can at times to a modern reader make the story seem very pedantic in its expression.[53] But what will have struck the twelfth-century reader rather more forcibly is the extent to which the complex

---

by Benedeit, and especially his discussion at pp 22–23 and n. 31 of *Brendan*, ll. 199–200. **50** This means that the contrast between two supernumerary monks being condemned to hell at *Brendan*, ll. 199–200, and the fact that the destination of one of these supernumerary monks is left uncertain at Brendan, ll. 1505–10, is probably not a contradiction in the text, but rather a continuation of the more merciful stance adopted towards Judas in the approach to paradise. Hogetoorn, p. 119, attempts to reconcile these two passages by saying that the place where the third monk disappeared implies he was going to hell, but this presupposes that the reader knows where the monk disappeared; all the reader is told is when his disappearance was noticed.   **51** Larmat, pp 239–41, sees the journey having a moral sense representing Christian existence seeking salvation, and a mystic sense representing the soul seeking union with God. **52** As with the Bible, understanding the letter of the text is the *sine qua non* to understand moral, spiritual or eschatalogical senses. Ruhe, p. 27, sees the purpose of the text as didactic, because it spells out a wish to see hell as well as God's marvels. Without for a moment denying the didactic implications of this story, and in particular the potential of the laity being impressed as the monks are intended to be at ll. 473–78 by the marvels of God, it would be as well to remind ourselves that Brendan and his crew pass by hell and meet with Judas on his day of rest; they do not actually enter hell, notwithstanding Brendan's initial prayer at ll. 65–70; again the outcome of the story is to show its audience a milder God than the God of the Old Testament.   **53** See Wolf-Dieter Stempel, *Untersuchungen zur Satzverknüpfung im Altfranzösischen*. Archiv fur das Studium der neueren Sprachen und Literaturen, Beiheft 1 (Braunschweig, 1964), and Jean Rychner, *Formes et structures de la prose française médiévale. L'articulation des phrases narratives dans la* Mort Artu. Recueil de travaux publiés par la Faculté des Lettres,

nature of the text is matched by a rhetorically well-formed style. Various recent studies have identified the wide-ranging vocabulary of the text, which includes maritime vocabulary with two borrowings from English.[54] In terms of the accessibility of the text to a lay audience, Ruhe reminds us that Benedeit uses predominantly lay forms of address within the poem, and that manuscripts of Waters' second textual family end the text with a prayer.[55] While Ruhe treats the presentation of Brendan as a type of Moses as a means of ensuring a more recognisable narrative structure to the lay audience than the monastic *Navigatio* could have achieved, he also follows Waters in attributing the rich descriptions to an aristocratic audience, and the omission of liturgical details as the simple avoidance of the risk of boredom.[56] However, an audience capable of following typology as a basis of narrative structure is likely to have sufficient appreciation of clerical procedures to grasp the fact that on both these points Benedeit is following the precepts of high style in his writing.

There is also the role of numerology in the structure of the text, which exploits significant numbers from the Bible such as three and forty, but also fourteen representing twice seven, a perfect number.[57] The text itself can be divided into three roughly equal sections, which can again be divided into three subsections each.[58] A recent study by David Howlett saw in *Beowulf* the numerical basis of composition found in both Greek and Vulgate texts of the

Université de Neuchâtel, 32ᵉ fasc. (Neuchâtel and Genève, 1970), for a general account of these syntactic patterns and the stylistic implications of their use. Jones, 'Mechanics', p. 106, seems not to recognise just how often Benedeit still uses paratactic constructions. **54** See T.D. Hemming, 'Language and Style in the *Voyage of Saint Brendan* by Benedeit', in *Littera et Sensus. Essays on Form and Meaning in Medieval French Literature presented to John Fox*, ed. by D.A. Trotter (Exeter, 1989), pp 1–16, esp. pp 5–10, 11–16, for innovative vocabulary (including at p. 7 n. 9 a reference to first attestations for a very large number of Latinisms); Illingworth, pp 219–25, for vocabulary linked to the structural themes he identifies; and Larmat, pp 236–39, esp. pp 236–37, for vocabulary related to water. Larmat, pp 241–43, discusses the poetic quality of the text based on its vocabulary. The English borrowings are 'raps', meaning 'ropes' (*Brendan*, l. 461), and 'haspes', meaning 'hasps' (*Brendan*, l. 688). Both words are attested at the rhyme; see also Waters, p. clxxxii, including n. 1.   **55** Ruhe, pp 28–30; Waters, pp lx–lxiv and the prose translation printed by Waters.   **56** Ruhe, pp 25–26; Waters, pp cii–ciii.   **57** See Caulkins, pp 247–50, 250–60, for a discussion of the numbers in Benedeit's text relating respectively to people, for example, 14 and 17, and to time including the liturgical year, e.g. 3, 7 and 40, and on p. 257 the significance of the Octave of Pentecost. Hogetoorn, p. 120, notes the increased numerical precision of Benedeit's text as one of the features which distinguishes it from the *Navigatio*. See John MacQueen, *Numerology. Theory and outline history of a literary mode* (Edinburgh, 1985), for a general discussion of the significance of numerology in medieval literature, exemplified *inter alia* from the *Navigatio* (pp 18–25).   **58** See Illingworth, pp 217–19, who arrives at his subsections by identifying three recurrent themes (pp 219–23), presented (pp 225–27) through the two 'strata' of Brendan as abbot and Brendan as navigator. His analysis assumes (pp 218–19) that Brendan reached hell as well as heaven, which as has already been discussed in nn. 36 and 52 is not strictly correct.

Prologue to the Gospel according to St John,[59] and without making the same claim for the Anglo-Norman *Brendan* as a whole,[60] it is worthy of note that standard rhetorical parallelisms and repetitions do appear in the poem. This can be exemplified among other places in the description of the walls of paradise, with the precious stones mentioned in the account of the New Jerusalem in Revelation.[61] However, this is not the only occasion on which rich descriptions are introduced, exceeding the richness of the descriptions found in the *Navigatio*; such rich descriptions are a feature of subsequent twelfth-century courtly literature in French which is here appropriate to Benedeit's patron and which is also a feature of rhetorical practice.[62] The constraints of French verse, with the line defined by a final rhyme and a count of eight syllables to the line, force a certain patterning of expression anyway, but the particular form of the octosyllable adopted here is, with hindsight, unusual, because so-called feminine rhymes ending in a 'mute e' include that 'mute e' in the syllable count, thus making a real rhythmic difference between masculine and feminine rhymes, and this may reflect the influence of medieval Latin verse.[63] There can accordingly be no doubt that Benedeit, the author of the Anglo-Norman poem, is an educated man, who knows the importance of both number and rhythm in composition, as well as the ornaments of rhetoric.[64]

59 See D. R. Howlett, 'New Criteria for Editing *Beowulf*', in *The Editing of Old English. Papers from the 1990 Manchester Conference*, ed. by D.G. Scragg and Paul E. Szarmach (Cambridge, 1994), pp 69–84, esp. pp 69–72, who begins by showing chiastic writing used to deploy ideas in parallel structures in the Greek text of John 1.1–5, and then demonstrates the numerical balance of words, syllables and letters in each section before demonstrating a similar organisation in the Vulgate translation of the same passage and a wider use of chiastic structure in St John's Gospel as a whole; the origin of this style of writing is seen in the Hebrew text of Genesis 1.1–2.4, and this is explained in pp 82–84 as based on the perceived mathematical act of God's creation of the universe.   **60** The numerical calculation of the golden section (defined by Howlett on pp 71 and 83–84 as a section in which the number in the minor part (m) relates to the number in the major part (M) as the number in the major part relates to the number in the whole (m+M), such that $m/M=M/(m+M)$), as demonstrated by Howlett for words, syllables and letters, is in the case of Benedeit perhaps facilitated for syllables by the rigorous octosyllabic structure of his line, but the reduced flexibility involved in this structure may make it harder to control the number of words as compared to the texts Howlett is working on, and certainly the vagaries of Old French spelling make it in any case harder for an author to achieve a golden section for the number of letters.   **61** *Brendan*, ll. 1675–1708.   **62** See Waters, p. ciii, on enhancing the dignity of the work; for the underlying theory deducible from French texts, see Edmond Faral, *Les arts poétiques du xiie et du xiiie siècle. Recherches et documents sur la technique littéraire du moyen âge*. Bibliothèque de l'École des Hautes Études IVe section – Sciences historiques et philologiques, 238e fasc. (Paris, 1924), pp 75–85, esp. pp 83–85.   **63** See Waters, pp xxx–xxxvii, for a discussion of feminine lines in this and other texts, and his conclusion (p. xxxvi) that Benedeit is imitating medieval Latin verse. For confirmatory evidence of the role of Latin verse models, see Waters' accounts of the restrictions placed by Benedeit on the internal construction of the line (pp xxxvii–xliv), and of the richness of his rhymes (pp lii–lviii).   **64** Hemming, pp 1–5, stresses the distinctiveness of Benedeit's

Brendan the Navigator: a Twelfth-Century View 223

The artistry of Benedeit, and his depiction of a saint who becomes increasingly just but merciful in the course of his journey, raise the two interrelated questions of the often quoted precocity of Anglo-Norman literature, and the possible political implications of the poem for its first audience. In order to address these topics, it is necessary first of all to discuss the date and authorship of the Anglo-Norman poem. The text begins with an eighteen-line prologue, which will be quoted from the Waters edition, but with the

language, pointedly contrasting it with that of his contemporary Philippe de Thaon, and suggesting that Benedeit, at least for some features of phonology and morphology and for some perhaps Walloon or North-Eastern vocabulary, is not writing the French of England in the early twelfth century, despite the substantial evidence that he was writing in England for an audience with an English perspective; the conclusion drawn is that his style as evidenced by both syntax and vocabulary is one which Benedeit has himself created, and includes a range of sentence types, ranging from the paratactic to the periodic. The effect of this strange idiolect, as Hemming, p. 10, summarises it, is that the otherness of the text is enhanced, and that its literary distinction must have been a factor in the production of the Latin translations of Benedeit's work, three being identified by Short and Merrilees, *The Anglo-Norman Voyage*, p. 3 and n. 11. In support of Hemming, it may be noted that Benedeit's prologue shows evidence of chiastic writing, especially in *Brendan*, ll. 1–8, and to a lesser extent also in *Brendan*, ll. 9–18. *Brendan*, ll. 1–8 begin and end with a chiasmus ('Donna Aaliz la reïne' and 'Li apostoiles danz Benedeiz') which acts as a frame; they constitute a single sentence, whose main clause is ll. 1, 7 and 8. There are 42 words in these eight lines, which would give a golden section of 16 + 26, but in fact ll. 1, 7 and 8 have 14 words, and ll. 2–6 28 words, which gives a 1:2 ratio but not a golden section. Syntactically, ll. 2–6 are parallel adverbial complements introduced by 'par', but with a further subdivision into clauses depending on 'reïne' (24 syllables) and prepositional phrases depending on the preceding verbs (16 syllables) in ll. 2–4 and 5–6 respectively, which achieves a 3:2 ratio but does not quite match the golden section of 25 + 15. This sufficiently demonstrates the difficulties of applying Howlett's numerical calculations to a verse text in strict octosyllabic couplets, but it also shows how the word count can, like the syllable count, produce more simple ratios, even though the number of words in a section can vary. In the remainder of the prologue, no numerical effects of any sort have been identified, but chiastic writing has not been abandoned. *Brendan*, ll. 9–18, contains two sentences, respectively ll. 9–13 and ll. 14–18. The lines which contain the focus of the reader's attention in each sentence are linked by the rhyme (ll. 13–14) and respectively end and begin their sentences, thus giving a chiastic structure to the two sentences as a whole (4 + 1 lines followed by 1 + 4). If the remaining four lines of each sentence are taken as a unit, ll. 9–12 show the chiasmus of 'Que comandas' and 'li teons cumanz' acting as a frame, and internally the disposition of 'en letre mis' at the end of l. 10 and the beginning of l. 11 seems also intended as a chiasmus with a view to further structuring and highlighting the phrase, which is also being emphasised by repetition, and whose meaning has been discussed in note 13. In the final four lines of the prologue (ll. 15–18), parallel structures dominate in ll. 15 and 17, but there is still a reminder of chiasmus in the disposition of 'cil' in respectively the first and second half of ll. 17–18. The conclusion of this analysis is that the prologue is a virtuoso piece of writing by Benedeit, in which respect he is following rhetorical and Biblical precedent, e.g. Romans 1.1–7.

punctuation and word division supplied by the author of this article, as is the accompanying line-by-line translation.[65]

Donna Aaliz la reïne,	Lady Queen Adeliza,
2 Par qui valdrat lei divine,	Through whom divine law will prevail,
Par qui creistrat lei de terre,	Through whom earthly law will grow in force,
4 E remandrat tante guerre	And many a war be brought to an end
Por les armes Henri lu rei	Through the arms of King Henry
6 Par le cunseil qui ert en tei,	By the good counsel which will be in you,
Salüet tei mil e mil feiz	Greets you one thousand and one thousand times
8 Li apostoiles danz Benedeiz.	The Lord apostle Benedict.
Que comandas, ço ad enpris	What you ordered, he has undertaken
10 Secund sun sens en letre mis,	And put into writing according to his understanding,
En letre mis e en romanz	Put into writing and into French
12 Esi cum fud li teons cumanz,	Just as was your command,
De saint Brendan le bon abeth.	Concerning Saint Brendan the good abbot.
14 Mais tul defent ne seit gabeth,	But may you forbid that he [Benedict] be mocked,
Quant dit que set e fait que peot:	When he says what he knows and does what he can:
16 Itel servant blasmer n'esteot;	Such a servant must not be blamed;
Mais cil qui peot e ne voile,	But someone who can but does not wish to,
18 Dreiz est que cil mult s'en doile.	It is right that he should suffer very much.

This prologue contains as one might expect the appropriate modesty topos for a servant who has carried out instructions to the best of his allegedly limited ability, but it also contains statements about the role of a queen in advising her husband, thus helping the king to fulfil what is strictly his role of enforcing both divine and human law, and of bringing about peace through winning or suppressing war. This implies that the queen's choice of text for translation may well have the same agenda, namely by showing through the success of the still mortal Brendan in reclaiming his just inheritance and converting people to true belief and salvation, that King Henry too will, having secured his

---

[65] For another translation, see Short and Merrilees, *Anglo-Norman Voyage*, p. 80. Both translations tacitly assume the variant 'Par' for 'Por' at the beginning of line 5; 'Par' is attested by his manuscripts C and D in the apparatus on p. 3 of Waters.

inheritance, bring a just yet merciful peace to his subjects, and that he will have divine authority for so doing.

As far as the dating and authorship of the poem are concerned, the authorship is unambiguously attributed to the Benedeit who greets the queen. However, his name, which according to Waters is relatively rare in English records of the appropriate period,[66] is not sufficiently distinctive for any of the candidates so far proposed to have been generally accepted by scholars.[67] His designation of 'apostoiles' is unusual.[68] According to the two principal dictionaries of Old French, 'apostoile' means 'apostle' or 'Pope'.[69] There seems no reason to doubt that the fundamental meaning of 'apostoile' is 'apostle', which has the etymological meaning of 'messenger' or 'envoy'; this meaning is attested in England, and seems more appropriate to the context of the prologue of the Anglo-Norman *Brendan* poem, where Benedeit is presenting himself as the errand boy, bearing the holy message as commanded.[70] The word is thus being used as part of a modesty topos to designate someone who is spreading the good word through his artistry and effort.[71]

The date of the work is normally assumed to be in the first half of the twelfth century, given a *terminus ad quem* of the late twelfth century from the paleographic dating of the oldest manuscript,[72] which means that the King Henry mentioned in the prologue can only be Henry I, since the Queen of Henry II was Eleanor of Aquitaine. The Queen Aaliz of the prologue is therefore normally identified as Henry I's second wife Adeliza of Louvain,

---

66 See Waters, p. xxvii. **67** See Legge, pp 8–9, including p. 9 n. 1, and Short and Merrilees, *Anglo-Norman Voyage*, pp 5–6. **68** See *Brendan* l. 8, and its proposed translation above. **69** Frédéric Godefroy, *Dictionnaire de l'ancienne langue française et de tous ses dialectes du IXe au XVe siècle*, i (Paris, 1880), pp 350c–351a, adds to these two meanings a contextual meaning derived from 'apostle', viz: 'saint considéré comme un grand défenseur de l'église'. T–L, i (1925), col. 464, attests 'Pope', and adds the further contextual meaning of 'Caliph'. Both dictionaries attest the separate word 'apostle' (Godefroy, viii (1893), complément, p. 152a, and T–L, i (1925), cols 463–64), but with only the one meaning of 'apostle'. **70** The OED, i (1933), p. 392, shows awareness of the etymological meaning of 'apostle' in the tenth and fourteenth centuries under meaning I. 1: 'A person sent', so this meaning may in Anglo-Norman be a calque from English, though it could also be a learned borrowing from Latin. At all events, the A-ND, i (1977), p. 32 attests from the late twelfth-century *Vie de Thomas Becket par Beneit* the form 'apostoile' under the heading 'apostle', with the meaning 'missionary, apostle', as the immediate context of the Beneit example requires. It is unfortunate that Short and Merrilees, *Anglo-Norman Voyage*, p. 5, used the evidence of this same Beneit example to say that the form 'apostoile' designates 'a papal emissary or envoy', given the absence of any evidence to show that 'a person sent' had to have been sent by a Pope; cf. Jones, 'Precocity', p. 145 and n. 3, where 'apostoile' has become a 'legate'. **71** See Faral, *Les arts poétiques*, pp 65 and 89, for the artistry involved here, where etymology is used as a form of 'interpretatio', and the tropes, with their principle of using words in a sense other than their proper meaning, are an essential type of difficult ornament. **72** Cologny (Genève), Fondation Martin Bodmer, MS 17.

which dates the poem to the period 1121–35, from the year of their marriage to that of the death of King Henry. However, of the four manuscripts to attest the prologue, one of the oldest, which can be dated *c*.1200 on palaeographical grounds, has the variant Mahalt for the Aaliz of the other manuscripts.[73] The obvious suggestion to make is that if the reading Mahalt is authorial, then the Queen in question will have been Henry's first wife Matilda, and the poem will have been composed sometime between their marriage in 1100 and Matilda's death in 1118. Professor Ritchie has argued that the term 'lei de terre' echoes a phrase in Henry's Charter of Liberties of 1100, and more significantly that as the daughter of Malcolm Canmore and St Margaret, and goddaughter of Robert duke of Normandy, Matilda was hailed as the person who would reconcile Norman and Saxon after the Conquest, as well as bring peace with the Scots; he adds that peace was secured by the Battle of Tinchebrai in 1106, which brought England and Normandy under Henry's sole rule, and that Brendan was the most picturesque of the Irish saints who evangelized Matilda's native Scotland.[74] Needless to say, it is difficult to confirm the personalities involved at this distance in time. Much will depend on exactly when in the periods 1100–18 or 1121–35 the work was commissioned. If at the moment of marriage, then it will be a matter of aspiration as the future tenses of the prologue strongly suggest, and not of any certain period of peace or victory.[75] The four complete manuscripts normally divide into two families, and the fragment which contains the name Mahalt, although not without its own individual errors, cannot certainly be ascribed to either of these families because it lacks the errors which characterize each family;[76] however the three complete manuscripts which do contain the prologue attest Aaliz, and this means that both identifiable textual families share this name. This would normally imply that Aaliz was indeed the name of the original patron, although it is not possible to exclude absolutely the thought that Mahalt was the first patron, but that her name was later replaced in manuscripts dating from the second half of the reign from which both textual families would be descended. However, this argument

---

[73] Oxford, Bodleian Library, MS Rawlinson D 913, fol. 85.   [74] R.L.G. Ritchie, 'The Date of the *Voyage of St Brendan*', *Medium Aevum*, 19 (1950), pp 64–66. The phrase cited on p. 64 is 'legem terrae', or 'law of the land', but this appears either a sufficiently general phrase for it to be unpersuasive as evidence of any connection between the Anglo-Norman *Brendan* and Henry's Charter of Liberties, or, if the technical meaning assigned to it on p. 65 is correct, too technical to have any connection at all with the *Brendan* poem.   [75] Both marriages of Henry I entailed aspirations for peace; in 1100 he needed to secure support for his reign against the probable claims of his elder brother Robert duke of Normandy, while in 1121 he needed a legitimate heir to ensure an undisputed and therefore peaceful succession. Both political contexts envisage civil strife, and accordingly the wish for Henry to bring many a war to an end, as expressed in *Brendan* ll. 4–5, is relevant on both occasions.   [76] Waters, pp lviii–lxxx, esp. pp lviii–lx, for the group AB; pp lx–lxiv, for the group DE; and pp lxxviii–lxxx for C, which is the fragment containing the name Mahalt.

could be reversed, by saying that by *c*.1200 a scribe might have forgotten the second queen of Henry I and used the name of the better known first queen, who was the mother of the Matilda who opposed Stephen in the calamitous civil war which followed the death of Henry; by *c*.1200 it would even be possible to suggest a further confusion, by which the scribe of that manuscript thought he was copying the name of Henry I's daughter Matilda, and her husband the King of the Romans and Holy Roman Emperor Henry V.[77] All in all, it seems better not to risk adopting what could be an individual scribal error, but to accept the reading of the two main manuscript families, and assume that the poem belongs to the years 1121–35, probably early in that period when there were still hopes of peace being secured by the birth of a legitimate son to succeed Henry I after the death of his heir William in 1120 in the wreck of the White Ship.

Arguably, however, Professor Ritchie is right to see the choice of Brendan as a subject linked to the theme of reconciliation of the nations. Immediately after the prologue at the beginning of the story proper we are told that Brendan was Irish and of royal lineage.[78] Many dark age saints were said to be of noble lineage, and royal lineage is helpful to gain the ear of a royal twelfth-century audience. But the choice of an Irish saint is not so obvious. In King Stephen's reign, Geoffrey of Monmouth produced his sub-Roman account of king Arthur conquering Britain and Gaul, allegedly on the basis of Welsh tradition. This gave Roman Britain superiority over Gaul, and provided Kings of England with a source of legitimacy independent from any that might be claimed by the French kings, which was clearly important to kings of England wishing to increase their freedom of manoeuvre in their French possessions against their French overlord. Indeed the tactic is ancient, since the early Merovingian rulers of France seem to have used the story of the Trojan origins of the Franks as a means of showing that they were entitled to parity of esteem with any Roman, since both Franks and Romans descended independently from Troy.[79] It may be, therefore, that the use of Irish material was perceived by Henry I as conveying a similarly independent status, since access to the interrelated histories of the different nations of the British Isles was not available to the French kings, and since the Irish had preceded the Vikings as travellers and had acted as missionaries in continental Europe, thus upstaging both Scandinavian and French claims over the kings of England.[80] However,

---

[77] The younger Matilda married the Emperor in 1114, and was widowed in 1125.
[78] *Brendan* ll. 19–32, where the contrast is created between the high station into which he was born, and the lowly position of monk which he chose in obedience to the Gospel, accepting the position of abbot only under duress.   [79] See Raymond Van Dam, *Saints and Their Miracles in Late Antique Gaul* (Princeton, 1993), p. 48.   [80] Although French claims related rather to the status of the Anglo-Norman and subsequently Planatagenet kings of England for their French possessions than to the crown of England itself, the potential for Scandinavian invasion remained for some time after the Norman Conquest of England, with the unsuccessful attempt earlier in 1066 by Harald Hardrada king of

since Ireland was not under the control of the English kings,[81] the Welsh material alleged by Geoffrey might well have seemed more promising to later generations. Meantime, for Henry's immediate purposes, the idea of a saint pursuing the universal inheritance of mankind stresses the unity of all mankind, and this seems very appropriate to a ruler who had to secure as much unity as he could.

Finally, the claim often made by anglophone historians of medieval French literature of the precocity of Anglo-Norman literature seems to be borne out by this particular text. In using the narrative octosyllabic couplet, for literature dedicated to a queen, which is stylistically highly wrought and theologically and politically ambitious, Benedeit is starting down the road which led to the courtly romance on Celtic themes in the second half of the century, with knightly heroes finding themselves through the discipline of the *aventure*. But he has not yet reached this individualistic position. His concerns are still universal, even if achieved through *aventure*, and to that extent he belongs to the worlds of the *Vie de Saint Alexis* and the *Chanson de Roland*, whose oldest extant copies were both produced in the first half of the twelfth century.[82] He is truly a Janus-like figure, but one whose interest in Celtic material, and use of an educated style and of a narrative form suitable for recitation to a select audience, unambiguously point the way to the future.

BIBLIOGRAPHICAL NOTE

The footnotes contain all works referred to in the article, except for Biblical references, which are all taken from: *Biblia Sacra Iuxta Vulgatam Versione*m ed. by R Weber, 2 vols (Stuttgart, 1969). I was unable to consult the following works listed in Otto Klapp, *Bibliographie der Französischen Literaturwissenschaft / Bibliographie d'histoire littéraire française*, (Frankfurt am Main, 1956–): (1) in Klapp, xxx (1992), item 1987: Claude Conter, 'Une lecture plurielle: *Le Voyage de Saint-Brandan*', *Études romanes*, i (Publications du Centre Universitaire de Luxembourg, Département des Lettres Romanes, 1989), pp 118–20; (2) in

---

Norway being followed by the planned invasion of 1086 by Cnut II king of Denmark, which was aborted only by Cnut's assassination at the moment of setting sail.   81 It was nevertheless a potential future area for conquest by Norman knights as happened in the 1170s under Henry II.   82 The oldest manuscript of the *Vie de Saint Alexis* is fos. 29–34 of the *St Albans Psalter*, now in St Godehard's, Hildesheim (no shelfmark); see Francis Wormald, with Otto Pächt and C.R. Dodwell, *The St Albans Psalter*, Warburg Institute Studies, xxv (London, 1960). The dating of the oldest manuscript of the *Chanson de Roland*, Oxford, Bodleian Library, MS Digby 23, is still contentious, but the most judicious recent survey of the evidence is M.B. Parkes, 'The date of the Oxford Manuscript of *La Chanson de Roland* (Oxford, Bodleian Library, MS Digby 23)', *Medioevo Romanzo*, 10 (1985), pp 161–75.

Klapp, xxiv (1986), item 1780: the unpublished thesis described in the following terms [sic]: Guy Vincent, Recherches sur la *Navigation de Saint Brendan* (MS Latin d'Alançon, Bibl. mun. 14–X–XI S, poème anglo-normand de Benedeit 1106–1121), Thèse Univ. d'Aix-Marseille II, 1982. From the *Catalogue Général des Manuscrits des Bibliothèques publiques de France: Départements*, ii (Paris, 1888), pp 488–91, it appears that MS 14 of the Bibliothèque municipale d'Alençon contains several individual manuscripts dated XIIe–XIe siècle [sic], beginning on fols 1–11 with a Latin life of St Brendan; Selmer, *Navigatio*, pp xxxiii–xxxiv, confirms that fols 1r–11v of Alençon MS 14 contain an 11th-century copy of the *Navigatio*, which he uses as his MS A. Without seeing the thesis, it is unclear how it relates to Benedeit's poem.

I was also unable to consult the following: *Il Viaggio di san Brandano*, a cura di Renata Bartoli e Fabrizio Cigni, Bibliothèque médiévale 12, Édition bilingue (Parma, 1994); Marie-Madeleine Castellani, 'Le voyage dans l'autre monde dans le "Voyage de Saint-Brandan"', *Uranie*, 4 (1994), pp 115–32; Glyn S. Burgess, 'Les fonctions des quatre éléments dans le "Voyage de saint Brendan" par Benedeit', *Cahiers de civilisation médiévale*, 38 (1995) pp 3–22; Glyn S. Burgess, '"Savoir" and "faire" in the Anglo-Norman Voyage of St Brendan', *French Studies*, 49 (1995), pp 257–74; Corinne Zemmour, '"Le Voyage de Saint-Brandan", du séjour des morts au paradis, en traversant la mer', *Speculum medii aevi*, 3 (1997), pp 167–82; Glyn S. Burgess, 'La souffrance et le repos dans "Le Voyage de saint Brendan" par Benedeit', in: *Miscellanea medievalia. Mélanges offerts à Philippe Ménard*. Études réunies par Jean-Claude Faucon, Alain Labbé et Danielle Quéruel, 2 vols Nouvelle bibliothèque du Moyen Âge, 46 (Paris, 1998), pp 262–77.

Shrine Rivalry in the North Sea World

ROBERT WORTH FRANK, JR

A notable feature of many medieval miracles is their strikingly 'reportorial' character, the provision of a density of detail that seems to go beyond the doctrinal function of the miracle itself. It is not a universal phenomenon and calls for explanation. Though it may increase the narrative effectiveness of the miracle, that does not appear to be its purpose. It is found most frequently in shrine miracles; it is, indeed, almost invariably present to some degree in them. This paper will attempt to define its function.

To illustrate this 'realistic' and 'reportorial' element I shall draw on miracles reported from shrines in the 'North Sea World' in the late twelfth century: the shrine of St Cuthbert in the cathedral of Durham, that of St Godric at Finchale near Durham, and St Thomas Becket's shrine at Canterbury. There will be references when pertinent to the shrine of St Andrew in Scotland.[1]

We must begin with a necessary discrimination among the mass of medieval miracles, a categorization based on the specific mode of delivery of the miracle to the medieval audience.[2] There were three basic forms of delivery. One was the shrine miracle, recorded and preserved by the shrine where the miracle occurred or to whose power the miracle was credited. A second form was the collection, a gathering of accounts of miracles from various shrines, from earlier collections, and/or from oral sources. The *Dialogus Miraculorum* of Caesarius of Heisterbach or William of Malmesbury's *De Laudibus et Miraculis Sanctæ Mariæ* would be examples of such collections.[3] The as yet unedited

---

[1] There was an early collection of St Cuthbert miracles by an unknown author, and another by Bede: *Two Lives of St Cuthbert*, ed. by Bertram Colgrave (Cambridge, 1940). This essay will draw on the later collection by Reginald of Durham, *Libellus de Admirandis Beati Cuthberti Virtutibus*, ed. by J. Stevenson, Surtees Society, no. 1 (London, 1835). For St Godric the collection is again by Reginald, *Libellus de Vita et Miraculis S. Godrici, Heremitæ de Finchali*, ed. by J. Stevenson, Surtees Society no. 20 (London, 1847). For Becket, see *Materials for the History of Thomas Becket, Archbishop of Canterbury*, ed. by J.C. Robertson and J.B. Sheppard, 7 vols, Rolls Society (London, 1875–85). [2] There is a useful list of miracles (shrines and collections) in Benedicta Ward, 'Primary Sources', in *Miracles and the Medieval Mind: Theory, Record and Event, 1000–1215* (Philadelphia, 1982), pp 288–99. [3] Caesarius of Heisterbach,

manuscript, Sidney Sussex College Cambridge 95, a gathering made early in the fifteenth century (1409?), would be another example. It originally contained 495 miracles, and included different versions of the same miracle.

The third form was the literary miracle, pious in purpose, but given a self-consciously literary treatment. The most familiar example would be Chaucer's *Prioress's Tale*. Another would be Gautier de Coinci's *Les Miracles de Nostre Dame*, in French, rhymed, and accompanied by poems praising and exalting the Virgin.[4]

There are a multitude of examples of the first category, the shrine miracles: the records of Canterbury (Becket), the compilations of miracles of the Virgin in France at Rocamadour, Laon, Soissons, Chartres, Coutances, St Pierre-sur-Dive; in England the Cuthbert miracles and the Godric miracles reported by Reginald of Durham, and many more. These have the advantage of being closest to the source, taken down oftentimes from the lips of the beneficiary of divine aid or from eyewitnesses of such aid. They are a record of the shrine's triumphs, an anthology of wondrous tales to tell pilgrim visitants, evidence that the shrine was a scene where divine power became manifest through the sacral figure honored there.

The pattern of a miracle narrative is very simple: human need, divine rescue. There is, however, often a striking difference between a shrine miracle, set down in the shrine's records, and a collection miracle. An example of each will illustrate this difference.

A miracle in the records of the shrine of St Thomas Becket at Canterbury tells of one Ailward, a hot-tempered man in Bedfordshire. A neighbor owed him a penny (worth a great deal more then, of course) but refused to pay him. One day, when the neighbor had left his house, after first barricading it with a crossbar, Ailward broke in, ripping off the crossbar and snatching a coat hanging from the wall, and made off with the crossbar, the coat, an awl, and some gloves as security for his debt. Apparently he also damaged the interior and destroyed some garden produce. The neighbor's children, who had been shut up playing in the house, got word to their father, who pursued Ailward and seized him. He wrested the coat from Ailward's hand, wounded him in the head, pierced his forearm with a drawn knife, bound him fast, and brought him with the goods he had stolen back to the house. A crowd gathered, among them an 'official' named Fulco. Because stealing something worth only a penny could not be punished by mutilation, Fulco suggested they secretly add to the stolen goods. So they placed beside these a small bundle of skins, a shawl, linen, and an ironclad instrument called a 'volganum', probably a 'biscuta', a two-edged sword.

Dialogus Miraculorum, ed. by J. Strange, 2 vols (Cologne, 1851); William of Malmesbury, *De Laudibus et Miraculis Sanctæ Mariæ*, ed. by José Canal, 2nd edn (Rome, 1968).
4 V. Frederic Koenig, ed., 4 vols (Geneva, 1966–70). The *Miracles* was composed between 1218 and 1228: 'Introduction', I, pp xxv–xxvi.

We follow Ailward's appearance before courts, his confession and counseling secretly by a priest named Paganus, his scourging himself fifteen times a day with a rod, his invocation of Mary and the saints, especially St Thomas, and his pledging himself to Thomas by winding a fillet of cloth round his body, branding himself on the thigh with a hot iron as a further pledge. Ultimately he was condemned and suffered public mutilation: blinding and castration, with the eyes and testicles buried in the earth.

Ailward did not cease invoking divine aid and calling on St Thomas all through this gruesome punishment. Afterward he was given shelter, we are told, by a man named Ailbricht. When ten days had passed, he saw in his sleep the blessed Thomas, whom he had called on continually. Clothed in white, Becket imprinted with his archbishop's crook the sign of the cross between Ailward's eyebrows, doing the same again just before dawn and saying, 'Good man, are you sleeping? Wake up. Tomorrow you're to keep watch with a lantern at the altar of the blessed Mary. Lo, Thomas comes to you and you receive sight'.

When the sun rose, the maidservant said, 'I saw in a dream, Ailward, that you recovered your sight'.

He replied, 'This is possible, just as all things are possible'. As the day was fading, his left eye itched. Scratching with his fingernail, he removed the wax and the emollient which had been placed there to draw out any festering. And seeing the sun's rays on the wall, he exclaimed, 'The Lord be praised! I can see!'

At which words his host, stunned, said, 'What's that? You're raving!' And drawing his hand before Ailward's eyes, he said, 'Look. What am I doing?'

'I see a hand moving', Ailward said.

The village elder (*decano*) was summoned, and a crowd gathered. Ailward was snatched up and led to the oratory. Very small eyes were growing, the right eye a deep black, the left parti-colored, as both had been since birth. And growing also were genitalia, which he exhibited for someone to touch, and which they could estimate as below the size of a rooster's testes.

What we have seen and heard, the narrator of Canterbury concludes, we must speak of and testify to. For he of whom we speak was sent to us, and stayed with us many days.[5]

For contrast, here is a charming miracle of the Virgin found in a number of collections.[6] It tells of a knight, once wealthy, who had fallen on hard times and found life no longer worth living. One day his servant told him that if he would

---

5 *History of Becket*, I, pp 155–58 (Book 2, 3).   6 Laurel Broughton of the Department of English at the University of Vermont is at work on a catalogue of miracles of the Virgin. Her list is not yet complete, but at this point it runs to over 1800 miracles (that is, 'tellings', versions, not separate narrations). Her catalogue lists fourteen 'tellings' of the miracle given here. This version is a free translation from the collection known as the pseudo-Celestinus. It is Chapter 19 in *S. Petri Caelestini [...] opuscula omnia*, ed. by Coelestinus (Telera, Naples, 1640), pp 199–219. I would like to thank Dr Broughton for sharing this catalogue with me.

go to a certain crossroads, he could be restored to a life of wealth and ease. He agreed.

At the crossroads, the Devil appeared and demanded that in return for the riches he was about to receive, he should first deny Christ. The knight did so. The Devil then demanded that he also deny the Virgin Mary. At this, the knight balked and would in no wise consent. Whereupon the Devil vanished, and the servant was never seen again.

The impoverished knight, despairing now of his soul as well as his body, wandered into a church and prayed before a statue of the Virgin and Child to be forgiven of his grievous sin. Another knight in the church quietly observed the scene from behind a pillar. He heard the Virgin of the statue begin to address the Christ-child.

'My son', she said, 'please forgive this poor man'.

'How can I, mother?' the Christ-child replied. 'He denied me to the Devil'. And petitioned again, the Child continued to refuse.

'Very well', the Virgin said. And she took the Child and laid Him down on a nearby altar. 'Unless you forgive him, I'll never take you to my bosom again'.

'Well, mother', the Child replied, 'you know I can deny you nothing. I do forgive him'. Then the Virgin took the Child once more in her arms.

The knight witnessing this stepped forth, took the penitent knight home, gave him money, and arranged a marriage. But on their wedding night the couple took religious vows and lived chaste lives ever after, withdrawn from the world.

There are obvious differences between the two narratives. The collection miracle is persistently general, abstract. The specific scenes have only a general significance: a crossroads (the frequent locale of interchange with the Devil) and a church – not named. It could be any church, any statue of Virgin and Child. The two knights are not named, nor is the woman given in marriage. Our attention is focused on the Virgin, her mercy, tenderheartedness, and peerless power. The dialogue between the Virgin and Child is the one really vivid moment – and it is a wondrous moment. There is, in sum, a striking lack of detail. This does not diminish the drama or the force of the narrative. It says what it wants to say admirably. But it is radically different from the shrine miracle. This is typical of collection miracles.

Ailward's story, on the other hand, is crowded with detail. We know names – Ailward; Fulco, who tampered with the evidence; Paganus, the name of the confessor priest; and Ailbricht, who gave Ailward shelter. We know what Ailward stole (a crowbar, awl, a coat, some gloves) and what was added to the stolen goods. We know about the children, how many times a day Ailward scourged himself, etc. Indeed, the detail may strike us as excessive, at moments embarrassing. Do we need it all? What is the point of it?

The question becomes only more pressing as we examine more shrine miracles. In them, however slight the entry, the petitioner's name and where he or she comes from are almost invariably given, together with the condition that is remedied: Sungiva from Fulewele (withered hand), Heccoc from Bedefeld (lost eyesight), Helyas, a youth from Stretun (weakened knee) – and so it goes, name after name.[7] More complex circumstances result in more details, apparently.

Why? There are, I believe, three forces that together account for the remarkable specificity and detail of many shrine miracles, their frequently 'realistic' quality, what I would call their 'reportorial' detail.

The first of these forces is medieval skepticism, skepticism specifically about miracles. We tend to assume that everyone in the Middle Ages was uniformly credulous, but this is not so. Almost everyone, if not everyone, believed in the *possibility* and the *reality* of miracle – not to believe so was heresy, or close to it. But this did not mean that one was obliged to believe in every claim that a miracle had occurred at a specific shrine. Claims of a miraculous cure or rescue were sometimes faked, or the incident could be explained in other ways.

The twelfth-century Welsh archdeacon and anecdotalist Walter Map provides an instructive case. Orthodox but skeptical, Map was once joined in Limoges by another skeptic, the bishop of Poitiers. The people of Limoges had brought a madman, foaming at the mouth, for cure to the blessed Peter, archbishop of Tarantaise. The bishop came to Walter, 'not to tempt God', Walter explained, 'but hoping to certify himself of what was common belief. He came to me', Map says, 'with these words: "My friend, do call the archbishop out to us that we may be able to bear witness for certain to what everyone asserts. I have sometimes seen illusory things happen when people declared they had seen miracles, and I always saw through the appearances, and never once have I seen a real miracle".' The madman was cured, and the bishop was moved to tears. He had seen, and this time, at last, he believed.[8]

Shrines – and saints – were aware of this skepticism. The story of Ailward that we began with was prefaced by a letter from the burgesses of Bedford confirming the truth of the miracle being reported. In the section on St Benignus in the *Nova Legenda Angliæ* we hear of a friar wasting away because of a long illness. When asked by his brothers why he didn't pray to St Benignus for health, he replied, 'In truth, just as he can't do me any good, so he can't do me any harm'. He paid for his lack of faith by a dream in which St Benignus appeared, clad in white garments, threatened him with the torments of hell, gave him a thorough dressing-down, and also gave him a good punch in the face. And when he woke up, he had a terrible fever that lasted a year.[9]

Shrines might anticipate a skeptical reception unless the miracle could be validated by witnesses and/or reinforced by convincing and confirmatory detail.

---

7 *Godrici*, p. 395.   8 Walter Map, *De Nugis Curialium*, ed. and trans. by M.R. James (Oxford, 1983), Dist. 2:3, pp 134–37.   9 *Nova Legenda Angliæ*, ed. by Carl Horstman[n] (Oxford, 1901), I, pp 113–14.

They kept records, and many of the largest shrines had a *notarius*, whose responsibility it was to cross-examine the pilgrim claiming to be the recipient of miraculous grace and to keep a written account of the miracle.

Such protective strategy would be useful in combating a second source of suspicion and disbelief that a shrine might have to contend with, the medieval belief in the omnipresence of demons serving the Devil, that is of *maleficia*, black magic, which coexisted with *beneficia*. Valerie Flint in *The Rise of Magic* has chronicled and documented the Church's struggle, when it first came into power, to wipe out the belief in magic. The belief in demons and magic was so strong, however, so pervasive, that the Church found it necessary to accept the reality of magic and foster belief in white magic, *beneficia*, as an effective counter-agent working against *maleficia*.[10] It was not always easy, however, to tell whether a suspension or reversal of the laws of nature was the result of divine grace acting through a saint or the work of demons doing the devil's business (though ultimately God's). A seeming miracle might not be a miracle at all.

The dilemma is illustrated neatly by a Becket miracle. It tells of a young man being held prisoner, unjustly charged with manslaughter. A pilgrim coming by, returning from Canterbury with an ampule of water mixed with St Thomas' blood, gave a sip to the young man. And he received from it, we are told, something he hadn't asked for: he drank it for health, but he received the release from his chains. For, says the narrator, the iron felt the power of the drink and sprang open. Three times the chains were replaced, and three times they were loosed. Harsh guards, a dark cave, heavy weights of iron did nothing. We are reminded by the informant that he whom the Son of God will free will truly be free. But what was a work of divine virtue was imputed to sorceries and charms. The King heard of these strange events, and, summoning the young man, said, 'Your witchcraft [*maleficia*] looses our chains and shatters our bars'.

But the young man replied, 'My sorceries [*maleficia*] are nothing, but the good works [*beneficia*] of St Thomas are great'.

'If St Thomas has freed him', the King ruled, 'let no man trouble him again'.[11]

The suspicion of witchcraft or of demonic influence in this case is understandable. The miraculous release reported did not occur *at* Canterbury or any other shrine. But sometimes even if the miracle did occur at a shrine there could be dark mutterings. At least this seems to have been true at Canterbury. We learn of attempts by the shrine's enemies – rival shrines, in all probability – to suppress the fame of St Thomas. They spread the rumor that the monks at Canterbury worked by magical incantations. No miracles really occurred: they were merely simulated by diabolical art. People coming to Canterbury were by means of the monks' incantations suddenly seized by insanity and then released by the monks' commands from what the monks had caused. So when their

10 Valerie Flint, *The Rise of Magic in Medieval Europe* (Princeton, 1991), *passim*.
11 *History of Becket*, I, pp 276–77 (3, cap 18).

devilish shaking stopped, they seemed cured when in truth no real sickness had oppressed them.[12]

And this takes us to the third element in the medieval context, what I believe to be the most powerful force responsible for circumstantial and 'realistic' reporting of miracles: the rivalry, sometimes fierce, among shrines. Christian miracle, we should remember, had lived with competition since its very beginnings. Miracle was not, after all, an exclusive prerogative of Christianity. Ancient Egypt, Babylon, India, Greece, and pre-Christian Rome all had their shrines and/or divinities, their oracles and prayers, whence came miraculous healings and rescues from shipwreck and natural disasters. Asclepius, Dionysius, Apollo, Serapis, and countless others were Christianity's competitors in its early centuries, and pagan gods and sacred springs and groves in Europe and Britain in later centuries.[13] In *Miracles and the Medieval World*, Sister Benedicta Ward observes that missionaries frequently presented the Christian saint to the unconverted 'as having greater powers through his miracles than the demons offered by magical deceits'.[14] When paganism was stamped out, however, competition did not cease.

Now it became competition for reputation and for pilgrim visitation among Christian shrines. The stakes were often high, and the motives behind the competition were mixed but powerful. Most basic was the devotion of monks or canons to their beloved saint and their belief in his or her special, privileged access to divine grace.

We should remember also that a shrine no longer visited, or only rarely, suffered a hurtful, costly public repudiation. The saint did not cease to be a saint, but the power and pride and esteem – and the wealth – which the shrine had once engendered diminished or faded away completely.

It was essential, then, that people should believe in the authenticity of the miracles claimed for the saint and the shrine. Anything that suggested they were false could be fatal. How important belief in the saint's power was in contributing to that power is a moot question. But belief in that power was all-important in bringing pilgrims to the shrine. For people invoked a saint's aid in the conviction that such aid was accessible and in the hope that it would be forthcoming.

A story Reginald of Durham tells reveals the pilgrim's pragmatic approach to miracle. A man of high rank and influence was suffering from leprosy at a time when Cuthbert of Durham, King Edmund of Bury, and Queen Ætheldreth of Ely were the most powerful saints in England. The nobleman had three wax candles of equal length and thickness made. He lighted them all

---

[12] *History of Becket*, II, p. 91 (2, cap 43). [13] See Hippolyte Delehaye, *Legends of the Saints* (London, 1907; reprint Notre Dame, 1961), pp 160–78, and Thomas Heffernan, *Sacred Biography: Saints and Their Biographers in the Middle Ages* (New York, 1988), pp 143–44 and notes 56–59. [14] Ward, *Miracles*, p. 10.

at the same time to determine which saint had the greatest power, that being the saint whose candle first burned out.[15] (It is an early instance, I would say, of consumer research. Indeed, a surprising number of proto-mercantile elements show up in what we might call the miracle market.) Since St Cuthbert's candle burned down first, you might well guess that the story appears in the record of his miracles.

Such self-promotion is a common feature of the shrine records. St Cuthbert's tell us of a man seeking relief from illness at Canterbury who is told in a vision by St Thomas to go to Cuthbert for help. The Canterbury records report the case of a priest's son whose prayers to the prestigious Virgin of Rocamadour go unanswered, but he is cured by St Thomas.[16] William of Canterbury, the narrator, adds diplomatically that the earlier saints, including the Virgin, hastened to work miracles in their time, but now leave this to more recent saints so that they too may be held to be marvelous. Rocamadour, in turn, reports that it was successful where the Church of the Holy Cross in Jerusalem was not.[17] Even churches dedicated to the same figure, the Virgin Mary, were rivals with each other.

There is evidence of this competitive spirit in our North Sea World, if I may stretch this to include Canterbury. The geographical area involved includes the following sites: Canterbury, Durham, Finchale, St Andrews, and the coast of Norway. The rivalry suggests – I would say reveals – an awareness of the North Sea world.

Durham (Cuthbert's shrine) felt in rivalry with the new, booming shrine of St Thomas Becket at Canterbury. On six occasions recorded in Reginald of Durham, in one way or another – sometimes, we are told, on the recommendation of St Thomas himself – Cuthbert rather than Thomas becomes the miracle worker. At one time or another Reginald of Durham compares St Cuthbert with St Benedict and with St Martin of Tours.[18] On one occasion, Cuthbert shares the credit with St Lawrence.[19] He also is in harmony with St Nicholas or equal with him on six occasions.[20] And St Brendan himself in a vision tells an unjustly imprisoned man to stop calling on him for aid and to call on St Cuthbert, for he is more famous and more powerful and, in the performance of miracles, much more illustrious and effective.[21]

On the other hand, Cuthbert's shrine, much the most established and prestigious in the North of England, did not feel threatened by the recently established shrine of St Godric at Finchale. It is mentioned only three times, all failures. Once it is to tell of a young man seriously ill who went twice to St Godric, but wasn't helped and then was cured by St Cuthbert. And both

---

15 *Cuthberti*, pp 38–39.   **16** *History of Becket*, I, pp 289–90.   **17** *Les Miracles de Notre-Dame de Roc-Amadour au XIIe Siècle*, ed. by Edmond Albe (Paris, 1907), no 2: 19, p. 212.   **18** *Cuthberti*, pp 231 and 187, respectively.   **19** *Cuthberti*, p. 244.   **20** *Cuthberti*, pp 62, 66, 68, 72, 74, and 146.   **21** *Cuthberti*, p. 92.

St Thomas and St Godric fail on another occasion while Cuthbert triumphs, St Godric's failure being especially embarrassing, for the young man goes to St Godric's because recent rumors had told of new signs of miraculous events there. But nothing happened, and the young man went on to Durham.[22]

Finchale is also the loser in the quietly dramatic account of a woman of Brunton afflicted with the falling sickness, who heads for the shrine of St Godric. Stopping overnight in the village of Thorp, she is told in a dream that she will be cured before she reaches Finchale. Passing through Durham the next morning, she suddenly hears the bells of St Cuthbert's church pealing for the introit of high mass. She turns aside, and arriving at the west wall of the cathedral, falling down and getting up again as she goes, she merited being released from her infirmity.[23] (Women were not allowed at St Cuthbert's shrine, which was in the monastic part of the cathedral, but she has come as close as she can to his tomb from the outside – an especially moving touch. And a dramatic assertion of St Cuthbert's power.)[24]

And there were many other saints to be considered. Sister Benedicta Ward has called attention to the competitive tone in the reporting of seventeen other of Cuthbert's miracles.[25]

Overshadowed by Cuthbert's long established shrine at Durham and the phenomenal success of Becket's at Canterbury, Godric's shrine was understandably the rival of both. Becket died in 1172, Godric in 1170. There is evidence in the Finchale narrative of the shrine's struggle to achieve recognition for Godric's special access to divine grace and to hold its own against its powerful competitors. The challenge is met in several ingenious ways, most notably with Becket, who appears in a total of fifteen of Godric's miracles. St Thomas is in a sense co-opted. In one vision St Thomas refers to Godric as 'meo consortium', my comrade, and in another vision a man tells Godric that he has been cured by St Thomas, 'tui consocii in coelistibus [sic]', your companion in heaven.[26] Three miracles are split between the two, Thomas, for example, curing one contracted hand and knee, Godric the other hand and knee, thus showing – one of the narratives is careful to point out – that Thomas and Godric were equals before God.[27] In nine of the miracles, the cures occur at Godric's shrine after Becket's had been visited in vain, but several times the suggestion is made that this is a gracious gesture by St Thomas, who is deferring to Godric.[28] There is no claim that Godric is superior. There is a firm assertion, however, of equality. The shrine is protecting its own interests.

St Cuthbert is treated with equal tact. Some cures occur at Finchale after disappointment at Durham, but perhaps this was Cuthbert being gracious to

---

22 *Cuthberti*, pp 271–72.   23 *Cuthberti*, p. 270.   24 Ward, *Miracles*, p. 63.   25 Ward, *Miracles*, p. 63.   26 *Godrici*, pp 459–60, 410–11.   27 *Godrici*, pp 376, 397–98, 432–33.   28 *Godrici*, pp 376, 409, 412, 423, 427–29, 441, 445, 459–60.

Godric. But, again, Godric is equal to Cuthbert in divine favor.[29] And several Godric miracles occur at Durham with no mention of Cuthbert.[30]

Twice in the Godric-Cuthbert records miracles involve persons in or from Norway who have heard, in one instance, of Cuthbert's powers, and once of Godric's.[31] And what of St Andrews? Godric apparently had visited St Andrews, 'maxime famosus illud domicilium Sancti Apostoli Andreæ', several times in his earlier days as a merchant, we are told, and had made offerings there pleasing to God. But his keeper of records seems to have felt no need to be diplomatic about the shrine of St Andrew. Three times Reginald tells of pilgrims who went to St Andrews but failed to be cured and had to make their way to Finchale to receive aid.[32] No record of miracles at St Andrews has, alas, survived. That it was a scene of miraculous cures the 'failures' confirm.

In such a competitive atmosphere, a shrine had to insure that its miracles could not be successfully challenged. Shrines sometimes tested the validity of a miracle by questioning the person professing to have experienced it, or checking later to see if it was permanent and real, or interrogating others who knew the person.[33] In the Canterbury records we find the attendants reluctantly refusing to accept the story of a poor woman who had traveled there at great sacrifice and hardship to tell of St Thomas' miraculous restoration to life of her ten-year-old son, injured and drowned in a millrace at Litchfield. But there were no neighbors to vouch for the story. Though the people at Canterbury were impressed by the circumstantiality of her account and by her difficult journey, they were afraid her story was a 'plant' by some rival shrine, designed to embarrass them, to be exposed as a fraud and lead to popular distrust.[34]

Convincing their audience of the truth of the miracle they are claiming is therefore a major concern of the recorders of such events. The skeptic had to be convinced or at least answered effectively. The suspicion of demonic involvement had to be exorcised. And a possibly reluctant suspension of disbelief among the champions of other shrines had to be achieved. As an essential element in the process, circumstantial detail was most useful. And it had to be true to observed life at the very least and was most often probably true to actual event. I would argue therefore for the validity of such detail as we find in 'This woman in the household of the Abbot of Jedworth returned sound and healthy, and she and her household were regaled with the butter and cheese from full-fat milk she had brought with her'.[35]

What then can it give us of value? For one, the detail communicates a sense of the living reality of the dead past, a sense of momentary closeness to a

---

29 *Godrici*, pp 379, 387–88, 396, 408, 454, 459–60.   30 *Godrici*, pp 352, 377, 378; and several involving women, pp 373, 377.   31 *Cuthberti*, p. 251, and *Godrici*, pp 349–50.   32 *Godrici*, pp 276, 426–27, and 445–46.   33 Pierre-André Sigal, *L'homme et le miracle dans la France médiévale* (Paris, 1985), pp 147–55.   34 *History of Becket*, I, pp 346–47 (Book 4, 34).   35 *Cuthberti*, p. 288.

distant age. As though caught in the flash of a stroboscopic light, a scene lost in time bursts upon our vision. A young knight from a good family, eager for glory, comes to a town in Normandy named Blangy, where a tournament is in progress. He is not armed like the others, but is furnished only with a lance and shield, no breast plate. But, confidently, he suddenly enters between the lines of combat. However, someone comes at him from the other side and the young man receives a lethal wound, the point of the lance penetrating the skin of his belly under the navel from one side almost to the other. His intestines break out through the wound, hanging over the front of his saddle, and a hand placed over the wound cannot hold them back. Victory in battle is changed to lamentation and the martial concerns are set aside. A grieving crowd runs to him. Arms embrace the wounded man, half alive, and taking him up from the saddle, place him on his shield and lower him to the ground. A priest gives him confession and the last rites.[36]

Miracle is not class-bound. It ranges relatively freely through class lines, as in this account of a poor woman in Teviotdale, deprived of wealth and a husband. She had a few sheep that supplemented her income. On the borders there were many fierce and ravenous wolves. The richest people could hire caretakers to guard their sheep and didn't lose any. But she was too poor to hire anyone.

So each day, as she drove her sheep out to pasture, she would say with great fervor, 'St Cuthbert, because I have no other protector, I commit the care of my sheep to you. For your piety's sake, guard and protect them from every attack, and send them home to me safe and sound'.

For some time her sheep were always unharmed. Although the ravaging wolves often seized the sheep of others, they didn't presume to ravage or harm the widow's. At last, one day a band of wolves yielded to a more raging greed than usual. Circling the wide boundaries of the fields, they discovered the widow's sheep, deprived (widowed) of a herdsman. They began to attack seven sheep. But harrying them for a long time through pathless and unpassable ways, they could never seem to seize one of them. At last all these sheep gathered together as a unit and collected within the walls of the chapel of St Cuthbert as if fleeing to their herdsman. Surprisingly (*mirum in modum*) the wolves following them fiercely all remained yelping outside the walls.[37]

One thing certainly that the shrine miracles, taken together, reveal is that the natural and supernatural live together in the most comfortable and familiar contiguity. They permeate each other's space. It is impossible to say of any scene or situation, here the supernatural cannot be. The Canterbury collections tell of an ox being saved, a cow, a lamb, a drowned suckling pig, a gander, not to mention a covey of lost hawks restored, revived, one with its broken leg

---

36 *Godrici*, pp 427–28. Through Godric's help, the young man recovers.   37 *Cuthberti*, pp 288–89.

mended.[38] And there is Reginald of Durham's charming story of a monk named Bartholomew who lived as a hermit on Farne and had a pet bird who came every day at mealtime and ate from his hand and was 'diligent to sit on the table and joke [*jocari*] with him as if by practice [*usu*] changed in nature'.[39]

Such miracles are classified as 'joca sanctorum', saints' jokes. Sister Benedicta Ward comments, 'In certain shrine collections joca show the saint to be concerned with trivia'. Though miracles were not mocked, 'this application of powers of sanctity to trivial incidents was a subject of mirth as well as edification. [... They were] a way of expressing the relationship between the saint and his or her devotees in terms appealing to all'.[40] These 'trivial' miracles reveal how deeply the supernatural penetrated the realm of the natural. They are flood-level marks. They confirm the coherence of the universe and assert that there is no human concern beyond divine attention.

One final miracle in support of all that I have claimed. Its Canterbury narrator begins, 'A miracle concerning a trifling matter occurred in a village'. The report is rather amusing. Someone had given a cheese to the wife of a man named William. She had turned it over to her young daughter, Beatrice, for safekeeping. Beatrice, once she had put the cheese away, turned to her play and games, as happens at that age, and immediately forgot completely where she had stored it. Some days had passed when the girl remembered the cheese. But she simply couldn't remember where she had put it. She was afraid that if the cheese were lost, she would be punished with a beating. So she told her secret to one of her brothers, a child like herself, whom she loved more than the others and who was especially fond of her. She asked him if *he* remembered the place where she had put it. He answered that he didn't know. The Friday of the following week was approaching, when, they were afraid, the stored cheese would be demanded. They searched every place, again and again. They turned the house upside down (*evertunt domum*). They looked for the cheese, but they couldn't find it. They held lengthy consultations, and held them frequently. They could think of absolutely no plan.

But then the girl had an idea, and thinking it over, it seemed a good one: that they should go all the way to the aforementioned man (that is, the man who had given them the cheese in the first place), though he was a good distance away, and ask him for a cheese just like the first one.

But the boy said, 'No, no, no [*nequaquam*], let's go do this, it's much more likely to work. I've heard – and it's already spread all over the world – that God's saint, Thomas the martyr, shines for his many, many miracles. If we wanted devoutly to seek him out for his help, surely we won't be at all sorry because what we ask for will be refused. Let's pray earnestly for his mercy so

---

[38] *History of Becket*, I, pp 343–44; 358–59; 393–94; 388–92.   [39] *Cuthberti*, pp 247–48.
[40] Ward, *Miracles*, pp 211–12.

that he'll make us dream where the cheese might be'. This childish plan pleased both youngsters. After saying the Lord's prayer, they went straight to bed.

And so the saint, most beautiful in countenance and clothing, stood by the sleeping girl and said, 'Why are you unhappy?' She told him the reason for her grieving, namely, the loss of the cheese and the fear of punishment. Then the saint pointed out an old pot in which it had been customary a long time ago for butter to curdle and be made. 'Don't you remember', he said, 'that you put the cheese in that old pot? Get up, you'll find it there'.

Roused from sleep, she ran to the place he had pointed out. Snatching up the cheese, she quickly ran back to her brother, saying, 'Hugo, I've really found the cheese!'

The boy said, 'Sure [*vere*], I knew where you'd find it'.

The girl wondered at his response. 'How', she said, 'did you know that?'

The boy said, 'A very nice-looking man dressed like a priest, stood by me and asked me the reason for my unhappiness. And when he learned why, he pointed out the cheese to me and said, 'Get up. You'll find it in that old pot!'

'That's right!' the girl said, 'and while I was sleeping, the same man showed up and used those same words'. Then they woke their mother and unfolded to her what happened from the very beginning. Their mother did the same to the village priest, Edricus. The priest in turn called in the boy and girl separately and heard one and the same thing from both of them without the slightest variation. When he came to Canterbury, he made everyone to whom he told the story laugh'.[41]

Aside from its charm, the story gives us a rare, precious glimpse of real children in the late twelfth or early thirteenth century. We don't see all that many children in medieval literature or chronicle.

We often have in shrine miracles a kind of reportage not available much of anywhere else in medieval documents. Shrine miracles have been little studied from this perspective. They often give us glimpses of life in the Middle Ages interesting in themselves, valuable because unposed. And the shrine rivalry responsible for their existence is revealed as an important dimension of miracle culture, an amalgam of spirituality and pragmatism. And, in the present instance, a glimpse of the North Sea World.

---

41 *History of Becket*, II, pp 153–59 (Book 3, 51).

The *South English Legendaries*

THOMAS R. LISZKA

Most scholars are familiar with *The South English Legendary* as it appears in the three-volume edition of by Charlotte D'Evelyn and Anna J. Mill, published between 1956 and 1959.[1] The edition is based on Corpus Christi College Cambridge MS 145 and British Library MS Harley 2277 (known by their sigla as C and H).[2] The Harley manuscript, dated about 1300, is the second oldest *SEL* manuscript and the earliest orderly text. However, because of some serious lacunae, especially at the beginning of the manuscript, and some careless copying throughout the manuscript, the editors substituted the similar, but later Corpus Christi manuscript as their primary base text. They then supplemented it from the Harley text.

Before this edition, the only apparently complete edition was that of Carl Horstmann, published in 1887, with the title *The Early South-English Legendary or Lives of Saints*.[3] It was an edition based on the oldest *SEL* manuscript, Bodleian Library MS Laud.Miscellaneous 108, usually dated around 1280. Its lacunae were filled from three other manuscripts, including the Harley.[4]

The Early English Text Society, a respected society of folk who usually know what they are talking about, published both editions. In both, the work edited is called the *South English Legendary*, singular, and not the *South English Legendaries*, as I title this article. Nevertheless, I do so to stress the existence and significance of variety among the manuscript texts of the work that collectively have come to be called by the name *South English Legendary*. I will discuss these two editions as points of departure.

* * *

1 *The South English Legendary*, ed. by Charlotte D'Evelyn and Anna J. Mill, 3 vols, EETS 235, 236, and 244 (London, 1956–59).　2 In the following discussion, especially the notes, I make some use of the sigla established in Manfred Görlach, *The Textual Tradition of the South English Legendary*, Leeds Texts and Monographs n. s. 6 (Leeds, 1974), pp viii–x, and in O.S. Pickering and Manfred Görlach, 'A Newly-Discovered Manuscript of the *South English Legendary*', *Anglia*, 100 (1982), pp 109–23.　3 Carl Horstmann, ed., *The Early South-English Legendary or Lives of Saints*, EETS o. s. 87 (London, 1887).　4 The others are British Library Cotton Julius D IX and Bodleian Library English Poetry a.1 ('The Vernon Manuscript').

I have listed the contents of the familiar D'Evelyn and Mill edition in Appendix 1. The collection begins with a prologue, in some manuscripts identified as the *Banna Sanctorum*. It is not so titled in the Corpus Christi College manuscript. But the editors, nevertheless, have supplied the title in square brackets. The edition is of a festial, that is, a collection of readings for the feasts of the church. Most of these feasts, of course, are saints' days, so most of the readings are saints' lives. The cycle of feasts is not arranged according to the church calendar, which begins with Advent, but according to the secular calendar, beginning 1 January. (The dates of the feasts are not indicated in the edition proper or in the edition's table of contents, but I have indicated them in Appendix 1 for reference.) There are also readings for many of the fixed feasts, such as Circumcision and Epiphany, and for the moveable feasts of Septuagesima, Lent, and Easter, and there is one combined reading for the Greater and Lesser Litanies, which are fixed and moveable feasts, respectively. (I have highlighted all of the non-saints' lives in Appendix 1.) The readings for the moveable feasts of Septuagesima, Lent, and Easter have been placed in an approximately appropriate position, following the feast of the Annunciation, or as it is often called, St Mary Day in Lent, and the text for both Litanies follows the life of St Mark because the Greater Litany also falls on his feast day, 25 April. The Lesser Litany, or Rogationtide, is a moveable feast which falls on the three days before Ascension Thursday. The collection then runs through the 29 December feast of St Thomas Becket and ends with an apparent appendix of texts for two 'luþer bridðes' or 'wicked birds', as they are sometimes called, Judas and Pilate. All texts are in rhymed couplets, usually with seven beats per line.

The D'Evelyn and Mill edition is said to be exclusively of a *sanctorale* collection. *SEL* scholars take some liberties with the terms *sanctorale* and *temporale* from the way they are used in the liturgical service books. There the *sanctorale* includes the readings for almost all of the fixed feasts arranged according to their calendar dates, and the *temporale* is a separate, usually preceding collection that includes the readings for the moveable feasts which 'move' around the calendar, in relation to the day of the week that Christmas falls on and the date of the year that Easter falls on. But as you have seen, the manuscripts on which D'Evelyn and Mill based their edition have most of this content inserted into the *sanctorale* cycle. Thus, we use the term *sanctorale* to refer to all those texts worked into the collection of saints' lives. The term *temporale* refers to all those texts in a separate collection preceding the saints' lives, whether they concern moveable feasts or not. The Corpus Christi manuscript and, consequently, the D'Evelyn and Mill edition lack a separate *temporale* section. But, as we shall see, several *South English Legendary* manuscripts do have a *temporale* collection preceding the *sanctorale*.[5]

5 O.S. Pickering, 'The *Temporale* Narratives of the *South English Legendary*', *Anglia*, 91 (1973), pp 425–55; and his 'The Expository *Temporale* Poems of the *South English*

I wish to use these editions by D'Evelyn and Mill and by Horstmann as starting points for this discussion because – while they lack the textual authority of the surviving manuscripts – they present the texts, whether correct, corrected, or corrupt, to which most of us by necessity refer. They present our visual image of the *South English Legendary*. They are, therefore, responsible for some basic assumptions that we make about the *SEL*. I have displayed the D'Evelyn and Mill edition first, though later in date, because its orderly presentation of texts makes for a clearer image. But I wish to discuss Carl Horstmann's older edition of the less orderly text first.

Perhaps the most basic assumption we make about a work is its name. Although I don't believe that Carl Horstmann intended to do so, his edition gave the collection its modern name, *South English Legendary*. Horstmann intended his title, *The Early South-English Legendary*, merely to describe generically, temporally, and geographically what was in his edition, in order to differentiate it from the northern and Scottish collections of homilies and saints' lives, and other collections such as Mirk's *Festial*. Other scholars before him, such as Madden and Furnivall, and a few after him were forced to use similar descriptive, rather than real titles because the manuscripts themselves preserve only slight evidence of an accepted medieval title.[6]

There are twenty-five manuscripts that preserve likely places to look for a title – that is, on folia with a medieval table of contents and on folia where one can find, or where one might have hoped to find an *incipit* or *explicit* for the entire collection. Of these twenty-five manuscripts, only six preserve possible titles. But the titles preserved appear to be merely generic descriptions of the contents of the manuscripts, not unlike the ones Horstmann and the other early scholars used. 'Vita Sanctor*um*' appears in two manuscripts, British Library MSS Harley 2277 (H) and Egerton 2810 (M). The Harley manuscript also contains the expanded description, 'vit*e* s*anctorum* [...] & Allie Historie'. Magdalene College Cambridge MS Pepys 2344 (P) twice uses 'Legenda s*anctorum*'. And Bodleian Library MS Laud.Miscellaneous 463 (D) has 'legenda s*anc*tor*um* in lingua Anglicana'. Finally, because of the *SEL*'s similarity to Jacobus de Voragine's important Latin collection, Lambeth Palace MS 223 (G) simply appropriates Jacobus' title for the *SEL*, calling it 'legenda Aurea'. One manuscript, unique in containing exclusively *temporale* texts, St John's College Cambridge MS 28 (I), refers to its collection simply as 'temporale in Anglicis'.[7]

Given the manuscript evidence then, or the lack thereof, we are intrigued to find Horstmann's footnote to the very first sentence of the Introduction to his edition. In it, he states that 'The Title of the complete collection was perhaps

---

Legendary', *Leeds Studies in English*, n. s. 10 (1978), pp 1–17. I refer to the *temporale* texts as they have been defined and titled by O.S. Pickering in 1973, rather than the using the older definitions and titles.   6 See below.   7 H: fol. 227ʳ (explicit) and fol. 232ᵛ (contents). M: fol. 3ᵛ (contents). P: p. [iii] (contents) and p. 1 (above first item, a title in

the *Mirrour of Saints' Lives*.[8] None of the surviving manuscripts preserves this title, but one might fancy that the nineteenth-century editor was aware of some subsequently lost medieval reference to the collection, which he would reveal at a later date. Horstmann apparently intended to edit all the manuscripts known to him and to write a comprehensive introduction in the last volume.[9] Alas, he did not fulfill that intention. But perhaps had he done so, in his final volume, the long-lost reference to a *Mirrour of Saints' Lives* would be revealed, and quite possibly along with it, Fermat's proof for his last theorem. But, this flight of fancy aside, in the absence of any manuscript authority for the *Mirrour of* title, we must conclude that Horstmann was merely making a harmless speculation on the analogy of similar medieval works with *Mirrour* or *Speculum* in their titles.

Now, while I am not aware that any subsequent scholar has ever referred to the collection as the *Mirrour of Saints' Lives*, the title *South English Legendary*, taken from Horstmann's title for his edition, gradually, but completely has caught on. In 1886, the year before Horstmann's edition, F.J. Furnivall referred to Horstmann's forthcoming work as the 'Early English *Lives of Saints*'.[10] In 1901, George McKnight still referred to the collection as 'the Southern Cycle'.[11] And in 1916, John Edwin Wells used the terms 'The Southern Legend Collection' and 'The Southern Legendary' in his *A Manual of the Writings in Middle English*.[12] But references to anything other than the *South English Legendary* or *SEL* after that are rare. The title, of course, was confirmed when Charlotte D'Evelyn and Anna J. Mill entitled their edition simply *The South English Legendary*, without comment or disclaimer. We might note that, in J. Burke Severs' updating of Wells' *Manual*, the names *South English Legendary* and *SEL* appear regularly in place of Wells' generic descriptions.[13] And of course Manfred Görlach in the most extensive modern study of the work and its manuscripts, *The Textual Tradition of the South English Legendary*, uses that name exclusively.

* * *

place?). D: fol. 157^r (explicit). G: fol. 297^r ('here endeþ'). I: fol. 79^r (explicit). 8 Horstmann, *Early South-English Legendary*, p. vii. 9 Horstmann, *Early South-English Legendary*, p. vii. The title page of his edition also identifies this edition as Volume 'I'. However, the series was not continued. 10 F.J. Furnivall, 'Early English Text Society: Statement for 1887 and 1888', in *The Lives of Women Saints of Our Contrie of England*, ed. by Carl Horstmann, EETS o. s. 86 (London, 1886), the second of four unnumbered pages prior to p. i. 11 *King Horn, Floriz and Blauncheflur, the Assumption of Our Lady, First ed. in 1866, by J. Rawson Lumby, and now re-ed. from the manuscripts*, ed. by George McKnight, EETS o. s. 14 (London, 1901), p. xxviii. 12 John Edwin Wells, *A Manual of the Writings in Middle English: 1050–1400* (London, 1916), pp 292, 317, etc. 13 J. Burke Severs, gen. ed., *A Manual of the Writings in Middle English 1050–1500*, II, Section IV.4 'The Southern Temporale' by Laurence Muir, pp 403–07, Section V 'Saints' Legends' by Charlotte D'Evelyn and Frances A. Foster, pp 410–57 (Hamden, CT, 1970).

Now the adoption of the name *South English Legendary* may seem like a mere historical curiosity, but with a name comes an identity. After Horstmann's edition, the collection was no longer merely a group of individual items. It was a whole. Previous editors and Horstmann himself had published various individual *SEL* items (for lack of another name) from the Laud.Miscellaneous 108 and other manuscripts. But now for the first time a collection, appearing complete, was published. It could be identified, considered, and discussed as a thing with a name, albeit modern. Now I do not mean to suggest that D'Evelyn, Mill, Severs, Görlach and other modern scholars were or are unaware that the *South English Legendary* is a modern title; they certainly are so. Nevertheless, their treatment of the work has been influenced by the identity implicit in that name.

Especially significant to the formation of that identity was Horstmann's decision to exclude certain items from his edition. Appendix 2 contains a summarized list of contents for the Laud.Miscellaneous 108 manuscript. (In the appendix, summarized contents are identified with italic capitals.) We can be fairly certain that at the beginning of the manuscript seven items have been lost because the items are numbered throughout, beginning with item number 8. The first surviving piece is a fragment of a poem on the *Ministry and Passion* of Christ, which begins and ends imperfectly. Then, in a separate quire, a narrative on the *Infancy of Christ* follows.

After these two texts comes the manuscript's important, but puzzling *sanctorale* collection. (In this appendix and the next several, I use a dotted line to show the place where the *sanctorale* collection begins.) The *sanctorale* of this manuscript has a number of texts, preserved in earlier versions than the more familiar ones available in the D'Evelyn and Mill edition. Also, as has often been noted, although the Laud *sanctorale* appears disorganized, it has a unique prologue located not at the beginning of the collection, but in the middle. (Its position cannot be accounted for by a simple misbinding of quires.) Despite its position, the prologue describes an organization according to the calendar year. This organization is not realized in the manuscript as a whole, but there are some clusters of texts that preserve some vestiges of a calendar order. The manuscript ends with some religious didactic works, two romances, three appended saints' lives, the poem 'Somer Soneday', and some assorted scribbles and fragments.[14]

Appendix 2 also shows which items Horstmann included in his edition and which ones he excluded. The exclusions are highlighted in boldface. For most of the excluded texts, such as the romances *Havelok the Dane* and *King Horn*, Horstmann's decision to exclude is easily defended. On the other hand, the exclusion of the first two items, the *Ministry and Passion* fragment and the poem on the *Infancy of Christ*, seems significant. For these two poems appear to

---

14 Thomas R. Liszka, 'MS Laud.Misc. 108 and the Early History of the *South English Legendary*', *Manuscripta*, 33 (1989), pp 75–91. Previous scholarship is also summarized there.

represent remnants of a *temporale* section. And if the *temporale* also included the seven lost items, it would have been of substantial size.[15]

In addition to Laud.Miscellaneous 108, there are five other *SEL* manuscripts in which a *temporale* collection precedes a *sanctorale*. But this arrangement of *SEL* texts is not now represented in any edition. British Library MS Egerton 1993 (E) is a good example (Appendix 3). Preceding the *Banna Sanctorum*, the first item in the *sanctorale*, we find the *Old Testament History*, a poem that begins with the Creation and Fall and then follows with the stories of important patriarchs and prophets, in this manuscript running from Adam through Abacuc. After that comes the *Abridged Life of Christ*, a poem on the *Conception of Mary*, and the *Expanded Nativity* version of the *Nativity of Mary and Christ* poem that appears in some other *SEL* manuscripts.

None of the manuscripts beginning with a *temporale* section has the same poems in the same order, but as you look at them, certain similarities emerge. For example, Trinity College Cambridge Manuscript 605 (R) (Appendix 4) has the *Old Testament History* followed again by material associated with Jesus and Mary before the *Banna Sanctorum*. In this manuscript, the beginning of the *Abridged Life of Christ* and one of the Miracles of our Lady, a text that in other manuscripts usually appears in the *sanctorale*, precede the *sanctorale* cycle. On the other hand, some *temporale* items – the conclusion of the *Abridged Life of Christ*, the poem on the *Nativity of Mary and Christ*, and the *Trinity Conception of Mary* – have been worked into the *sanctorale* cycle in December contexts, where they appear to have functioned as texts for Christmas and the Feast of the Conception (25 and 8 December, respectively). And a small portion of the *Ministry and Passion* poem was appended to the collection.

Lambeth Palace 223 (G) (Appendix 5) begins atypically with the *temporale* poems on the Moveable Feasts, which in other manuscripts often appear in the *sanctorale* cycle. It then, however, reverts to the familiar pattern: *Old Testament History*, followed by material of one sort or another on the lives of Christ and Mary, preceding the *sanctorale* cycle.

Two other manuscripts have vestiges of the same order (Appendices 6 and 7). Each begins with the *Old Testament History*. The Vernon manuscript (V) follows with the *Vernon Life of Mary* before the *sanctorale*, and Winchester College MS 33a (W) follows its *Old Testament History* with the lives of Pilate and Judas, which frequently appear among texts on Christ's passion, whether presented in *temporale* or *sanctorale* contexts.

And finally, the unique manuscript exclusively composed of *temporale* texts, St John's College Cambridge MS 28 (I) (Appendix 8), begins familiarly with the *Old Testament History*, includes the *Nativity of Mary and Christ* and the *Ministry and Passion* poems, and supplements the passion story with the St

15 Pickering, 'Expository *Temporale*', pp 4–5.

The South English Legendar*ies*

Longinus and Pilate vitae, and the stories of *The Harrowing of Hell and the Destruction of Jerusalem*. The collection is completed with the Moveable Feasts *temporale*.

The variety among the various *temporale* collections would even today make it difficult, perhaps impossible, for an editor to select one particular collection, if that editor hoped to present a definitive *South English temporale* collection. Nevertheless, it should have been apparent to Horstmann that in many manuscripts some *temporale* collection – with a basic chronological order of *Old Testament History*, followed by material from the lives of Christ and Mary – was clearly part of the complete literary work – by whatever title that work should be called.

If we pay attention to how scribes and readers have referred to these *temporale* texts in the manuscripts – in marginal titles, running titles, and titles appearing in lists of contents and in the other marginal indexes to the content of the texts – we will find even more evidence of the homogeneity of the *temporale* and *sanctorale* collections. The medieval reader appears to have accepted the *temporale* texts as much the same kind of thing as the *sanctorale* texts.

Appendix 9 shows the contents of Trinity College Cambridge MS 605 (R) again, this time emphasizing its *temporale* collection. The appendix also identifies the titles given in the manuscript for the various texts. It has both running titles and some marginal titles, and there are two lists of contents at the end of the manuscript. Only the first was completed. Its relevant titles appear here in the third column. The middle column has the titles that we find in the body of the manuscript. There, the text that we refer to as *Old Testament History* is identified as several continuous texts with the titles: 'Adam & Eve', 'Noe', 'Abraham', 'Iacob', 'Ioseph', 'Moyses', 'Dauid', 'Salamon', 'Roboam', and 'Daniel'. The selection from the *Abridged Life of Christ* has the title '*Salutatio Marie*'. Most of these titles appearing in or with the text also appear in the completed list of contents. However, we find there additional references to 'Isaac', 'Sampson', 'Saul', 'Absolon', 'Helise' (that is, Elisha), and 'Helie' (that is, Elijah).[16]

It seems clear that, while the audience probably recognized smaller units and separate sections in the manuscript, they also saw a unity to the whole. They recognized the *temporale* and *sanctorale* as one continuous series of vitae of holy people: those living before Christ and Mary, Christ and Mary themselves, and those living after Christ and Mary. Note by comparison that in the margins, running title, and list of contents of the *sanctorale* the saints are referred to simply as 'Hillary', 'Wolston', 'Fabian', etc. – not as 'St Hillary', 'St Wolston', 'St Fabian', etc. Thus, the presentations of two groups of holy people are as closely assimilated as they can be.

---

16 The completed table of contents is on fol. 275^r; the incomplete table, on fol. 275^v. Its *temporale* titles appear to be the same as those in the completed table. However, much of its text is illegible on my microfilm copy, and I have not seen the manuscript itself.

This manuscript is not alone in its homogeneous presentation of the *temporale* and *sanctorale* texts. Lambeth Palace 223 is also a good example (Appendix 10). There is no medieval list of contents, but running titles are used throughout, and marginal titles are frequent (although other referential marginalia are sometimes indistinguishable from the latter). After the manuscript's atypical beginning with the Moveable Feasts, the scribe gives an especially complete titling or indexing of the *Old Testament History*, using the names of the main characters. The names of 'Loth', 'Esau', 'Iosue', 'Gedeon', 'Ionathas', 'Nathan', 'Ieroboam', and 'Ionas' are added to those we noted in the previous manuscript. In the next part of the manuscript, we find a selection entitled 'Ierome'. At first glance, the selection might seem chronologically inappropriate, in a place where we expect material from the life of Christ and Mary. However, 'Ierome' is a small stand-alone portion of the *Abridged Life of Christ*. Furthermore, although it would better fit the pattern for which I am arguing if Christ's or Mary's name had been used in the title, we should at least note that the content is referred to by the name of a person, the author Ierome, rather than by the thematic title, the 'Fifteen Signs of Judgment', as the text is also known. The texts following 'Ierome' all do include either Christ, Jesus, or Mary in their titles.

Winchester College MS 33a's (W) brief selection of *Old Testament History* texts has interlinear or marginal titles (Appendix 11). Included are the expected 'Vita de Adam', 'Noe', 'Abraham', and 'Joseph' texts. The text identifying 'Rebecca' as a central character spans the units usually referred to as 'Isaac', 'Jacob', and 'Esau' in the other manuscripts. The unique title suggests that the compiler exercised some subjective judgment as to who the main character in the text was. Nevertheless, the compiler still presents the text as the story of somebody. The 'Vita Pilati' and 'De Iuda Scarioth' are appropriate parts of the story of Christ's passion, which is composed of stories of bad people, as well as good. The pattern continues in the *sanctorale* where the first three titles are 'Vita Sancti Oswaldi', 'Vita Sancti Edwardi regis Anglie', and 'Vita Sancti Cuthberti episcopi'.

I have not supplied an appendix showing the titles used in British Library MS Egerton 1993 (E) and St John's College Cambridge MS 28 (I) because they are exceptions to the pattern. The Egerton manuscript has only one marginal title similar to the ones I have been discussing, the title 'Liber Salamou*n*'. Instead, there are many marginal statements of reference, such as 'Portam auream' and 'Fuit in die Herodes rex'. These do not seem intended as titles. They can appear almost anywhere, and they are usually not near large capitals. Still, the presentation in the *sanctorale* is like that of the *temporale*. No titles accompany the saints' lives. Instead, there are merely reference statements such as 'Mirac*u*l*u*m', 'Narratio', and 'Lamentatio' next to the text.

The St John's *temporale* manuscript (I) also uses few names of main characters as titles of texts. Instead, 'De creacione mundi' appears to be the main title of the *Old Testament History*, and much annotation and other indexing, such as 'Adam accepit pomum' and 'Nudi erant', appear in the margins. However, a possible title, 'Abraham', does appear next to a major capital at the beginning of his episode, and 'Isakar Ioachym et Anna' (or simply 'Ioachym et Anna', since there is a large space between the words 'Isakar' and 'Ioachym') appears as a title for the *Nativity of Mary and Christ*.

Finally, the Vernon manuscript (V) is deceptive (Appendix 12). There are no titles in the collection proper, but there is a large index to the huge book's collection. It appears at first glance to use people's names as titles for the items in the *temporale* only exceptionally. The collection begins with 'de creacione coeli & terre & de aliis operibus sex dierum'. Most titles after that are in English and descriptive of the action, such as 'Hou þe deuel bygylede Eue' and 'Of þe deþ of Moyses'. Nevertheless, although they appear to be in the minority, we still find used as titles almost all of the names that we are used to finding. (These appear in boldface.) Included are 'Of noe', 'Oof abraham', 'Of Ysaac', 'Of Iacob', 'Off Sampson', 'Of Saul', 'Of Dauid', 'Of Ieroboam', 'Of Helye', 'Of Daniel', 'Of Abacuc þe profete', 'Of Ioachim and of Anna', and again 'Of anna'.[17] In all probability then, the compiler of the index started from a list of names used as titles, but then supplemented it in an extremely thorough fashion.

* * *

Given then these three facts – the common core and arrangement of *temporale* texts in the manuscripts that have them, the number of manuscripts that begin with or otherwise preserve a separate *temporale* collection, and the consistency of presentation between the *sanctorale* and *temporale* texts – Horstmann's decision not to include the two *temporale* texts beginning the Laud manuscript in his edition of the *Early South-English Legendary* may seem surprising. (See Appendix 2 again.) Horstmann knew and, in fact, had described the contents of all but one of these manuscripts. Only the Winchester manuscript was unknown to him.

He also knew that, in the Laud manuscript, at least the first of the two texts in question, the *Ministry and Passion* fragment, was related to the collection he was editing. For in his 'List of Contents' of the Laud manuscript, he specifically identified that first text as a 'fragment of the Temporale'.[18] Indeed, Horstmann had described the contents of this manuscript several times previous to his 1887 *Early South-English Legendary* edition. And in every instance, the first sixty-one items, including these first two texts and running through to St Hippolitus, were listed and considered together as one continuous work. He did so in 1872, again in 1873, and again in 1875.[19] This last time, he stated explicitly

---

[17] Mary S. Serjeantson, 'The Index of the Vernon Manuscript', *Modern Language Review*, 32 (1937), pp 222–61.   [18] Horstmann, *Early South-English Legendary*, p. xiii.   [19] Carl Horstmann, 'Die Legenden des Ms. Laud 108', *Archiv für das Studium der Neueren Sprachen und Literaturen*, 49 (1872), pp 395–414; Carl Horstmann, ed., *Leben*

> Ms. *Laud 108* enthält bis *fol. 198* die Hauptmasse der Legenden, im Ganzen *61*, darauf drei religiöse Gedichte, die Epen *Havelok* und *King Horn*, dann *fol. 238b* drei weitere Legenden von einer spätern Hand des 15. Jhdts.
>
> ('Ms Laud 108 contains up to folio 198 the main part of the legends, sixty-one in all, after that three religious poems, the heroic poems *Havelok* and *King Horn*, then following folio 238b three further legends in a later hand of the fifteenth century'.)[20]

Well then, if these first two items were among the sixty-one items he considered to make up 'the main part of the legends', why did Horstmann exclude them from his edition of the 'Legendary'?

One might speculate that he excluded the first item, *Ministry and Passion*, because it was a fragment, which would therefore have made an awkward beginning for his edition. Had he wanted to include the poem, it would have been possible for him to fill its lacunae since the St John's College Cambridge manuscript preserves a complete version of the poem. (He did supply very long passages of the Dunstan, Austin, Brendan, Nicholas, Eustace, and Edmund of Abingdon texts from four other manuscripts.) But then, he would have the embarrassing situation of an edition of the Laud text beginning with several pages of text from another manuscript. Furthermore, he could not supply the seven items lost before this first surviving text.

Another possibility is that Horstmann had previously published editions of several of the omitted items. He published *King Horn* in 1872 and the *Sayings of St Bernard* and the *Vision of St Paul* in 1874, both in *Archiv für das Studium der Neueren Sprachen und Literaturen*. As parts of books, he published the *Ministry and Passion*, under the title *Leben Jesu*, in 1873, and the *Infancy of Christ*, under the title *Kindheit Jesu*, in 1875.[21] So the availability of these texts elsewhere in print may have helped to justify his decision to make this an edition of the *sanctorale* only.[22]

Jesu, ein Fragment und Kindheit Jesu, I. Theil, *Leben Jesu* (Münster, 1873), pp 3–7; Carl Horstmann, ed., *Altenglische Legenden* (Paderborn, 1875), pp xi–xiii.   **20** Horstmann, *Altenglische Legenden*, p. xi. Translation mine.   **21** Carl Horstmann, 'King Horn nach Ms. Laud 108' *Archiv für das Studium der Neueren Sprachen und Literaturen*, 50 (1872), pp 39–58. Carl Horstmann, 'Die Sprüche des h. Bernhard und die Vision des h. Paulus nach Ms. Laud 108', *Archiv für das Studium der Neueren Sprachen und Literaturen*, 52 (1874), pp 33–38. Horstmann, *Leben Jesu, ein Fragment und Kindheit Jesu*, I. Theil, *Leben Jesu*. It does not appear that the second volume was published. *Kindheit Jesu* was published in Horstmann, *Altenglische Legenden*, pp 1–61.   **22** Of course, Horstmann also edited elsewhere the life of St Mary Magdalene and St Patrick's Purgatory from this manuscript, but included them in *Early South-English Legendary* edition as well. 'Magdalena' in Carl Horstmann, ed., *Sammlung Altenglischer Legenden* (Heilbronn, 1878), pp 148–62. 'IV Das Fegefeuer des h. Patrick […] c. aus Ms. Laud 108

To speculate further and, perhaps, more wildly, it is possible that Horstmann was under some pressure to limit the material in the edition. Almost every scholar who reads his introduction will pause to note Horstmann's long and curious defense of his undertaking. Clearly some negativism must have inspired his statement, which begins: 'I know that most Englishmen consider it not worth while to print all these Legends; I know they regard them as worthless stuff, without any merit [...]'.[23] But most scholars are not aware of a similar disparaging attitude toward the project, expressed by Horstmann's series editor, F.J. Furnivall. In EETS editions published prior to Horstmann's edition, Furnivall described various recently published and forthcoming editions in the EETS series. These descriptions do not accompany later reprints of EETS editions. One version of Furnivall's statement reads:

> The Subscribers to the Original Series must be prepared for the issue of the whole of the Early English *Lives of Saints*, sooner or later. The Society cannot leave out any of them, even though some are dull. The Sinners would doubtless be much more interesting.

Now there is some intentional tongue-in-cheek here, also evidenced elsewhere in Furnivall's statement, and to his credit, Furnivall concedes some value to the saints' lives. He especially evokes that great justification of most nineteenth-century editions of medieval English literature, that is, the obtaining of *linguistic* information:

> But in many Saints' Lives will be found interesting incidental details of our forefathers' social state, and all are worthful for the history of our language. The Lives may be lookt on as the religious romances or storybooks of their period.[24]

Nevertheless, Furnivall's laboring to find an appropriate justification for the work might support the speculation that Horstmann had some encouragement

---

Purgatorium sci Patrici abbatis' in Horstmann, *Altenglische Legenden*, pp 177–211. **23** Horstmann, *Early South-English Legendary*, p. xi.   **24** [F.J. Furnivall], 'Original and Extra Series Books, 1893–5' in *The Minor Poems of the Vernon Manuscript*, ed. by Carl Horstmann, EETS o. s. 98 (London, 1892), p. 5 (of 10 numbered pages prior to p. i). A similar version appears in F.J. Furnivall, 'Statement for 1887 and 1888' in Horstmann, *The Lives of Women Saints of our Contrie of England*, pp 2–3 (of 4 unnumbered pages prior to p. i). For the tongue-in-cheek tone, compare Furnivall's comment on the many recent editions with German rather than English editors: 'Members will also note with pleasure the annexation of large tracts of our Early English territory by the important German contingent under General Zupitza, Colonels Kölbing and Horstmann, volunteers Hausknecht, Einenkel, Haenisch, Kaluza, Hupe, Adam, Holthausen, &c. &c.', in 'Original and Extra Series Books, 1893–5', p. 5.

to limit the size of his edition, while still presenting a selection that could be defended as complete.

Probably though, the least fanciful and simplest explanation is that Horstmann planned nothing at all sinister, that I am overreacting, and that he was simply interested in editing the *sanctorale* only. Many other editors before and after him have chosen to do selected editions. He did, after all, give his edition the alternate title '*or Lives of Saints*'.

Perhaps so. Nevertheless, it is at least regrettable that Carl Horstmann chose to do so. As a result of his selection, and of his edition's appearance of completeness, and finally of the *sanctorale*'s becoming identified as a literary work with a name, most subsequent scholars have accepted the *sanctorale* portion of the *SEL*, *de facto*, as the complete collection. Again, it is not that modern scholars aren't aware that the name is modern and that the *temporale* items are related. But these awarenesses have not stopped them (and here I include myself among the guilty) from treating the collection as if the *temporale* were not a part of the complete work – a work worthy of its own name and identity, but which today lacks both.[25]

* * *

Among the most important to so treat the *SEL* are those who are also most responsible for confirming the impression that the *SEL* is basically a *sanctorale* collection.

When Charlotte D'Evelyn and Anna J. Mill undertook their edition in the 1950s, they did so at the behest of the Committee on Editing Medieval Texts from the Medieval Section of the Modern Language Association of America. The Committee was composed of such notables as John Edwin Wells, Carleton Brown, Sir William Craigie, and Sanford B. Meech.[26] It is easy to imagine that the Committee and the editors understood their project as consistent with, but a necessary compromise to the work planned by Carl Horstmann.

When Horstmann said that he hoped to 'find my way through this mass of materials', the numerous and diverse manuscripts which he had been discussing, 'and to lay open the relation of the principal MSS., in the Introduction to the last volume' he apparently meant that he intended to edit all the manuscripts known to him in separate volumes.[27] While completing that plan would have been impractical, the Committee on Editing Medieval Texts saw an obvious and immediate need for a more representative edition, with only Horstmann's edition of one important, but apparently disorganized and otherwise atypical manuscript in print. They and the editors sought 'to make available for further

---

25 I refer to the *Banna Sanctorum* as a 'Prologue' in Thomas R. Liszka, 'The *South English Legendary*: A Critical Edition of the Prologue and the Lives of Saints Fabian, Sebastian, Gregory the Great, Mark, Quiriac, Paul, and James the Great' (unpublished doctoral dissertation, Northern Illinois University, 1980), *passim*.   **26** D'Evelyn and Mill, *South English Legendary*, I, p. v.   **27** Horstmann, *Early South-English Legendary*, p. vii.

study the earliest orderly text of *The South English Legendary*'. This was, Charlotte D'Evelyn and Anna J. Mill say, their 'whole purpose'.[28] In doing so, in preparing an edition based on the Harley and Corpus Christi manuscripts, they performed an extremely useful service: they improved our understanding of the *SEL* immeasurably. For, in most of its manuscripts, the *SEL* was not, after all, simply a jumble of texts, as the Laud manuscript may appear to be. Indeed, there are a number of key manuscripts that resemble the D'Evelyn and Mill edition, having an orderly arrangement of *sanctorale* items, and lacking a separate *temporale*. These I shall discuss shortly.

But, as we have already seen, there are also a number of manuscripts in which an orderly *temporale* does precede the *sanctorale*. Now, these later editors agreed with Horstmann that there would still be generations of work to do on the *SEL* after they completed their task. But if D'Evelyn and Mill weren't going to edit a manuscript with an orderly collection of *temporale* and *sanctorale* texts, such as the Vernon or Lambeth manuscripts, or if they weren't going to complement their own edition with an edition of the St John's College manuscript's *temporale* collection, why didn't they at least call for such editions? One must wonder if D'Evelyn and Mill might not have recognized a need for the availability of the *temporale* collection, if there were not already in print an edition of something called *The South English Legendary* from which the *temporale* had been excluded.

Manfred Görlach's work is monumental in scope. By collating or sample collating each *sanctorale* item in each of the more than sixty *SEL* manuscripts known at the time of his study and by surveying each of these manuscripts for evidence relevant to date, dialect, and provenance, Görlach has given us useful working hypotheses as to the early history of the collection and its subsequent development. If Horstmann, D'Evelyn, and Mill agreed that 'it will require more brains, the brains of several generations to come, before every question relative to this collection can be decided',[29] clearly Manfred Görlach accomplished one or two generations' shares of the work single-handedly. Nevertheless, Görlach has systematically studied only the *sanctorale* items. Moreover, in his list of the manuscripts, he classifies several manuscripts which have a single *sanctorale* text among other items as 'Manuscripts Containing Single Items of the SEL'. [One such is National Library of Scotland MS Advocates 23.7.11 (Az). It has an excerpt from a *sanctorale* item, the St Michael legend, set among various medical and astrological texts.] But he classifies manuscripts such as Bodleian Library Laud.Miscellaneous 622 (Lx), which contains *temporale* items in non-*SEL* contexts, among the 'Miscellanies Erroneously Claimed to Contain SEL Texts'.[30] Again, one wonders if either the scope of Görlach's study or his

28 D'Evelyn and Mill, *South English Legendary*, I, p. v. 29 Horstmann, *Early South-English Legendary*, p. vii. D'Evelyn and Mill, *South English Legendary*, I, p. v. 30 Görlach, *Textual Tradition*, pp ix–x, 51–63, 118, 128, and *passi*m. His subsequent major work on the *SEL* continues to be thorough studies focused on the *sanctorale*. See, most recently,

classification of manuscripts would have been different if Horstmann had not excluded the *temporale* from his edition.

* * *

Let us now revisit the D'Evelyn and Mill edition (Appendix 1). Even though they did their work in an era when more scholars thought such things possible, Charlotte D'Evelyn and Anna J. Mill knew that they were not preparing a 'definitive edition' of the *South English Legendary*. They based their edition on only four of the manuscripts known to them, with some additional attention to the Laud text edited by Horstmann. They were simply trying to present something more representative of the texts preserved in several important manuscripts, texts whose arrangement is consistent with the plan for the work described both in the Laud prologue and in the *Banna Sanctorum*, a collection arranged according to the calendar year. The editors wished to give the scholarly world something better to work from than Horstmann's edition of an apparently disorganized text, and of course my point is that, for better or for worse, scholars have done so.

Although among the surviving *sanctorale* collections, just as in the *temporale* collections, no two manuscripts preserve the same texts in the same order, a fact which Charlotte D'Evelyn notes,[31] there are a number of manuscripts with collections or fragments of collections reasonably similar to her and Anna J. Mill's edited text. It is indeed an edition representative of these manuscripts. Of the twenty-six major manuscripts, six begin their collection with the *Banna Sanctorum*, and several of the acephalous manuscripts appear to have done so as well.[32] Twenty-two of the manuscripts, including most of the manuscripts with separate *temporale* collections, are largely in calendar order, despite some variations, breakdowns, lacunae, etc.[33] Of the three remaining manuscripts having *sanctorale*, all – including the Laud manuscript – contain at least some groups of texts arranged in calendar order.[34]

British Library Cotton Julius D ix (J) is a good example of the kind of collection represented by the D'Evelyn and Mill edition (Appendix 13). It is a *sanctorale* collection, beginning with the *Banna Sanctorum*, here identified, though not in the main scribe's hand, as the 'Prologus libri', and having the Moveable Feasts inserted into the cycle. It is arranged in calendar order, beginning 1 January. And its contents are similar to those of the edition. Depending upon how we count them, it has about eighty of the same texts, and its differences are relatively minor. Only nine D'Evelyn and Mill texts are lacking. In the cycle proper, there are eleven saints' lives not in D'Evelyn and Mill, all of them in the July through December part of the cycle. Only two texts appear in a different calendar position (In D'Evelyn and Mill, the three parts

---

Studies in Middle English Saints' Legends, Anglistische Forschungen 257 (Heidelberg, 1998), especially pp 25–57.   [31] Charlotte D'Evelyn, 'Introduction' in *The South English Legendary*, ed. by Charlotte D'Evelyn and Anna J. Mill, III, p. 3.   [32] MSS DCJQTY.   [33] MSS GFVSUAJCQNTPKYHODMXERZ.   [34] MSS BLW.

of Michael appear together, but here the second part of Michael is in its proper calendar position, commemorating the feast of Michael in Monte Tumba. Conversely, in D'Evelyn and Mill, the Exaltation of the Holy Cross appears in its proper September position, but here the three Holy Cross texts appear together in the May position of the Invention or Finding of the Holy Cross.) Finally, as in many *SEL* manuscripts, texts that obviously came to hand after the scribe had completed the cycle are appended after the December section. Here, seven are appended.

* * *

But what kinds of manuscripts and what phenomena are not represented well by the D'Evelyn and Mill edition?

As I have argued elsewhere, because the *Banna Sanctorum* came to function as a prologue in many of the manuscripts that lack a *temporale* section and because we have become accustomed to thinking of the *South English Legendary* as a *sanctorale* collection, the fact that the *Banna* was written to be a transition from the *temporale* to the *sanctorale* became obscured. In one of two elaborate metaphors that make up the major part of the poem, salvation history is compared to a battle. When a king goes into battle, first, he sends his archers; then, he enters himself; finally, he sends his knights of the rear guard. The poem explains that the three groups correspond to the patriarchs and prophets, Christ himself, and the martyrs who followed, all going to battle against the devil. The metaphor nicely unites the three parts of the collection in those manuscripts that have *Old Testament History* and material from the lives of Christ and Mary preceding the collection of saints' lives.[35] However, in the D'Evelyn and Mill edition and the manuscripts it resembles, the point is lost.

Furthermore, in comparison to the eleven items in the Cotton Julius manuscript but not in the D'Evelyn and Mill edition, there are among the various *SEL* manuscripts more than thirty *sanctorale* texts not in D'Evelyn and Mill.[36] These deserve to be better known.[37] Nevertheless, since most manuscripts are like the Cotton Julius manuscript in that they typically contain only a small number of these legends, the absence of most of these thirty plus texts from the D'Evelyn and Mill edition does not seriously compromise it as a representative edition.

On the other hand, a most significant absentee from the D'Evelyn and Mill edition is the piece known as the *Southern Passion*. It was derived from the *temporale* text known as the *Ministry and Passion*, probably for incorporation

---

35 See Pickering, 'Expository *Temporale*' and Thomas R. Liszka, 'The First "A" Redaction of the *South English Legendary*: Information from the "Prologue",' *Modern Philology*, 82 (1985), pp 407–13. **36** The exact number is difficult to calculate since deciding what is and what is not an *SEL* item becomes a factor. Görlach identifies most of the items with a '+' in *Textual Tradition*, pp vii–viii and *passim*. **37** Görlach has announced an intention to edit the texts that do not appear in either the D'Evelyn and Mill edition or the Horstmann edition: Manfred Görlach, ed., *An East Midland Revision of the South English Legendary*, Middle English Texts 4 (Heidelberg, 1976), p. 7.

into the *sanctorale*.[38] The *Southern Passion* is a very long poem, which has been the subject of a separate EETS edition by Beatrice Daw Brown where it runs to 2,566 lines.[39] Curiously, the poem does appear in the Harley manuscript, the oldest orderly manuscript, about which D'Evelyn and Mill originally planned their edition. In that manuscript it occupies more than 20 folia. But when they changed their plan, by substituting the Corpus Christi manuscript as their base text, the *Southern Passion* disappeared from the *Legendary*, making the *temporale* even less conspicuous in the collection. Its appearance out of context in a separate edition makes its text accessible to scholars. However, the *Southern Passion* is a poem that exists in a context. It survives in twelve manuscripts. Eleven of these are major *SEL* manuscripts in which the poem forms the largest part of the series of moveable feasts inserted into the *sanctorale* Easter cycle. The other is a miscellany in which the *Southern Passion* follows the *SEL* St Michael, Annunciation, Septuagesima and Lent texts.[40] In other words, the *SEL* Michael and Easter cycle texts are included in the miscellany. Thus, while we have a *Southern Passion* edition, we lack an edition of the *South English Legendary* with the largest portion of its Easter cycle intact.

Also obscured from view in the D'Evelyn and Mill edition of an orderly *SEL* text is the existence of largely disorderly manuscripts in which the processes of collecting and arranging were ongoing. I have referred already to those manuscripts that have an appendix of a few texts after what is or appears to have been a reasonably consistent *sanctorale* cycle. There are twelve such manuscripts.[41] But look again at Trinity College Cambridge 605 (R) (Appendix 14). After the *temporale*, its *sanctorale* begins in typical D'Evelyn and Mill fashion with a forty-three item January to July section in which calendar order is followed. But then eighteen texts follow which were either copied from sources, one or two at a time, or were taken from a source in which that kind of collection occurred. In either case, when this second group of texts was added, the compiler abandoned any hope of producing a calendrically organized finished product in this manuscript. Then follow twenty-eight items presented in calendar order from May through December, when again the compiler appears to have had an extensive orderly source at hand. The texts following next either began an appendix to that orderly source and were copied here along with the orderly content, or they come from new sources and begin here an appendix to the Trinity manuscript. (Note that the Brendan and Patrick texts appear consecutively at the beginning of this section, a subject I will discuss

---

[38] O. S. Pickering, ed., *The South English Ministry and Passion*, Middle English Texts 16 (Heidelberg, 1984), pp 33–35. [39] Beatrice Daw Brown, ed., *The Southern Passion*, EETS o. s.169 (London, 1927). [40] MSS BDHKNOPTVYZ and the miscellany Uz. [41] MSS ACDGHJ(M/Bd)NO(Q/Qa/Ba)VZ. MSS M and Bd were originally parts of the same manuscript, as were MSS Q, Qa, and Ba. See Görlach, *Textual Tradition*, pp 90, 95–97, 107–108, 115. The Q/Qa/Ba manuscript appears to have had a lengthy

The South English Legendaries 259

below.) The manuscript continues in and out of calendar order, with 17 and 18 March, 9 July and 1 August, three November texts, and two Miracles of the Virgin before a final series of October to December texts, concluding with texts that are frequently appended after December.

A more extreme example is Bodleian Library Bodley 779 (B) (Appendix 15). It has more *sanctorale* items than any other *SEL* manuscript. And it begins with the aforementioned Brendan and Patrick duo; then after eleven additional randomly collected items, it has nine English saints in calendar order from January to July, eight November saints and one December saint in calendar order, six saints in random order, five January saints, thirteen March through May items in order (counting the Exaltation of the Holy Cross as a May item), two random items, six August through September items in order, five random items (including a portion of the *Southern Passion* misbound), twelve October items in order interrupted by one November item, thirty-one items mostly in random order but including many unique items (indicated with italics) and a long collection of popes and several English saints, nine December items in order, and finally seventeen randomly collected items including a stretch of four English saints' lives and a small November section. It is clearly not an accident that, if we ignore the randomly ordered sections of this manuscript, we see that the collector passed through the calendar twice: 1) January to July, November to December, and 2) January, March to May, August to September, October, and December.

There are two similar manuscripts in which the processes of collecting and arranging are apparent. One of them is the important, but enigmatic Laud. Miscellaneous 108 manuscript.[42] I submit that its relative state of order or disorder would not seem such an anomaly to scholars if the similarly ordered or the disordered *SEL* texts were better known.

For example, we can see in these manuscripts and in the more organized manuscripts having a single appendix that certain texts such as Brendan and Patrick either circulated independently of the *SEL* or formed the cores of circulating *SEL* booklets. In four manuscripts Brendan and Patrick follow one another, and in three of these (the other being non-determinable) the two texts begin the entire collection or begin an appendix.[43] They never fall in the middle of an appendix. In three other manuscripts, one or the other text begins an appendix,[44] and only once does a single text fall in a non-calendrical and nondescript location.[45] Similar observations could be made of other longer *SEL* texts, such as the Thomas Becket and the Michael texts, as well.

appendix, including *sanctorale* and *temporale* items and the romance *Gy of Warwick*. **42** The other is MS W   **43** In MSS LRB, Brendan and Patrick begin units. The scribe of Wa made an obvious error in copying Brendan. On the same folio, after 24 unique lines from Julian the Hospitaller, the Brendan text continues, beginning with line 661. Brendan, thus, does not begin a unit in Wa. It is uncertain how it appeared in Wa's exemplar. See Görlach, *Textual Tradition*, pp 115–16.   **44** MSS VZU.   **45** Patrick

These kinds of facts about the arrangement and development of *SEL* collections in manuscripts and sections of manuscripts that appear disorganized, as well as the fact of alternate calendrical arrangements, beginning with Advent in two manuscripts, Christmas in one, and September in two others are not available to scholars working from the orderly D'Evelyn and Mill edition.[46]

* * *

Of course, one edition can't do everything. And we touch now upon the debate raging among editors in medieval studies and, indeed, in literary studies generally. Should an editor attempt to correct and present an ideal text, one consistent with an author's final intentions? Or should an editor simply present a text that actually existed in some point in time? Nowadays, more textual critics argue that editors should do the latter. There are many technical dimensions to the argument, but most of them reduce to: how can we ever really know what someone intended? And even if we guess right on the first seven disputed readings, our having done so is not a guarantee that we won't guess wrong on the next seven, or even that the author intended the non-disputed readings, which we do not see a need to question. Furthermore, the assumptions on which the 'science' of stemmatics and the newer alternatives to it are based have been questioned.

But there is one basic difference between the editorial situation in, say, Chaucer studies and the *South English Legendary* that, in the case of the *SEL*, makes the argument moot. If I am editing a Chaucer text, even if I despair that I never can know what Chaucer 'wrote' or 'intended', even if I don't think that either the surviving materials or the science to analyze them can be trusted, I still know that at the head of the manuscript tradition, at the top of the stemma, stands a literary genius, whose accomplishments justify our efforts, ingenuity, and good intentions.

But the *South English Legendary* is not such a work. The earliest manuscript is in such a state that, unless new materials are discovered, not even the most optimistic recensionist could ever hope to recreate the original state of the text. Furthermore, from what we can guess about that original state, it is clear that greater geniuses reside further down on the stemma than at the top. I would prefer to have recreated, for example, the *SEL* text intended by whoever wrote the *Banna Sanctorum* or the one on which the reviser whom O.S. Pickering dubs the 'Outspoken Poet' worked.[47] These were or would have been superior

appears in a June context in V. 46 MSS EP begin with Advent. MS Y begins with the *Banna Sanctorum*, referred to as 'De Natiuitate', followed by the legends of Sts Stephen, John, and Thomas Becket (26, 27, and 29 December, respectively). MSS US each begin with the September feast of St Michael. 47 See, respectively, Thomas R. Liszka, 'The First "A" Redaction of the *South English Legendary*: Information from the "Prologue",' and O. S. Pickering, 'The Outspoken *South English Legendary* Poet', in *Late-Medieval Religious Texts and Their Transmission*, ed. by A.J. Minnis (Cambridge,

artistic achievements to the original state of the text. But more relevant than my personal preferences is the fact that – as we have seen – later compilers of the *Legendary*, unlike those later authors who tried to pass their own work off as Chaucer's, did not respect the genius of those who came before them. To the later *SEL* compilers, the *SEL* was an open text, one that not merely could, but should be improved, adapted, and suited to local use. As a result, there were produced many *South English Legendaries* that deserve to be better known.

APPENDIX 1

Contents: *The South English Legendary*, ed. by D'Evelyn and Mill

		Prologue/ [Banna Sanctorum]
1	January	**Circumcision/3eres Day**
6	January	**Epiphany**
14	January	Hillary
19	January	Wulfstan
20	January	Fabian
20	January	Sebastian
21	January	Agnes
22	January	Vincent
27	January	Julian the Confessor
29	January	Julian the Hospitaller
1	February	Bridget
3	February	Blaise
5	February	Agatha
10	February	Scolastica
14	February	Valentine
16	February	Juliana
24	February	Mathias
28	February	Oswald the Bishop
2	March	Chad
12	March	Gregory
15	March	Longinus
17	March	Patrick
18	March	Edward the Martyr
20	March	Cuthbert

1994), pp 21–37. It is doubtful, but unknown, if either revision was ever finally realized. It is also possible that these were the same people and perhaps the same person responsible for Görlach's 'A' redaction. See Görlach, *Textual Tradition*, *passim*, and his *Studies in Middle English Saints' Legends*, pp 47–48.

21 March		Benedict
25 March		**Annunciation**
		Septuagesima
		Lent
		Easter
2 April		Mary of Egypt
19 April		Alphege
23 April		George
25 April		Mark
		Rogationtide/Litanies
29 April		Peter the Dominican
1 May		Philip and James
3 May		**Holy Cross: Early History and Invention**
4 May		Quiriac
16 May		Brendan
19 May		Dunstan
25 May		Aldhelm
26 May		Austin
11 June		Barnabas
		Theophilus/Miracles of the Virgin
22 June		Alban
24 June		John the Baptist
29 June		Peter
29 June		Paul
9 July		Swithun
17 July		Kenelm
20 July		Margaret
22 July		Mary Magdalene
24 July		Christina
25 July		James the Great
25 July		Christopher
29 July		Martha
5 August		Oswald the King
10 August		Lawrence
15 August		**Assumption**
24 August		Bartholomew
1 September		Giles
14 September		**Holy Cross: Exaltation**
21 September		Matthew
29 September		Michael I, II, III
30 September		Jerome
9 October		Denis

The South English Legendaries 263

18 October	Luke
21 October	Ursula/11,000 Virgins
28 October	Simon and Jude
31 October	Quentin
1 November	**All Hallows**
2 November	**All Souls**
6 November	Leonard
11 November	Martin
16 November	Edmund the Bishop
20 November	Edmund the King
23 November	Clement
25 November	Katherine
30 November	Andrew
6 December	Nicholas
13 December	Lucy
21 December	Thomas
25 December	Anastasia
26 December	Stephen
27 December	John
29 December	Thomas Becket
	Judas
	Pilate

APPENDIX 2

Contents: Bodleian Library MS Laud.Miscellaneous 108 (L) and
The Early South-English Legendary, ed. by Carl Horstmann

ITEMS 1–7, LOST
Ministry and Passion, *imperfect at beginning and ending*   excluded
Infancy of Christ, *in a different meter*   excluded

Holy Cross, Invention, *imperfect at beginning*   HORSTMANN'S *EARLY SEL*
St Quiriac
Holy Cross, Exaltation
St Dunstan
   15 SAINTS' LIVES
St Thomas Becket
Prologue, *unique*
Circumcision
Epiphany

St Fabian
St Sebastian
   39 SAINTS' LIVES
St Mary Magdalene
St Hippolitus

Sayings of St Bernard   excluded
Vision of St Paul   excluded
Debate of Body and Soul   excluded
Havelok the Dane   excluded
King Horn   excluded

St Blaise, *in second hand*   HORSTMANN'S *SEL* APPENDIX
St Cecelia, *in second hand*

St Alexius, *in second hand, a different meter and rhyme scheme*   excluded
Somer Soneday, *in second hand*   excluded
Miscellaneous lines of verse   excluded

APPENDIX 3

Contents: British Library MS Egerton 1993 (E)

Old Testament History
Abridged Life of Christ, *lines 1–480*
Conception of Mary
Expanded Nativity [of Mary and Christ]

Banna Sanctorum
St Andrew (30 Nov)
St Nicholas (6 Dec)
    5 SAINTS, December/ Advent
    74 SAINTS and OTHER LEGENDS, January-October
    END OF MS LOST

APPENDIX 4

Contents: Trinity College Cambridge MS 605 (R)

Old Testament History, *with insertions*
Abridged Life of Christ, *beginning*
Miracle of Our Lady: Oxford Scholar

The South English Legendar*ies* 265

Banna Sanctorum
Circumcision (1 Jan)
   33 SAINTS' LIVES, January – May
   47 SAINTS' LIVES, mostly out of order
St Lucy (13 Dec)
St Thomas the Apostle (21 Dec)
St Stephen (26 Dec)
Nativity of Mary and Christ
Abridged Life of Christ, *ending*
St Thomas Becket (29 Dec)
St Brendan (16 May)
St Patrick (17 Mar)
St Edward the Martyr (18 Mar)
   15 SAINTS' LIVES, mostly November and October, but out of order
St Birin (3 Dec)
Trinity Conception of Mary
St Silvester (31 Dec)
Ministry and Passion, *Pater Noster portion*
Judas
Pilate

APPENDIX 5

Contents: Lambeth Palace MS 223 (G)

Moveable Feasts / Septuagesima
Lent
Easter
Rogationtide

Old Testament History
Abridged Life of Christ, *conclusion*
Vernon Life of Mary, *Prologue*
Nativity of Mary and Christ
Lambeth Assumption of Mary

Banna Sanctorum
Circumcision (1 Jan)
   SAINTS' LIVES, January – December
St Eustace (1 Nov)

APPENDIX 6

Contents: Bodleian Library MS English Poetry a.1 (the Vernon MS) (V)
SEL contents only

Old Testament History
Vernon Life of Mary

Banna Sanctorum
Circumcision (1 Jan)
  SAINTS' LIVES, *January – December, with some losses*
St Thomas Becket (29 Dec), *ending lost*
St Silvester (31 Dec), *lost*
  APPENDIX OF VARIOUS SAINTS, *lost*

APPENDIX 7

Contents: Winchester College MS 33a (W)

Old Testament History
Pilate
Judas

---

  16 SAINTS' LIVES, *mostly February–June, disorganized*
Banna Sanctorum
Circumcision (1 Jan)
Epiphany (6 Jan)
Sts Fabian & Sebastian (20 Jan)
St Agnes (21 Jan)
  NON-SEL MATERIAL

APPENDIX 8

Contents: St John's College Cambridge MS 28 (I)

Old Testament History
Nativity of Mary and Christ
Ministry and Passion

St Longinus

The South English Legendaries

Pilate
Harrowing of Hell and the Destruction of Jerusalem

Movable Feasts / Septuagesima
Lent
Easter
Rogationtide

APPENDIX 9

Titles of Contents: Trinity College Cambridge MS 605 (R)

Modern Title	Title in Text	Title in List of Contents
Old Testament History	Adam & Eve	Adam & Eue
	Noe	Noe
	Abraham	Abraham
		Isaac
	Iacob	Iacob
	Ioseph	Ioseph
	Moyses	Moyses
		Sampson
		Saul
	Dauid	Dauyd
		Absolon
	Salamon	Salamon
	Roboam	Roboam
		Helise
		Helie
	Daniel	Daniel
Abridged Life of Christ, *beginning* **Miracle of Our Lady: Oxford Scholar**	Salutatio Marie	Salutatio Marie
Banna Sanctorum		Banna Sanctorum
Circumcision (1 Jan)		ȝeres Day
Epiphany (6 Jan)		Twelþe Day
St Hilary (14 Jan)	Hyllary	Hilary
St Wulfstan (19 Jan)	Wolston	Wolston
St Fabian (20 Jan)	Fabian	Fabian

ETC.

APPENDIX 10

Titles of Contents: Lambeth Palace MS 223 (G)

Modern Title	Title in Text
Moveable Feasts / Septuagesima	ffestes meuable
Lent	Lentoun
Easter	Aster
Rogationtide	Holy Þoresday; **Also** Rogacionis
Old Testament History	Adam
	Noe
	Abraham
	Loth
	Isaac
	Iacob
	Esau
	Ioseph
	Moyses
	Iosue
	Gedeon
	Sampson
	Saul
	Ionathas
	Dauid
	Kyng Dauid
	Nathan
	Salomon
	Ieroboam
	Elye
	Ionas
	Helisee
	Danyel
Abridged Life of Christ/	Ierome
XV Signs of Judgment	
Vernon Life of Mary, *Prologue*	Concepcio Sancte Marie
Nativity of Mary and Christ	Concepcio Sancte Marie
	Vita Beate Marie
	Concepcio Xpisti
	Natiuitas domini nostri Ihesu Xpisti
	Purificatio beate Marie
	Puericia domini nostri Ihesu Xpisti
Lambeth Assumption of Mary	Assumpcio beata Marie

THEN *SANCTORALE* CYCLE

APPENDIX 11

Titles of Contents: Winchester College MS 33a (W)

Modern Title	Title in Text
Old Testament History	Vita de Adam Noe Abraham Rebecca Joseph
Pilate	Vita Pilati
Judas	De Iuda Scarioth
St Oswald (19 Feb) St Edward Martyr (18 March) St Cuthbert (20 March)	Vita Sancti Oswaldi Vita Sancti Edwardi regis Anglie Vita Sancti Cuthberti episcopi.

ETC.

APPENDIX 12

Titles of Contents: Bodleian MS English Poetry a.1 (Vernon MS) (V)

Modern Title	Title in List of Contents
Old Testament History	De creacione coeli & terre & de aliis operibus sex dierum Qualiter deus posuit adam in paradiso & precepit ei ne comederet &c Hou þe deuel bygylede Eue How adam knew hym self naked aftur is trespas How god reprouede Adam and Eue ant þe deuel Hou adam gat caym and abel **Of noe** and of þe flood **Oof abraham** **Of Ysaac** **Of Iacob** Hou rebecca sende iacob to laban Hou iacob wrastlede wyt þe angel Of iosepes Swyfnes and he was sold Hou þe chyldren of israel wente into Egypte Off þe burþe of moyses

How god aperede to moyses in þe busk
Hou god sende moyses to kyng pharao forto delyuere his people
De plagis egipti
Hou moyses 3af þe lawe in the desert
Off þe prophecie off balaam
Of þe deþ of moyses
Off Sampson   Of Saul   Of Dauid
Hou absolon pursuwede his fader
Hou dauid made sorwe for absolones deþ
Hou dauid noumbrede þe people off israel
Of þe coronacioun of kyng Salomon
Of þe dom of salomon bytwene tweye commun wymmen
Of salomones ded   **Of Ieroboam**
Of Helye   And hou he was rapt in to þe eyr
Hou heliseus multeplyede oyle
Of Daniel   Of Abacuc þe profete

Vernon　þat alle þe profetes prophecieden of crist
Life of　Of þe feste of þe concepcion of vre lady
Mary　**Of ioachim and of Anna**
　　　Hou þe angel tolde ioachym þat he scholde gete vre lady   Of
　　　　　ioachimmes offrynge   **Off anna**   Of þe natiuite off vre
　　　　　lady   And hou vre lady was offred in to þe temple
　　　Hou vre lady ladde heore lyf in þee temple
　　　Hou vre lady was wedded to ioseph
　　　De legacione gabrielis & incarnacone ihesu christi
　　　Hou ioseph wolde ha forsake vre lady
　　　Of þe natiuite of vre lord ihesu crist
　　　Of his circumcision   Hou he was offred in þe temple to
　　　　　Symeon   Hou he was baptised   Off þe sorwe þat ovr
　　　　　lady hadde when heo say vr sone on þe cros
　　　Hou crist on þe cros bytok hys moder to seynt Jon to kepe

ETC.

APPENDIX 13

Contents: British Library MS Cotton Julius D ix (J)
(D & M = the D'Evelyn and Mill edition of the *South English Legendary*)

Prologus Libri (later hand)/ [Banna Sanctorum]
1 January   Circumcision/3eres Day
6 January   Epiphany

14 January	Hillary
19 January	Wulfstan
20 January	Fabian
20 January	Sebastian
21 January	Agnes
22 January	Vincent
27 January	Julian the Confessor
29 January	Julian the Hospitaller
1 February	Bridget
3 February	Blaise
5 February	Agatha
10 February	Scolastica
14 February	Valentine
16 February	Juliana
24 February	Mathias
28 February	Oswald the Bishop
2 March	Chad
12 March	Gregory
17 March	Patrick
18 March	Edward the Martyr
20 March	Cuthbert
21 March	Benedict
25 March	**Annunciation**
	Septuagesima
	Lent
	Easter
2 April	Mary of Egypt
19 April	Alphege
23 April	George
25 April	Mark
	Rogationtide/Litanies
29 April	Peter the Dominican
1 May	Philip and James
3 May	Holy Cross: Early History and Invention
14 September	**Holy Cross: Exaltation** MOVED **to Invention**
4 May	Quiriac
16 May	Brendan
19 May	Dunstan
25 May	Aldhelm
26 May	Austin
11 June	Barnabas
24 June	John the Baptist

29 June	Peter	
29 June	Paul	
20 July	Margaret	
22 July	Mary Magdalene	
24 July	Christina	
25 July	James the Great	
25 July	Christopher	
27 July	**Seven Sleepers**	not in D & M
10 August	Lawrence	
15 August	Assumption	
24 August	Bartholomew	
1 September	Giles	
21 September	Matthew	
26 September	**Justine**	not in D & M
29 September	Michael I	
2 October	**Leger**	not in D & M
4 October	**Francis**	not in D & M
6 October	**Fides**	not in D & M
9 October	**Denis**	
16 October	**Michael II**	MOVED to M. in Monte Tumba
18 October	Luke	
21 October	Ursula/11,000 Virgins	
28 October	Simon and Jude	
31 October	Quentin	
20 May	**Ailbri3t/ Ethelbert in twice**	not in D & M
1 November	All Hallows	
2 November	All Souls	
6 November	Leonard	
1 November	**Eustace**	not in D & M
11 November	Martin	
13 November	**Brice**	not in D & M
16 November	Edmund the Bishop	
20 November	Edmund the King	
22 November	**Caecilia**	not in D & M
23 November	Clement	
25 November	Katherine	
27 November	**Jakes**	not in D & M
30 November	Andrew	
3 December	**Birin**	not in D & M
6 December	Nicholas	
13 December	Lucy	

The South English Legendaries

21 December	Thomas		
25 December	Anastasia		
26 December	Stephen		
27 December	John		
29 December	Thomas Becket		
30 December	Egwine		
31 December	Silvester		

APPENDIX

20 May	Ailbriȝt/Ethelbert	in twice	**not in D & M**
1 February	**Ignatius**	unique text	**not in D & M**
19 October	Frideswide		**not in D & M**
29 September?	Michael III		
5 January	Edward the Confessor		**not in D & M**
11 April	Guthlac		**not in D & M**
	Theophilus/Miracles of the Virgin		**miracles first**

In D & M. Not in Cotton Julius D ix

15 March	Longinus
22 June	Alban
9 July	Swithun
17 July	Kenelm
29 July	Martha
5 August	Oswald the King
30 September	Jerome
	Judas
	Pilate

APPENDIX 14

Contents: Trinity College Cambridge 605 (R)

Old Testament History   *TEMPORALE*
Abridged Life of Christ, part 1
Miracle of the Virgin: Oxford Scholar

	Banna Sanctorum	*SANCTORALE*	JANUARY TO JULY
1 January	Circumcision/ȝeres Day		
6 January	Epiphany		
14 January	Hillary		
19 January	Wulfstan		

20 January	Fabian	
20 January	Sebastian	
21 January	Agnes	
22 January	Vincent	
27 January	Julian the Confessor	
29 January	Julian the Hospitaller	
1 February	Bridget	
2 February	Candlemas, Purification	
3 February	Blaise	
5 February	Agatha	
10 February	Scolastica	
14 February	Valentine	
16 February	Juliana	
24 February	Mathias	
28 February	Oswald the Bishop	
2 March	Chad	
12 March	Gregory	
15 March	Longinus **in twice**	
20 March	Cuthbert	
21 March	Benedict	
25 March	Annunciation	
	Septuagesima	
	Lent	
	Easter	
2 April	Mary of Egypt	
19 April	Alphege	
23 April	George	
25 April	Mark	
	Rogationtide/Litanies	
29 April	Peter the Dominican	
1 May	Philip and James	
19 May	Dunstan	
25 May	Aldhelm	
	Theophilus/Miracles of the Virgin	
17 June	Botulf	
17 July	Kenelm	
25 July	Christopher	
27 July	Seven Sleepers	
1 September	Giles	**SUPPLEMENTING & FILLING GAPS: 1, 2, or 3 at a time**
29 July	Martha	
29 September	Michael I, II, III	

The South English Legendaries 275

6	October	Fides	
9	October	Denis	
18	October	Luke	
3	May	Holy Cross: Early History, Invention	
14	September	Holy Cross: Exaltation	
4	May	Quiriac	
15	August	Assumption	
24	August	Bartholomew	
27	December	John	
24	June	John the Baptist	
29	June	Peter	
29	June	Paul	
6	December	Nicholas	
30	November	Andrew	
15	March	Longinus **in twice**	
26	May	Austin	MAY TO DECEMBER
11	June	Barnabas	
22	June	Alban	
20	July	Margaret	
22	July	Mary Magdalene	
25	July	James the Great	
1	August	Athelwold **in twice**	
4	August	Dominic	
10	August	Lawrence	
13	August	Hippolyt	
21	September	Matthew	
30	September	Jerome	
2	October	Leger	
4	October	Francis	
1	November	Eustace	
16	November	Edmund the Bishop	
13	November	Brice **slightly out of place**	
20	November	Edmund the King	
24	July	Christina **out of place, but from a virgin section?**	
22	November	Caecilia	
25	November	Katherine	
13	December	Lucy	
21	December	Thomas	
26	December	Stephen	
25	December	Nativity of Mary and Christ	
		Abridged Life of Christ, part 2	
29	December	Thomas Becket	

16	May	**Brendan**	APPENDIX?
17	March	**Patrick**	
18	March	Edward the Martyr	
		Miracles of the Virgin: Devil in Service	
9	July	Swithun	
1	August	Athelwold **in twice**	
6	November	Leonard	NOVEMBER
11	November	Martin	
23	November	Clement	
		Miracles of the Virgin: BV comes to the Devil	
		Miracles of the Virgin: Saved by Learning Two Words	
19	October	Frideswide	OCTOBER to DECEMBER
21	October	Ursula/11,000 Virgins	
28	October	Simon and Jude	
31	October	Quentin	
20	May	Ailbri3t **out of place?**	
1	November	All Hallows	
2	November	All Souls	
3	December	Birin	
8	December	Trinity Conception of Mary	
31	December	Silvester	
		Ministry and Passion/Pater Noster APPENDIX	
		Judas	
		Pilate	

APPENDIX 15

Contents: Bodleian Library Bodley 779 (B)

16	May	Brendan	
17	March	Patrick	
24	July	Christina	RANDOM
5	August	Oswald the King	
1	January	Circumcision/3eres Day	
25	December	Expanded Nativity Extract, Christmas portion	
		In Principio	
		Southern Passion, part 1	

The South English Legendaries

29	December	Thomas Becket
29	September	Michael I, II
1	November	All Hallows
2	November	All Souls
3	February	Blaise

19	January	Wulfstan	**JANUARY to JULY, ENGLISH SAINTS**
28	February	Oswald the Bishop	
18	March	Edward the Martyr	
19	April	Alphege	
19	May	Dunstan	
25	May	Aldhelm in **twice**	
26	May	Austin	
17	July	Kenelm	
9	July	Swithun **in twice**	

6	November	Leonard	**NOVEMBER to DECEMBER**
11	November	Martin	
16	November	Edmund the Bishop	
20	November	Edmund the King	
23	November	Clement	
25	November	Katherine	
27	November	Jakes	
30	November	Andrew	
6	December	Nicholas	

25	July	Christopher	**RANDOM**
27	July	Seven Sleepers	
1	May	Philip and James	
29	June	Paul	
29	January	Julian the Hospitaller	
1	February	Bridget	

21	January	Agnes	**JANUARY**
14	January	Hillary	
20	January	Fabian	
20	January	Sebastian	
22	January	Vincent	

20	March	Cuthbert	**MARCH to MAY**
21	March	Benedict	
25	March	Annunciation	

	Septuagesima	
	Lent	
	Easter	
2 April	Mary of Egypt	
23 April	George	
25 April	Mark	
	Rogationtide/Litanies	
29 April	Peter the Dominican	
3 May	Holy Cross: Early History and Invention	
14 September	Holy Cross: Exaltation	
27 January	Julian the Confessor	RANDOM
12 March	Gregory	
10 August	Lawrence	AUGUST to SEPTEMBER
13 August	Hippolyt	
15 August	Assumption	
24 August	Bartholomew	
1 September	Giles	
26 September	Justine and Ciprian	
11 April	Guthlac	RANDOM
1 November	Eustace	
4 August	Dominic	
24 February	Mathias, **beginning**	
	Southern Passion, part 2, misbound	
24 February	Mathias, **ending**	
4 October	Francis	OCTOBER, with unique texts in italic
6 October	Fides	
9 October	Denis	
11 October	*Nicasie and his Companions*	
14 October	*Calixtus*	POPE
3 November	*Vonefreda*	
18 October	Luke	
22 October	*Hillarion*	
25 October	*Crissaunt and Dari3e*	
21 October	Ursula/11,000 Virgins	
25 October	*Crispin and Crispinyan*	
26 October	*Euarist*	POPE
28 October	Simon and Jude	

The South English Legendar*ies*

RANDOM, many unique texts in bold

25 September	*Firmim*		
28 April	*Vital*		
25 May	Aldhelm **in twice**	ENGLISH	
20 July	Margaret	ENGLISH	
20 August	*Oswin*	ENGLISH	
24 June	John the Baptist		
26 June	*John and Paul*		
28 June	*Leo*	POPE	
19 February	*Marius and his wife and two sons*		
29 June	Peter		
9 July	Swithun **in twice**	ENGLISH	
22 June	Alban		
?	*Illurin*	POPE	
15 January	*Paulin the ermyte*		
31 December	*Silvester*	POPE	
1 October	*Remigi*		
11/17? April	*Anicet*	POPE	
22 April	*Sother*	POPE	
22 April	*Gay*	POPE	
23 January	*Emerinciane*		
11 January	*Hyginus*	POPE	
10 December	*Melchiades*	POPE	
11 December	*Damas*	POPE	
29 November	*Saturnin and cicin*		
31 July	*Innocent*	POPE	
30 May	*Felix*	POPE	
29 July	*Simplice and Faustine*		
30 July	*Abdon and Cemen*		
30 July	*Ierman*		
1 August	*Athelwold*		
29 July	Martha		
8 December	Conception of Mary	DECEMBER	
13 December	Lucy		
21 December	Thomas		
25 December	Anastasia, **beginning, cancelled**		
25 December	Nativity of Mary and Christ		
25 December	Anastasia		
26 December	Stephen		
27 December	John		
28 December	*Holy Innocents*		

22 July	Mary Magdalene	
3 December	Birin	
8 December	Conception of Mary, **extract**	
2 October	Leger	
5 January	Edward the Confessor	ENGLISH
23 June	Aeldri/Etheldred	ENGLISH
19 October	Frideswide	ENGLISH
15 June	Edburga	ENGLISH
31 October	Quentin	
4 May	Quiriac	
13 November	Brice	
22 November	Caecilia	
27 November	Barlaam and Josaphat	
13 July	Mildred	
11 June	Barnabas	
31 May	Petronella/Parnel	
17 June	Botulf	

St John's House Papers, St Andrews

1. R.G. Cant, *The Writing of Scottish History in the Time of Andrew Lang*, £1

2. R.G. Cant, *The New Foundation of 1599 in Historical Perspective*, £1

3. L.J. Macgregor and B.E. Crawford, *Ouncelands and Pennylands*, £2.50

4. R.J. Macrides, *The Scottish Connection in Byzantine and Modern Greek Studies*

5. B.E. Crawford, *Scotland in Dark Age Europe*, £8

6. B.E. Crawford, *Scotland in Dark Age Britain*, £9

7. S. Taylor, *The Uses of Place-names*, £9.99

8. B.E. Crawford, *Conversion and Christianity in the North Sea World*, £9

Where still available, copies of nos. 1-8 may be obtained from Department of Mediaeval History, University of St Andrews, 71 South Street, St Andrews, Fife KY16 9AL, Scotland.

9. T.R. Liszka and L.E.M. Walker (eds), *The North Sea World in the Middle Ages*

Index of Names and Places

This index sets out to include names of persons, places and primary sources to which reference is made in the text of each chapter. Italics are used both for historical forms of place-names and for primary sources, whether published or unpublished. Manuscript locations are shown separately.

Abaddon 84
Abercorn (*Aebbercurnig*) (W. Lothian) 13, 127, 129 (Map 7.2), 130, 140, 159–60; peculiar of Dunkeld 130; Romanesque doorway at 130–31, Fig.7.1 (p.131); Hopetoun aisle at 131; episcopal see at 131; sculptured cross-shafts and hogbacks at 131–34, 143, 159, 161, Fig. 7.2 (p.132)
Aberdeen 129 (Map 7.2), 165
Aberdeen Breviary (AB) 176 and n, 178n, 180–84 *passim*, 194, 195–201
Aberdeenshire: people of 192
Aberdour (Fife), barony, church and parish of 188; Hospital of St Martha in 188; Pilgrims' Well ('le pilgramyswell') at 188–89, 198n; *and see* St Fillan's Well
Aberlemno (Angus) 129 (Map 7.2); Pictish cross-slab at 132, 143
Abernethy (Perthshire) 129 (Map 7.2); round tower at 139
Abimelech, Old Testament character 80n
Abiron 220
Abraham, Old Testament figure: in *SEL* texts 249–51
Abridged Life of Christ 248–49
Absalom (Absolon), Old Testament figure: in *SEL* texts 249
Achaia 69
Acheson *see* James
Achilleidos 69
Achilles 60, 63–65, 68
Adam and Eve 249
Adam, first man 216, 220; in *SEL* texts 248–50
Adeliza (*Aaliz la reine*) of Louvain, wife of Henry I 13, 211, 223n, 224–27

Adomnán, abbot of Iona *see* Columba, St, *Life* of
Adrian, 'ghost saint' 190
Aeneas 67
Æþelberht, king of Kent 119
Æþelrœd II, 'the Unready', king of England 102, 122
Æþelstan, king of England 13, 101, 108, 113, 114, 123, 125
Æþelweard, ealdorman, 'the Chronicler' 89
African folk-tales 26
Agamemnon 60, 65–66, 68
Ágrip af Nóregs konunga sögum 111–18 *passim*, 124–25
Ahimelech, Old Testament character 70, 80n
Ailbe, St, of Emly (Co. Tipperary) 179
Ailbricht, character in a Canterbury miracle 232–33
Ailward, character in a Canterbury miracle 231–33
Airyolland, Mochrum (Wigtownshire) 177 (Map 9.1: Key 22, p. 208), *and see* Kilfillan, Sorbie
Airyolland, New Luce (Wigtownshire) 177 (Map 9.1: Key 21, p. 208), *and see* Kilfillan, Old Luce and Sorbie
Ajax Telamon 63
Alan son of Waltheof, lord of Allerdale 148
Alba (*Albain*) 178, 179
Alcluith 'the rock of the Clyde' (Dumbarton) 130
Aldred, scribe 94, 95, 105
Alexander I, king of Scots 141
Alexander II, king of Scots 181
Alexander de Néhou 158n

Alexander Gillespie of Elie, merchant skipper and author of the *Journal* 170–74
Alexander Menzies, lord of Glendoquhart 206
Alexander the Great 55
Alexis, St *see* Vie de Saint Alexis
Álfífa (OE Ælfgifu), mother of Svein Álfífuson 119
Alfred, king of Wessex 98, 114n, 119, 122
Allerdale (Cumbria) 148
Alloa (Central Scotland) 170
Allt Fhaolàin ('Fillan's burn'), Ardchattan & Muckairn (Argyll) 177 (Map 9.1: Key 2, p. 202)
Alne (Yorkshire) 148
Alreksstaðir 124
Amalfi 27
America 211
Amphitrite, wife of Poseidon 84
Amphymacus 67
Andrew of Wyntoun, chronicler 141–42
Andrew, St: cult of 134, 135, 140; *Legend of* 139; in *SEL* texts 230, 239
Andromache 69
Angles 90
Anglesey 27
Anglo-Saxon Chronicle (*ASC*) 89, 90, 98, 101, 104, 113–14n, 122
Anglo-Saxons 89, 114–26 *passim*, 226; manuscript illumination of 76; church architecture of 127; *and see* England
Angus 134
Anlaf Sihtricsson, king of Northumbria 114n
Anna (Anne), St: in *SEL* texts 251
'Anna of Elie, The', merchant ship 170, 172; *and see* James Acheson
Annals of Ulster (A.U.) 179, 181
Anstruther (Fife) 166, 170
Antenor 67
Antichrist 12, 72–87
Antonine Wall 130
Apocalypse 78; *and see* Byzantium
Apocalypse illustrations 74–77, 86; *and see* Manuscripts: Trier, Valenciennes
Apollo 63, 65, 81, 236
Apollyon 84

Aquinas, Thomas 54
Aratus of Soloi, *Phaenomena* 85
Ardbraccan, Co. Meath 178
Argyll, diocese of 177 (Map 9.1)
Ari Þorgilsson (*inn fróði* 'the wise'), historian 110, 111 and n, 112, 114
Arion 82
Aristotle 54–56
Armageddon 86
Arthur, king 48, 52, 227
Asclepius 236
Aðalsteinn *see* Æþelstan
Atholl 193 and n
Atlantic Ocean 211, 212
Augustine, St: *Commentary on the Psalms* 80 and n, 81; *and see* Manuscripts: Valenciennes
Austin, St: in *SEL* texts 252
Axmouth (Devon) 159
Ayenbite of Inwit 56

Babylon 236; *and see* Whore of Babylon
Babylonia: creation myth of 77
Baldwin of Ford, archbishop of Canterbury 27
Balmaclellan, parish of (Kirkcudbrightshire) 208 (24)
Balmaha, Buchanan parish (Stirlingshire) 183n
Baltic Sea 14, 165, 166, 171, 172
Bamburgh (Northumberland) 94
Bangor abbey 182
Banna Sanctorum 244, 248, 256–57, 260
Bannockburn, battle of 187, 197n
Barfillan, Houston (Renfrewshire) 177 (Map 9.1: Key 19, p. 208)
Barintus, character in the *Navigatio* and *Voyage de Saint Brendan* 215, 216
Barlaam and Josaphat 259
Bartholomew, Durham monk and hermit on Farne 241
Battle of Brunanburh 101, 107
Battle of Maldon 88, 103, 104
Beatrice, character in a Canterbury miracle 241
Beatus *see* Spain
Becket, Thomas, St: miracles of 230–32, 235, 237–39, 241; in *SEL* texts 244, 259

Index

Bede, historian 90, 96, 130, 132, 181
Bedford 234
Bedfordshire 231
Beggary Island (Co. Wexford) 197n
Belial 85
Benedeit (Benedict, *Benedeiz*), poet and 'apostoile' 222–25, 228; *and see Voyage de Saint Brendan*
Benedict Biscop, abbot of Monkwearmouth 76
Benedict, St 237
Benignus, St 234
Benoît de Sainte-Maure 52–53
Beowulf 96, 104–05, 221
Berach, Irish saint 201n
Bergþora 16–17
Bern, abbot of Reichenau 24
Bernard, St *see Sayings of*
Bernard Pallissy, potter 168
Bernicia 93, 94, 95, 105
Bersöglisvísur 114
Berwick (Scotland, now Northumb.) 165
Bestiary, imagery of 81
Bible 53–54, 220 and n, 221; books of: *Genesis* 77n, 82, 216n, 219, 222n; *Exodus* 216n, 218; *Numbers* 220; *Deuteronomy* 216n; *Samuel* 70; *Job* 77 and n, 81; *Psalms* 70–87 *passim*; for commentary *see* Augustine, Cassiodorus; *Isaiah* 77 and n; *Ezekiel* 78n, for commentary *see* Gregory the Great; *Matthew* 78; *Luke* 216n; *John* 222 and n; *Epistles of St Paul* 76; *Revelation* 72–87 *passim*, 216, 219, 222
Björketorp, runic stone 95
Blangy (Normandy) 240
Boece 197n
Boethius 63
Bohemond of Taranto 27
Boniface, St 97
Book of Devotion see Robert Blackadder
Book of Kells 152
Book of Leinster 178 and n
Book of Sir Tristram de Lyones 47–51
Bordeaux (France), 166, 171–73 *passim*
Botham (York) 100
Brazil: wood from 172

Brechin (Angus) 129 (Map 7.2), 134; round tower at 139; hogbacks at 161
Bremen 165
Brendan, abbot of Clonfert, Irish saint, and character in subsequent literary texts 13, 211–13, 224, 226–27, 237; in *SEL* texts 252, 258–59; *see also Vita Sancti Brendani; Navigatio Sancti Brendani; Voyage de Saint Brendan*
Brian Boru, Irish king 18
Britain (*also* British Isles) 11, 52, 88, 128 (Map 7.1), 129, 227, 236; title of 'King of all ...' 123
Britons 42, 165
Brittany 212
Brix (Cotentin), 156, Map 7.3
Brother Robert 34, 44–47, 51
Bruce (Brus) family 156, 158; *and see* Robert
Bruce of Annandale, armorial bearings of 188n, Fig 9.2 (p.188)
Brunanburh 101; *see also Battle of Brunanburh*
Brunton 238
Buchan, harrying of 192; *and see* Deer
Burghal Hidage 122
Bury St Edmunds (Suffolk) 236
Byrhtnoþ, ealdorman of Essex 103
Byzantium: artistic influence of 72, 74, 82; Apocalypse literature of 82; coins from 124

Cadiz 170
Caedmon's Hymn 100
Caen (Normandy) 156 (Map 7.3); church of St Étienne at 153, 154 (Fig. 7.11)
Caesarius of Heisterbach 230
Cahors (France) 148–49n
Caintigern (*see also* Kentigerna), daughter of Cellach Cualann 181–82
Caintigern, queen of Fiachnae king of the Dál nAraide 182
Calliope, mother of Orpheus 58
Canaanites 77
Canada 186n
'Caniculus', ?Latin version of Fillan (Fáelán) 200n

Canterbury (Kent) 13, 96, 97, 230–32, 235, 237–42
Capetian kings 28
Capricorn, constellation of 85
Carlisle 148
Carolingians: book illustration of 74, 84; *and see* Apocalypse illustrations
Carr Rocks (Fife) 165
Cassandra 60
Cassiodorus: *Commentary on the Psalms* 80 and n, 84; *and see* Manuscripts: Durham
Cassiopeia 85
Catalogus Regum Norwagensium 111
Catena see Olympiodorus of Alexandria
Cavers Castle 191
Cellach Cualann, last Uí Máile king of Leinster 181 and n, 182 and n
Celts 212n
Cerveteri, Laconian cup from 84
Cethes, father of Medea 58–59
Cetus, constellation of 85
Chanson de Roland 40, 228
Charlemagne 34, 40, 42
Charles I, king 166–70 *passim*
Charles II, king 170
Charles, count of Anjou 25
Chartres (France) 231
Chaucer, Geoffrey 53, 56–57, 59, 64, 67, 231, 260
Cherbourg *see* Voeu
Cheshire 99
Chester-le-Street (Durham) 94
Chevelere Assigne 26
Chrétien de Troyes *see Li Contes del Graal*
Christ *see* Jesus Christ
Christian Small, wife of Alexander Gillespie 171, 174
Cicero 55
Cill-Chaointeort (*Kilkinterne*), parish of Kintail (Ross and Cromarty) 182
Circe 68
Cistercians: influence on sculptural style 152
Cîteaux *see Moralia in Job*
Clarina *see Valentin und Namenlos*
Cleopatra Glossary 88

Clerk's Tale (Geoffrey Chaucer) 56–57
Clerk, character in *Canterbury Tales* 57
Clio 58
Clonfert (Galway), abbey of 212
Clontarf, battle of 18, 106
Clúain Móescna *see* Kylmisken
Clytemnestra 66
Cnut (Knud) II (*d*.1086), king of Denmark 23, 228n
Cnut (Knud, Knútr), king of Denmark, England and Norway 102, 104, 106, 119
Coemgen, Irish saint 201n
Colchis, home of Medea 60
Coldingham (Berwick.) 129 (Map 7.2), 140
Coleville-sur-Mer (Manche) 156 (Map 7.3), 158
Columba, St 164, 188, 193–94, 212; community of 86; relics of 130; the *Brecbennoch* of *see* Monymusk; Adomnán's *Life* of 193; the post-Columban church 130
Comgán, cult of 183
Comgall, St, founder of Bangor Abbey, 182
Compostela (Spain) 166; *and see* St Andrews
Comyns, family of 191–92
Con(n)an, St 183n
Conception of Mary 248
Confessio Amantis (John Gower) 56
Congan *Lectio* (Cong. Lect.) 180, 181, 183, 196n, 200n
Conganus (Congan, Comgán), St, uncle of Fillan 176, 180, 181, 182 and n, 183, 194, 200; *and see* Congan *Lectio*
Corbie abbey (N. France) 70
Corbie Psalter (*also* Master) 12, 72, 74, 80, 81, 82, 84, 86; *and see* Manuscripts: Amiens
Corc son of Lughaidh, king of Munster 179n
Coreyheynan (*Coire Sheanain*), in Gleann a' Chlacain (Perthshire) 177 (Map 9.1: Key 16, pp. 205–06), 187 (Map 9.2)
Cornwall 35, 36, 40–41, 45–46, 49–50
Cospatric II, earl of Lothian and Dunbar 147

Index 287

Cospatric III, earl of Lothian and Dunbar 147, 153
Cospatric Maldredson, earl of Northumberland 147
Cospatric son of Waltheof (and brother of Alan) 147–48, 153
Cossans (Angus) 143
Cotentin (Normandy) 153–60, Map 7.3 (p.156); barons of (*Constantinienses*) 158
Counterblasts to Tobacco see James VI and I
Courtesy, allegorical figure 43
Coutances (Normandy) 231; bishops of *see* Hugh de Morville
Crail (Fife) 166, 167 (Fig. 8.1), 170
Crianlarich 184n, 187 (Map 9.2)
Criseyde 56
Croftindewar (*Cryetindowar* in *Auchincairn* [Acharn], *croit an dèoraidh* 'croft of the dewar') in Glendochart (Perthshire) 206 (Key 16.b)
Cruthin *see* Dál nAraide
Cumberland 148
Cumbria 153
Cumbric 175, 192
Cuthbert, St 130, 141; cult of 127, 140, 141; community of 94, 140; patrimony of 140; *Lives* of 130; miracles of 230–31, 236–40; in *SEL* texts 250; *and see* Dalmeny
Cytherea, temple at 65

Dál nAraide, main tribe of the Cruthin, 182
Dál Riata 193; Gaels of 193–94
Dalgety Bay (Fife) 164
Dalmeny (W Lothian) 129 (Map 7.2); church of St Cuthbert at 13, 127, 145, 147–48, 149–51 (Figs 7.9 and 7.10(b-e)), 152–53, 159, 161, 163; parson of 145; patronage and lordship of 145, 147
Dan, Jewish tribe 82
Danelaw 12, 98–107 *passim*
Daniel, Old Testament figure: in *SEL* texts 249
Danir, Dene 89

Danish Sound 172
Dante Alighieri 57
Danzig 172
Dares 12, 52, 60, 63
Dathan 220
David I, earl of Huntingdon/Northampton, king of Scots 127, 140–45, 148, 153, 155, 156/58n, 165, 185; assize of 186n
David, king of Israel 42, 70, 134; in *SEL* texts 249, 251
De antiquitate Glastonie ecclesie (William of Malmesbury attrib.) 116–17
De Creacione mundi 250
De creacione coeli & terre & de aliis operibus sex dierum 251
De Gestis Regum Anglorum (William of Malmesbury) 113
De Juda Scarioth 250
De Laudibus et Miraculis Sanctæ Mariæ (William of Malmesbury) 230
Dee estuary 106
Deer monastery (Buchan) 192
Deira 93
Denmark (*also* Danes, Danish men) 89, 90, 91, 123
Deor 102, 103
Devil 42, 51, 232, 235–36; in *SEL* texts 251
Devon 158
Dewar ('deore', *dèoraidhean*), hereditary keeper of the relics of St Fillan 186 and n, 194, Fig. 9.3 p. 189; *and see* Croftindewar, Dewarnafargs Croft, Dewarvernan's Croft, Donald M'Sobrell, MacGregor
Dewarnafargs Croft (*Dewar-Nafargs-croft, croit dèoraidh na Fairg(e)*, 'croft of the dewar of the shrine) at Auchlyne in Glendochart (Perthshire) 206 (Key 16.c)
Dewarvernan's Croft (*lie Dewaris-croft* in *lie Suy, croit dèoraidh a'Bhearnain* 'croft of the dewar of the bell') at Suie in Glendochart (Perthshire) 206 (Key 16.d)
Dialogus Miraculorum (Caesarius of Heisterbach) 230

Dictys 12, 52
Dicuil, Irish geographer 211
Diomede 60
Dionysius 236
Discretion, allegorical figure 43
Doeg the Edomite 70, 71, 72, 74, 80, 86
Donald M'Sobrell, dewar of the Cogerach (*coigreach*), staff or crozier 206 (Key 16.a)
Dorchester 89
Dorset 89, 158
Doune (*Downe*) Castle, Kilmadock (Perthshire) 191; chapels dedicated to St Fillan at 191, 207 (Key 17)
Drummond Missal 179, 180n
Dublin, Viking kingdom of 105, 106
Dumbarton *see Alcluith*
Dùn-Fhàolain (*Dundurn*) by St Fillan's, Comrie (Perthshire) 177 (Map 9.1: Key 14, p. 205), 184, 187 (Map 9.2), 193, 198; site of hill-fort, St Fillan's Chapel, Well and Seat: 205 (14)
Dunbar (Lothian) 169
Dundee 129 (Map 7.2), 165, 166, 169
Dundurn *see* Dùn-Fhàolain
Dunfermline abbey (Fife) 13, 129 (Map 7.2), 140–43, 144 (Fig 7.7), 145, 146 (Fig 7.8), 152, 153, 163; abbot of 147; shrine of St Margaret at 165
Dunfermline Register 145
Dunkeld (Perthshire) 129 (Map 7.2); diocese of 130; cathedral seal of 132n
Dunstan, St 252
Durham Cassiodorus see Manuscripts: Durham
Durham: architecture and sculpture of the cathedral at 13, 127, 140–45, 152, 153, 155 (Fig. 7.12), 163; chapter house: caryatids in 145; *and see* Cuthbert, St
Durham, Treaty of 148
Dysart (Fife) 172

Early South-English Legendary or Lives of Saints (ed. by Carl Horstmann) 243, 245, 247, 251, 263–64
East Anglia 103, 181; Danes in 123

East Neuk (Fife) 170, 171
Ecclesiastical History (Eusebius of Caesaria) 23
Ecgbert, king of Northumbria 131
Edgar, king of England 117, 122
Edgar, king of Scots 140
Edgar the Ætheling 141
Edinburgh 129 (Map 7.2), 169, 172; collegiate church of St Giles at 145n
Edmund, king of England 114n, 123
Edmund, St, of Abingdon, archbishop of Canterbury 252
Edmund the Martyr, St, king of East Anglia 236
Edricus, character in a Canterbury miracle 242
Edward the Confessor, St, king of England 106, 119; in *SEL* texts 250
Edward the Elder, king of England 122, 123
Egill Skalla-Grímsson, Icelander and Norse skaldic poet 103
Egypt 236
Eider river, Schleswig 91
Eirík *blóðöx* ('Bloodaxe'), king of Norway and later of Northumbria, brother of Hákon Haraldsson 103, 113; sons of (Eiríkssons) 115, 120
Eiríkr *skakki*, earl 29
Elbe 90
Eleanor of Aquitaine, wife of Henry II 225
Elgin (Morayshire) 143; museum at 164
Elias (Elijah), prophet and witness of the Book of Revelation 76, 80, 86
Elie (Fife) 166, 171
Elijah (Helie, Helye), Old Testament figure: in *SEL* texts 249, 251
Elisha (Helise), Old Testament figure: in *SEL* texts 249
Elsinore 172
Ely (Cambridgeshire) 236
Emmies Islands (Norway) 173
England (*also* English) 11–14 *passim*, 25, 41, 44, 49, 55, 88–107 *passim*, 113–17 *passim*, 119, 122, 132, 134, 140, 174, 176, 213, 221, 226–28, 231, 236–37

Index

English Channel 14, 70
Enoch, prophet and witness of the Book of Revelation 76, 80, 86
Eoghanacht, Munster royal house of 196n
Épinal-Erfurt Glossaries 88
Erchadia Borialis (northern Argyll) 200n
Erchembald, knight 30
Ernfillan, Crossmichael (Kirkcudbrightshire) 177 (Map 9.1: Key 12, p. 204)
Esau, Old Testament figure: in *SEL* texts 250
Eson, father of Jason 58
Essex 103
Etheldreda (Ætheldreth), St 236
Ethernan, St 189–90
Europe 11, 14, 236
Eusebius of Caesarea, historian 23
Eustace, St 252
Eve, first woman: in *SEL* texts 249, 251
Ewich (Iuich, *Eyich*, *Eicht*) in Strath Fillan/Glendochart (Perthshire) 186, 187 (Map 9.2), 206 (Key 16.e)
Exchequer Rolls of Scotland 187–88 and 187n
Expanded Nativity of Mary and Christ 248
Eysteinn Haraldsson, king of Norway 12, 21, 22, 24, 28–32
Eyvind *skáldaspillir* Finnson, skald 116

Fabian, St: in *SEL* texts 249
Faelain *amlabair* (*Fáelán... in t–amlabar ánsin*), 'Fillan the dumb', *also* 'Faolàn of Ratherran' 178–79, 194
Fáelán mac Colmáin, king of Leinster 201n
Fáelán of Clúain Móescna (Kylmisken, Meath), Irish saint 178
Fáelán, son of Conchenn daughter of Cellach Cualann 182n
Fagrskinna 23, 112–120 *passim*, 125
Family Sagas, genre of 108
Farne (Northumberland) 241
Fartullagh (*Fir Tulach*) (Co. Westmeath) 178
Fate, allegorical figure 63, 65, 68
Felanus, son of Kentigerna 200n

'Feradach', father of Leamhain, 'king of Pictland' 196n
Feriach (*Feriacus*, *Feriatus*), father of Fillan 196
Fermat, Pierre de 246
Festial (Mirk) 245
Fiachnae, king of the Dál nAraide, 182
Fife 13, 127–63 *passim*, 164–74 *passim*
Fife Ness 165
Fifteen Signs of Judgment 250
Fillan (Faelain, Fáelán, Faelanus, Faolàn, Felan, Feolanus, Fhaolain, Fillanus, Fulanus, Philanus, St 13, 175–210 *passim;* for 'Caniculus', ?Latin version of Fillan (Fáelán), *see* 200n; cult of as evidenced by place-names, dedications and fairs: 177 (Map 9.1: Key, pp. 202–08); relics of: arm or hand reliquary 186, 188n, 197–98n, 206 (16.b), Figs 9.2, 9.3 (pp.188–89); bell 186, 194, 204 (13), 206 (16.d); portable altar, manuscript or wooden bowl (*meser, mazer*) 186, 205–06 (16.a); shrine 186, 206 (16.d); staff or crozier 186 and n, 194, 206–07 (16.e); wooden image of 204–05 (13); *see also* Strath Fillan for lands associated with the relics; *see also:* Dewar; Fillan *Legenda* or *Lectio*
Fillan, brother of Fursu (Fursey) and Ultán 181
Fillan *Legenda* or *Lectio* 178n, 180, 195–201
Fínan, St 191
Finchale (Durham) 13, 230, 237–39
Fintán (Mundu), St 180, 197 and n, 199; community of 180
Firth of Forth 105, 130, 132
Fitjar, battle of 115, 124
Forgan, parish of (originally called Naughton), St Fillan's Kirk at 177 (Map 9.1: Key 9, p. 204), 190
Fors 22
Fort William, main road from (A 82) 185 (Fig. 9.1)
Forth river 93, 140, 141, 147, 164–66 *passim,* 169; *and see* Firth of Forth
Forth-Clyde valley 105

Fortrenn 193, 194; and Fife, Picts of 193
Fortrose 183
Fortune, allegorical figure 52, 57, 60, 62–66, 68
Fothad II, bishop of St Andrews 139
Fræðarberg (in the Frostaþingslög), battle of 120
France (*also* French) 12, 13, 25, 52, 69, 165, 227, 231; literary texts 213–28 *passim;* pottery from 168
Franks 41, 227
Frederick Barbarossa 28
Frederick II (Holy Roman) Emperor, grandson of 25
Friarton (Tay Estuary) 164
Frisian islands (*also* Frisians) 90, 91
Friuli 25
Frostaþing, Frostaþingslög, Norwegian law code 17, 118, 122n
Frostaþingslög, law district in N.W. Norway 118, 120, 122n
Frosterley (Durham): marble from 142
Fulcher of Chartres, historian 19, 24, 27, 32
Fulco, character in a Canterbury miracle 231, 233
Furseus, son of Kentigerna 200n
Fursu, brother of Fillan 181, 183
fylki, division of Gulaþingslög 121

Gaels 193
Galahad, 215n
Gandin 35
Gaul 227
Gautier de Coinci 231
Gellone Sacramentary see Manuscripts: Paris
Genelun 40, 42
Genesis (Book of) *see* Bible
Geoffrey of Monmouth, author of *History of the Kings of Britain*, 227–28
Geoffrey the Fat, chronicler 158n
Gerald of Wales, author, archdeacon of Brecon 27, 30, 31
Germany (*also* Germanic tribes) 11, 12, 25, 36–37, 40, 90, 91, 92; coins from 124; cooking ware from 168

Gest Hystoriale 52
Gesta Dei per Francos (Guibert of Nogent) 20
Gesta Francorum et aliorum Hierosolimitanorum 27
Gideon (Gedeon), Old Testament figure: in *SEL* texts 250
Gille Fáelàin, personal name 208 (Key 24)
Girona Beatus see Spain
Gironde river 145
Glasgow, cathedral church of 183, 184; diocese of 177 (Map 9.1); *and see* Robert Blackadder; main road to (A 82) 185 (Fig. 9.1)
Glastonbury abbey 116
Gleann Fhaolàin, 'Fillan's glen', Ardchattan & Muckairn (Argyll) 177 (Map 9.1: Key 2, p. 202)
Glen Dochart, Glendochart, 'Glen Drochta' (*[G]lendochred, glendeochquhy*), Killin parish (Perthshire) 177 (Map 9.1: Key 16 a-e, pp. 205–07), 179, 184 and n, 186n, 187 (Map 9.2), 191–4 *passim*, 200; abbot and monastery of 185 and n, 186 and n; *see also* Killin/Glendochart, Strath Fillan
Glen Ogle 193
Glenduckie (*Glendooquhy*), Flisk parish (Fife) 200n
Godric, St 230–31, 237–39
Golgotha 27
Goliath, Old Testament figure 42
Göta river, Norway 120
Gothic Revival, style of 142
Gottfried von Straßburg 12, 33–51 *passim*
Govan (by Glasgow) 134
Gower, John 56
Greece (*also* Greeks) 53, 57, 59–65, 67–68, 236
Greek mythology 26
Gregory I, the Great, Pope: *Homilies on Ezekiel* 78–81 *and see* Manuscripts: New York; *Moralia in Job* 81–82, 86 *and see* Manuscripts: Dijon
Grettis saga 108n
Griselde, character in the *Clerk's Tale* 56–57

Index 291

Guibert of Nogent 19, 20, 32
Guido delle Colonne 12, 53, 59–62, 64, 66–67
Gulaþingslög, law district in W. Norway 118, 120, 121, 123
Gulaþingslög, Norwegian law code 121, 122 and n
Gunnar Hámundarson 15, 18
Gunnhild, widow of Eirík *blóðöx* ('Bloodaxe') 125; serving boy of 125
Gunnlaugs saga ormstunga 102
Gurmun of Ireland 35
Guy of Steenvoorde 39
Guðrum 113n
'Gyles, The' (Pittenweem), merchant's house 170, 171 (Figure 8.3)

Habbakuk (Abacuc), Old Testament figure: in *SEL* texts 248, 251
Hadrian of Naples, abbot of St Augustine's Canterbury 96
Hæsten, Viking leader 114n
Hákon Hákonarson, king of Norway 109
Hákon Haraldsson (Hákon *inn góði* 'the Good', Hákon *Aðalsteins fóstri* 'Athelstan's foster-son'), king of Norway 13, 108–26
Hákon the Mighty, earl of Hlaðir, grandson of the earlier Hákon, earl of Hlaðir 110
Hákon, earl of Hlaðir 115, 118, 119
Hákonarhella 124
Hall Þorarinsson 110
Hampshire 158
Hapsburg family 25
Harald Hardrada, king of Norway 227n
Harald hárfagri ('Finehair'), king of Norway, father of Hákon Haraldsson 109, 113
Harald Sigurðsson, king of Norway 110
Harrowing of Hell and the Destruction of Jerusalem 249
Hávamál 102
Havelok the Dane 247, 252
heaven 221n
Hebrews 42
Heccoc, character in a miracle of Godric of Finchale 234

Hector 60–66, 68–69
Hecuba 65
Heimskringla 21, 24, 31, 32, 108–26 *passim*
Helen of Troy 64–65
hell 217, 218, 219, 220n, 221n, 234, 248
Helyas, character in a miracle of Godric of Finchale 234
Henry I, king of England 13, 148, 153, 158, 211, 224–28
Henry II, king of England 225, 228n
Henry III, emperor 24
Henry V, emperor 227
Henry V, king of England (and Prince of Wales) 12, 53, 55, 68–69
Herculaneum: mosaic floors at 84
Hercules 59
Hereford *Mappa Mundi* 211n
Herefordshire School (of sculpture) 159n
Herman the Iron 39
Herod 250
Hesione 61, 64–65, 67–68
Hexham (Durham): sculptural style of 131
Hillary, St: in *SEL* texts 249
Hinba (Argyll), island of 212
Hippolitus, St 251
Hippolytus 82
Historia de Antiquitate Regum Norwagensium 109–111, 114, 117, 124, 125
Historia destructionis Troiae (Guido delle Colonne) 12, 53
Historia Ecclesiastica (Bede) 181
Historia Hierosolymitana (Fulcher of Chartres) 19, 24
Historia Naturalis (Pliny the Elder) 31
Historia Norwegiae 110, 111–12, 114, 117, 119, 124, 125
Hjalti Skeggjason 16–17
Hlaðir, earls of 115, 119; *and see* Hákon, Sigurð
Hoccleve, Thomas 55
Holland 91, 169–73 *passim*
Holy Land 19, 26
Homer 52
Homilies on Ezekiel see Gregory the Great
Hospital of St Martha *see* Aberdour
Hou þe deuel bygylede Eue 251

Hugh de Morville, bishop of Coutances 156n
Hugh de Morville, constable of Scotland 153
Hugo, character in a Canterbury miracle 242
Huí Tortain (Co Meath) 178 and n
Humber 93
Huntingdon, earls of *see* David I
Hǫfuðlausn 102

Ibar (*Ybarus*), Irish saint and bishop 196–97 and n; putative Scottish bishop 197n
Iceland 45, 89, 212n; sagas of 12, 13, 15–32 *passim*, 108–26 *passim*
Immram Snédgusa ocus Meic Riagla 86
Inbhir Fhaolàin, 'Fillan's burn–mouth' (*Invereoland, Inverellan*), Ardchattan & Muckairn (Argyll) 177 (Map 9.1: Key 2, p. 202)
Inchaffray, abbey of 184, 185 and n, 187
Inchcailloch (*innis cailleach* 'island of nuns', 'ad insulam *Inchcailzeoch* in Louchloumont in Leuenax') in Loch Lomond, Lennox 177 (Map 9.1), 182, 196, 201n; parish and kirk of (now Buchanan parish, Stirlingshire) 183–4
Inchcolm abbey (Fife) 129 (Map 7.2), 188; hogback at 133 (Fig.7.3), 134, 161
India 236; folk tales of 26
Infancy of Christ 247, 252
Ingi, king of Norway 21, 22, 24
Inguaeones 90
Ioachym et Anna 251
Iona 130, 164, 193, 200n
Ireland (*also* Irish) 11–14 *passim*, 26, 35, 44–46, 49–50, 70, 86, 134, 164, 175, 176, 178, 179, 180, 184, 194, 196 and n, 211, 212, 217, 226–228
Irenaeus 82
Isaac (Ysaac), Old Testament figure: in *SEL* texts 249–51
Isakar Ioachym et Anna 251
Island of Sheep, location in the *Navigatio* and in *Brendan* 217
Isle of Ailbe, location in *Brendan* 217n, 218

Isle of Grapes, location in the *Navigatio* 218
Isle of May 105; Benedictine priory (cell of Reading abbey) at May/Pittenweem 165, 189–90; lighthouse on 166, 168 (Fig. 8.2)
Isle of the Blest, location in the *Navigatio* 212
Isle of Three Choirs, location in the *Navigatio* 218, 219
Isle of Wight 158
Íslendingabók ('Book of the Icelanders') 110 *and see* Ari Þorgilsson
Isolde 33–51 *passim*
Issachar (Isakar), Old Testament figure: in *SEL* texts 251
Italy 52
Itinerarium Kambriae, The Journey through Wales (Gerald of Wales) 27, 30–31
Iuch *see* Ewich

Jacob (Iacob) Old Testament figure: in *SEL* texts 249–51
Jacobus de Voragine 245
James IV, king of Scots 194
James VI and I, king 166; author of *Counterblasts to Tobacco* 169
James Acheson, skipper of 'The Anna' 170
James Kennedy, bishop of St Andrews 190
'James of Pittenweem, The', merchant ship 170, 172, 173
January, allegorical figure 57
Jason 53, 58–60
Jedburgh abbey (Roxb.) 147; sculptural decoration at 159n
Jedworth monastery: abbot of 239
Jeroboam (Ieroboam), Old Testament figure: in *SEL* texts 250–51
Jerome (Ierome), St 250
Jersey 174
Jerusalem 27, 237, 249; Solomon's Temple at 80; Church of the Holy Cross at 237; and see *Harrowing of Hell and the Destruction of Jerusalem*
Jesus Christ 15, 23, 24, 25, 27, 38, 76, 81, 84, 97, 199–201 *passim*, 216n, 217, 219, 220, 233, 235; in *SEL* texts 247, 248, 249–50, 252, 257

Index

Joachim (Ioachym), St: in *SEL* texts 251
Job (Book of) *see* Bible
John Cook, merchant skipper 170
John MacFarlane, tobacconist 169
John of Salisbury 55
John, son of Thomas Randolph, earl of Moray 188
John, St *see* Bible: *John* (Gospel); *Revelation*
Jonah (Ionas) Old Testament figure 81, 83 (Fig. 4.5); in *SEL* texts 250
Jonathas (Ionathas), Old Testament figure: in *SEL* texts 250
Joseph, Old Testament figure: in *SEL* texts 249–50
Joshua (Iosue) Old Testament figure: in *SEL* texts 250
Journal, the see Alexander Gillespie of Elie
Judas 218n, 219, 220n; in *SEL* texts 244, 248, 250
Judith of Brittany, wife of Duke Richard II of Normandy 155
Julius Agricola, Roman governor of Britain 164
Justice, allegorical figure 43
Jutes 90
Jutland 90, 91

Karl der Grosse 42
Katherine, princess of France, queen of England 69
Kelso abbey (Roxb.) 152n
Kennedy, family of 190
Kenneth mac Alpin, king of Picts and Scots 130
Kentigern, St 183
Kentigerna (*see also* Caintigern), St, mother of Fillan, 176, 178n, 180–81, 182, 183–84, 194, 196 and n, 200 and n, 201n; hypocoristic of 183
Kentigerna *Lectio* (Kent. *Lect.*) 178n, 180, 196n, 200n, 201n
Kilchoan, 'church of Comgan' (Ross and Cromarty) 182–3 and n
Kilellan (Islay) 203
Kilellan (*Kelenan, Kilhelan, Kylhelan*), Houston (Renfrewshire) 177 (Map 9.1: Key 19, pp. 207–08), 191, 192;

St Fillan's fair, Chair and Well at 208 (Key 19); *and see* Kilfinan, Cowal (Argyll)
Kilellan (*Killelan*, 'church of Fillan'), Campbeltown (Argyll) 177 (Map 9.1: Key 3, p. 202)
Kilenaillan (*Killane, Killenaillan*), Kilninian & Kilmore (Mull, Argyll) 177 (Map 9.1: Key 5, p. 203)
Kilfillan (*chill Foelan i Laigis*) 'church of Fillan' (Co. Leix, Munster) 179
Kilfillan (*Kilphillen*), Old Luce (Wigtownshire) 177 (Map 9.1: Key 23, p. 208)
Kilfillan (*Kirkfolan*), Sorbie (Wigtownshire) 177 (Map 9.1: Key 24, p. 208)
Kilfillan Bridge, Kilfillan Burn, Kilfillan Hill *see* Kilfillan, Sorbie (Wigtownshire)
Kilfinan (*Kilelan, Kylfelan, Kyllellan*), Cowal (Argyll) 191, 207 (19)
Kilfinan (*Kilphillen*), Old Luce (Wigtownshire) 177 (Map 9.1: Key 23, p. 208)
Killilan (*Killewlan*), 'the church of Fillan', Kintail (Ross and Cromarty) 176, 177 (Map 9.1: Key 20, p. 208), 182 and n, 183
Killin (Killin/Glendochart) (Perthshire) 177 (Map 9.1: Key 15, p. 205), 179n, 186, 193; parish of 183, 186, 187 (Map 9.2); church of 184; fair, mill and healing stones at 205
Killinallan (*Cillean Ailean*), Kilmarrow & Kilmeny (Islay, Argyll) 177 (Map 9.1: Key 4, p. 202)
Kilrenny (Fife): churchyard at 173
Kilsyth, battle of 170
Kindheit Jesu 252
King Horn 247, 252
Kings' Sagas, genre of 108, 109, 125 *and see Heimskringla*
Kinneil (Penneltun, *Peanfahel*) 130
Kinrymont (Fife) *see* St Andrews
Kirkton of Strath Fillan 186, 198n, Fig. 9.1; priory at 187
Kisping, serving boy of Gunnhild 125

Knight's Tale (Geoffrey Chaucer) 67
Konigsberg 172
Konrad, Priest 40
Kunegunde 35, 38
Kylmisken (*Clúain Móescna*) (Co. Westmeath) 178 and n

Làirg Fhaolàin ('Fillan's pass), Ardchattan & Muckairn (Argyll) 177 (Map 9.1: Key 2, p. 202)
Lais (Marie de France) 214
Lambert of St Omer 72, 81–82; *and see Liber Floridus*
Lamedon 59–60, 66, 68
Lamedonte 69
Lancashire 99
Langland, William 57
Laocoon 159
Laon (France) 231
Lawrence, St 237
Lay of Havelock the Dane 25
Leabhar Breac 179 and n, 181; *see also Martyrology of Óengus*
Leamhain 196n
Leben Jesu 252
Lectiones 176; *and see* Conganus, Fillan and Kentigerna
Legend of St Andrew 139
Legenda Aurea (Jacobus de Voragine) 245
Legenda of the saints 176
Leiden 11; *Aratus* manuscript from 85
Leinster (*also* Leinstermen, *Laynenses*) 181, 182 and n, 193n, 196n; *and see* Book of
Leith (Edinburgh) 165–73 *passim*
leiðangr, naval defence system in Norway and Denmark 119–22
Lennox, earls of 179n
Leuchars church (Fife) 127, 129 (Map 7.2); sculptural decoration at 152–53 and n
Leviathan 12, 77, 78, 80–87 *passim*
Li Contes del Graal (Chrétien de Troyes) 214
Liber Floridus 72, **75** (Fig. 4.3), 81–82, 86; *and see* Manuscripts: Chantilly, Ghent, Wolfenbüttel
Liber Salamoun 250
Liège 74

Life and Miracles of St Godric (Reginald of Durham) 27
Limoges (France) 234
Lindisfarne (Northumberland) 94, 97; abbey 130, 140; *Gospels* 131
Litchfield (Hampshire) 239
Loch Alsh, Lochalsh (*Lochelch*) (Wester Ross, formerly 'northern Argyll') 177 (Map 9.1: Key 20, p. 208), 181, 182–183, 200n
Loch Duich (Wester Ross) 177 (Map 9.1: Key 20, p. 208), 182,
Loch Earn 187 (Map 9.2), 193,
Loch Lomond, island in 196n; *and see* Inchcailloch
Loch Long (Wester Ross) 177 (Map 9.1: Key 20, p. 208), 182, 183
Loch Rannoch 183n
Loch Tay 187 (Map 9.2), 193
Loders (Dorset) 159
Loire river (France) 145
London 94, 102, 171–74 *passim*
Longforgan (Perthshire) 207 (18)
Longinus, St: in *SEL* texts 248–49
Lorn 193
Lot, Old Testament figure: in *SEL* texts 250
Lotan, Old Testament monster 77
Lothian 13, 106; authority of king of Scots over 140
Lothian/Dunbar, earls of 147, 148 *and see* Cospatrick
Love, allegorical figure 65
Lower Largo (Fife) 130
Lumphinnans (*Lumfilan, Lumphenen, Lumphenane, Lu[m]fennan, [L]umfulan, Lumfillans, Lumphinnanis*), Ballingry (Fife) 177 (Map 9.1: Key 8, p. 203), 190–91
Luncarty (*Lonfortin*) (Perth) kirk and parish of 177 (Map 9.1: Key 18, p. 207), 191; *see* St Fillan's Burn
Lydgate, John 12, 52–69 *passim*

M.O. *see Martyrology of Óengus*
M.T. *see Martyrology of Tallaght*
Mac Ríagla, character in the *Immram Snédgusa ocus Meic Riagla* 86

Index

MacGregor, dewar of the *Meser*, 205
Machquha, 183n, *and see* Kentigerna
Mære (in Trøndelag, Norway) 153
Magnús Erlingsson, king of Norway 31, 118
Magnús Óláfsson, king of Norway 118, 119
Malcolm I, king of Scots 123
Malcolm III Canmore, king of Scots 127, 141, 142, 148, 226
Malcolm IV, king of Scots 127, 147, 148 and n, 153
Maldon 103; *see also Battle of Maldon*
Malory, Sir Thomas 12, 34, 47–51
Man, Viking kingdom of 105
manngerð, assessment unit for naval defence 121, 122
Manuscripts:
    Amiens, Bibliothèque Municipale 18 (*Corbie Psalter*): 70, 71 (Fig. 4.1), 72–77
    Cambridge, Corpus Christi College 145: 243–44, 255, 258
    Cambridge, Corpus Christi College 173 (*Anglo–Saxon Chronicle*): 98
    Cambridge, Magdalene College Pepys 2344: 245
    Cambridge, Sidney Sussex College 95: 231
    Cambridge, St John's College 28: 245, 248, 250–52, 266–67
    Cambridge, Trinity College 605: 248–49, 258, 264–65, 267, 273–76
    Chantilly, Museé Condé 724 (*Liber Floridus*): 82
    Cologny (Genève), Fondation Martin Bodmer 17: 225 and n
    Dijon, Bibliothèque Municipale 168 (*Cîteaux Moralia in Job*): 82
    Durham, Dean and Chapter Library A. IV. 19 (*Durham Ritual*): 94
    Durham, Dean and Chapter Library B.II.30 (*Durham Cassiodorus*): 76
    Edinburgh, National Library of Scotland Advocates 23.7.11: 255
    Exeter, Dean and Chapter Library 3501 (*Exeter Book*): 101–02
    Ghent, University Library 92 (*Liber Floridus*): 72, 75 (Fig. 4.3)
    Hildesheim, St Godehard (*St Albans Psalter*): 228 and n
    London, British Library Cotton Julius D ix: 256–57, 270–73
    London, British Library Cotton Nero D IV (*Lindisfarne Gospels*): 94
    London, British Library Cotton Tiberius C.VI (*Cotton Psalter*): 76
    London, British Library Egerton 1993: 248, 250, 264
    London, British Library Egerton 2810: 245
    London, British Library Harley 2277: 243, 245, 255, 258
    London, British Library Rawlinson D 913: 226 and n
    London, Lambeth Palace 223: 245, 248, 250, 255, 265, 268
    New York, Pierpont Morgan Library Glazier 6 (*Gregory the Great, Homilies on Ezekiel*): 78, 79 (Fig.4.4), 80
    Oxford, Bodleian Library Auctarium D. II 19 (*Rushworth Gospels*): 94
    Oxford, Bodleian Library Bodley 779: 259, 276–80
    Oxford, Bodleian Library Digby 23: 228 and n
    Oxford, Bodleian Library Digby 230: 59
    Oxford, Bodleian Library English Poetry a.1 (*Vernon Manuscript*): 248, 251, 255, 266, 269–70
    Oxford, Bodleian Library Laud.Miscellaneous 108: 243, 247–48, 251–52, 255–56, 259–60, 263–64
    Oxford, Bodleian Library Laud.Miscellaneous 463: 245
    Oxford, Bodleian Library Laud.Miscellaneous 610: 179
    Oxford, Bodleian Library Laud.Miscellaneous 622: 255
    Paris, Bibliothèque Nationale, lat. 1 (*Vivian Bible*): 84

Manuscripts: *(cont.)*
  Paris, Bibliothèque Nationale, lat. 10087 (*Cartulary of Montebourg*): 158–59 and n
  Paris, Bibliothèque Nationale, lat. 12048 (*Gellone Sacramentary*): 84
  St Andrews University Library 38352 (*Alexander Gillespie's Journal*): 170
  Trier, Stadtbibliothek 31 (*Trier Apocalypse*): 74
  Troyes Cathedral 12 (*Psalter*): 70, 73 (Fig. 4.2)
  Valenciennes, Bibliothèque Municipale 39 (*St Augustine, Commentary on the Psalms*): 81, 83 (Fig. 4.5)
  Valenciennes, Bibliothèque Municipale 99 (*Valenciennes Apocalypse*): 74, 76
  Winchester, Winchester College 33a: 248, 250, 251, 266, 269
  Wolfenbüttel, Herzog August Bibliothek Guelf 1. Gud. lat. 2 (*Liber Floridus*): 82
Map, Walter 234
Margaret, St, queen of Scots 141–43, 148, 165, 226
Marie de France see *Lais*
Mark, king 38, 40, 42–43, 45, 48–49
Mark, St 244
Marker region of Norway 29, 31
Marmoutier abbey (France) 155
Mars, Greek god 53, 57
Marsilius of Padua 55
Martin of Tours, St 237
Martinvast (Cotentin) 156 (Map 7.3), 159
Martyrology of Óengus (Félire Óengussa) (MO) 178 and n, 179, 184; *see also* Leabhar Breac
Martyrology of Tallaght (MT) 178 and n, 180, 184
Mary, mother of Jesus 196: miracles of 230–33, 237; in *SEL* texts 248–50, 257, 259
Matilda (*Mahalt*) of Scotland, daughter of Malcolm Canmore and Margaret of Scotland, first wife of Henry I 226–27

Matilda, daughter of Henry I, wife of Emperor Henry V and Geoffrey of Anjou 227
Matthew, St 58
May/Pittenweem see Isle of May
Means, allegorical figure 43
Medea 53, 58–59
Mediterranean Sea 52
Meigle (Perthshire): hogback at 134; Pictish grave-marker at 161 (Fig. 7.16)
Melrose abbey (Roxb.) 130
Menelaus 60, 64–66
Merchant's Tale (Geoffrey Chaucer) 57
Metamorphoses (Ovid) 58
Mettle, allegorical figure 43
Michael, St: in *SEL* texts 255, 257–59
Ministry and Passion 247–48, 251–52, 257
Miracles de Nostre Dame (Gautier de Coinci) 231
Mirk 245
Mirrour of Saints' Lives 246
Modwenna, St 207 (18)
Moissac (France) 148–52n
Monkwearmouth monastery 76
Montebourg abbey (Manche) 156 (Map 7.3), 158–59
Monymusk (Aberdeenshire) 129 (Map 7.2); reliquary from (the *Brecbennoch*) 132 and n; *and see* Columba, St
Moralia in Job see Gregory the Great
Moray 13, 176, 192
Moray Firth 165
Morgan 35, 43
Morolt (*Morold, Marhalt*) 33–51 *passim*
Morton (Fife) 164
Morville (Cotentin) 156 (Map 7.3), 158
Moses (Moyses), Old Testament figure 215n, 218n, 220, 221; in *SEL* texts 249, 251
'Muckle Yett', Elie (Fife) 174
Mull, 193
Mundu see Fintan
Munster 179 and n, 181
Myrmidons 58

Namenlos see *Valentin und Namenlos*
Nantes 172
Nathan, Old Testament figure: in *SEL* texts 250

Index

Nativity of Mary and Christ 248, 251
Nature, allegorical figure 61
Naughton (*Adnacthen*, 'Nechtan's Ford'), parish of, *see* Forgan
Navan (Co. Meath) 178
Navigatio Sancti Brendani, tenth-century legendary pilgrimage text, 13, 211–13, 215–22, 229
Nechtansmere, battle of 129 (Map 7.2), 130, 131
Need, allegorical figure 57
Néhou (Cotentin) 156 (Map 7.3), 158; *and see* Alexander de Néhou
Nestor 60
Netherlands 25, 172
New Jerusalem 216, 219, 222
New Testament 78, 87, 219, 220; *and see* Bible; books of
Newfoundland 211
Nicholas, St 237, 252
Nicomachean Ethics (Aristotle) 54
Nidarholm (Trondheim) 111
Nigg 143
Nith-(*Niud-*)folk 130
Niðarnes 110
Njáll Þorgeirsson 15–18, 21
Njáls saga 12, 15, 17, 18, 21, 24, 32
Noah (Noe), Old Testament figure: in *SEL* texts 249, 250, 251
Normandy (*also* Normans) 11, 106, 128 (Map 7.1), 134, 153–60, 163, 226, 240
Norse settlement, society, language and literature 12, 15–32 *passim*, 88–126 *passim*
Norsemen (*also* Norþmenn, 'men from the north'), 89, 90, 102, 104, 134
North Sea (*also* North Sea World) 11, 14, 52, 70, 86, 87, 88, 90, 91, 95, 129, 131, 164–74 *passim*, 211, 212, 230, 237, 242
Northumbria 95, 105; art of 132, 134
Norway 11, 13, 21–32 *passim*, 45, 89, 90, 106, 108–26, 171–73 *passim*, 237, 239
Nova Legenda Angliæ 234
Numbers (Book of) *see* Bible

Odd son of Kol son of Hall of Siða 110
Óengus 178

Oengus son of Natfraoch 179
Of Abacuc þe profete 251
Oof Abraham 251
Of Anna 251
Of Daniel 251
Of Dauid 251
Of Helye 251
Of Iacob 251
Of Ieroboam 251
Of Ioachim and of Anna 251
Of Noe 251
Off Sampson 251
Of Saul 251
Of þe deþ of Moyses 251
Of Ysaac 251
Offa of Angeln 91
Ögvaldsnes (in the Gulaþingslög), battle of 120
Ohthere (*Óttarr*) 98
Óláf Haraldsson, St, king of Norway 31, 111n, 118, 119, 124
Óláf Tryggvason, king of Norway 124
Old Testament 77, 219, 220 and n; *and see* Bible
Old Testament History 248–51, 257
Olympiodorus of Alexandria, *Catena* 82
Onuist/Oengus I son of Fergus, king of the Picts 135
Oracle of Baalbeck (Greek Apocalypse text) 82
Orderic Vitalis, chronicler 23, 158
Orkney 172, 212
Orosius, *Historiae adversum paganos* 98
Orpheus 58
Oseberg (Norway) 161, 162 (Figs 7.17, 7.18)
Ostend 174
Ostia: mosaic floors at 84
Oswald, St: in *SEL* texts 250
Othea 53, 57
Ottonian emperors 24
Ovid 52, 58–59
Owun, scribe 94, 105
Óðinn (Wotan) 17

Paganus, priest, character in a Canterbury miracle 232–33
Palamides 65
Palestine 23

Panonia 61
paradise 211n, 212, 216, 217, 218, 219; of Birds (location in *Brendan*) 217, 218
Paris (France) 111
Paris, Trojan hero 64, 66–67
Patrick, St: in *SEL* texts 258–59
Paul the Hermit 219
Paul, St *see* Bible; *see Vision of*
Peleus 58–59
Penitential of Thomas of Chobham 214n
Penneltun (*Peanfahel*) see Kinneil
Perth (Perthshire) 165
Peter, archbishop of Tarantaise 234
Phaenomena see Aratus of Soloi
Phila *see Valentin und Namenlos*
Philip de Colville 153
Philippe de Thaon 223
Pictland (*also* Picts) 101, 129, 130, 134, 141, 192, 193; art of 134, 135, *and see* Meigle; cross-slabs from, *see* Aberlemno, Cossans, Elgin, Shandwick, Nigg
Piers Plowman (William Langland) 57
Pilate: in *SEL* texts 244, 248–50
Pilgrims' Well ('le pilgramyswell') *see* Aberdour
Pinabel 41–42
Pittenweem (Fife) 166–70 *passim*, 177 (Map 9.1: Key 10, p. 204); cave of 189; merchant houses at Fig. 8.3 (p. 171); *and see* May/Pittenweem
Placebo, allegorical figure 57
Plantagenets 227n
Pliny the Elder 31
Poitiers, bishop of 234
Politics (Aristotle) 54–55
Polyxena 64–65
Poseidon, God of the Sea 82, 84, 85
Priam 53, 60–61, 65–68
Priest Konrad 40
Prioress's Tale (Geoffrey Chaucer) 231
Procopius, historian 90
Prudence, Dame, allegorical figure 56
Psalms (Book of) *see* Bible
Psalms, Commentaries on 80–81, 83 (Fig. 4.5), *and see* Augustine, Cassiodorus
Psalter *see* Manuscripts: Amiens, London, Troyes

Pseudo-Ephraem (Greek Apocalypse text) 82
Purgatorio (Dante Alighieri) 57
purgatory 217

Queensferry, Queen's Ferry (W. Lothian) 130, 147
Querqueville *Karkarevil* (Cotentin) 155–56, 156 (Map 7.3), 158n,

Rath Erenn (?Rottearns, Ardoch) (?Dundurn) 184
Ráth Erenn (*Ráith Érenn*), Ratherran 179
Rathmore of Moylinny (Co. Antrim) 182
Reading Abbey (England) *see* May/Pittenweem
Rebecca, Old Testament figure: in *SEL* texts 250
Redvers, de, family and lordships of 158
Regement of Princes (Thomas Hoccleve) 55
Reginald of Durham, hagiographer 27, 141, 231, 236–37, 239, 241
Rehoboam (Roboam), Old Testament figure: in *SEL* texts 249
Renfrewshire 192
Restenneth priory (Angus) 129 (Map 7.2), 139
Revelation (Book of) *see* Bible
Reviers (Calvados) 158
Rhine 90
Rhineland 96; delftware from 168
Richard de Redvers I 158, 159
Richard de Tolewast 158
Richard II, duke of Normandy 155
Richardis 38
Right, allegorical figure 43
Robert I Bruce (de Brus) 153, 155, 156 and n
Robert I, king of Scots (Robert Bruce) 184, 186–8, 190, 191, 192, 194
Robert Blackadder, bishop of Glasgow, *Book of Devotion* of 183n
Robert Bruce of Liddesdale, illegitimate son of Robert I king of Scots 187–88
Robert Ford, skipper 173; tombstone of Fig.8.4 (p. 173)

Index

Robert Pantre, priest of Holy Trinity, St Andrews 190
Robert, bishop of St Andrews 137, 139
Robert, Brother 34, 44–47, 51
Robert, duke of Albany, earl of Menteith 191
Robert, son of Humphrey of Tollevast 155 and n
Robert, son of William I, duke of Normandy 226
Rocamadour (France) 231, 237
Roger de Moubray 147
Roger II, king of Sicily 24
Rögnvald Guðröðsson, king of Northumbria 114n
Roland 34, 40–41; *and see Chanson de Roland*
Roman d'Énée 214
Roman de Troie (Benoît de Sainte–Maure) 53
Rome (*also* Romans) 44, 52, 129, 180, 227, 236; St Peter's at 28, 143, 163; shipping of 164, 165
Ross, cathedral chapter of 183
Rottearns, Ardoch (Perthshire) 184
Rotterdam 172, 173, 174

Saemund Sigfússon (*inn fróði* 'the wise'), historian 110, 111, 112, 114
Saladin, ruler of Egypt and Syria 27
Salutatio Marie 249
Sampson, Old Testament figure: in *SEL* texts 249, 251
Santiago (Spain) 166; *and see* Compostela
Saintes (Saintonge): pottery from 168
Satan 74, 220
Saul, Old Testament figure, 42, 70; in *SEL* texts 249, 251
Saur, talking dog who became king (*Heimskringla*) 112
Saxons 90
Sayings of St Bernard 252
Scandinavia (*also* Scandinavians) 12, 13, 88–107 *passim*, 227; artistic influence of 134, 152; place names of 163; cooking ware from 168
Scoti (*Ybernences*) 196 and n; *and see* Ireland (Irish)

Scotland (*also* Scots) 11, 13, 14, 106, 123, 127–63, 164–74 *passim*, 175–210 *passim*, 226, 230; Maps 7.2 (p.129), 9.1 (p.177); *and see* Troy Book
Scott, Sir Walter 166
Seafarer 102
Secreta secretorum 55
Septimius Severus, Roman emperor 165
Serapis 236
Seville: pottery from 168
Shandwick (Ross and Cromarty) 143
Sheol 85
Sherborne (Dorset): bishop of 122
Shetlands 212
Shiel river 182
Sicily 19, 24
Sigefridus, bishop of Norway and monk of Glastonbury 116–17
Sighvatr Þórðarson, Icelandic poet 102, 114
Sigurð, earl of Hlaðir, son of Earl Hákon 115, 120
Silverius, St 180
Símun 22
Sir Gawain and the Green Knight 52
Siracht (Strath, Strath Fillan) 200 and n
Skarphéðinn 16–18, 21, 32
skipreiða, assessment unit for naval defence 120–23
Skipton (W. Yorks.) 99
Snédgus, character in the *Immram Snédgusa ocus Meic Riagla* 86
Snorri Sturluson, Icelandic chieftain and writer 21, 108, 111
Socrates 54
Soissons (France) 231
Solomon's Temple *see* Jerusalem
Solomon, Old Testament figure, 53, 69; in *SEL* texts 249–50
Solway Firth 106
Solway river 130
Somer Soneday 247
Song of Roland see Chanson de Roland
South English Legendary (ed. by Charlotte D'Evelyn and Anna J Mill) 244–46, 254, 256–58, 260–63
South English Legendary (*Legendaries*) (*SEL*) 14, 243–80 *passim*
Southern Passion 257–59

Spain: *Beatus* manuscripts and imagery of 76–77; *Girona Beatus*, 84; amphorae from 165; pottery from 168

Spesar þáttr 108n

Spey river 164

St Andrews (Kinrymont, *Cennrígmonaid*) 11, 13, 14, 127, 129 (Map 7.2), 237, 239; 'the Compostela of the north' 129; pilgrimage to 148, 165 ; sarcophagus at 134–35, 135 (Fig. 7.4), 143; shrine church of St Regulus (St Rule's church/St Rule's Tower) at 134–140, 136 (Fig. 7.5), 138 (Fig. 7.6), 156; Augustinian priory of 139, 190; prior of 147; medieval diocese of 130, 140–41, 177 (Map 9.1); consecration of cathedral at 190; sculptural decoration of cathedral at 152; bishops *see* Fothad, Robert; altar of St Fillan in the parish kirk of Holy Trinity at 190, 204 (Key 11); archaeology near 164

St Eysteinn's spring (*St Østein's kilde*) 31

St Fillan *see* Fillan

St Fillan's Burn (*Sanct-phillanis-burn*), Redgorton (Perthshire) 177 (Map 9.1: Key 18, p. 207); *and see* Luncarty

St Fillan's Cave, Pittenweem (Fife) 177 (Map 9.1 Key 10, p. 204); *and see* Pittenweem

St Fillan's Chair, Houston *see* Kilellan (Renfrewshire)

St Fillan's Chapel, Comrie (Perthshire) 177 (Map 9.1: Key 14, p. 205); *and see* Dùn-Fhàolain

St Fillan's Chapels *see* Doune Castle

St Fillan's Kirk, Aberdour (Fife) 177 (Map 9.1: Key 7, p. 203)

St Fillan's Kirk, Forgan (Fife) 177 (Map 9.1: Key 9, p. 204)

St Fillan's Pool (*Poll Fhaolain*), Strath Fillan, 197n

St Fillan's Well, Aberdour (Fife) 177 (Map 9.1: Key 7, p. 203); *and see* Aberdour

St Fillan's Well, Houston *see* Kilellan (Renfrewshire)

St Fillan's Well (*Sanct-Phillanis-well*), Largs (Ayrshire) 177 (Map 9.1: Key 6, p. 203)

St Fillan's Well, Lochlee (Angus) 177 (Map 9.1: Key 1, p. 202)

St Fillan's Well (*Tobair Fhaolàin*), Struan, Blair Atholl (Perthshire) 177 (Map 9.1: Key 13, p. 204); *and see* Dùn-Fhàolain

St Fillan's, Comrie (Perthshire) 177 (Map 9.1: Key 14, p. 205), 187 (Map 9.2)

St Giles' collegiate church *see* Edinburgh

St Mary's abbey *see* York

St Peter's *see* Rome

St Pierre-sur-Dive 231

St Regulus' church (St Rule's) *see* St Andrews

St Þorleifr's Chapel (*Hellig Thorlofs Capel*) 31

Standard, battle of the 147

Stephen, count of Blois 19

Stephen, king of England 148, 227

Stephen, son of Erchembald 30

Strath Fillan, Strathfillan (*Straithfulane, Strathfulane, Straphilane, Straphilane*), Killin parish (Perthshire) 182–188, 189, 193; Fig. 9.3 (p. 185); church/chapel of 184–85, 188, 201, 205; priory of 185, 190, 200n; lands in associated with the relics of St Fillan: 177 (Map 9.1: Key 16 (a)-(e), pp 205–06), Map 9.2 (p. 187); *and see* Glen Dochart

Strathclyde 101, 192

Strathearn (*Sraith Eret, Srath hErenn*) 178 and n, 184, 192–93

Stricker 42

Struan, Blair Atholl (Perthshire) 177 (Map 9.1: Key 13, p. 204); iron hand-bell (*Buidhean,* 'litttle yellow one') at 204; fair day (*Féill Fhaolàin*) at 204; well at, *see* St Fillan's Well

Sturlunga saga 23

Suie (*suidhe* 'seat') in Glen Dochart (Perthshire) 187 (Map 9.2), cemetery and chapel at 206

Index

Summa theologiae (Thomas Aquinas) 54
Sungiva, character in a miracle of Godric of Finchale 234
Sutton Hoo 96
Svein Álfífuson, king of Norway 118, 119
Sveinn Haraldsson, king of Denmark 89, 106
Sverrir Sigurðarson, king of Norway 28–29, 31
Sverris saga 28–31
Sweden 25

Tabula Othiniensis 23
Tacitus, Roman historian 164
Tale of Melibee (Geoffrey Chaucer) 56
Tallaght near Dublin, 192
Tangiers 170
Tarantaise 234
Taras, son of Poseidon, God of the Sea 82
Tarent (Tarentum, Calabria) 82
Tay river (*and* Estuary) 164
Tehom 77, 78 and n
Telamon 61, 64, 68–69
Telegonus 68–69
Testament of Love (Thomas Usk) 56
Teviotdale 240
Texel, the 171
Themes, bishop of 40
Theodore of Tarsus, archbishop of Canterbury 96
Theodricus Monachus, historian 111
Theseus 67
Thessaly 69
Thomas de Tollevast 156 and n
Thomas of Brittany 34, 44–45, 47
Thomas of Chobham see *Penitential of*
Thomas Randolph, earl of Moray 188
Thomas Russell, merchant apprentice 170
Thomas Tucker, Cromwellian official 170
Thorp[e] (Durham) 238
Thule (*Tyle*) 179
Tiamat, Babylonian sea monster 77
Tinchebray, *Tinchebrai* (Normandy), battle of 226

Tollevast (Cotentin) 155–56 (Map 7.3), 157 (Fig. 7.13), 158–59, 160 (Figs. 7.14, 7.15), 163
Toulouse: scriptorium of *see Homilies on Ezekiel*
Tours: scriptorium of 74
Trier Apocalypse see Manuscripts: Trier
Trinity Conception of Mary 248
Tristams saga ok Isöndar (Brother Robert) 12, 44–47, 50
Tristan (Gottfried von Straßburg) 12, 33–51 *passim*
Tristan (Thomas of Brittany) 34, 44
Tristan (*Tristam, Tristram*) 12, 33–51 *passim*
Tristan, legend of 108n
Tristan, Old French version 34, 47–48
Troilus 61, 63–65
Trøndelag (Norway) *see* Værnes, Mære
Trondheim 111
Troy (*also* Trojans) 12, 52–69 *passim*, 227
Troy Book (John Lydgate) 12, 52–69 *passim*; Scottish fragments 60
Troyes Cathedral *see* Manuscripts
Truchseß 35
Trumwine, 'bishop of the Picts' 131
Tryggvi, king of the Vík, nephew of Hákon Haraldsson 120
Turgis de Toutfresville 155n
Turgot, prior of Durham, biographer 141, 148
Tweed river 130
Tyninghame church (E. Lothian) 129 (Map 7.2), 152
Tyrennus, subking of Leinster, father of Kentigerna 182n, 196n
Þangbrand, priest responsible for the conversion of Iceland 110
Þorgeir *afraðskoll* 110
Þorleif the wise 118
Þrœndalög, district around Trondheim 115, 116, 118

Ulcanus (Ultán), son of Kentigerna 200n
Ultán, brother of Fillan 181, 183
Ulysses 53, 68–69
Urban II, pope 26

Ushant 174
Usk, Thomas 56

Værnes (in Trøndelag, Norway) 153
Valencia: pottery from 168
Valenciennes Apocalypse see Manuscripts: Valenciennes
Valentin *see Valentin und Namenlos*
Valentin und Namenlos 29–30
Valentine and Orson 25
Valhalla 116
Veøy, island of (Romsdal) 117
Vernon (Vexin) 158
Vernon Life of Mary 248
Vie de Saint Alexis 228
Vík, area around the Oslo Fjord in S.E. Norway 22, 120
Vikings 12, 70, 86, 88–107 *passim;* 113, 122, 125, 127, 132, 159, 166, 211, 227
Virgil 52
Vision of St Paul 252
Vita de Adam 250
Vita Eustaci (*Placidus saga*) 18
Vita Pilati 250
Vita Sancti Brendani, ninth–century *Life of St Brendan* 212
Vita Sancti Cuthberti episcopi 250
Vita Sancti Edwardi regis Anglie 250
Vita Sancti Oswaldi 250
Vitae (*Lives*) of the saints 176
Vitalis, St 180
Vivian Bible see Manuscripts: Paris
Voeu abbey (Cherbourg) 156
Voyage de Saint Brendan, Anglo-Norman poem by Benedeit 211–29
Vulcan 43
Vǫlundarkviða 103

Wales (*also* Welsh) 212, 227–28
Walter Bower, chronicler 191
Walter, character in the *Clerk's Tale* 56
Waltheof (Waldeve): name 153n
Waltheof, earl of Northumbria 23
Waltheof (Waldeve), lord of Allerdale 147
Waltheof, son of Cospatric, lord of Inverkeithing 147
Waltheof, sons of: *see* Alan, Cospatrick
Wanderer 101–02
Weeke (Isle of Wight) 159
Weser river 165
Wessex 105, 107; royal house of 141
West Linton (Peebleshire) 134
Westmoreland 148
Whore of Babylon 80, 85
Widsiþ 102
Wife of Bath (Chaucer) 59
Will, allegorical figure 57
William I, king of England 23
William Banks, pipemaker 169
William de Redvers 158
William Douglas 188
William Elphinstone, bishop of Aberdeen 176
William Lamberton, bishop of St Andrews 190
William of Malmesbury 113, 116, 230
William, character in a Canterbury miracle 241
William, monk of Canterbury 237
William, son of Henry I, 227
Willibrord, St 97
Willing Heart, allegorical figure 43
Wolston, St: in *SEL* texts 249
Worcestershire 99
Wyntoun *see* Andrew of

Ymaginatif, allegorical figure 57
York 93; St Mary's abbey at 155; Viking kingdom of 103, 105
Yorkshire 100, 133; Romanesque churches of 148

Zeeland 169
Zeus 85